STATISTICAL RECORD

OF THE

ARMIES OF THE UNITED STATES

CAMPAIGNS OF THE CIVIL WAR

SUPPLEMENTARY VOLUME

STATISTICAL RECORD

OF THE

ARMIES OF THE UNITED STATES

BY

FREDERICK PHISTERER,

LATE CAPTAIN U. S. ARMY

CASTLE BOOKS

CAMPAIGNS OF THE CIVIL WAR.—
SUPPLEMENTARY VOLUME.
STATISTICAL RECORD OF THE ARMIES OF THE
UNITED STATES

This edition published in 2002 by Castle Books,
A division of Book Sales Inc.
114 Northfield Avenue, Edison, NJ 08837

First published in 1883.
Written by Frederick Phisterer.

ISBN: 0-7858-1585-6

Printed in the United States of America.

THE

FOLLOWING PAGES,

COMPILED FROM ARMY ORDERS, REGISTERS

OF REGULARS AND VOLUNTEERS,

REPORTS OF THE PROVOST-MARSHAL

AND THE ADJUTANT-GENERAL U. S. ARMY,

MEDICAL HISTORY OF THE REBELLION, AND OTHER SOURCES,

ARE

RESPECTFULLY DEDICATED

TO HIS COMRADES

OF THE

Grand Army of the Republic,

BY

FREDERICK PHISTERER,

LATE CAPTAIN U. S. ARMY, REGULAR BRIGADE, FOURTEENTH CORPS,
ARMY OF THE CUMBERLAND.

CONTENTS.

PART I.

NUMBERS AND ORGANIZATION OF THE ARMIES OF THE UNITED STATES.

PART II.

CHRONOLOGICAL RECORD OF ENGAGEMENTS, BATTLES, ETC., IN THE UNITED STATES, 1861 TO 1865.

PART III.

RECORD OF THE GENERAL OFFICERS OF THE ARMIES OF THE UNITED STATES DURING THE WAR OF THE REBELLION.

PART I.

NUMBERS AND ORGANIZATION OF THE ARMIES OF THE UNITED STATES.

STATISTICAL RECORD.

CALLS FOR TROOPS.

On April 15, 1861, President Lincoln issued his proclamation for 75,000 militia for three months. Under this call there were furnished by the loyal States 91,816 men, as follows:

STATES.	Quota.	Men furnished.
Maine...	780	771
New Hampshire	780	779
Vermont	780	782
Massachusetts	1,560	3,736
Rhode Island	780	3,147
Connecticut	780	2.402
New York	13,280	13,906
New Jersey	3,123	3,123
Pennsylvania..	12,500	20,175
Delaware	780	775
Maryland	3,123	.....
West Virginia	2,340	900
District of Columbia..........	......	4,720
Ohio..	10,153	12,357
Indiana...	4,683	4,686
Illinois...	4,683	4,820
Michigan..........................	780	781
Wisconsin............................	780	817
Minnesota..	780	920
Iowa....	780	968
Missouri	3,123	10,591
Kentucky	3,123	.....
Kansas	......	650
Tennessee..	1,560	.....
Arkansas...	780	.....
North Carolina....................................	1,560	.....
Total	73,291	91,816

On May 3, 1861, the President issued another call for troops, which was confirmed by act of Congress, approved August 6, 1861. Under this call, and under acts approved July 22 and 25, 1861, 500,000 men were required; and there were furnished for six months, 2,715 men; for one year, 9,147 men; for two years, 30,950 men; and for three years, 657,868 men; making a total of 700,680 men.

STATES AND TERRITORIES.	Quota.	MEN FURNISHED FOR				Total.
		Six mos.	One year.	Two years.	Three years.	
Maine	17,560	....	....	......	18,104	18,104
New Hampshire	9,234	....	....	......	8,338	8,338
Vermont	8,950	....	....	......	9,508	9,508
Massachusetts	34,868	....	....	......	32,177	32,177
Rhode Island	4,955	....	....	......	6,286	6,286
Connecticut	13,057	....	....	......	10,865	10,865
New York	109,056	....	....	30,950	89,281	120,231
New Jersey	19,152	....	....	......	11,523	11,523
Pennsylvania	82,825	....	....	......	85,160	85,160
Delaware	3,145	....	...	......	1,826	1,826
Maryland	15,578	....	....	......	9,355	9,355
West Virginia	8,497	....	....	......	12,757	12,757
District of Columbia	1,627	....	....	......	1,795	1,795
Ohio	67,365	....	863	......	83,253	84,116
Indiana	38,832	....	1,698	......	59,643	61,341
Illinois	47,785	....	....	......	81,952	81,952
Michigan	21,857	....	....	......	23,546	23,546
Wisconsin	21,753	....	.	......	25,499	25,499
Minnesota	4,899	....	1,167	......	5,770	6,937
Iowa	19,316	....	....	......	21,987	21,987
Missouri	31,544	2,715	199	......	22,324	25,238
Kentucky	27,237	....	5,129	......	29,966	35,095
Kansas	3,225	....	....	......	6,953	6,953
Nebraska Territory	......	....	91	......	....	91
	611,827	2,715	9,147	30,950	657,868	700,680

Special authority was granted to the States of New York, Illinois, and Indiana, in May and June, 1862, to furnish men for three months' service. Under this authority, there were furnished by

New York 8,588
Indiana.. 1,723
Illinois 4,696
                                                 _____
Total................................ 15,007

Under the call of July 2, 1862, for 300,000 men, for three years, there were furnished by the States and Territories 421,465 men, as follows:

States and Territories.	Quota.	Men furnished.	States and Territories.	Quota.	Men furnished.
Maine............	9.609	6,644	Dist. of Columbia.	890	1,167
New Hampshire...	5,053	6,390	Ohio	36,858	58,325
Vermont	4,898	4,369	Indiana	21,250	30,359
Massachusetts	19,080	16,519	Illinois	26,148	58,689
Rhode Island......	2,712	2,742	Michigan	11,686	17,656
Connecticut	7,145	9,195	Wisconsin..	11,904	14.472
New York....	59.705	78,904	Minnesota........	2,681	4,626
New Jersey........	10,478	5.499	Iowa............	10,570	24,438
Pennsylvania......	45,321	30.891	Missouri	17.269	28.324
Delaware..........	1,720	2,508	Kentucky	14,905	6,463
Maryland	8,532	3,586	Kansas...........	1,771	2,936
West Virginia......	4,650	4,925	Nebraska Ter.....	......	1,838
Total				334,835	421,465

Under the call of August 4, 1862, for 300,000 militia for nine months' service, there were furnished by the States 87,588 men, as follows:

States.	Quota.	Men furnished.	States.	Quota.	Men furnished.
Maine............	9.609	7,620	Dist. of Columbia.	890	......
New Hampshire...	5,053	1,736	Ohio	36,858	......
Vermont	4,898	4,781	Indiana	21,250	337
Massachusetts	19,080	16,685	Illinois...........	26,148	......
Rhode Island......	2,712	2,059	Michigan	11,686	......
Connecticut	7,145	5,602	Wisconsin	11,904	958
New York	59,705	1,781	Minnesota........	2,681	......
New Jersey........	10,478	10,787	Iowa.............	10,570	......
Pennsylvania	45,321	32,215	Missouri	17,269	......
Delaware	1,720	1,799	Kentucky	14,905	......
Maryland..........	8,532	......	Kansas...........	1,771	......
West Virginia	4,650	......	Nebraska Ter.....	......	1,228
Total				334,835	87,588

Under the President's proclamation of June 15, 1863, for militia for six months' service, there were furnished by, and credited to, the States 16,361 men; no quotas were made, and the men were furnished as follows:

Massachusetts	103	Ohio	2,726
Pennsylvania	3.708	Indiana	3,767
Maryland	1,615	Missouri.............	3,284
West Virginia....	1,148		
Total...			16,361

The Missouri troops, although credited under this call, were not furnished until November, 1864.

October 17, 1863, and February 1, 1864, calls were made for 500,000 men, in the aggregate, for three years. In these calls there are embraced the men raised by draft in 1863, and under them there were furnished and credited 369,380 men, as follows:

STATES.	Quota.	Men furnished.	Men paid commutation.	Total.
Maine	11,803	11,958	1,986	13,944
New Hampshire	6,469	6,406	571	6,977
Vermont	5,751	6,726	1,885	8,611
Massachusetts	26,597	17,711	3,703	21,414
Rhode Island.............	3,469	3,223	463	3,686
Connecticut	7,919	10,326	1,513	11,839
New York	81,993	59,839	15,912	75,751
New Jersey...............	16,759	9,187	....	9,187
Pennsylvania	64,979	36,723	17,672	54,395
Delaware	2,463	2,138	435	2,573
Maryland............... ..	10,794	6,244	1,106	7,350
West Virginia	5,127	3,988	....	3,988
District of Columbia	4,256	4,570	318	4,888
Ohio	51,465	32,809	......	32,809
Indiana	32,521	23,023	......	23,023
Illinois	46,309	28,818	......	28,818
Michigan.................	19,553	17,686	1,644	19,330
Wisconsin	19,852	10,389	5,080	15,469
Minnesota......	5,451	3,054	......	3,054
Iowa.....................	16,097	8,292	......	8,292
Missouri................. .	9,813	3,823	......	3,823
Kentucky	14,471	4,785	......	4,785
Kansas...................	3,523	5,374	. ....	5,874
Total.............	467,434	317,092	52,288	369,380

Under the call of March 14, 1864, for 200,000 men for three years' service, there were credited to the States 292,193 men, who were furnished as follows :

STATES.	Quota.	Men furnished.	Men paid commutation.	Total.
Maine.....................	4,721	7,042	......	7,042
New Hampshire	2,588	2,844	121	2,965
Vermont	2,300	1,601	89	1,690
Massachusetts	10,639	17,322	1,615	18,937
Rhode Island.......	1,388	1,906	......	1,906
Connecticut	3,168	5,294	......	5,294
New York	32,794	41,940	2,267	44,207
New Jersey...............	6,704	9,550	4,170	13,720
Pennsylvania	25,993	35,036	10,046	45,082
Delaware	985	652	951	1,603

STATES.	Quota.	Men furnished.	Men paid commutation.	Total.
Maryland......................	4,317	9,365	2,528	11,903
West Virginia..............	2,051	3,857	......	3,857
District of Columbia	1,702	1,142	......	1,142
Ohio	20,595	31,193	6,290	37,483
Indiana	13,008	14,862	......	14,862
Illinois	18,524	25,055	......	25,055
Michigan..................	7,821	7,344	323	7,667
Wisconsin	7,941	10,314	......	10,314
Minnesota	2,180	2,469	1,027	3,496
Iowa	6,439	11,579	......	11,579
Missouri..................	3,925	10,137	......	10,137
Kentucky	5,789	6,448	3,241	9,689
Kansas....................	1,409	2,563	......	2,563
Total....	186,981	259,515	32,678	292,193

The troops credited to the State of Missouri in this call include 5,679 militia, furnished for six months; 2,311 for nine months; 1,954 for one year; which were credited to the State as 2,174 three years' men.

There were mustered into the United States service, between April 23 and July 18, 1864, for one hundred days' service, 83,612 militia, as follows :

STATES.	Quota.	Men furnished.
New Hampshire..	......	167
Massachusetts..	4,000	6,809
New York................................	12,000	5,640
New Jersey	......	769
Pennsylvania..........................	12,000	7,675
Maryland	......	1,297
Ohio	30,000	36,254
Indiana..	20,000	7,197
Illinois.......................	20,000	11,328
Wisconsin...	5,000	2,134
Iowa...	10,000	3,901
Kansas.................................	......	441
Total..............	113,000	83,612

The men credited to New Hampshire above were, however, furnished for three months' service only.

On the 18th July, 1864, 500,000 men were called for ; this call was reduced by the excess of credits on previous calls, and under it the States were credited with 386,461 men furnished, as follows :

STATES.	Quota.	MEN FURNISHED FOR				Paid commu- tation.	Total.
		One year.	Two years.	Three years.	Four years.		
Maine	11,116	8,320	131	2.590	1	11	11,053
New Hampshire....	4.648	1.921	25	4,027	....	......	5,973
Vermont...........	2,665	1,861	18	2.081	11	......	3.971
Massachusetts......	21,965	6,990	108	24,641	....	......	31,739
Rhode Island........	1,423	1,223	196	851	....	......	2,310
Connecticut........	5,583	493	20	10,318	24	2	10,857
New York...........	77,539	45,089	2,125	36,547	74	5	83,843
New Jersey	14,431	9,587	1,184	4.357	....	11	15,119
Pennsylvania	49,993	44,489	439	10,416	198	171	55,707
Delaware	2.184	1,558	9	593	15	......	2,175
Maryland	10,947	6,198	246	3,727	64	31	10,266
West Virginia......	2,717	1,726	28	202	....	......	1,956
District of Columbia.	2.386	979	59	937	343	19	2,537
Ohio...............	27,001	25.431	748	4,644	....	176	30,999
Indiana............	25,662	18,099	597	7,158	....	690	26,544
Illinois.............	21,997	12,558	535	2.323	....	49	15,465
Michigan	12,098	5,960	57	6.492	....	23	12,532
Wisconsin..........	17,590	10,905	86	5,832	....	16	16,839
Minnesota	4,018	2,791	205	239	....	3	3,238
Iowa	5,749	3,995	60	168	....	67	4,290
Missouri	25,569	7.782	1,295	14,430	....	......	23,507
Kentucky	9,871	5,060	169	10,137	....	24	15,390
Kansas	....	29	3	319	....	......	851
Total	357,152	223,044	8,340	153,049	730	1.298	386,461

Under the call of December 19, 1864, for 300,000 men, there were furnished 212.212 men, as specified below. The necessity for more men ceased to exist before most of the States had completed their quotas.

STATES.	Quota.	MEN FURNISHED FOR				Paid commu- tation.	Total.
		One year.	Two years.	Three years.	Four years.		
Maine	8,389	4,898	141	1,884	3	10	6,956
New Hampshire.....	2,072	492	9	775	28	......	1,304
Vermont...	1,832	962	29	550	9	......	1,550
Massachusetts......	1,306	1,535	43	2,349	2	......	3,929
Rhode Island........	1,459	739	92	732	....	......	1,563
Connecticut.........	....	34	7	1,282	2	......	1,325
New York......	61,076	9,150	1,645	23,321	67	13	34,196

STATES.	Quota.	MEN FURNISHED FOR				Paid commutation.	Total.
		One year.	Two years.	Three years.	Four years.		
New Jersey	11,695	6,511	1,075	3,527	155	15	11,283
Pennsylvania	46,437	26,666	204	3,903	44	282	31,099
Delaware	938		376	5	30	....	......	411
Maryland	9,142	3,236	430	1,275	....	3	4,944
West Virginia	4,431	2,114	8	415	....	......	2,537
District of Columbia	2,222	692	12	116	2	1	823
Ohio	26.027	21,712	641	2,214	....	13	24,580
Indiana	22,582	20,642	243	2,329	....	94	23,308
Illinois	32,902	25,940	356	2,022	....	6	28,324
Michigan	10,026	6,767	41	1,034	....	18	7,860
Wisconsin	12,356	9,666	15	240	....	1	9,922
Minnesota	3,636	2,689	12	68	....	2	2.771
Iowa	......	772	15	67	....	......	854
Missouri	13,984	3.161	44	1,002	....	......	4,207
Kentucky	10,481	1,987	7	5,609	....	......	7,603
Kansas	1,222	622	26	223	....	2	883
Total	284,215	151,363	5,110	54,967	312	460	212,212

During the war there were also furnished volunteers and militia by the following States and Territories, which, after the first call, had not been called upon for quotas when general calls for troops were made, viz.:

STATES AND TERRITORIES.	MEN FURNISHED FOR								Total.
	Sixty days.	Three mos.	100 days.	Four mos.	Six mos.	Eight mos.	One year.	Three years.	
Tennessee	....	....	739	....	....	....	6,039	24.314	31,092
Arkansas	.. .	....	....	....	374	....	213	7,702	8.289
N. Carolina	....	....	....	....	....	....	....	3,156	3,156
California	....	....	....	....	....	....	....	15,725	15.725
Nevada	....	....	....	....	....	....	.. .	1,080	1.080
Oregon	....	....	....	42	....	....	....	1,768	1,810
Wash. Ter	....	....	....	....	....	....	....	964	964
Colorado Ter	....	....	1,156	....	186	....	....	3,561	4,903
Dakota Ter	....	....	....	....	....	....	....	206	206
N. Mexico Ter.	....	1,593	....	....	803	....	....	4.165	6,561
Alabama	....	....	....	....	....	....	1,447	1,129	2,576
Florida	....	....	....	....	....	....	....	1,290	1,290
Louisiana	296	....	....	....	....	373	....	4.555	5.224
Mississippi	...	....	....	....	....	...	....	545	545
Texas	....	....	....	....	....	....	499	1,466	1,965
Indian Nation	....	....	....	... .	....	....	....	3,530	3,530
Col'd Troops	1,749	....	....	....	....	....	....	91,692	93,441
Total	2,045	1,593	1,895	42	1,363	373	8,198	166,848	182,357

1*

SUMMARY of the number of men called for by the President of the United States, and furnished by, and credited to, the States and Territories during the War of the Rebellion.

STATES AND TERRITORIES.	Quota.	MEN		Total.	Aggregate reduced to a three years' standard.
		Furnish'd.	Paid commutation.		
Maine	73.587	70,107	2,007	72,114	56,776
New Hampshire	35,897	33,937	692	34 629	30,349
Vermont	32,074	33,288	1,974	35,262	29,068
Massachusetts	139,095	146,730	5,318	152,048	124,104
Rhode Island	18,898	23,236	463	23,699	17,866
Connecticut	44,797	55,864	1,515	57,379	50,623
New York	507,148	448,850	18,197	467,047	392,270
New Jersey.............	92,820	76,814	4,196	81,010	57,908
Pennsylvania	385,369	337,936	28,171	366,107	265,517
Delaware	13,935	12,284	1,386	13,670	10.322
Maryland..............	70,965	46,638	3,678	50,316	41,275
West Virginia	34,463	32,068	......	32,068	27,714
District of Columbia	13,973	16,534	338	16,872	11,506
Ohio	306.:22	313,180	6,479	319,659	240,514
Indiana................	199,788	196,363	784	197,147	153,576
Illinois	244,496	259,092	55	259,147	214,133
Michigan	95,007	87,364	2,008	89,372	80,111
Wisconsin	109,080	91,327	5,097	96,424	79,260
Minnesota	26,326	24,020	1,032	25,052	19.693
Iowa	79,521	76,242	67	76,309	68,650
Missouri...............	122,496	109,111	......	109,111	86,530
Kentucky..............	100.782	75,760	3,265	79,025	70,832
Kansas................ .	12,931	20.149	2	20,151	18,706
Tennessee	1,560	31,092	......	31,092	26.394
Arkansas	780	8,289	......	8,289	7,836
North Carolina	1,560	3.156	......	3,156	3,156
California.............	......	15.725	......	15,725	15.725
Nevada................	......	1,080	......	1,080	1,080
Oregon	......	1,810	......	1,810	1,773
Washington Territory...	......	964	......	964	964
Nebraska Territory	......	3,157	......	3.157	2,175
Colorado Territory	......	4.903	......	4,903	3,697
Dakota Territory	......	206	......	206	206
New Mexico Territory...	......	6,561	......	6,561	4,432
Alabama	......	2,576	. ....	2,576	1,611
Florida	......	1,290	......	1,290	1,290
Louisiana..............	......	5,224	......	5,224	4,654
Mississippi	......	545	......	545	545
Texas	......	1,965	......	1,965	1,632
Indian Nation	......	3,530	......	3,530	3,530
Colored Troops	......	93,441	......	93,441	91,789
Total...............	2,763,670	2,772,408	86,724	2,859,132	2,320,272

The numbers given opposite "Colored Troops" in the foregoing table and the one preceding it show, not the total number of colored troops enlisted, but simply the number of those who were organized at various stations in the States in rebellion, and who could not be at the time, and were not, assigned or specifically credited to States.

The total number of colored troops enlisted during the war was 186,097.

As will be noticed in the preceding tables, some of the States and Territories, to whom no quotas were assigned, furnished men; which fact will account for the apparent excess of the men furnished over the number called for.

In the regular army there were enlisted during the war about 67,000 men; of these, probably not more than two-thirds were credited to the States.

For men furnished for service for a shorter period than ninety days, with a few exceptions, States received no credit. Many men were furnished for a service of thirty days, notably so in the summer of 1863. How many men were thus furnished it is not practicable to state, but an estimate may be based on the number (17,213 officers and men) furnished by the State of New York.

The accounts of all the States probably do not agree with the account of the Adjutant-General of the army; still the latter's account must be taken and accepted as correct.

Nevertheless, it is safe to say that the total number of men furnished by the States and Territories for the armies of the United States, after deducting those credited for service in the navy, will exceed 2,850,000 men.

In this number, men who re-enlisted are counted twice, or even more often. To give the number of individual persons who served in the army during the war is not practicable, nor is it of any practical benefit.

ORGANIZATIONS MUSTERED INTO THE SERVICE OF THE UNITED STATES.

During the war the following numbers of organizations were raised in the States and Territories and mustered into the service of the United States for various periods; these organizations do not, however, represent all the men furnished, for large numbers were sent as recruits to fill and strengthen old organizations already in the field.

Maine.

Cavalry—for over three years' service, 1 regiment; for three years' service, 1 regiment; total, 2 regiments.

Heavy Artillery—for over three years' service, 1 regiment.

Garrison Artillery—for three years' service, but served only one year, 3 companies.

Light Artillery—1 battalion of 7 batteries, of whom six served over three years.

Sharpshooters—1 battalion of 6 companies, for three years' service.

Infantry—for three years' service, but served longer, 7 regiments; for three years' service, 14 regiments and 4 companies; for nine months' service, 8 regiments; for three months' service, 1 regiment; for three years' service, coast-guard battalion, 7 companies; unassigned companies, for one year's service, 5; total infantry, 30 regiments and 16 companies.

Total—33 regiments, 7 batteries, and 25 companies.

New Hampshire.

Cavalry—for three years' service, 1 regiment.

Heavy Artillery—for three years' service, 1 regiment.

Light Artillery—for three years' service, 1 battery.

Infantry—for three years' service, 7 regiments, which served longer; for three years' service, 7 regiments; for nine months' service, 2 regiments; for three months' service, 1 regiment; for ninety days' service, 2 companies; for sixty days' service, 2 companies; total infantry, 17 regiments and 4 companies.

Total—19 regiments, 1 battery, and 4 companies.

Vermont.

Cavalry—for over three years' service, 1 regiment.

Heavy Artillery—for three years' service, 1 regiment; for one year's service, 1 company; total, 1 regiment and 1 company.

Light Artillery—for over three years' service, 1 battery ; for three years' service, 1 battery ; for two years' service, 1 battery ; total, 3 batteries.

Infantry—for over three years' service, 7 regiments; for three years' service, 7 regiments ; for nine months' service, 2 regiments ; for three months' service, 1 regiment ; total, 17 regiments.

Total—19 regiments, 3 batteries, and 1 company.

Massachusetts.

Cavalry—for over three years' service, 2 regiments ; for three years' service, 2 regiments ; for three years' service, colored, 1 regiment ; for three months' service, 1 battalion ; total, 5 regiments and 1 battalion.

Heavy Artillery—for over three years' service, 1 regiment ; for three years' service, 2 regiments and 6 companies ; for one year's service, 1 regiment and 2 companies ; total, 4 regiments and 8 companies.

Light Artillery—for over three years' service, 5 batteries ; for three years' service, 10 batteries ; for nine months' service, 1 battery ; for six months' service, 1 battery ; for three months' service, 1 battalion ; total, 1 battalion and 17 batteries.

Sharpshooters—for three years' service, 2 companies.

Infantry—for over three years' service, 15 regiments ; for three years' service, 23 regiments ; for three years' service, colored, 2 regiments ; for one year's service, 1 regiment and 14 companies ; for nine months' service, 22 regiments ; for six months' service, 1 company ; for one hundred days' service, 15 companies ; for three months' service, 5 regiments and 2 companies ; for ninety days' service, 13 companies ; total, 68 regiments and 45 companies.

Total—77 regiments, 2 battalions, 17 batteries, and 55 companies.

Rhode Island.

Cavalry—for over three years' service, 1 regiment ; for three years' service, 2 regiments ; for three months' service, 1 squadron ; total, 3 regiments and 2 companies.

Heavy Artillery—for over three years' service, 2 regiments.

Light Artillery—for over three years' service, 1 regiment ; for three months' service, 1 battery ; total, 1 regiment and 1 battery.

Infantry—for over three years' service, 1 regiment ; for three years' service, 2 regiments ; for nine months' service, 2 regiments ; for three months' service, 3 regiments ; for three years' service, Independent Company Hospital Guards ; total, 8 regiments and 1 company.

Total—14 regiments, 1 battery, and 3 companies.

Connecticut.

Cavalry—for over three years' service, 1 regiment.

Heavy Artillery—for over three years' service, 1 regiment ; for three years' service, 1 regiment ; total, 2 regiments.

Light Artillery—for over three years' service, 1 battery ; for three years' service, 1 battery ; for one year's service, 1 battery ; total, 3 batteries.

Infantry—for over three years' service, 9 regiments ; for three years' service, 7 regiments ; for three years' service, colored, 1 regiment ; for nine months' service, 7 regiments ; for three months' service, 3 regiments ; total 27 regiments.

Total—30 regiments and 3 batteries.

New York.

Cavalry—for over three years' service, 9 regiments and 1 company; for three years' service, 18 regiments and 2 companies; for one year's service, one regiment of 5 companies; for three months' service, 2 companies; total, 27 regiments and 10 companies.

Heavy Artillery—for over three years' service, 3 regiments; for three years' service, 10 regiments; total, 13 regiments.

Light Artillery—for over three years' service, 2 regiments; for over three years' service, 14 batteries; for three years' service, 19 batteries; for two years' service, 1 battery; for three months' service, 1 battery; total, 2 regiments and 35 batteries.

Engineers—for over three years' service, 2 regiments; for three years' service, 1 regiment; for two years' service, 1 regiment; total, 4 regiments.

Sharpshooters—for three years' service, 4 companies of 1st United States Sharpshooters and 4 additional companies; total, 8 companies.

Infantry—for over three years' service, 45 regiments; for three years' service, white, 93 regiments; for three years' service, colored, 3 regiments; for two years' service, white, 33 regiments; for two years' service, but served longer, 3 regiments; for one year's service, 6 regiments and 3 companies; for nine months' service, 2 regiments; for one hundred days' service, 10 regiments and 4 companies, for three months' service, 23 regiments; for thirty days' service, 30 regiments; total, 248 regiments and 7 companies.

Total—294 regiments, 35 batteries, and 25 companies.

New Jersey.

Cavalry—for three years' service and over, 1 regiment; for three years' service, 2 regiments; total, 3 regiments.

Light Artillery—for three years' service and over, 2 batteries; for three years' service, 3 batteries; total, 5 batteries.

Infantry—for three years' service and over, 5 regiments; for three years' service, 13 regiments and 4 companies; for one year's service, 4 regiments; for nine months' service, 11 regiments; for one hundred days' service, 1 regiment; for three months' service, 4 regiments; 38 regiments and 4 companies.

Total—41 regiments, 4 companies, and 5 batteries.

Pennsylvania.

Cavalry—for three years' service and over, 12 regiments; for three years' service, 9 regiments and 1 company; for one year's service, 1 company; for six months' service, 2 regiments and 8 companies; for one hundred days' service, 5 companies; for three months' service. 1 company; for ninety days' service, 7 companies; for the emergency, or thirty days' service, 5 companies; total, 23 regiments and 28 companies.

Heavy Artillery—for three years' service and over, 1 regiment; for three years' service, 1 regiment; for one year's service, 2 regiments; for six months' service, 2 companies; for three months' service, 1 company; for ninety days' service, 2 companies; total, 3 regiments and 5 companies.

Light Artillery—for three years' service and over, 1 regiment and 6 batteries; for three years' service, 3 batteries; for one year's service, 1 battery; for six months' service, 1 battery; for one hundred days' service, 3 batteries; for ninety days' service, 2 batteries; for thirty days' service, or the emergency, 3 batteries; total, 1 regiment and 19 batteries.

Infantry—for three years' service and over, 48 regiments; for three years' service, 51 regiments and 2 companies; for three years' service, colored, 10 regiments; for one year's service, 18 regiments and 4 companies; for nine months' service, 34 regiments and 5 companies; for six months' service, 21 companies; for one hundred days' service, 5 regiments and 9 companies; for three months' service, 25 regiments; for ninety days' service, 28 regiments and 18 companies; for thirty days' service, or the emergency, 8 regiments and 3 companies; total, 227 regiments and 62 companies.

Total—254 regiments, 95 companies, and 19 batteries.

Delaware.

Cavalry—for three years' service, 1 battalion of 7 companies; for thirty days' service, 1 company; total, 8 companies.

Heavy Artillery—for three years' service, 1 company.

Light Artillery—for three years' service, 1 battery.

Infantry—for three years' service and over, 2 regiments; for three years' service, 2 regiments; for one year's service, 4 companies; for nine months' service, 2 regiments; for one hundred days' service, 1 regiment; for three months' service, 1 regiment; for thirty days' service, 1 regiment; total, 9 regiments and 4 companies.

Total—9 regiments, 13 companies, and 1 battery.

Maryland.

Cavalry—for three years' service and over, 1 regiment; for three years' service, 2 regiments and 4 companies; for six months' service, 1 regiment; total, 4 regiments and 4 companies.

Light Artillery—for three years' service and over, 2 batteries; for three years' service, 2 batteries; for six months' service, 2 batteries; total, 6 batteries.

Infantry—for three years' service and over, 7 regiments and 1 company; for three years' service, 8 regiments; for one year's service, 1 regiment; for six months' service, 2 regiments; for one hundred days' service, 2 regiments; total, 20 regiments and 1 company.

Total—24 regiments, 5 companies, and 6 batteries.

District of Columbia.

Cavalry—for three years' service, 1 regiment; for three months' service, 1 company; total, 1 regiment and 1 company.

Infantry—for three years' service and over, 2 regiments; for three months' service, 33 companies; total, 2 regiments and 33 companies.

Total—3 regiments and 34 companies.

West Virginia.

Cavalry—for three years' service and over, 4 regiments; for three years' service, 2 regiments and 2 companies; for six months' service, 1 regiment; total, 7 regiments and 2 companies.

Light Artillery—for three years' service and over, 3 batteries; for three years' service, 5 batteries; total, 8 batteries.

Infantry—for three years' service and over, 4 regiments; for three years' service,

11 regiments and 2 companies; for one year's service, 1 regiment; for three months' service, 1 regiment; total, 17 regiments and 2 companies.
Total—24 regiments, 4 companies, and 8 batteries.

Virginia.

Infantry—one independent company for three years' service. The Light Artillery furnished by West Virginia was known also as Virginia Light Artillery.

North Carolina.

Cavalry—for three years' service, 2 regiments of mounted infantry.
Infantry—for three years' service, 2 regiments.
Total—4 regiments.

Georgia.

Infantry—for three years' service, 2 companies.

Florida.

Cavalry—for three years' service, 2 regiments.

Alabama.

Cavalry—for one and three years' service, 1 regiment; for one year's service, 5 companies.
Total—1 regiment and 5 companies.

Mississippi.

Cavalry—for three years' service, 1 battalion of 2 companies.

Louisiana.

Cavalry—for three years' service, 2 regiments.
Infantry—for three years' service, 3 regiments.
Total—5 regiments.

Texas.

Cavalry—for three years' service, 1 regiment and 5 companies; for one year's service, 4 companies.
Total—1 regiment and 9 companies.

Arkansas.

Cavalry—for three years' service, 4 regiments.
Light Artillery—for three years' service, 1 battery.
Infantry—for three years' service, 3 regiments; for six months' service, 2 companies; total, 3 regiments and 2 companies.
Total—7 regiments, 2 companies, and 1 battery.

Tennessee.

Cavalry and Mounted Infantry—for three years' service, 13 regiments and 4 companies; for one year's service, 7 regiments and three companies; for one hundred days' service, 1 regiment; total 21 regiments and 7 companies.
Light Artillery—for three years' service, 5 batteries.
Infantry—for three years' service and over, 2 regiments; for three years' service, 7 regiments; total 9 regiments.
Total—30 regiments, 7 companies, and 5 batteries.

Kentucky.

Cavalry and Mounted Infantry —for three years' service and over, 5 regiments ; for three years' service, 5 regiments and 4 companies ; for one year's service, 6 regiments and 6 companies ; total, 16 regiments and 10 companies.

Light Artillery—for three years' service and over, 2 batteries; for three years' service, 4 batteries ; for one year's service, 1 battery ; total, 7 batteries.

Infantry—for three years' service and over, 9 regiments ; for three years service, 21 regiments and 1 company ; for three years' service, colored, 2 regiments ; for one year's service, 12 regiments ; for nine months' service, 1 regiment ; total, 45 regiments and 1 company.

Total—61 regiments, 11 companies, and 7 batteries.

Ohio.

Cavalry—for three years' service and over, 7 regiments and 4 companies ; for three years' service, 6 regiments and 1 company ; for six months' service, 9 companies ; for three months' service, 2 companies ; for sixty days' service, 2 companies ; total, 13 regiments and 18 companies.

Heavy Artillery—for three years' service, 2 regiments.

Light Artillery—for three years' service and over, 1 regiment and 15 batteries ; for three years' service, 9 batteries ; for four months' service, 1 battery ; for sixty days' service, 2 batteries ; total, 1 regiment and twenty-seven batteries.

Sharpshooters—for three years' service, 3 companies.

Infantry—for three years' service and over, 60 regiments ; for three years' service, 60 regiments and 6 companies ; for three years' service, colored, 2 regiments ; for one year's service, 25 regiments ; for six months' service, 2 regiments ; for one hundred days' service, 42 regiments ; for three months' service, 27 regiments ; for thirty days' service, 2 companies ; total, 218 regiments and 8 companies.

Total—234 regiments, 29 companies, and 27 batteries.

Michigan.

Cavalry—for three years' service and over, 4 regiments ; for three years' service, 8 regiments and 2 companies ; total 12 regiments and 2 companies.

Heavy Artillery—for three years' service and over, 1 regiment.

Light Artillery—for three years' service and over, 1 regiment ; for three years' service, 11 batteries ; total, 1 regiment and 11 batteries.

Engineers—for three years' service and over, 1 regiment; for three years' service, 1 company ; total 1 regiment and 1 company.

Sharpshooters—for three years' service, 1 regiment and 2 companies ; for one year's service, 2 companies ; total, 1 regiment and 4 companies.

Infantry—for three years' service and over, 13 regiments ; for three years' service, 17 regiments and 2 companies ; for three years' service, 1 regiment colored troops ; for one year's service, 2 regiments ; for three months' service, 1 regiment ; total, 34 regiments and 2 companies.

Total—50 regiments, 9 companies, and 11 batteries.

Indiana.

Cavalry—for three years' service and over, 3 regiments : for three years' service, 10 regiments ; for one year's service, 1 company ; total, 13 regiments and 1 company.

Heavy Artillery—for three years' service and over, 1 regiment.

Light Artillery—for three years' service and over, 11 batteries; for three years' service, 14 batteries; for one year's service, 1 battery; total, 26 batteries.

Infantry—for three years' service and over, 40 regiments; for three years' service, 42 regiments; for three years' service, 1 regiment colored troops; for one year's service, 18 regiments and 5 companies; for six months' service, 4 regiments; for one hundred days' service, 8 regiments; for three months' service, 8 regiments; for sixty days' service, 6 companies; for thirty days' service, 2 regiments and 5 companies; total, 123 regiments and 16 companies.

Total—137 regiments, 17 companies, and 26 batteries.

Illinois.

Cavalry—for three years' service and over, 12 regiments; for three years' service, 5 regiments; total, 17 regiments.

Light Artillery—for three years' service and over, 2 regiments and 1 battery; for three years' service, 6 batteries; for three months' service, 1 battery; total, 2 regiments and 8 batteries.

Infantry—for three years' service and over, 53 regiments; for three years' service, 67 regiments and 1 company; for three years' service, 1 regiment colored troops; for one year's service, 12 regiments; for one hundred days' service, 13 regiments and 2 companies; for three months' service, 11 regiments and 2 companies; for thirty days' service, 1 company; for fifteen days' service, 3 companies; total 157 regiments and 9 companies.

Total—176 regiments, 9 companies, and 8 batteries.

Missouri.

Cavalry—for three years' service and over, 9 regiments; for three years' service, 19 regiments and 25 companies; for twenty months' service, 2 regiments; for three months' service, 1 company; total, 30 regiments and 26 companies.

Light Artillery—for three years' service, 3 batteries; for three months' service, 3 batteries; total, 6 batteries.

Engineers—for three years' service and over, 1 regiment.

Infantry—for three years' service and over, 9 regiments; for three years' service, 23 regiments, 16 companies; for three years' service, 4 regiments colored troops; for one year's service, 12 regiments; for six months' service, 3 regiments; for three months' service, 11 regiments and 4 companies; for one hundred days' service, 1 regiment; total 63 regiments and 20 companies.

Total—94 regiments, 6 batteries, and 46 companies.

Wisconsin.

Cavalry—for three years' service and over, 4 regiments.

Heavy Artillery—for three years' service and over, 1 regiment.

Light Artillery—for three years' service and over, 10 batteries; for three years' service, 2 batteries; total, 12 batteries.

Infantry—for three years' service and over, 15 regiments; for three years' service, 21 regiments; for one year's service, 12 regiments; for nine months' service, 1 regiment; for one hundred days' service, 3 regiments; for three months' service, 1 regiment; total, 53 regiments.

Total—58 regiments and 12 batteries.

Iowa.

Cavalry—for three years' service and over, 5 regiments ; for three years' service, 4 regiments ; total, 9 regiments.

Light Artillery—for three years' service and over, 3 batteries; for three years' service, 1 battery ; total, 4 batteries.

Infantry—for three years' service and over, 15 regiments; for three years' service, 24 regiments ; for three years' service, 1 regiment, colored troops ; for one hundred days' service, 5 regiments ; for three months' service, 1 regiment ; total, 46 regiments.

Total—55 regiments and 4 batteries.

Minnesota.

Cavalry—for three years' service and over, 4 companies ; for three years' service, 1 regiment and 6 companies ; for one year's service, 1 regiment ; total, 2 regiments and 10 companies.

Heavy Artillery—for one year's service, 1 regiment.

Light Artillery—for three years' service and over, 2 batteries; for three years' service, 1 battery ; total, 3 batteries.

Infantry—for three years' service and over, 5 regiments ; for three years' service, 5 regiments , for one year's service, 1 regiment ; total, 11 regiments.

Total—14 regiments, 10 companies, and 3 batteries.

California.

Cavalry—for three years' service and over, 1 regiment ; for three years' service, 1 regiment and 4 companies ; total, 2 regiments and 4 companies.

Infantry—for three years' service and over, 4 regiments ; for three years' service, 5 regiments ; total, 9 regiments.

Total—11 regiments and 4 companies.

Kansas.

Cavalry—for three years' service and over, 4 regiments ; for three years' service, 5 regiments ; total, 9 regiments.

Light Artillery—for three years' service and over, 2 batteries ; for three years' service, 1 battery ; total, 3 batteries.

Infantry—for three years' service and over, 3 regiments ; for three years' service, two regiments, colored troops ; for three years' service, 5 regiments ; for one hundred days' service, 5 companies ; total, 10 regiments and 5 companies.

Total—19 regiments, 5 companies, and 3 batteries.

Oregon.

Cavalry—for three years' service, 1 regiment.

Infantry—for three years' service, 1 regiment.

Total—2 regiments.

Nevada.

Cavalry—for three years' service, 6 companies.

Infantry—for three years' service, 3 companies.

Total—9 companies.

Washington Territory.

Infantry—for three years' service and over, 1 regiment.

New Mexico Territory.

Cavalry—for three years' service, 1 regiment; for six months' service, 1 regiment; for three months' service, 5 companies; total, 2 regiments and 5 companies.
Infantry—for three years' service, 5 regiments; for three months' service, 1 regiment and 11 companies; total, 6 regiments and 11 companies.
Total—8 regiments and 16 companies.

Nebraska Territory.

Cavalry—for three years' service and over, 1 regiment; for three years' service, 4 companies; for nine months' service, 1 regiment; total, 2 regiments and 4 companies.
Infantry—for one year's service, 2 companies.
Total—2 regiments and 6 companies.

Colorado Territory.

Cavalry—for three years' service and over, 1 regiment; for three years' service, 1 regiment; for one hundred days' service, 1 regiment; total, 3 regiments.
Light Artillery—for three years' service, 1 battery
Infantry—for six months' service, 2 companies.
Total—3 regiments, 1 battery, and 2 companies.

Dakota Territory.

Cavalry—for three years' service, 2 companies.

In addition to these organizations from States and Territories there were in the service of the United States:

United States Veteran Volunteer Infantry.

(FIRST ARMY CORPS, HANCOCK.)

Engineers— for three years' service, 1 regiment.
Infantry—for three years' service, 9 regiments.
Total—10 regiments.

United States Volunteer Infantry.

Sharpshooters—2 regiments, which have been included in State organizations.
Infantry—for three years' service, 4 regiments and 1 company ; for one year's service, 2 regiments.
Total—6 regiments and 1 company.

U. S. Colored Troops.

There were in all 167 organizations, but 31 of these which have been included in State organizations, are omitted here :
Cavalry—for three years' service, 6 regiments.
Heavy Artillery—for three years' service, 11 regiments and 4 companies.

Light Artillery—for three years' service, 10 batteries.
Infantry—for three years' service, 100 regiments and 16 companies ; for one year's service, 1 company ; for one hundred days' service, 1 company ; for sixty days' service, 2 regiments : total, 102 regiments and 18 companies.
Total—119 regiments, 22 companies, and 10 batteries.

Veteran Reserve Corps.

In this Corps there were 24 regiments and 187 companies, which were, however, composed of men credited to volunteer organizations.

Regular Army.

In the Regular Army there were :
Cavalry—for three years' service and over, 6 regiments.
Artillery—for three years' service and over, 5 regiments.
Infantry—for three years' service and over, 19 regiments.
Total—30 regiments.

TABULAR STATEMENT OF ORGANIZATIONS
IN THE SERVICE
OF THE UNITED STATES DURING THE REBELLION.

STATES AND TERRITORIES.	CAVALRY. Regiments.	Companies.	ARTILLERY. Regiments.	Companies.	Batteries.	INFANTRY. Regiments.	Companies.	TOTAL. Regiments.	Companies.	Batteries.
Maine	2	..	1	3	7	30	22	33	25	7
New Hampshire	1	..	1	..	1	17	4	19	4	1
Vermont	1	..	1	1	3	17	..	19	1	3
Massachusetts	5	4	4	8	19	68	47	77	59	19
Rhode Island	3	2	3	..	1	8	1	14	3	1
Connecticut	1	..	2	..	3	21	..	30	..	3
New York	27	10	15	..	35	252	15	294	25	35
New Jersey	3	..	..	..	5	38	4	41	4	5
Pennsylvania	23	28	4	5	19	227	62	254	95	19
Delaware	..	8	..	1	1	9	4	9	13	1
Maryland	4	4	..	..	6	20	1	24	5	6
District of Columbia	1	1	..	..	..	2	33	3	34	..
West Virginia	7	2	..	..	8	17	2	24	4	8
Virginia	..	..	..	..	..	..	1	..	1	..
North Carolina	2	..	.	..	..	2	..	4	..	..
Georgia	..	..	..	..	..	..	2	..	2	..
Florida	2	..	..	..	..	..	..	2	..	..
Alabama	1	5	..	..	..	..	..	1	5	..
Mississippi	..	2	..	..	..	..	..	..	2	..
Louisiana	2	..	..	..	..	3	..	5	..	..
Texas	1	9	..	..	..	..	..	1	9	..
Arkansas	4	..	..	..	1	3	2	7	2	1
Tennessee	21	7	..	..	5	9	..	30	7	5
Kentucky	16	10	..	..	7	45	1	61	11	7
Ohio	13	18	3	..	27	218	11	234	29	27
Michigan	12	2	2	..	11	36	7	50	9	11
Indiana	13	1	1	..	26	123	16	137	17	26
Illinois	17	..	2	..	8	157	9	176	9	8
Missouri	30	26	..	..	6	64	20	94	46	6
Wisconsin	4	..	1	..	12	53	..	58	..	12
Iowa	9	..	..	..	4	46	..	55	..	4
Minnesota	2	10	1	..	3	11	..	14	10	3
California	2	4	..	..	..	9	..	11	4	..
Kansas	9	..	..	..	3	10	5	19	5	3
Oregon	1	..	..	..	..	1	..	2	.9	..
Nevada	..	6	..	..	..	..	3	..	..	..
Washington Territory	..	..	..	..	..	1	..	1	..	..
New Mexico Territory	2	5	..	..	..	6	11	8	16	..
Nebraska Territory	2	4	..	..	..	..	2	2	6	..
Colorado Territory	3	..	..	..	1	..	2	3	2	1
Dakota Territory	..	2	..	..	..	..	..	..	2	..
U. S. Vet. Volunteer Infantry	..	..	..	..	..	10	..	10	..	..
U. S. Volunteer Infantry	..	..	..	..	..	6	1	6	1	..
United States Colored Troops	6	..	11	4	10	102	18	119	22	10
U. S. Army, Regulars	6	..	5	..	..	19	..	30	..	..
Total	258	170	57	22	232	1666	306	1981	498	232

Reduce the 170 companies of cavalry to regiments, 12 companies to a regiment, will give 14 regiments and 2 companies, which added to the 258 regiments will give a total of cavalry, mounted infantry, rifles, and lancers of.................. 272 regiments, 2 companies.

Reduce the 22 companies and 232 batteries of artillery to regiments, 12 companies to a regiment, will give 21 regiments and 2 companies, which added to the 57 regiments will give a total of artillery of................................... 78   "   2   "

Reduce the 306 companies of infantry to regiments, 10 companies to a regiment, will give 30 regiments and 6 companies; this, added to the 1,666 regiments, will give a total infantry of........1,696   "   6   "

Making a grand total of .... 2,047 regiments.

Nine regiments of infantry of the regular army were organizations of 24 companies each; taking this into consideration and allowing for errors it may be said that during the war organizations equivalent to 2,050 regiments entered into the service of the United States: the regular army included and the veteran reserve corps excluded.

The Secretary of War, in his report dated November 22, 1865, makes the following remarks, which show more than anything else the spirit animating the people of the loyal States: "On several occasions, when troops were promptly needed to avert impending disaster, vigorous exertion brought them into the field from remote States, with incredible speed. Official reports show that after the disasters on the Peninsula, in 1862, over 80,000 troops were enlisted, organized, armed, equipped, and sent into the field in less than a month. 60,000 troops have repeatedly gone to the field within four weeks. 90,000 infantry were sent to the armies from the five States of Ohio, Indiana, Illinois, Iowa, and Wisconsin, within twenty days. When Lee's army surrendered, thousands of recruits were pouring in, and men were discharged from recruiting stations and rendezvous in every State."

MILITARY DIVISIONS, DEPARTMENTS, AND DISTRICTS OF THE UNITED STATES.

DURING the war, the several States and Territories of the United States were divided into military divisions, military departments and districts. These divisions were, from time to time, changed, abolished, and renewed. The divisions made by order of the President of the United States were as follows:

MILITARY DIVISIONS.

GEOGRAPHICAL DIVISION.—General Order No. 47, War Department, July 25, 1861, directs that the Departments of Washington and North-Eastern Virginia should constitute this division, and be under the command of Major-General McClellan, with headquarters at Washington, D.C.

DEPARTMENT OF THE MISSISSIPPI.—In spring, 1862, this department was enlarged for a time, so as to bring the armies of the Ohio, of the Tennessee, and of the Mississippi under the command of Major-General Halleck, for combined operations.

MILITARY DIVISION OF THE MISSISSIPPI.—October 16, 1863, General Order No. 337, War Department, the Departments of the Ohio, of the Cumberland, and of the Tennessee were constituted the military division of the Mississippi, under the command of Major-General Grant. March 12, 1864, Major-General W. T. Sherman was placed in command of the division. June 27, 1865, it was to consist of the Departments of the Ohio, of the Missouri, and of Arkansas, with headquarters at St. Louis, Mo.

MIDDLE MILITARY DIVISION.—The Middle Department and the Departments of Washington, of the Susquehanna, and of West Virginia, were constituted this division, August 7, 1864, and Major-General P. H. Sheridan placed in command of it.

MILITARY DIVISION OF WEST MISSISSIPPI.—May 7, 1864, General

Order No. 192, War Department, created this division, composed of the Departments of Arkansas and the Gulf, and assigned Major-General E. R. S. Canby to the command of it.

MILITARY DIVISION OF THE ATLANTIC.—General Order No. 118, War Department, June 27, 1865, constituted this division, to be composed of the Departments of the East, Virginia, North Carolina, South Carolina, and Mountain Department; to be commanded by Major-General Geo. G. Meade, with headquarters at Philadelphia, Pa.

MILITARY DIVISION OF THE GULF.—Constituted, June 27, 1865, of the Departments of Mississippi, Louisiana, Texas, and Florida, with Major-General P. H. Sheridan in command, and headquarters at New Orleans.

MILITARY DIVISION OF THE TENNESSEE.—Constituted, June 27, 1865, to embrace the Departments of the Tennessee, Kentucky, Georgia, and Alabama; Major-General G. H. Thomas to command; headquarters at Nashville, Tenn.

MILITARY DIVISION OF THE PACIFIC.—Constituted, June 27, 1865, of the Departments of the Columbia and California, and commanded by Major-General H. W. Halleck, with headquarters at San Francisco, Cal.

MILITARY DEPARTMENTS, ETC.

into which the several States and Territories of the United States were divided during the War of the Rebellion:

(*By States.*)

Maine.—This State was in the Department of the East from January 1, 1861, to October 1, 1861; Department of New England to February 20, 1862; not in any department to January 3, 1863; Department of the East to the close of the war.

New Hampshire.—In the Department of the East from January 1, 1861, to October 1, 1861; Department of New England to February 20, 1862; not in any department to January 3, 1863; Department of the East to the close of the war.

Vermont.—In the Department of the East from January 1, 1861, to October 1, 1861; Department of New England to February 20, 1862; not in any department to January 3, 1863; Department of the East to the close of the war.

Massachusetts.—In the Department of the East from January 1, 1861, to October 1, 1861; Department of New England to February 20, 1862; not in any department to January 3, 1863; Department of the East to the close of the war.

Rhode Island.—In the Department of the East from January 1,

1861, to October 1, 1861 ; Department of New England to February 20, 1862; not in any department to January 3, 1863 ; Department of the East to the close of the war.

Connecticut.—In the Department of the East from January 1, 1861, to October 1, 1861 ; Department of New England to February 20, 1862 ; not in any department to January 3, 1863 ; Department of the East to the close of the war.

New York.—In the Department of the East from January 1, 1861, to October 26, 1861 ; Department of New York to January 3, 1863 ; Department of the East to the close of the war.

New Jersey.—In the Department of the East from January 1, 1861, to October 26, 1861; not in any department to February 1, 1862; Department of the Potomac to March 22, 1862; Middle Department to February 6, 1863 ; Department of the East to the close of the war.

Pennsylvania.—In the Department of the East from January 1, 1861, to April 19, 1861 ; Department of Washington to April 27, 1861 ; Department of Pennsylvania to August 17, 1861 (excepting that part lying west of a line drawn from the point of intersection of the Southern Pennsylvania and Western Maryland lines to the northeast corner of McKean County, which was in the Department of the Ohio from May 9, 1861, to July 25, 1861) ; [1] not in any department to February 1, 1862 ; Department of the Potomac to March 22, 1862; Middle Department to June 9, 1863 ; that part lying east of Johnstown and the Laurel Hill range of mountains in the Department of the Susquehanna to December 1, 1864, and that part west of said line in the Department of the Monongahela to April 6, 1864, when the latter section was merged into the Department of the Susquehanna, and the entire State so continued till December 1, 1864; Department of Pennsylvania to the close of the war.

Delaware.—In the Department of the East from January 1, 1861, to April 19, 1861 ; Department of Washington to April 27, 1861 ; Department of Pennsylvania to August 17, 1861 ; Department of the Potomac to March 22, 1862; Middle Department to the close of the war, excepting the post of Fort Delaware, which was regarded as an independent command subsequent to March 12, 1864.

---

[1] Although the Department of Pennsylvania was discontinued August 17, 1861, yet part of its territory (State of Pennsylvania) was not formally added to the Department of the Potomac, to which the remainder was transferred, until February 1, 1862. It appears, however, that by an order from the Headquarters of the army of August 24, 1861, General Dix's command (formerly the Department of Pennsylvania) was assigned to the Department of the Potomac, and on the 8th of November, 1861, that officer changed the caption of his orders from " Headquarters Department of Pennsylvania " to " Headquarters Division."

Maryland.—January 1, 1861, to April 9,1861.—The entire State in the Department of the East.

April 9, 1861, to April 27, 1861.—The entire State in the Department of Washington.

April 27, 1861, to July 25, 1861.—Fort Washington and the adjacent country as far as Bladensburg, inclusive, in the Department of Washington ; the country for twenty miles on each side of the railroad from Annapolis to the City of Washington as far as Bladensburg in the Department of Annapolis (changed to the Department of Maryland July 19, 1861) ; the remainder in the Department of Pennsylvania.

July 25, 1861, to August 17, 1861.—The counties of Washington and Allegheny in the Department of the Shenandoah ; all of Prince George's County, including the section of country lying east of the District of Columbia and south of a line twenty miles from the south side of the railroad from Annapolis to the City of Washington as far as Bladensburg, and the counties of Montgomery and Frederick, in the Department of Washington ; the remainder in the Department of Pennsylvania.

August 17, 1861, to March 3, 1862.—The entire State in the Department of the Potomac.

March 3, 1862, to March 11, 1862.—That part lying west of Flintstone Creek, in Allegheny County, in the Department of Western Virginia ; the remainder in the Department of the Potomac.

March 11, 1862, to March 22, 1862.—That part lying west of Flintstone Creek, in Allegheny County, in the Mountain Department ; the remainder in the Department of the Potomac.

March 22, 1862, to April 4, 1862.—The Eastern Shore and counties of Cecil, Harford, Baltimore, and Anne Arundel, in the Middle Department ; that portion west of Flintstone Creek, in Allegheny County, in the Mountain Department, and the remainder in the Department of the Potomac.

April 4, 1862, to June 26, 1862.—That part west of the Blue Ridge and east of Flintstone Creek in the Department of the Shenandoah ; that part west of Flintstone Creek in the Mountain Department ; the country between the Potomac and Patuxent in the Department of the Rappahannock, and the remainder in the Middle Department.

June 26, 1862, to September 2, 1862.—The sections embraced within the limits of the Departments of the Shenandoah, Rappahannock, and Mountain Department (as described in the foregoing paragraph), were under the jurisdiction of the Commanding General Army of Virginia ; the remainder continued in the Middle Department.

September 2, 1862, to February 2, 1863.—The district of country lying within a line beginning at Fort Washington, on the Potomac, and running thence to Annapolis Junction, and thence to the mouth of

Seneca Creek, in the defences of Washington ; the rest in the Middle Department.[1]

February 2, 1863, to June 24, 1863.—The district of country north of the Potomac River from Piscataway Creek to Annapolis Junction, and thence to the mouth of the Monocacy, in the Department of Washington ; the remainder in the Middle Department.

June 24, 1863, to July 23, 1863.—That part lying west of Hancock, Washington County, in the Department of West Virginia ; that north of the Potomac River from Piscataway Creek to Annapolis Junction, and thence to the mouth of the Monocacy, in the Department of Washington ; the remainder in the Middle Department.[1]

July 23, 1863, to August 3, 1863.—The county of St. Mary's in the St. Mary's District; that part west of Hancock, Washington County, in the Department of West Virginia; that north of the Potomac River from Piscataway Creek to Annapolis Junction, and thence to the mouth of the Monocacy, in the Department of Washington ; the remainder in the Middle Department.

August 3, 1863, to December 21, 1863.—The county of St. Mary's in the District of St. Mary's; that part west of the Monocacy River in the Department of West Virginia ; that north of the Potomac River from Piscataway Creek to Annapolis Junction, and thence to the mouth of the Monocacy, in the Department of Washington ; the remainder in the Middle Department.

December 21, 1863, to June 21, 1864.—The county of St. Mary's in the Department of Virginia and North Carolina ; that part west of the Monocacy River in the Department of West Virginia ; that north of the Potomac River from Piscataway Creek to Annapolis Junction, and thence to the mouth of the Monocacy, in the Department of Washington ; the remainder in the Middle Department.

June 21, 1864, to close of war.—That portion between the Patuxent, the Chesapeake Bay, and the Potomac River, including the prisoners' camp at Point Lookout and south of a line from Annapolis Junction to the mouth of the Monocacy, in the Department of Washington ; that west of the Monocacy in the Department of West Virginia ; the remainder in the Middle Department.[2]

---

[1] During the Maryland campaign, from September 3 to November 2, 1862, the Army of the Potomac also operated in the Counties of Montgomery, Frederick, and Washington ; and during the Gettysburg campaign, from June 25 to July 19, 1863, in the Counties of Montgomery, Frederick, Carroll. and Washington.

[2] At the time of the rebel invasion of Maryland and threatened attack on the City of Washington, in July, 1864, troops of the Sixth and Nineteenth Army Corps and the Department of West Virginia also operated in the Counties of Montgomery and Frederick. In the early part of August, 1864, the First Division, Cavalry Corps, Army of the Potomac. marched from Washington, D. C., *via* Tenallytown and Poolesville to Harper's Ferry.

District of Columbia.—In the Department of the East from January 1, 1861, to April 9, 1861 ; Department of Washington to August 17, 1861 ; Department of the Potomac to April 4, 1862 ; Department of the Rappahannock to June 26, 1862 ; Military District of Washington to September 2, 1862 ; Defences of Washington to February 2, 1863, and Department of Washington to the close of the war.

Virginia.—This State seceded April 17, 1861, and the whole of its territory (except the military post of Fort Monroe, which was continuously held by the Government) passed into the hands of the rebel authorities. The first advance of United States troops within its borders occurred on the night of the 23d of May, 1861. A force belonging to the Department of Washington took possession of Arlington Heights, and the following morning (May 24) the city of Alexandria was also occupied. From this time to the close of the war the entire State, to a greater or less extent, was occupied by the opposing armies moving to and fro, and rendering it difficult to accurately define the various changes of departmental lines occurring therein. The following summary, however, may be considered approximately, if not absolutely, correct.

January 1, 1861, to April 9, 1861.—The entire State in the Department of the East.

April 9, 1861, to May 9, 1861.—Alexandria County (originally in the District of Columbia) in the Department of Washington ; the remainder in the Department of the East.

May 9, 1861, to May 22, 1861.—Alexandria County in the Department of Washington ; so much of Western Virginia as lies north of the Great Kanawha, north and west of the Greenbrier, and west of a line thence northward to the southwest corner of Maryland, and west of the Western Maryland and Western Pennsylvania lines, in the Department of the Ohio ; the remainder in the Department of the East.

May 22, 1861, to May 27, 1861.—Alexandria County in the Department of Washington ; so much of Western Virginia as lies north of the Great Kanawha, north and west of the Greenbrier, and west of a line thence northward to the southwest corner of Maryland, and west of the Western Maryland and Western Pennsylvania lines, in the Department of the Ohio ; the district of country within sixty miles of Fort Monroe, including that post in the Department of Virginia ; the remainder in the Department of the East.

May 27, 1861, to July 25, 1861.—So much of Western Virginia as lies north of the Great Kanawha, north and west of the Greenbrier, and west of a line thence northward to the southwest corner of Maryland, and west of the Western Maryland and Western Pennsylvania lines, in the Department of the Ohio ; the district of country within sixty miles of Fort Monroe, including that post in the Department of Virginia ;

that portion east of the Allegheny Mountains and north of the James
River (except Fort Monroe and within sixty miles thereof) in the Department of Northeastern Virginia; the remainder in the Department
of the East.

[NOTE.—On July 2, 1861, the Army under General Robert Patterson, commanding the Department of Pennsylvania, crossed the Potomac at Williamsport,
Md., and operated in Berkeley and Jefferson Counties, returning to the Maryland side of the river on July 21, 1861, by way of Harper's Ferry.]

July 25, 1861, to August 17, 1861.—So much of Western Virginia as
lies north of the Great Kanawha, north and west of the Greenbrier, and
west of a line thence northward to the southwest corner of Maryland, and west of the Western Maryland and Western Pennsylvania
lines, in the Department of Ohio; the district of country within sixty
miles of Fort Monroe, including that post, in the Department of Virginia; that portion east of the Alleghenies and north of the James (except Fort Monroe and within sixty miles thereof, and such parts as may
be covered by the Army or Department of the Shenandoah in its operations) in the Department of Northeastern Virginia; the Shenandoah
Valley and such other parts as may be covered by the Army commanded
by General Banks in its operations in the Department of the Shenandoah.

August 17, 1861, to September 19, 1861.—So much of Western Virginia as lies north of the Great Kanawha, north and west of the Greenbrier, and west of a line thence northward to the southwest corner of
Maryland, and west of the Western Maryland and Western Pennsylvania
lines, in the Department of the Ohio; the district of country within
sixty miles of Fort Monroe, including that post, in the Department of
Virginia; that portion east of the Alleghenies and north of the James
(excepting Fort Monroe and within sixty miles thereof, and including
the Shenandoah Valley) in the Department of the Potomac.

September 19, 1861, to November 9, 1861.—That part lying west of
the Blue Ridge Mountains in the Department of Western Virginia; the
district of country within sixty miles of Fort Monroe, including that
post, in the Department of Virginia; that portion east of the Blue
Ridge Mountains and north of the James (except Fort Monroe and
within sixty miles thereof) in the Department of the Potomac.

November 9, 1861, to March 3, 1862.—That part lying west of the
Alleghenies in the Department of Western Virginia; the district of
country within sixty miles of Fort Monroe, including that post, in the
Department of Virginia; that portion east of the Alleghenies and north
cf the James (except Fort Monroe and within sixty miles thereof) in the
Department of the Potomac.

March 3, 1862, to March 22, 1862.—The district of country within
sixty miles of Fort Monroe, including that post, in the Department of

Virginia; that part north of the James River (except Fort Monroe and within sixty miles thereof) and east of a line commencing at the north on the Potomac River opposite the mouth of the Flintstone Creek, and running thence southwardly along the South Branch Mountain, Town Hill Mountain, Branch Mountain or Big Ridge, and North or Shenandoah Mountain, Purgatory Mountain, Blue Ridge, and the Alleghenies, in the Department of the Potomac; and that part west of the lines just defined in the Department of Western Virginia.

[NOTE.—On March 11, 1862, the designation of the Department of Western Virginia was changed to the Mountain Department, but no alteration of Departmental lines was made, so far as related to the State of Virginia.]

March 22, 1862, to April 4, 1862.—The Eastern Shore (Accomac and Northampton Counties) in the Middle Department; the district of country within sixty miles of Fort Monroe (on the mainland), including that post, in the Department of Virginia; that part north of the James River (except Fort Monroe and within sixty miles thereof), and east of a line commencing at the north on the Potomac River, opposite the mouth of Flintstone Creek, and running thence southwardly along the South Branch Mountain, Town Hill Mountain, Branch Mountain or Big Ridge, the North or Shenandoah Mountain, Purgatory Mountain, Blue Ridge, and the Alleghenies, in the Department of the Potomac, and that part west of the line just defined in the Mountain Department.

April 4, 1862, to June 1, 1862.—The Eastern Shore (Accomac and Northampton Counties) in the Middle Department; the district of country within sixty miles of Fort Monroe (on the mainland), including that post, in the Department of Virginia; that part north of the James River (except Fort Monroe and within sixty miles thereof) and east of the Fredericksburg and Richmond Railroad in the Department of the Potomac; that part west of the Potomac River and the Fredericksburg and Richmond Railroad, and east of the Blue Ridge, in the Department of the Rappahannock; that part west of the Blue Ridge and east of a line commencing at the north on the Potomac River, opposite the mouth of Flintstone Creek, and running thence southwardly along the South Branch Mountain, Townhill Mountain, Branch Mountain or Big Ridge, the North or Shenandoah Mountain, Purgatory Mountain, Blue Ridge and the Alleghenies, in the Department of the Shenandoah, and that part west of the line just defined in the Mountain Department.

[NOTE.—The Advance Corps of the Army of the Potomac, changing its line of operations to the Peninsula, arrived at Fort Monroe, March 23, 1862, and from that date until June 1, 1862, the Army of the Potomac operated within the limits previously comprehended in the Department of Virginia. On the last-named date the limits of the Department of Virginia were extended, and all the forces therein placed under the command of General McClellan.]

June 1, 1862, to June 8, 1862.—The Eastern Shore (Accomac and

Northampton Counties) in the Middle Department; that part south of the Rappahannock and east of the railroad from Fredericksburg to Richmond, Petersburg, and Weldon, in the Department of Virginia; that part north of the Rappahannock, west of the railroad from Fredericksburg to Richmond, and east of the Blue Ridge, in the Department of the Rappahannock; that part west of the Blue Ridge and east of a line commencing at the north on the Potomac River, opposite the mouth of Flintstone Creek, and running thence southwardly along the South Branch Mountain, Town Hill Mountain, Branch Mountain or Big Ridge, the North or Shenandoah Mountain, Purgatory Mountain, Blue Ridge, and the Alleghenies, in the Department of the Shenandoah, and that part west of the line just defined in the Mountain Department.

June 8, 1862, to June 26, 1862.—The Eastern Shore (Accomac and Northampton Counties) in the Middle Department; that part south of the Rappahannock and east of the railroad from Fredericksburg to Richmond, Petersburg, and Weldon, in the Department of Virginia; that part north of the Rappahannock, west of the railroad from Fredericksburg to Richmond, and east of the Blue Ridge (excluding the Piedmont District and the Bull Mountain Range), in the Department of the Rappahannock; that part west of the Blue Ridge (including the Piedmont District and the Bull Mountain Range on the east) and east of the road known as Valley pike, and running from the Potomac (opposite Williamsport, Maryland) to Staunton (excluding that place), and of a line thence southward until it reaches the Blue Ridge, and thence with the line of the railroad to the southern boundary of the State, in the Department of the Shenandoah, and that part west of the line just defined in the Mountain Department.

[NOTE.—The limits and boundaries of the Departments of the Rappahannock, the Shenandoah, and the Mountain Department as herein described were not strictly adhered to. Certain movements of the enemy west of the Blue Ridge made it necessary to disregard departmental lines, and troops of the three departments named operated in the Luray and Shenandoah Valleys during the whole or greater part of the time here embraced.]

June 26, 1862, to September 19, 1862.—The Eastern Shore (Accomac and Northampton Counties) in the Middle Department; that part south of the Rappahannock and east of the railroad from Fredericksburg to Richmond, Petersburg, and Weldon, in the Department of Virginia.

[NOTE.—On June 26, 1862, the forces belonging to the Departments of the Rappahannock, the Shenandoah, and the Mountain Department were consolidated into one army, under the designation of the "Army of Virginia," the troops of the Mountain Department forming the First Army Corps, the Department of the Shenandoah the Second Army Corps, and the Department of the Rappahannock the Third Army Corps. This arrangement was continued until September 2, 1862, when the Army Potomac (which had in the latter part of August moved from the Peninsula or Department of Virginia) and Army of Virginia were consolidated, the latter being merged into the former, and the entire force (except those in the defences of Washington) put in motion through Maryland to repel the invasion of that State by the enemy.]

September 19, 1862, to February 2, 1863.—The Eastern Shore (Accomac and Northampton Counties) in the Middle Department; that part south of the Rappahannock and east of the railroad from Fredericksburg to Richmond, Petersburg, and Weldon, in the Department of Virginia; all of Western Virginia in the Department of the Ohio, and so much of the remainder as lies north of the James River and was covered by the Army of the Potomac in its operations, in the Department (or Army) of the Potomac.

February 2, 1863, to March 16, 1863.—The Eastern Shore (Accomac and Northampton Counties) in the Middle Department; that part south of the Rappahannock and east of the railroad from Fredericksburg to Richmond, Petersburg, and Weldon, in the Department of Virginia; the district of country lying east of a line beginning at the confluence of Goose Creek and the Potomac, and running south along the creek and Bull Run Mountains to the mouth of the Occoquan, in the Department of Washington; all of Western Virginia in the Department of the Ohio, and so much of the remainder as lies north of the James River and was covered by the Army of the Potomac in its operations, in the Department (or Army) of the Potomac.

March 16, 1863, to June 9, 1863.—The Eastern Shore (Accomac and Northampton Counties) and Western Virginia in the Middle Department; that part south of the Rappahannock and east of the railroad from Fredericksburg to Richmond, Petersburg, and Weldon, in the Department of Virginia; the district of country lying east of a line beginning at the confluence of Goose Creek and the Potomac, and running south along the creek and Bull Run Mountains to the mouth of the Occoquan, in the Department of Washington, and so much of the remainder as lies north of the James River and was covered by the Army of the Potomac in its operations, in the Department (or Army) of the Potomac.

[NOTE.—From this point Western Virginia is taken up as a separate State, which see following.]

June 9, 1863, to July 15, 1863.—The Eastern Shore (Accomac and Northampton Counties) in the Middle Department; that part south of the Rappahannock and east of the railroad from Fredericksburg to Richmond, Petersburg, and Weldon, in the Department of Virginia; the district of country lying east of a line beginning at the confluence of Goose Creek and the Potomac, and running south along the creek and Bull Run Mountains to the mouth of the Occoquan, in the Department of Washington, and so much of the remainder as lies north of the James

2*

River and was covered by the Army of the Potomac in its operations, in the Department (or Army) of the Potomac.

July 15, 1863, to December 21, 1863.—The Eastern Shore (Accomac and Northampton Counties) in the Middle Department; that part south of the Rappahannock and east of the railroad from Fredericksburg to Richmond, Petersburg, and Weldon, in the Department of Virginia; the district of country lying east of a line beginning at the confluence of Goose Creek and the Potomac, and running south along the creek and Bull Run Mountains to the mouth of the Occoquan, in the Department of Washington, and so much of the remainder as lies north of the James River and was covered by the Army of the Potomac in its operations, in the Department (or Army) of the Potomac.

[NOTE.—On August 3, 1863, that part of the State in the vicinity of Harper's Ferry was formally transferred to the Department of West Virginia. See State of West Virginia following.]

December 21, 1863, to close of war.—That part south of the Rappahannock and east of the railroad from Fredericksburg to Richmond, Petersburg, and Weldon, including the Eastern Shore (Accomac and Northampton Counties), in the Department of Virginia and North Carolina; the district of country lying east of a line beginning at the confluence of Goose Creek and the Potomac, and running south along the creek and Bull Run Mountains to the mouth of the Occoquan, in the Department of Washington.

[NOTE.—During this epoch the Army of the Potomac operated along the line of the Orange and Alexandria Railroad as far south as the Rapidan River to May 4, 1864. It then moved *via* the Wilderness, Spottsylvania Court-House, Hanover Court-House, and Cold Harbor to the line of the James River, investing the cities of Richmond and Petersburg from June 16, 1864, to April 3, 1865, and finally reached Appomattox Court-House (where hostilities terminated) April 9, 1865. The Army of the James (Department of Virginia and North Carolina to January 12, 1865, and thereafter Department of Virginia) operated in conjunction with the Army of the Potomac from May, 1864, to the end of the war. The Middle Military Division, created August 7, 1864, comprehended all the troops operating in the valley of the Shenandoah.

About the 1st of October, 1864, an expedition, composed of troops of the District of Kentucky, Department of the Ohio, moved from Kentucky into the southwestern section of Virginia, and proceeded as far as Saltville, whence it returned to Kentucky. In December, 1864, another expedition, composed of a force from the Department of the Cumberland moving from Tennessee, and a force from the Department of the Ohio moving from Kentucky, operated in the southwestern portion of the State along the line of the East Tennessee and Virginia Railroad to Saltville. Also, in March and April, 1865, a detachment of the First Cavalry Division, Department of the Cumberland, moving from Tennessee, proceeded along the line of the East Tennessee and Virginia Railroad to a point within four miles of Lynchburg.]

West Virginia.—The act of Congress approved December 31, 1862, providing for the admission of the State of "West Virginia," was subsequently ratified by the people and announced by the President April 20, 1863, to take effect from and after sixty (60) days from that date. (For its departmental connections prior to this transaction see page 33, *ante*.)

March 16, 1863, to June 24, 1863.—All of the State in the Middle Department, except the counties of Hancock, Brooke, and Ohio, which were transferred to the Department of the Monongahela, June 9, 1863.

June 24, 1863, to August 3, 1863.—That part lying west of a line drawn north and south through Hancock, Maryland, except the counties of Hancock, Brooke, and Ohio, in the Department of West Virginia; that part lying east of said line in the Middle Department; the counties of Hancock, Brooke, and Ohio, in the Department of the Monongahela.

August 6, 1863, to October 12, 1863.—The entire State, except the counties of Hancock, Brooke, and Ohio, in the Department of West Virginia; the exceptions in the Department of the Monongahela.

October 12, 1863, to close of war.—The entire State in the Department of West Virginia.

North Carolina.—This State seceded May 21, 1861. Previous, however, to the passage of the ordinance of secession the United States forts on the coast (Caswell, Johnston, and Macon) and the arsenal at Fayetteville had been seized by the State authorities. Its departmental connections, etc., were as follows:

January 1, 1861, to May 22, 1861.—The entire State in the Department of the East.

May 22, 1861, to January 7, 1862.—That part within a radius of sixty miles from Fort Monroe, Virginia, in the Department of Virginia; the remainder (except Hatteras Inlet, captured August 29, 1861, by troops from the Department of Virginia) not in any Department.

January 7, 1862, to July 15, 1863.—The entire State known as the Department of North Carolina.

July 15, 1863, to January 12, 1865.—The entire State in the Department of Virginia and North Carolina.

January 12, 1865, to January 31, 1865.—The entire State in the Department of the South.

January 31, 1865, to close of war.—The entire State formed the Department of North Carolina.

[NOTE.—From March 2, 1865, till early in May, 1865, the army composed of the Fourteenth, Fifteenth, Seventeenth, and Twentieth Corps, and Kilpatrick's (Third) Division of Cavalry, under Major-General W. T. Sherman, commanding the Military Division of the Mississippi, also operated in the State, marching entirely through from South Carolina to Virginia. In March and April, 1865, the First Cavalry Division, Department of the Cumberland, moving from East Tennessee, penetrated the western portion of the State as far east as Salisbury.]

South Carolina.—This State seceded December 20, 1860, and steps were at once taken to have the United States troops withdrawn from the posts in Charleston Harbor. This the Government refused to do. On the night of December 26, 1860, the garrison of Fort Moultrie was transferred to Fort Sumter, and on the 27th and 30th, respectively, Castle Pinckney and the arsenal in Charleston was seized by the State authorities. This was followed by the investment of Fort Sumter, which finally capitulated on April 13, 1861, after sustaining a vigorous bombardment for thirty-four hours. The entire State was now in the hands of the insurgents. Up to this time it had formed a part of the Department of the East.

The first attempt on the part of the Government to regain a foothold within the State was inaugurated on October 29, 1861, at which time a military and naval expedit on, commanded respectively by Brigadier-General W. T. Sherman and Commodore S. F. DuPont, set sail from Hampton Roads, and after an engagement with the enemy's forts, occupied Hilton Head, Port Royal, Beaufort, and the adjacent islands. The troops garrisoning these captured positions were known as the "Expeditionary Corps" until March 15, 1862, when the State was announced as forming a part of the Department of the South, and so continued to the close of the war. Meantime, from January 15, 1865, to March 2, 1865, the army composed of the Fourteenth, Fifteenth, Seventeenth, and Twentieth Corps, and Kilpatrick's (Third) Division of Cavalry, under Major-General W. T. Sherman, commanding the Military Division of the Mississippi, operated in the State, marching entirely through it, from Georgia to North Carolina.

Georgia.—This State seceded January 18, 1861. On January 3, 1861, the State authorities seized Fort Pulaski, and on January 24, 1861, a force of State troops also took possession of the U. S. Arsenal at Augusta, which act placed the entire State, with all the Government property, in the hands of the insurgents.

The State was subsequently embraced in the following military departments, etc.:

March 15, 1862, to close of war.—That portion bordering on the Atlantic in the Department of the South; the remainder not (actually) in any department till October 24, 1862, when such parts of Northern Georgia as might be occupied by U. S. troops were placed in the Department of the Cumberland.

[NOTE.—On May 7, 1864, the major portion of the army, known as the Military Division of the Mississippi, commanded by Major-General W. T. Sherman, entered the State from the north, and, after a series of hard-fought battles, reached the sea-coast at Savannah, December 21, 1864.]

Florida.—On January 7, 1861, the ordinance of secession was passed by this State, and within a few days thereafter several of the military posts of the United States, including the Navy Yard at Pensacola, were seized by the State authorities. The garrisons of Forts Pickens, Jefferson, and Taylor, being strong enough to defend them, were maintained throughout the war.

The military departmental connections of the State were as follows :

January 1, 1861, to April 11, 1861.—The entire State in the Department of the East.

April 11, 1861, to January 11, 1862.—The entire State in the Department of Florida.

January 11, 1862, to March 15, 1862.—Key West, the Tortugas, and the mainland on the west coast as far as Appalachicola, and to Cape Canaveral on the east coast, in the Department of Key West; the remainder in the Department of Florida.

March 15, 1862, to August 8, 1862.—The entire State in the Department of the South.

August 8, 1862, to March 16, 1863.—West Florida in the Department of the Gulf; the remainder in the Department of the South.

March 16, 1863, to February 10, 1865.—Key West, the Tortugas, and West Florida in the Department of the Gulf; the remainder in the Department of the South.

February 10, 1865, to May 17, 1865.—Key West, the Tortugas, and West Florida in the Division of West Mississippi ; the remainder in the Department of the South.

[NOTE.—By treaty with Spain, February 22, 1819, the United States acquired possession of the territories of Eastern and Western Florida. Down to 1821, the Appalachicola River divided the two territories, but in that year General Jackson (then Governor) constituted the Suwanee River the line of division. In 1824 Congress (see Statutes at Large, vol. iv., chap. 163, p. 45) divided Florida into three judicial districts, the Eastern embracing all of Florida east of the Suwanee River, the Middle that part of the territory west of the Suwanee and east of the Appalachicola Rivers, and the Western that portion of Florida west of the Appalachicola. In the absence of positive data, it is assumed that the creation of the three judicial districts form the basis of the usual division of that State into East, Middle, and West Florida.]

Alabama.—The ordinance of secession was formally adopted by this State January 11, 1861. Already the United States Arsenal at Mount Vernon, and Forts Gaines and Morgan, in Mobile Bay, had been seized by Alabama State troops. At this time the State was embraced within the limits of the Department of the East. Its coast-line was held by the enemy until August 8, 1864, when Fort Gaines, in Mobile Bay, was captured and occupied by United States troops. On the 23d of the same month Fort Morgan also surrendered. This portion of the State was included in the Department of the Gulf until February 10, 1865, when it became a part of the Military Division of West Mississippi.

On May 17, 1865, it was transferred back to the Department of the Gulf. Possession of the northern portion of the State was obtained by the National forces at a much earlier period.

Immediately after the fall of Fort Henry, Tennessee, in February, 1862, gunboats were sent up the Tennessee River as far as Florence, Ala., and again, on April 1, 1862, a combined military and naval expedition moved from Pittsburg Landing, Tenn., to Chickasaw, Ala., but no permanent lodgment was effected. The first foothold of importance gained by the Federal troops in Northern Alabama occurred on April 8, 1862, when the Third Division (General O. M. Mitchel) of the Army of the Ohio, Department of the Mississippi, moving from Murfreesboro, Tenn., crossed the State line and occupied Huntsville and other points. The troops in that section of country continued as a part of the Department of the Mississippi until October 24, 1862, when such portions of Northern Alabama as were or might be in possession of the United States troops was announced as constituting a part of the Department of the Cumberland, and so remained until the close of the war.

Mississippi.—The ordinance of secession was passed by this State January 9, 1861. The only military post in the State at this time was a fort under construction on Ship Island, in Mississippi Sound. It was seized by an armed body of secessionists January 20, 1861. Having been abandoned by the enemy, a force from the United States steamer Massachusetts took possession of the island, September 17, 1861, and held it until relieved by a brigade of troops under command of Brigadier-General J. W. Phelps, on December 3, 1861. On February 23, 1862, the coast-line of Mississippi was made a part of the Department of the Gulf, and so continued until May 17, 1865, when the entire State was merged into that Department.

The northern portion of the State was first entered in April, 1862, soon after the battle of Pittsburg Landing, fought April 6th and 7th, by the Armies of the Tennessee, the Mississippi, and the Ohio, of the Department of the Mississippi. From this time till October 16, 1862, such portions of this section of country as were in possession of the Federal troops were comprehended within the limits of the Department of the Mississippi, whose designation was changed on the last-named date to the Department of the Tennessee, and so remained until November 28, 1864, when it was transferred to the Department of the Mississippi. This arrangement continued until January 17, 1865, when such parts of the State as were occupied by troops under the command of Major-General George H. Thomas, were included in the Department of the Cumberland, and that part along the Mississippi River occupied by the troops of the Military Division of the West Mississippi was embraced in the Department of the Mississippi. This construction of departmental lines remained unchanged until May 17, 1865, when the entire State was merged into the Department of the Gulf.

Louisiana.—The ordinance of secession was adopted by this State January 26, 1861. A short time previous to the passage of the act, Forts Jackson and St. Philip, Jackson Barracks at New Orleans, and the Arsenal and Barracks at Baton Rouge, were taken possession of by the State authorities. The United States Marine Hospital, the Mint, and Custom-house at New Orleans, and Forts Macomb and Pike, on Lake Pontchartrain, and other posts were subsequently seized. The entire State remained in the hands of the enemy until April 25, 1862, on which day a portion of the Western Gulf Squadron, under Flag-Officer D. G. Farragut, having passed Forts Jackson and St. Philip, appeared before the city of New Orleans and demanded its surrender. On April 28th Forts Jackson and St. Philip fell into the hands of the Federal forces, and on May 1st the city of New Orleans was formally occupied by the troops under General B. F. Butler, commanding the Department of the Gulf. The southern portion of the State remained in the Department of the Gulf to the close of the war.

On June 20, 1862, an expedition consisting of troops belonging to the Department of the Gulf, and commanded by General Thomas Williams, accompanied by a naval force under Flag Officer Farragut, left Baton Rouge, and proceeding up the Mississippi River, landed at a point opposite Vicksburg, Mississippi, where an attempt was made to construct a cut-off canal and capture Vicksburg ; both of which having failed, the combined force returned to Baton Rouge during the following month.

No further operations in Northern Louisiana by United States troops took place until December 25, 1862, when the right wing, Army of the Tennessee, under General W. T. Sherman, landed at Milliken's Bend, and, after cutting the Vicksburg and Shreveport Railroad, re-embarked, and proceeding to the vicinity of Vicksburg, Mississippi, made an unsuccessful assault on the enemy's works at Chickasaw Bluffs. After the capture of Arkansas Post, in January, 1863, the Army of the Tennessee, under General U. S. Grant, landed at Young's Point, Louisiana, and commenced the final campaign against Vicksburg. This section of the State was thenceforth embraced within the limits of the Department of the Tennessee up to November 28, 1864, when it became a part of the Department of the Mississippi, and so remained until the close of the war.

Texas.—The ordinance of secession was passed by this State February 1, 1861. On the 18th of that month Brigadier-General David E. Twiggs, commanding the Department of Texas, which comprehended the entire State, surrendered all the military posts and public property to the State authorities.

By the articles of agreement the troops were to be allowed to march to the coast, and there take transportation North. Some detachments garrisoning the interior posts were unavoidably delayed in leaving the State, and on April 25th a force, consisting of two companies of the 1st, three of the 3d, and two of the 8th Infantry—seven in all—under command of Major C. C. Sibley, 3d Infantry, which had embarked, and was about to leave Texas under the provisions of the agreement above cited, was seized by a superior armed force of Texans, under Van Dorn, near the port of Saluria, and compelled to give their paroles not to bear arms, etc., until exchanged or released by order of the President of the Confederate States. Upon complying with these requirements this force was permitted to proceed North.

On May 9th another detachment, composed of six companies of the 8th Infantry, commanded by Captain I. V. D. Reeve, while *en route* to the coast for the purpose of leaving the State, was met at San Lucas Spring, fifteen miles west of San Antonio, by a superior armed body of the enemy, also under Van Dorn, and forced to surrender unconditionally. These troops were not paroled, but held to await the orders of the President of the Confederate States, who subsequently directed that they be held as hostages. Some of the officers and a part of the enlisted men were afterward released on parole, but the greater portion of them were kept in confinement until February, 1863. Colonel C. A. Waite, 1st Infantry, who succeeded General Twiggs in command of the Department of Texas, and several other officers on duty at San Antonio, were arrested on April 23, 1861, and forcibly required to give their paroles.

Exclusive control of the State was held by the enemy from this time until the summer of 1862, when a column of troops from California, under command of Brigadier-General J. H. Carleton, marched to the Rio Grande, and took possession of the town of Franklin and Forts Bliss, Quitman, and Davis. Although all of these posts were not occupied, yet the foothold thus gained in the northwestern corner of Texas was maintained throughout the war, and formed a part of the Department of New Mexico till the close of hostilities.

On February 23, 1862, the coast line and so much of the State as might be occupied by the U. S. forces under General Butler was placed in the Department of the Gulf. But with the exception of the port and town of Galveston, held by a naval force from October 10, 1862, to January 1, 1863, and which was reinforced late in December, 1862, by a small detachment of Infantry, no portion of the coast was recovered by the U. S. troops until November 3, 1863, on which day an expedition, consisting of the Second Division, Thirteenth Army Corps, commanded by General N. J. T. Dana, effected a landing at Brazos, Santiago Island, and pushing inland, took possession of Brownsville. Later in the month other troops of the Thirteenth Army Corps landed on Mustang and St. Joseph's Islands, and succeeded in capturing Fort Esperanza, at the head of Matagorda Bay. Other points in this vicinity were subsequently taken and occupied.

The forces engaged in these operations belonged to the Department of the Gulf, and that locality, together with other portions subsequently added (excepting the northwestern part, heretofore mentioned), was embraced within the limits of said department till the close of the war.

Arkansas.—The ordinance of secession was passed by this State May 6, 1861, the United States Arsenal at Little Rock, and the military post of Fort Smith having been previously seized by the State authorities. Its departmental connections were as follows:

January 1, 1861, to July 3, 1861.—The entire State in the Department of the West.

July 3, 1861, to November 9, 1861.—The entire State in the Western Department.

November 9, 1861, to March 11, 1862.—The entire State in the Department of the Missouri.

March 11, 1862, to September 19, 1862.—The entire State in the Department of the Mississippi.

September 19, 1862, to January 6, 1864.—The entire State in the Department of the Missouri, excepting Fort Smith, transferred to the Department of Kansas, January 1, 1864.

January 6, 1864, to April 17, 1864.—The entire State, excepting Fort Smith (see preceding paragraph), in the Department of Arkansas.

April 17, 1864, to close of war.—The entire State in the Department of Arkansas.

Tennessee.—On January 1, 1861, this State formed a part of the Department of the East. Although its ordinance of secession was not adopted by the people, to whom submitted, until the 8th of June, 1861, yet, as early as April its Governor had refused the requisition of President Lincoln for troops to suppress the rebellion, and had also ordered the seizure of certain funds belonging to the United States which were in possession of the Collector at Nashville, and on the 1st of May the Legislature passed a resolution directing the Governor to enter into a military league with the Confederate States, subjecting the whole military force of the State to the control of the rebel authorities. The subsequent departmental connections of the State were as follows:

August 15, 1861, to November 9, 1861.—The entire State in the Department of the Cumberland.

November 9, 1861, to March 11, 1862.—The entire State in the Department of the Ohio.

(By the capture of Fort Henry, on the Tennessee River, February 6, 1862, soon followed by the surrender of Fort Donelson, on the Cumberland, a force of United States troops under General U. S. Grant, belonging to the Department of the Missouri, gained control of the western part of the State.)

March 11, 1862, to June 8, 1862.—That portion of the State lying west of a north and south line indefinitely drawn through Knoxville, in the Department of the Mississippi, and that portion east of said line in the Mountain Department.[1]

June 8, 1862, to October 16, 1862.—The entire State in the Department of the Mississippi, excepting Cumberland Gap and vicinity, transferred to the Department of the Ohio, August 19, 1862.

October 16, 1862, to November 16, 1863.—That portion of the State west of the Tennessee River in the Department of the Tennessee, and that portion east of said river in the Department of the Cumberland.

November 16, 1863, to November 28, 1864.—Such parts of the State (i. e., East Tennessee) as were occupied by the troops of the Army of the Ohio, in the Department of the Ohio; the middle portion, extending westward to the Tennessee River in the Department of the Cumberland, and that part west of the Tennessee River in the Department of the Tennessee.

November 28, 1864, to January 17, 1865.—That portion of the State west of the Tennessee River in the Department of the Mississippi; the central portion in the Department of the Cumberland, and the eastern part in the Department of the Ohio.

January 17, 1865, to February 10, 1865.—That portion of the State east of the Tennessee River in the Department of the Cumberland, the remainder in the Department of the Mississippi.

February 10, 1865, to close of war.—The entire State in the Department of the Cumberland.

Kentucky.—At the beginning of the rebellion this State assumed a position of neutrality, and refused to take part on either side; but this position was not recognized by the Government of the United States.

On the 1st of July, 1861, Lieutenant William Nelson, U. S. Navy (afterwards Brigadier-General of Volunteers), was authorized by the War Department to raise and organize into regiments, Volunteers from Tennessee and Kentucky. He proceeded to Bryantsville, Garrard County, and there established a camp called "Camp Dick Robinson." The first armed invasion of the State was made by the rebel General Polk, who seized the towns of Columbus and Hickman on the 4th of September, 1861. This was followed on the 6th by the occupation of Paducah by a force of United States troops, under General U. S. Grant,

---

[1] Although this division of the State was made in orders, yet the only troops operating in Eastern Tennessee (i. e., Cumberland Gap and vicinity) belonged to the Army of the Ohio, of the Department of the Mississippi, so that, in fact, no portion of the State was in the Mountain Department.

belonging to the District of Southeast Missouri, in the Western Department.

On May 28, 1861, so much of the State as was embraced within one hundred miles of the Ohio River was announced as constituting the Department of Kentucky. Its subsequent departmental connections were as follows:

August 15, 1861, to November 9, 1861.—The entire State in the Department of the Cumberland, except that portion lying within fifteen miles of Cincinnati, Ohio, transferred to the Department of the Ohio September 19, 1861, and the forces operating in the vicinity of the junction of the Tennessee, Cumberland, Ohio, and Mississippi Rivers, which belonged to the Western Department.

November 9, 1861, to March 11, 1862.—That portion of the State west of the Cumberland River in the Department of the Missouri, and that part east of the Cumberland River in the Department of the Ohio.

March 11, 1862, to June 8, 1862.—That portion of the State lying west of a north and south line indefinitely drawn through Knoxville, Tenn., in the Department of the Mississippi, and that portion lying east of said line in the Mountain Department.[1]

June 8, 1862, to August 19, 1862.—The entire State in the Department of the Mississippi.

August 19, 1862, to October 16, 1862.—All of the State east of the Tennessee River in the Department of the Ohio; the remainder in the Department of the Mississippi.

October 16, 1862, to August 7, 1864.—That portion of the State west of the Tennessee River in the Department of the Tennessee; the remainder in the Department of the Ohio, excepting the town of Covington and the country around it within a radius of ten miles, annexed to the Northern Department June 25, 1864.

August 7, 1864, to January 17, 1865.—The entire State in the Department of the Ohio.

January 17, 1865, to February 10, 1865.—The entire State in the Department of the Cumberland.

February 10, 1865, to close of war.—The entire State in the Department of Kentucky.

Ohio.—January 1, 1861, to May 3, 1861.—The entire State in the Department of the East.

May 3, 1861, to March 11, 1862.—The entire State in the Department of the Ohio.

March 11, 1862, to June 26, 1862.—That part of the State lying east

---

[1] Although this division of the State was made in orders, yet the only troops operating in Eastern Kentucky belonged to the Army of the Ohio, of the Department of the Mississippi, so that in fact no portion of the State was in the Mountain Department.

of a north and south line indefinitely drawn through Knoxville, Tennessee, in the Mountain department, that part west of said line in the Department of the Mississippi.[1]

June 26, 1862, to August 10, 1862.—That part of the State lying east of a north and south line indefinitely drawn through Knoxville, Tennessee, not in any department, the remainder in the Department of the Mississippi.[1]

August 19, 1862, to June 9, 1863.—The entire State in the Department of the Ohio.[2]

June 9, 1863, to June 24, 1863.—The counties of Columbiana, Jefferson, and Belmont, in the Department of the Monongahela; the remainder in the Department of the Ohio, except Gallipolis and the Ohio shore opposite the mouth of the Kanawha, which was in the Middle Department.[2]

June 24, 1863, to January 12, 1864.—The counties of Columbiana, Jefferson, and Belmont, in the Department of the Monongahela; the counties of Monroe, Washington, Athens, Meigs, Gallia, and Laurence, in the Department of West Virginia; the remainder of the State in the Department of the Ohio until November 16, 1863, when that Department was reorganized, and this portion of the State, which had constituted a part of it, being excluded, was not embraced within the limits of any department until the formation of the Northern Department, January 12, 1864.

January 12, 1864, to close of war.—The entire State in the Northern Department.

Michigan.—January 1, 1861, to April 13, 1861.—The entire State in the Department of the East.

April 13, 1861, to November 9, 1861.—Not in any department.

November 9, 1861, to March 11, 1862.—The entire State in the Department of the Ohio.

March 11, 1862, to June 26, 1862.—That part of the State lying east of a north and south line indefinitely drawn through Knoxville, Tenn., in the Mountain Department, that part west of said line in the Department of the Mississippi.

---

[1] By a literal interpretation of the President's War Order No. 3, of March 11, 1862, the State of Ohio was unequally divided between the Department of the Mississippi and the Mountain Department, but no evidence exists that the Commanding General of either department exercised control over any forces in the State. On the contrary, the Governor of Ohio seems to have held a semi-military jurisdiction over the troops stationed at Camp Chase, Johnson's Island, etc.

[2] By telegram from War Department of May 15, 1863, Gallipolis and the Ohio shore opposite the mouth of the Kanawha was placed in the Middle Department, and so continued until the formation of the Department of West Virginia, June 24, 1863, with which this section of country was merged.

June 26, 1862, to August 19, 1862.—That part of the State lying east of a north and south line indefinitely drawn through Knoxville, Tenn., not in any department, the remainder in the Department of the Mississippi.

August 19, 1862, to November 16, 1863.—The entire State in the Department of the Ohio.

November 16, 1863, to January 12, 1864.—Not in any department.

January 12, 1864, to close of war.—The entire State in the Northern Department.

Indiana.—January 1, 1861, to May 3, 1861.—The entire State in the Department of the East.

May 3, 1861, to March 11, 1862.—The entire State in the Department of the Ohio.

March 11, 1862, to August 19, 1862.—The entire State in the Department of the Mississippi.

August 19, 1862, to November 16, 1863.—The entire State in the Department of the Ohio.

November 16, 1863, to January 12, 1864.—The entire State in no department.

January 12, 1864, to close of war.—The entire State in the Northern Department, except the post of Jeffersonville, transferred to the Department of the Ohio, February 8, 1864, and then, together with the post of New Albany, to the Department of Kentucky, March 24, 1865.

Illinois.—January 1, 1861, to May 3, 1861.—The entire State in the Department of the East.

May 3, 1861, to July 3, 1861.—The entire State in the Department of the Ohio.

July 3, 1861, to November 9, 1861.—The entire State in the Western Department.

November 9, 1861, to March 11, 1862.—The entire State in the Department of the Missouri.

March 11, 1862, to August 19, 1862.—The entire State in the Department of the Mississippi.

August 19, 1862, to November 16, 1863.—The entire State in the Department of the Ohio, excepting the post of Alton, transferred to the Department of the Missouri, September 19, 1862, and the post of Cairo, annexed to the Department of the Tennessee, October 16, 1862. (The first-named place remained in the Department of the Missouri throughout the war, and the latter was merged into the Northern Department August 7, 1864.)

November 16, 1863, to January 12, 1864.—The entire State, exclusive of the foregoing exceptions, not in any department.

January 12, 1864, to close of war.—The entire State, exclusive of the exceptions above noted, in the Northern Department.

Wisconsin.—January 1, 1861, to November 9, 1861.—The entire State virtually not in any department.

November 9, 1861, to March 11, 1862.—In the Department of the Missouri.

March 11, 1862, to August 19, 1862.—In the Department of the Mississippi.

August 19, 1862, to September 6, 1862.—In the Department of the Ohio.

September 6, 1862, to close of war.—In the Department of the Northwest.

Iowa.—January 1, 1861, to July 3, 1861.—The entire State in the Department of the West.

July 3, 1861, to November 9, 1861.—In the Western Department.

November 9, 1861, to March 11, 1862.—In the Department of the Missouri.

March 11, 1862, to September 6, 1862.—In the Department of the Mississippi.

September 6, 1862, to close of war.—In the Department of the Northwest.

Missouri.—January 1, 1861, to July 3, 1861.—The entire State in the Department of the West. (On June 6, 1861, an order was issued extending the limits of the Department of the Ohio so as to embrace the State of Missouri, but not being carried into effect the State remained in the Department of the West until the formation of the Western Department, July 3, 1861.)

July 3, 1861, to November 9, 1861.—In the Western Department.

November 9, 1861, to March 11, 1862.—In the Department of the Missouri.

March 11, 1862, to September 19, 1862.—In the Department of the Mississippi.

September 19, 1862, to close of war.—In the Department of the Missouri.

Minnesota.—January 1, 1861, to July 3, 1861.—The entire State in the Department of the West.

July 3, 1861, to November 9, 1861.—In the Western Department.

November 9, 1861, to March 11, 1862.—In the Department of the Missouri.

March 11, 1862, to September 6, 1862.—In the Department of the Mississippi.

September 6, 1862, to close of war.—In the Department of the Northwest.

Kansas.—January 1, 1861, to July 3, 1861.—The entire State in the Department of the West.

July 3, 1861, to November 9, 1861.—In the Western Department.

November 9, 1861, to March 11, 1862.—In the Department of Kansas.

March 11, 1862, to May 2, 1862.—In the Department of the Mississippi.

May 2, 1862, to September 19, 1862.—In the Department of Kansas.

September 19, 1862, to January 1, 1864.—In the Department of the Missouri.

January 1, 1864, to January 30, 1865.—In the Department of Kansas.

January 30, 1865, to close of war.—In the Department of the Missouri.

California.—January 1, 1861, to close of war.—The entire State in the Department of the Pacific.

Oregon.—January 1, 1861, to close of war.—The entire State in the Department of the Pacific.

Nevada.—January 1, 1861, to close of war.—In the Department of the Pacific.

Arizona Territory.—(Created out of a part of New Mexico by act of Congress of March 3, 1863.)

January 1, 1861, to July 23, 1861.—In the Department of the Pacific.

July 23, 1861, to May 21, 1862.—Unoccupied by United States troops.

May 21, 1862, to January 14, 1863.—In the Department of the Pacific.

January 14, 1863, to January 20, 1865.—In the Department of New Mexico.

January 20, 1865, to close of war.—In the Department of the Pacific.

Nebraska Territory.—January 1, 1861, to July 3, 1861.—In the Department of the West.

July 3, 1861, to November 9, 1861.—In the Western Department.

November 9, 1861, to March 11, 1862.—In the Department of Kansas.

March 11, 1862, to May 2, 1862.—In the Department of the Mississippi.

May 2, 1862, to September 6, 1862.—In the Department of Kansas.

September 6, 1862, to October 11, 1862.—In the Department of the Northwest.

October 11, 1862, to January 1, 1864.—In the Department of the Missouri.

January 1, 1864, to January 30, 1865.—In the Department of Kansas.

January 30, 1865, to close of war.—In the Department of the Missouri.

Colorado Territory.—(Created by act of Congress of February 28, 1861.)

January 1, 1861, to July 3, 1861.—In the Department of the West.

July 3, 1861, to November 9, 1861.—In the Western Department.

November 9, 1861, to March 11, 1862.—In the Department of Kansas, excepting Fort Garland, transferred to the Department of New Mexico, February 14, 1862.

March 11, 1862, to May 2, 1862.—In the Department of the Mississippi, excepting Fort Garland, in the Department of New Mexico.

May 2, 1862, to September 19, 1862.—In the Department of Kansas.

September 19, 1862, to January 1, 1864.—In the Department of the Missouri.

January 1, 1864, to January 30, 1865.—In the Department of Kansas.

January 30, 1865, to close of war.—In the Department of the Missouri.

Dakota Territory.—January 1, 1861, to July 3, 1861.—In the Department of the West.

July 3, 1861, to November 9, 1861.—In the Western Department.

November 9, 1861, to March 11, 1862.—In the Department of Kansas.

March 11, 1862, to May 2, 1862.—In the Department of the Mississippi.

May 2, 1862, to September 6, 1862.—In the Department of Kansas.

September 6, 1862, to February 17, 1865.—In the Department of the Northwest.

February 17, 1865, to close of war.—That part east of the 104° of longitude in the Department of the Northwest, the remainder in the Department of the Missouri.

Idaho Territory.—(Created by act of Congress of March 3, 1863.)

January 1, 1861, to close of war.   In the Department of the Pacific.

Indian Territory.[1]—January 1, 1861, to July 3, 1861.—In the Department of the West.

July 3, 1861, to November 9, 1861.—In the Western Department.

November 9, 1861, to March 11, 1862.—In the Department of Kansas.

March 11, 1862, to May 2, 1862.—In the Department of the Mississippi.

May 2, 1862, to September 19, 1862.—In the Department of Kansas.

September 19, 1862, to January 1, 1864.—In the Department of the Missouri.

January 1, 1864, to April 17, 1864.—In the Department of Kansas.

April 17, 1864, to close of war.—In the Department of Arkansas.

Montana Territory.—(Created by act of Congress of May 26, 1864.)

June 1, 1861, to May 26, 1864.—Included within the limits of the departments which embraced the Territory of Dakota.

May 26, 1864, to February 17, 1865.—In the Department of the Northwest.

---

[1] In May, 1861. the troops garrisoning the military posts of the Territory (Forts Arbuckle, Cobb, and Washita) were withdrawn and marched to Fort Leavenworth, Kansas. The first reoccupation of any part of the Territory by U. S. troops occurred in June, 1862, when an expedition was fitted out in the State of Kansas (Department of Kansas) which penetrated the Territory to within a short distance of Fort Gibson. This force returned to Fort Scott, Kansas, August 11, 1862.

February 17, 1865, to close of war.—In the Department of the Missouri.

New Mexico Territory.—January 1, 1861, to November 9, 1861.— That portion of the Territory lying east of the 110° of longitude in the Department of New Mexico, and that part lying west of said line in the Department of the Pacific.

November 9, 1861, to close of war.—The entire Territory in the Department of New Mexico.

Utah Territory.—January 1, 1861, to July 27, 1861.—That portion of the Territory lying east of the 117° of longitude in the Department of Utah, and that part lying west of said line in the Department of the Pacific.

July 27, 1861, to February 17, 1865.—The entire Territory in the Department of the Pacific.

February 17, 1865, to close of war.—In the Department of the Missouri.

Washington Territory.—January 1, 1861, to close of war.—In the Department of the Pacific.

XIII.—3

MILITARY DEPARTMENTS ALPHABETI-CALLY ARRANGED.

The Departments were composed of part or the whole of the States and Territories named.

Alabama—see ALABAMA.

Annapolis—see MARYLAND.

Arkansas—see ARKANSAS, INDIAN TERRITORY.

California—see ARIZONA, CALIFORNIA, NEW MEXICO, NEVADA.

Columbia—see OREGON, WASHINGTON TERRITORY, IDAHO.

Cumberland, The — see ALABAMA, GEORGIA, KENTUCKY. MISSISSIPPI, TENNESSEE.

East, The—see NEW ENGLAND STATES, NEW YORK, NEW JERSEY.

Florida—see FLORIDA.

Georgia—see GEORGIA.

Gulf, The—see GULF STATES.

Kansas—see KANSAS, INDIAN TERRITORY, NEBRASKA, COLORADO, DAKOTA.

Kentucky—see KENTUCKY, INDIANA.

Key West—see FLORIDA.

Louisiana—see LOUISIANA.

Maryland—see MARYLAND.

Middle Department—see WEST VIRGINIA, MARYLAND, VIRGINIA, DELAWARE, PENNSYLVANIA.

Mississippi, The—see TENNESSEE, KENTUCKY, MISSISSIPPI.

Missouri, The—see MISSOURI, IOWA, MINNESOTA, WISCONSIN, ILLINOIS, ARKANSAS, KENTUCKY, COLORADO, NEBRASKA, KANSAS, UTAH, DAKOTA, MONTANA, NEW MEXICO.

Monongahela, The—see PENNSYLVANIA, OHIO, VIRGINIA.

Mountain Department—see WEST VIRGINIA, MARYLAND.

New England—see NEW ENGLAND STATES.

New York—see NEW YORK.

Northern Department—see OHIO, MICHIGAN, INDIANA, ILLINOIS.

North Carolina—see NORTH CAROLINA.

Northeastern Virginia—see VIRGINIA.

New Mexico—see NEW MEXICO, ARIZONA.

Northwest, The—see WISCONSIN, IOWA, MINNESOTA, NEBRASKA, DAKOTA.

Ohio, The—see OHIO, INDIANA, ILLINOIS. MISSOURI, PENNSYLVANIA, WEST VIRGINIA, MICHIGAN, KENTUCKY, WISCONSIN.

Pacific, The—see CALIFORNIA, WASHINGTON TERRITORY, OREGON, ARIZONA.
Pennsylvania—see MARYLAND, DELAWARE, PENNSYLVANIA.
Potomac, The—see PENNSYLVANIA, NEW JERSEY, MARYLAND.
Rappahannock, The—see VIRGINIA, DISTRICT OF COLUMBIA.
Shenandoah, The—see MARYLAND, VIRGINIA.
South, The—see SOUTH CAROLINA, GEORGIA, FLORIDA, NORTH CAROLINA.
South Carolina—see SOUTH CAROLINA.
Susquehanna, The—see PENNSYLVANIA.
Tennessee, The—see ILLINOIS, TENNESSEE, MISSISSIPPI, KENTUCKY.
Texas—see TEXAS.
Virginia—see VIRGINIA.
Virginia and North Carolina—see NORTH CAROLINA, VIRGINIA.
Washington—see MARYLAND, DISTRICT OF COLUMBIA, VIRGINIA.
West, The—see KANSAS, INDIAN TERRITORY, NEBRASKA, COLORADO, DAKOTA,
    NEW MEXICO, MINNESOTA, WISCONSIN, IOWA, ARKANSAS.
Western Virginia—see VIRGINIA, WEST VIRGINIA.
Military District of Kentucky—see KENTUCKY.

MILITARY DIVISION OF THE UNITED STATES FORCES.

DURING the war the forces called for by the President of the United States were organized first into armies, and later into army corps and armies. The troops sent to a military department were usually called the army of the department in which they operated or were located ; the corps were known by numbers, and were part of the army of a department, or sometimes constituted the army.

The armies of the United States were commanded by

THE PRESIDENT,

as Commander-in-Chief under the Constitutional provision ; and under him, as General Commanders, by

BREVET LIEUTENANT-GENERAL WINFIELD SCOTT,
until November 6, 1861.

MAJOR-GENERAL GEORGE B. McCLELLAN,
until March 11, 1862.[1]

MAJOR-GENERAL HENRY W. HALLECK,
from July 11, 1862, to March 12, 1864.

LIEUTENANT-GENERAL and GENERAL U. S. GRANT,
until March 4, 1869.

---

[1] There was no General Commander during the interval between March 11 and July 12, 1862.

PRINCIPAL ARMIES OF THE UNITED STATES.

Army of the Potomac.

This army was virtually called into existence in July, 1861, and was organized by Major-General George B. McClellan, its first commander; November 5, 1862, Major-General A. E. Burnside took command of it; January 25, 1863, Major-General Joe Hooker was placed in command, and June 27, 1863, Major-General George G. Meade succeeded him.

Army of Virginia.

General Orders No. 103, War Department, August 12, 1862, directs the forces under Major-Generals Fremont, Banks, and McDowell, including the troops then under Brigadier-General Sturgis at Washington, to be consolidated and called the Army of Virginia, under the command of Major-General John Pope; and in the first part of September, 1862, the troops forming this army were transferred to other organizations, and the army as such discontinued.

Army of the Ohio.

General Orders No. 97, War Department, November 9, 1861, directed General Don Carlos Buell to assume command of the Department of the Ohio. The troops serving in this department were organized by him as the Army of the Ohio, General Buell remaining in command until October 30, 1862, when he was succeeded by General W. S. Rosecrans. This Army of the Ohio became, at the same time, the Army of the Cumberland. A new Department of the Ohio having been created, Major-General H. G. Wright was assigned to the command thereof; he was succeeded by Major-General Burnside, who was relieved by Major-General J. G. Foster of the command of the Department and Army. Major-General J. M. Schofield took command January 28, 1864, and January 17, 1865, the Department was merged into the Department of the Cumberland.

Army of the Cumberland.

The Army of the Ohio, commanded by General Don Carlos Buell, became, October 24, 1862, the Army of the Cumberland, and was placed under the command of Major-General W. S. Rosecrans; it was also organized at the same time as the Fourteenth Corps. In January, 1863, it was divided into three corps, the Fourteenth, Twentieth, and Twenty-first; in September, 1863, the Twentieth and Twenty-first Corps were consolidated into the Fourth Corps. October, 1863, General George H. Thomas took command of the army, and the Eleventh and Twelfth Corps were added to it. In January, 1864, the Eleventh and Twelfth Corps were consolidated and known as the Twentieth Corps.

Army of the Tennessee.

Originally the Army of the District of Western Tennessee, fighting as such at Shiloh, Tenn., it became the Army of the Tennessee upon the concentration of troops at Pittsburg Landing, under General Halleck; and when the Department of the Tennessee was formed, October 16, 1862, the troops serving therein were placed under the command of Major-General U. S. Grant. October 24, 1862, the troops in this Department were organized as the Thirteenth Corps; December 18, 1862, they were divided into the Thirteenth, Fifteenth, Sixteenth, and Seventeenth Corps. October 27, 1863, Major-General William T. Sherman was appointed to the command of this army; March 12, 1864, Major-General J. B. McPherson succeeded him; July 30, 1864, McPherson having been killed, Major-General O. O. Howard was placed in command, and May 19, 1865, Major-General John A. Logan succeeded him.

Of the minor armies the following are mentioned in the records in connection with the more important operations :

Army of the Mississippi.

Operations on the Mississippi River in spring, 1862; before Corinth, Miss., in May, 1862; Iuka and Corinth, Miss., in September and October, 1862.

Army of the Gulf.

Siege of Port Hudson, La., May, June, and July, 1863.

Army of the James.

Consisting of the Tenth and Eighteenth Corps and Cavalry, Major-General Butler commanding. Operations in conjunction with Army of the Potomac.

Army of West Virginia.

At Cloyd's Mountain, May 9 and 10, 1864.

Army of the Middle Military Division.

At Opequan and Cedar Creek, September and October, 1864.

ARMY CORPS.

SECTION 9 of the act approved July 17, 1862, which reads as follows: "And be it further enacted, that the President be and he is hereby authorized, to establish and organize Army Corps according to his discretion"—legalized and allowed the organization of troops into Army Corps, and under this authority the following corps were organized:

First Army Corps.

August 12, 1862.—The troops of the Mountain Department were to constitute the First Corps, under command of Major-General Fremont.

April 15, 1863.—Major-General John F. Reynolds assigned to command.

March 23, 1864.—Discontinued, and troops transferred.

November 28, 1864.—Reorganized under the command of Major-General Hancock.

Second Army Corps.

August 12, 1862.—The troops of the Shenandoah Department were to constitute the Second Corps, under command of General Banks.

September 12, 1862.—The President ordered that this corps should be known hereafter as the Eleventh, and that the corps arranged in General Order No. 101, of March 13, 1862, Headquarters Army of the Potomac, as the Second, should be known as such.

June 28, 1865.—Discontinued.

Third Army Corps.

August 12, 1862.—The troops under General McDowell, except those within the city and fortifications of Washington, were to form this corps, and to be under his command.

September 12, 1862.—The President ordered that this corps should be known hereafter as the Twelfth; and that the corps arranged as the Third in General Orders No. 101, of March 13, 1862, Headquarters Army of the Potomac, should be known as such.

March 23, 1864.—Discontinued, and troops transferred.

Fourth Army Corps.

September 12, 1862.—The President directed that the corps arranged as the Fourth in General Orders No. 101, of March 13, 1862, Headquarters of the Army of the Potomac, should be known as such.

August 1, 1863.—Discontinued, and the troops transferred to other corps.

September 28, 1863.—The Twentieth and Twenty-first Corps consolidated and constituted the Fourth Corps, under command of Major-General Gordon Granger.

August 1, 1865.—Discontinued.

Fifth Army Corps.

July 22, 1862.—The President directed that the corps arranged in G. O. No. 125, Headquarters Army of the Potomac, of the forces commanded by Brigadier-General Porter, should be known as the Fifth Corps.

June 28, 1865.—Discontinued.

Sixth Army Corps.

July 22, 1862.—The President directed that the corps arranged in G. O. No. 125, Headquarters Army of the Potomac, of the forces commanded by Brigadier-General Franklin, should be known as the Sixth Army Corps.

June 28, 1865.—Discontinued.

Seventh Army Corps.

July 22, 1862.—The President directed that the forces under Major-General Dix should constitute the Seventh Corps.

August 1, 1863.—Discontinued, and the troops transferred to the Eighteenth Corps.

January 6, 1864.—The troops in the Department of Arkansas to constitute this corps, commanded by Major-General Steele.

August 1, 1865.—Discontinued.

Eighth Army Corps.

July 22, 1862.—The President directed that the forces under Major-General Wool should constitute the Eighth Corps.

March 12, 1863.—Major-General Lewis Wallace, commanding Middle Department, assigned to command.

July 11, 1864.—Major-General E. O. C. Ord assigned to command of the corps, and of all the troops in the Middle Department.

July 28, 1864.—Major-General Wallace resumed command of the corps, and all the other troops in the Middle Department.

August 1, 1865.—Discontinued.

Ninth Army Corps.

July 22, 1862.—The President directed that the troops under Major-General Burnside, and belonging to the Department of North Carolina, should be known as the Ninth Corps.

July 27, 1865.—Discontinued.

Tenth Army Corps.

September 3, 1862.—It was ordered that the forces in the Department of the South should constitute the Tenth Army Corps, to be commanded by Major-General O. M. Mitchell.

3*

December 3, 1864.—Discontinued.

March 27, 1865.—Reorganized of all troops in the North Carolina not belonging to the Second, Ninth, and Twenty-third Corps and General Sherman's army, with Major-General A. H. Terry in command.

August 1, 1865.—Discontinued.

Eleventh Army Corps.

September 12, 1862.—The troops of the Shenandoah Department, commanded by Major-General Banks, were constituted this corps.

April 4, 1864.—Consolidated with the Twelfth, and constituted the Twentieth Corps.

Twelfth Army Corps.

September 12, 1862.—The troops under General McDowell, with some exceptions, were constituted this corps.

April 4, 1864.—Consolidated with the Eleventh, and constituted the Twentieth Corps.

Thirteenth Army Corps.

October 24, 1862.—The troops under command of Major-General Grant, commanding Department of the Tennessee, were to constitute this corps.

December 18, 1862.—Major-General J. A. McClernand assigned to the command of the Thirteenth Corps, and the forces under General Grant organized into the Thirteenth, Fifteenth, Sixteenth, and Seventeenth Corps.

June 11, 1864.—Temporarily discontinued, and troops transferred.

February 18, 1865.—Reorganized, and Major-General Gordon Granger placed in command.

July 20, 1865.—Discontinued. *No badge adopted.*

Fourteenth Army Corps.

October 24, 1862.—The troops under Major-General Rosecrans, commanding the Department of the Cumberland, were ordered to constitute this corps.

January 9, 1863.—This corps divided into three corps: the Fourteenth, Twentieth, and Twenty-first; the Fourteenth to be commanded by Major-General G. H. Thomas.

August 1, 1865.—Discontinued.

Fifteenth Army Corps.

Constituted December 18, 1862, from troops of General Grant's command, and
Major-General W. T. Sherman assigned to its command.
August 1, 1865.—Discontinued.

Sixteenth Army Corps.

Constituted December 18, 1862, from troops of General Grant's command, and
Major-General S. A. Hurlbut assigned to its command.
November 7, 1864.—The Corps organization abolished.
February 18, 1865.—Reorganized, and Major-General A. J. Smith in command.
July 20, 1865.—Discontinued.

Seventeenth Army Corps.

Constituted December 18, 1862, from troops of General Grant's command, and
Major-General J. B. McPherson assigned to command.
August 1, 1865.—Discontinued.

Eighteenth Army Corps.

December 24, 1862.—The President ordered that the troops in North Carolina
should constitute the Eighteenth Army Corps, and assigned Major-General
J. G. Foster to the command.
August 1, 1863.—The Seventh Army Corps transferred to this corps.
July 17, 1864.—The troops of the Department of North Carolina and Virginia serv-
ing with the Army of the Potomac in the field, to constitute this corps,
and Major-General William F. Smith assigned to command.
December 3, 1864.—Discontinued.

Nineteenth Army Corps.

January 5, 1863.—Ordered that the troops in the Department of the Gulf shall
constitute this corps, to be commanded by Major-General N. P. Banks.

July 11, 1864.—Major-General Gilmore assigned to temporary command of the part of the corps in the Department of Washington.

July 13, 1864.—Brigadier-General W. H. Emory placed in command of this portion of the corps.

November 7, 1864.—Brevet Major-General Emory appointed to command; headquarters with the army of Sheridan, in the field. The organization in the Military Division of West Mississippi known as the Nineteenth Corps, abolished.

March 20, 1865.—Discontinued.

Twentieth Army Corps.

January 9, 1863.—The Army of the Cumberland divided into three corps: the Fourteenth, Twentieth, and Twenty-first. The Twentieth to be commanded by Major-General A. McD. McCook.

September 28, 1863.—Consolidated with the Twenty-first, and constituted the Fourth Corps.

April 4, 1864.—Re-formed of the Eleventh and Twelfth Corps by consolidation, and Major-General J. Hooker placed in command.

June 1, 1865.—Discontinued.

Twenty-first Army Corps.

January 9, 1863.—The Army of the Cumberland, divided into three corps, the Fourteenth, Twentieth, and Twenty-first; the latter to be commanded by Major-General T. L. Crittenden.

September 28, 1863.—Consolidated with the Twentieth, and constituted the Fourth Corps. *No badge adopted.*

Twenty-second Army Corps.

February 2, 1863.—The troops in the Department of Washington to constitute this Corps, under command of Major-General Heintzelman.

Twenty-third Army Corps.

April 27, 1863.—The troops in Kentucky, not belonging to the Ninth Corps, were constituted the Twenty-third Corps, commanded by Major-General G. L. Hartsuff; by Major-General Stoneman, from Jan. 28, 1864; by Major-Gen. Schofield, from April 4, 1864; by Maj.-Gen. J. D. Cox, from Mar. 27, 1865.

June 8, 1863.—The troops within the Department of the Ohio, not belonging to the Ninth Corps, were to form this corps.

August 1, 1865.—Discontinued.

Twenty-fourth Army Corps.

December 3, 1864.—The white infantry of the Tenth and Eighteenth Corps with the Army of the James consolidated and constituted this corps, under the command of Major-General E. O. C. Orr.

August 1, 1865.—Discontinued.

Twenty-fifth Army Corps.

December 3, 1864.—The colored troops of the Department of Virginia and North Carolina were organized into a corps and constituted the Twenty-fifth, Major-General G. Weitzel commanding.

January 8, 1866.—Discontinued.

Cavalry Corps, Army of the Potomac.

April 15, 1863.—Major-General George Stoneman was assigned to the command of this corps, consisting of the cavalry of the Army of the Potomac.

April 4, 1864.—Major-General P. H. Sheridan was assigned to command.

The following organizations not corps organizations in the sense of the Act of Congress given above, adopted badges as follows:

Wilson's Cavalry Corps.   Engineers and Mechanics.   Signal Corps.

STRENGTH OF THE ARMY AT VARIOUS DATES.

THIS Table, from the report of the Provost-Marshal-General, will give the reader an idea of the number of men in service, present and absent, at certain periods during the war:

DATES.	PRESENT.			ABSENT.			AGGREGATE.		GRAND TOTAL.
	Regulars.	Volunteers.	Total.	Regulars.	Volunteers.	Total.	Regulars.	Volunteers.	
Jan. 1, 1861.	14,663	....	14,663	1,704	....	1,704	16,367	....	16,367
July 1, 1861.	14,108	169,480	183,388	2,314	849	3,163	16,422	170,329	186,751
Jan. 1, 1862.	19,871	507,333	527,204	2,554	46,159	48,713	22,425	553,492	575,917
Mar. 31, 1862.	19,585	514,399	533,984	3,723	99,419	103,142	23,308	613,818	637,126
Jan. 1, 1863.	19,169	679,633	698,802	6,294	213,095	219,389	25,463	892,728	918,191
Jan. 1, 1864.	17,237	594,013	611,250	7,399	242,088	249,487	24,636	836,101	860,737
Jan. 1, 1865.	14,661	606,263	620,924	7,358	331,178	338,536	22,019	937,411	959,460
Mar. 31, 1865.	13,880	643,867	657,747	7,789	314,550	322,339	21,669	958,417	980,086
May 1, 1865.	....	....	797,807	...	....	202,709	....	....	1,000,516

AVERAGE MEAN STRENGTH OF THE VARIOUS CLASSES OF TROOPS.

The following table, prepared by Lieut. Chas. A. L. Totten, U. S. Army, will show the average mean strength of the classes of troops serving during the Rebellion. In this compilation, the regulars are considered as in service from January 1, 1861, to January 1, 1865—forty-eight months; the volunteers from July 1, 1861, to March 31, 1865,—forty-five months; the colored troops from September, 1862, to December, 1867,—sixty-three months:

Character of Troops.	Present.	Absent.	Aggregate.
Regulars	17,735	5,194	22,929
Volunteers	544,704	196,803	741,507
White troops	562,439	204,997	764,436
Colored troops	35,640	6,699	42,339
Mixed troops	598,079	211,696	808,775

EFFECTIVE STRENGTH OF THE ARMY.

The following table, also prepared by Lieut. Chas. A. L. Totten, of the U. S. Army, and based on the preceding table, will assist to a conception of the number of men effective in every thousand of mean aggregate strength :

Troops.	Absent.	Sick in Hospital.	Total.	Consequent effective strength per 1,000 of troops concerned.
Regulars	226	64	290	710
Volunteers.........	265	89	354	646
White	264	86	350	650
Colored............	158	46	204	796
Mixed	258	80	338	662

HONORS CONFERRED BY THE CONGRESS OF THE UNITED STATES IN PUBLIC ACTS.

Approved December 24, 1861.

Joint Resolution expressive of the recognition by Congress of the gallant and patriotic services of the late Brigadier-General Nathaniel Lyon, and the officers and soldiers under his command at the battle of Springfield, Missouri.

Approved February 22, 1862.

Joint Resolution giving the thanks of Congress to the officers, soldiers, and seamen of the Army and Navy of the United States, for the heroic gallantry that . . . has won the recent series of brilliant victories over the enemies of the Union and Constitution.

Approved July 12, 1862.

Joint Resolution to provide for the presentation of "Medals of Honor," in the name of Congress, to the enlisted men of the army and volunteer forces, who have distinguished or may distinguish themselves in battle during the present rebellion.

Approved March 3, 1863.

Joint Resolution giving the thanks of Congress to Major-General William S. Rosecrans, and the officers and men under his command, for their gallantry and good conduct in the battle of Murfreesboro, Tennessee.

Approved March 3, 1863.

An Act authorizing the President to confer brevet rank upon such volunteer and other officers in the United States service as have been, or may hereafter be, distinguished by gallant actions or meritorious conduct.

Approved December 17, 1863.

Joint Resolution of thanks to Major-General Ulysses S. Grant, and the officers and soldiers who have fought under his command during this Rebellion ; and providing that the President shall cause a medal to be struck, to be presented to Major-General Grant in the name of the People of the United States of America.

Approved January 28, 1864.

Joint Resolution of thanks to Major-General Nathaniel P. Banks, and the officers and soldiers under his command at Port Hudson.

Approved January 28, 1864.

Joint Resolution of thanks to Major-General Ambrose E. Burnside, and the officers and men who have fought under his command, for their gallantry, good conduct, and soldier-like endurance.

Approved January 28, 1864.

Joint Resolution, expressive of the thanks of Congress to Major-General Joseph Hooker, Major-General Geo. G. Meade, Major-General Oliver O. Howard, and the officers and soldiers of the Army of the Potomac, for the skill, energy, and endurance in covering Washington and Baltimore, and for the skill and heroic valor displayed at Gettysburg, Pa.

Approved February 19, 1864.

Joint Resolution of thanks to Major-General W. T. Sherman, and the officers and soldiers who served under him, for their gallant and arduous services in marching to the relief of the Army of the Cumberland and at the battle of Chattanooga.

Approved March 3, 1864.

Joint Resolution of thanks of Congress to the Volunteer Soldiers who have re-enlisted in the army.

Approved June 11, 1864.

Joint Resolution or thanks of Congress to Lieutenant-Colonel Joseph Bailey, Fourth Wisconsin Volunteers, for distinguished services in the recent campaign on the Red River, by which the gunboat flotilla under Rear-Admiral David D. Porter was rescued from imminent peril.

Approved January 10, 1865.

Joint Resolution tendering the thanks of the people and of Congress to Major-General William T. Sherman, and the officers and soldiers of his command, for their gallant conduct in their late brilliant movement through Georgia.

Approved January 24, 1865.

Joint Resolution to present the thanks of Congress to Brevet Major-General Alfred H. Terry, and to the officers and men under his command, for the unsurpassed gallantry and skill exhibited by them in the attack upon Fort Fisher, and for their long and faithful services and unwavering devotion to the cause of the country.

Approved March 3, 1865.

Joint Resolution of thanks to Major-General Geo. H. Thomas, and the army under his command, for the signal defeat of the rebel army under General Hood.

Approved April 21, 1866.

Joint Resolution of thanks to Major-General Winfield S. Hancock for his services with the Army of the Potomac in 1863.

Approved May 30, 1866.

Joint Resolution expressive of the gratitude of the Nation to the officers, soldiers, and seamen of the United States, by whose valor and endurance, on land and on sea, the rebellion has been crushed.

LOSSES.

In Part VI. of the Final Report of the Provost Marshal-General of the Army, General James B. Fry, to the Secretary of War, dated March 17, 1866, appears the following statement of casualties in the military forces:

CAUSES.	REGULARS			WHITE VOLUNTEERS			COLORED TROOPS			AGGREGATE		
	Officers.	Enlisted men.	Total.	Officers.	Enlisted men.	Total.	Officers.	Enlisted men.	Total.	Officers.	Enlisted men.	Total.
Killed	157	1,890	2,047	3,345	54,056	57,401	124	1,790	1,914	3,626	57,736	61,362
Died of wounds				1,595	32,095	33,690	46	1,037	1,083	1,641	33,132	34,773
Died of disease	88	2,749	2,832	2,141	152,013	154,154	90	26,211	26,301	2,314	180,973	183,287
Accidentally killed				12	294	306				12	294	306
Executed by sentence		1	1		6	6					7	7
Missing in action	33	1,266	1,299	72	4,085	4,157	18	1,275	1,293	123	6,626	6,749
Honorably discharged	2	1,201	1,203	10,805	159,764	170,569	427	2,378	2,805	11,234	163,343	174,577
Discharged for disability	2	5,089	5,091	3,058	209,102	212,160	166	6,889	7,055	3,226	221,080	224,306
Dishonorably discharged		275	275	186	2,023	2,209	18	191	209	204	2,489	2,693
Dismissed	122		122	2,143		2,143	158		158	2,423		2,423
Cashiered	6		6	252		252	16		16	274		274
Resigned	390		390	21,090		21,090	801		801	22,281		22,281
Deserted	5	16,360	16,365	187	170,029	170,216	24	12,440	12,464	216	198,829	199,045
Total of casualties	800	28,831	29,631	44,886	783,467	828,353	1,888	52,211	54,099	47,574	864,509	912,083

In this table men who were mustered out at expiration of their term of service or at the close of the war are not included.

The foregoing statement gives the loss by death among

White officers and men, in which are included the officers of the colored troops, as they were almost without exception white 250,697

Colored men 29,038

Total 279,735

LOSSES BY DEATH—ADJUTANT-GENERAL'S REPORT.

The Adjutant-General of the United States Army, February 7, 1869, made a report to the Secretary of War, in which the total number of deaths are given as follows :

Among white officers and men	261,036	
Among colored men	33,380	
Total	294,416	
Of these there were *killed in battle*		44,238
Regulars, officers and men	1,355	
Volunteers, officers and men	41,369	
Colored enlisted men	1,514	
Died of wounds		33,993
Regulars, officers and men	850	
White volunteers, officers and men	32,106	
Colored enlisted men	1,037	
Died of disease		149,043
Regulars, officers and men	2,428	
White volunteers, officers and men	120,404	
Colored enlisted men	26,211	
Of other known causes		11,845
Of unknown causes		55,297

Under date of October 25, 1870, the Adjutant-General furnished the following statement to the Surgeon-General of the Army :

Total number of Deaths.

Regular army	267 commis'd officers ;		4,592 enlisted men.	Total,		4,859
Volunteer army,	8,553 "	"	256,427 "	"	"	264,980
Colored troops..	285 "	"	33,380 "	"	"	33,665
Total	9,105 "	"	294,399 "	"	" Aggregate,	303,504

Or among white officers and men	270,124
" colored men	33,380
	303,504

These numbers are to be understood as embracing the deaths from all causes, so far as it had been possible to collect information with regard to them up to the date of the report, October 25, 1870.

To explain the difference in the numbers in the various reports of the Provost-Marshal-General and Adjutant-General of the United States Army, it is necessary to remind the veterans of the war of the Rebellion, as they will well remember, that often men were reported missing in action, and even deserted, when in reality they had been killed in battle, or died in rebel prisons, or died in hospitals; or even at home while on furlough. Immediately after the close of the war vast numbers of applications for pension and back pay were made by the legal heirs of deceased soldiers. In cases where there was no record of the death of the soldier in the office of the Adjutant-General, evidence of the death was required, had to be furnished, and thus the record of the dead was daily rendered more nearly complete, and is to-day probably as complete as it ever will be. To accomplish this has been a most laborious work, and the officers of the various departments of the Adjutant-General's office, of the office of the Surgeon-General of the Army, of the Paymaster-General's Department, of the Second Auditor of the United States Treasury, and of the Commissioner of Pensions, all deserve credit for the great work well performed.

Losses by Death—Surgeon-General's Report.

The Surgeon-General of the United States Army, November 12, 1870, reports the loss, by death, of the Union army, according to his records, to be as follows:

Killed in action	35,408
Died of wounds	49,205
" suicide	302
" homicide	103
" executions	121
" disease	186,216

In these figures those who died while prisoners of war, or while at home on furlough, are not included; the number reported by the Surgeon-General as killed in action is based on indirect and second-hand information, never complete, and not always reliable. The Surgeon-General specifies the headings as follows:

Killed in action.

Regular army, officers and men	831	
White volunteers, officers and men	33,805	
Colored troops, enlisted men	772	
		35,408

Died of wounds.

Regular army, officers and men	1,174	
White volunteers, officers and men	46,271	
Colored troops, enlisted men	1,760	
		49,205

Died of Disease.

Regular army, officers and men	3,009	
White volunteers, officers and men	153,995	
Colored troops, enlisted men	29,212	
		186,216

Losses by Death—Quartermaster-General's Report.

The Quartermaster-General of the United States Army estimates that of those buried in the National Cemeteries about 300,000 were Union soldiers. To this should be added the number buried at their homes, and allowance should be made for those whose remains have not been found ; what this number is, is not practicable to ascertain.

Summary.

To form as nearly a correct estimate of the loss by death in the Union armies as it may be possible to do, the reports of the Adjutant-General and the Surgeon-General of the United States Army must be combined.

The Adjutant-General of the Army is likely to be more correct in his report of those killed in battle ; the reverse is the case of his report of those who died of wounds and disease, and for these it would be proper to take the report of the Surgeon-General.

The following summary may therefore be considered as correct as it will ever be practicable to make.

A Statement of Loss by Death.

	Regulars.	White Volunteers.	Colored troops.	Total.
Killed in battle	1,335	41,369	1,514	44.238
Died of wounds and injuries.	1,174	46,271	1,760	49,205
Suicide, homicide, and execution.........	27	442	57	526
Died of disease	3,009	153,995	29,212	186,216
Unknown causes	159	23,188	837	24,184
Total	5,724	265,265	33,380	304,369

The Adjutant-General reports that 26.168 men are known to have died while prisoners of war in the hands of the enemy.

The latest report from the War Department on record makes the total loss by death 303,504

The foregoing summary makes it .... 304,369 the difference arising from the fact that the Surgeon-General reports over 900 more regulars died during the war than the Adjutant-General.

The last report of the Adjutant-General on the subject is dated October 25, 1870, and during the preceding three months only one hundred names were added to his death list ; this would show that the list must be nearly complete, and that since then probably not more names have been added than will suffice to make the total number near 308,000 men ; these are, however, men whose death in the service has been absolutely substantiated.

All who served during the war know that at times men disappeared or failed to turn up, who, it was morally certain, had not deserted; still they could not be accounted for, never were heard of again, and undoubtedly lost their lives in some way and owing to the war. If we allow one-tenth of one per cent. of the total force enrolled, or perhaps still better, two men for each regimental organization, as loss of this nature, the total loss will foot up in round numbers 313,000 men, or about eleven per cent. of the number of men who were enrolled during the war.

PERCENTAGE.

In the "Medical History of the War," in the list of engagements, an effort is made to give the losses of wounded and captured or reported missing in action; although the numbers given there are in many instances not reliable, they will give a fair general idea of the losses incurred, which are as follows:

Wounded in action, 280,040; missing and captured, 184,791. Based on the foregoing, the figures of losses given heretofore, and the *total* number of men furnished by the States and Territories during the war it would appear that

Out of about every 65 men one man was killed in action.
" " " 56 " " died of wounds received in action.
" " " 13 " " " of disease and unknown causes.
" " " 9 " " " while in the service.
" " " 15 " " was captured or reported missing.
" " " 10 " " " wounded in action.
" " " 7 men captured one died while in captivity.

In his work "Strategos," Lieutenant Totten, of the United States Army, computes the *annual* loss *per one thousand men* of mean aggregate strength, actually enrolled or engaged, to have been as follows:

	Regulars.	Volunteers.	White.	Colored.	Mixed.
General mortality..................	47.6	75.4	74.6	176.3	79.7
Killed in battle....................	19.9	18.8	18.9	10.6	18.4
Died of wounds	11.7	11.2	11.2	10.8	10.8
Total loss by death, per 1,000 men per annum...................	79.2	105.4	104.7	197.7	108.9

In this computation the number of those who died of wounds is smaller than the number of killed in action. The latest report as set forth in the foregoing pages makes the loss by death from wounds larger than the loss by death in action; it is therefore probable the above computation is based on earlier reports of losses.

Reducing the total number of men furnished to an effective force, by allowing 662 men of each 1,000 men furnished to have been effective and likely to have been actively engaged, a number is obtained on which it would be proper to distribute the loss by killed in action, died of wounds, captured and wounded ; the deaths by disease and the total number of deaths may be placed on the whole number of men furnished by the States and Territories during the war ; this plan will give :

Killed in action, one man out of every 42.7 effective and actively engaged men ; died of wounds, one man out of every 38.1 effective and actively engaged men ; died of disease, etc., one man out of every 13.5 men of the total force furnished ; died while in service, one man out of every 9.3 men of the total force furnished ; captured, etc., one man out of every 10.2 effective and actively engaged men ; wounded in action, one man out of every 6.7 effective and actively engaged men ; died while a prisoner, one man out of about every 7 captured.

The proportion of violent deaths to deaths from other known causes is : of white troops alone, one out of every two and seven-tenths ; of colored troops alone, one out of every nine and eight-tenths ; of regulars alone, one out of every two and two-tenths ; of volunteers alone one out of every two and seven-tenths.

	Regulars.	White Volunt'rs.	Colored Troops.	Total.
Violent deaths.....................	2,556	88,082	3,331	93,969
Deaths from disease...............	3,009	153,995	29,212	186,216
Unknown cáuses...................	159	23,188	837	24,184
Total.....................	5,724	265,265	33,380	304,369

DEATHS IN HOSPITALS.

In the Hospitals of the Army 6,049,648 cases were treated by the officers of the Medical Department, and the deaths have been classified by the Surgeon-General as follows :

	WHITE TROOPS.		COLORED TROOPS.		TOTAL DEATHS.
	Cases treated.	Deaths.	Cases treated.	Deaths.	
CLASS I.—ZYMOTIC DISEASES. *Order No.* 1. Miasmatic Diseases ; this order is again subdivided into 23 divisions	3,285,376	92,150	369,659	16,537	108,687
Order No. 2. Enthetic diseases ; divided into 7 subdivisions	192,504	162	14,948	37	199
Order No. 3. Dietetic diseases ; subdivided into 6 divisions....................	42,944	1,124	16,460	416	1,540

DEATHS IN HOSPITALS. —(*Continued.*)

	WHTIE TROOPS.		COLORED TROOPS.		TOTAL DEATHS.
	Cases treated.	Deaths.	Cases treated.	Deaths.	
CLASS II.—CONSTITUTIONAL DISEASES.					
Order No. 1. Diathetic Diseases; subdivided into 8 divisions..........	288,287	1,226	35,922	581	1,807
Order No. 2. Tubercular diseases; divided into 3 subdivisions..............	19,890	5,418	3,859	1,296	6,714
CLASS III.—PARASITIC DISEASES.					
Divided into 5 divisions................	35,669	8	3,810	6	14
CLASS IV.—LOCAL DISEASES.					
Order No. 1. Diseases of nervous system; divided into 13 subdivisions...........	170,032	4,442	23,936	815	5,257
Order No. 2. Diseases of eye; subdivided into 7 divisions..........	88,701	2	7,599	1	3
Order No. 3. Diseases of ear; divided into 5 divisions	28,918	6	2,080	1	7
Order No. 4. Diseases of organs of circulation; subdivided into 11 divisions....	25,106	1,658	1,559	467	2,125
Order No. 5. Diseases of respiratory organs; divided into 11 subdivisions. ...	448,923	17,902	55,189	6,198	24,100
Order No. 6. Diseases of digestive organs; divided into 23 subdivisions	563,259	4,146	54,271	971	5,117
Order No. 7. Diseases of urinary and genital organs; subdivided into 13 divisions	29,875	430	3,016	131	561
Order No. 8. Diseases of bones and joints; divided into 9 subdivisions	8,079	47	950	15	62
Order No. 9. Diseases of integumentary system; subdivided into 7 divisions....	189,817	216	11,760	27	243
CLASS V.—WOUNDS, ACCIDENTS, AND INJURIES.					
Order No. 1. Wounds, accidents, and injuries; divided into 16 subdivisions..	400,933	36,688	24,337	1,427	38,115
Order No. 2. Homicide................	....	144	......	30	174
Order No. 3. Suicide.................	....	301	.....	9	310
Order No. 4. Execution of sentence.....	....	104	.....	39	143
Unclassified diseases...................	7,187	449	.....	....	449
	5,825,480	166,623	629,354	29,004	195,627
Of these cases and deaths there occurred in the year ending June 30, 1866.......	245,954	4,735	159,232	5,539	10,274
Leaving cases and deaths from May 1, 1861, until June 30, 1865.........	5,579,526	161,888	470,122	23,465	185,353

The largest number of deaths occurred from the following diseases :

	White Troops.	Colored Troops.	Total.
OF CLASS I.			
Typhoid fever—Order No. 1........................	27,056	2,230	29,336
Typho-malarial fever—Order No. 1..	4,059	1,301	5,360
Remittent fever—Order No. 1........	3,853	1,002	4,855
Congestive intermittent fever—Order No. 1........	3,370	794	4,164
Acute diarrhœa—Order No. 1..	2,923	1,368	4,291
Chronic diarrhœa—Order No. 1.........	27.558	3,278	30,836
Acute dysentery—Order No. 1....................	4,084	1,492	5,576
Chronic dysentery—Order No. 1..................	3,229	626	3,855
Erysipelas—Order No. 1.......................	1,860	247	2,107
Small-pox and varioloid—Order No. 1............ .	4,717	2,341	7,058
Measles—Order No. 1......................	4,246	931	5,177
OF CLASS II.			
Consumption—Order No. 2..................... ...	5,286	1,211	6,497
OF CLASS IV.			
Inflammation of brain—Order No. 1........... ...	1,269	262	1,531
Inflammation of lungs—Order No. 5..............	14,738	5,233	19,971
OF CLASS V.			
Gunshot wounds—Order No. 1....................	32,907	1,042	33,949
Total..................................	141,155	23,408	164,563

The foregoing tables do not embrace those died of wounds or disease while prisoners of war, or those who died while on furlough, leave of absence, or absent without leave.

DISCHARGES FOR DISABILITY.

The Adjutant-General, in a report dated October 25, 1870, gives the number of men discharged for disability during the war as 285,245 men, as follows :

Enlisted men of the regular army 6,541
     "   "   volunteer army...................... 269,197
     "   "   colored troops 9,807

The Surgeon-General collating the number thus discharged from the medical records, finds accounts of only 223,535, as follows :

White 215,312
Colored...................... 8,223

The numbers given by the Adjutant-General must be taken as more reliable or conclusive, and it would appear that one man out of about every ten men furnished was discharged for disability. The causes of the discharges reported by the Surgeon-General are, with the exception of 27,141, stated in the medical records, and will give a basis on which to place an estimate of the causes of all discharges for disability. These known causes of discharges are arranged in classes and orders, same as the causes of death, and from the following tables it appears that there were discharged for disability arising from

Gunshot wounds 34,209
Consumption 20,995
Diarrhœa 16,487
Debility 15,040
Rheumatism 12,653
Heart disease 10,797

TABLE SHOWING THE NUMBER AND CAUSES OF DISCHARGES.

CLASSES AND ORDERS.	No. of Discharges of—		
	White Vols.	Col-ored	Total.
Class I.—Zymotic d seases divided into three orders.... ...	36,804	1,078	37,882
" II.—Constitutional diseases divided into two orders...	36,281	1,789	38,070
" III.—Parasitic diseases..	6	2	8
" IV.—Local diseases, divided into nine orders	63,493	1,962	65,455
" V.—Wounds, accidents and injuries.................	48,374	1,479	49,853
" VI.—Developmental diseases.......................	30,354	1,913	32,267
Total	215,312	8,223	223,525

TABLE SHOWING THE MOST FREQUENT CAUSES OF DISCHARGES.

CLASSES AND ORDERS.	No. of Discharges of—		
	White Vols.	Colored.	Total.
Diarrhœa—Order 1, Class I..................	16,185	302	16,487
Dysentery— " 1, " I......	1,204	57	1,261
Debility— " 1, " I..................	14,500	540	15,040
Syphilis— " 2, " I..................	1,779	86	1,865
Rheumatism—Order 1, Class II.	11,779	874	12,653
Dropsy— " 1, " II.	2,224	109	2,333
Consumption— " 2, " II.	20,403	592	20,995
Epilepsy— " 1, " IV.................	3,872	174	4,046
Paralysis— " 1, " IV.................	2,838	69	2,907
Ophthalmia— " 2, " IV.................	1,463	25	1,488
Deafness— " 3, " IV.................	1,157	38	1,195
Heart disease— " 4, " VI.........	10,636	161	10,797

TABLE SHOWING THE MOST FREQUENT CAUSES OF DISCHARGES.—
(*Continued.*)

CLASSES AND ORDERS.	NO. OF DISCHARGES OF—		
	White Vols.	Colored.	Total.
Varicose veins—Order 4, Class IV..............	1,969	69	2,038
Varicocele— " 4, " IV..............	1,390	25	1,415
Asthma— " 5, " IV..............	1,220	42	1,262
Bronchitis— " 5, " IV..............	3,729	96	3,825
Inflammation of lungs—Order 5, Class IV.......	1,092	25	1,117
Hernia—Order 6, Class V.....................	9,002	358	9,360
Inflammation of liver—Order 6, Class V.........	1,354	29	1,383
Piles	1,555	43	1,598
Inflammation of kidneys—Order 7, Class IV.....	1,069	27	1,096
Anchylosis—Order 8, Class IV.	1,838	105	1,943
Diseases of spine—Order 8, Class IV...........	1,547	31	1,578
Ulcers—Order 9, Class IV....	1,138	46	1,184
Fractures—Class V............................	2,138	89	2,227
Gunshot wounds—Class V.....................	33,458	751	34,209
Amputations—Class V.........................	5,832	327	6,159
Wounds, unspecified—Class V..................	4,878	154	5,032
Old age—Class VI.	2,598	478	3,076

NATIONAL CEMETERIES.

SEPTEMBER 9, 1861, the Secretary of War directed that the Quarter-master-General of the Army shall cause to be printed and to be placed in every hospital of the army, blank books and forms for the purpose of preserving accurate and permanent records of deceased soldiers and their place of burial, and that he should also provide proper means for a registered head-board to be secured at the head of each soldier's grave.

Act of Congress, approved July 17, 1862, authorizes the President of the United States, whenever, in his opinion, it shall be deemed expedient, to purchase cemetery grounds, and to cause them to be securely enclosed, to be used as a national cemetery for the soldiers who shall die in the service of the country.

April 13, 1866, it was provided by Public Resolution No. 21 " that the Secretary of War be authorized to take immediate measures to preserve from desecration the graves of soldiers of the United States who fell in battle or died of disease during the War of the Rebellion, and to secure suitable burial-places, and to have these grounds enclosed, so that the resting-places of the honored dead may be kept sacred forever."

February 28, 1867, an act to establish and protect national cemeteries was approved, which provided in detail for the purchase of grounds, and the management and inspection of cemeteries ; also for the punishment of any person who should mutilate monuments or injure the trees and plants.

In accordance with the foregoing and the orders issued by the War Department from time to time, every effort has been made to collect the remains of the dead, to inter them decently, and to record all the facts known in connection with each grave. After no war, whether of ancient or modern times, have any such systematic exertions been made to secure the collection of the dead and their interment in permanent resting-places, as have been made by the Quartermaster Department of the United States Army under the above provisions of the law.

The latest report of the Quartermaster-General on the subject of the

Nation's Dead, shows that the following National Cemeteries have been established :

NAME OF CEMETERY.	INTERMENTS.		
	Known.	Unknown.	Total.
Annapolis, Md.........................	2,285	204	2,489
Alexandria, La........................	534	772	1,306
Alexandria, Va.	3,402	120	3.522
Andersonville, Ga.....	12,793	921	13,714
Antietam, Md.........................	2,853	1,818	4,671
Arlington, Va..	11,915	4,349	16,264
Ball's Bluff, Va.......................	1	24	25
Barrancas, Fla.....	798	657	1,455
Baton Rouge, La......................	2,469	495	2,964
Battle Ground, D.C...................	43	....	43
Beaufort, S. C........................	4,748	4,493	9,241
Beverly, N. J.........................	145	7	152
Brownsville, Tex........	1.417	1,379	2,796
Camp Butler. Ill......................	1 007	355	1,362
Camp Nelson, Ky......................	2,477	1,165	3,642
Cave Hill, Ky.........................	3,344	583	3,927
Chalmette, La.	6.837	5,674	12,511
Chattanooga, Tenn....................	7,999	4,963	12,962
City Point, Va......	3,778	1,374	5,152
Cold Harbor, Va......................	673	1,281	1,954
Corinth, Miss.........................	1,789	3,927	5,716
Crown Hill, Ind..........	681	32	713
Culpeper, Va..........................	456	911	1,367
Custer Battle Field, M. T..............	262	....	262
Cypress Hills, N. Y................... .	3,710	76	3,786
Danville, Ky..........................	335	8	343
Danville, Va..........................	1,172	155	1.327
Fayetteville, Ark.	431	781	1,212
Finn's Point, N. J...	....	2,644	2,644
Florence, S. C........................	199	2,799	2,998
Fort Donelson, Tenn...................	158	511	669
Fort Gibson, I. T.....	215	2,212	2,427
Fort Harrison, Va.....................	239	575	814
Fort Leavenworth, Kan................	835	928	1,763
Fort McPherson, Neb......	152	291	443
Fort Smith, Ark.......................	711	1,152	1,863
Fort Scott, Kan.......................	390	161	551
Fredericksburg, Va....................	2,487	12,770	15,257
Gettysburg, Pa........................	1,967	1,608	3,575
Glendale, Va	234	961	1,195
Grafton, W. Va........................	634	620	1,254
Hampton, Va..........................	4,930	494	5,424
Jefferson Barracks, Mo.........	8,584	2,906	11,490
Jefferson City, Mo...	349	412	761
Keokuk, Iowa.........	612	33	645
Knoxville, Tenn	2,090	1,046	3,136
Laurel, Md............................	232	6	238
Lebanon, Ky....................... ..	591	277	868
Lexington, Ky...........	805	108	913
Little Rock, Ark...........	3,265	2,357	5,602
Logan's Cross Roads, Ky...............	345	366	711

NAME OF CEMETERY.	INTERMENTS.		
	Known.	Unknown.	Total.
Loudon Park, Md.......................	1,637	166	1,803
Marietta, Ga.	7,188	2,963	10,151
Memphis, Tenn.	5,160	8,817	13,977
Mexico City	284	750	1,034
Mobile, Ala......................... ...	756	113	869
Mound City, Ill........................	2,505	2,721	5,226
Nashville, Tenn.	11,825	4,701	16,526
Natchez, Miss	308	2,780	3,088
New Albany, Ind......................	2,139	676	2,815
New Berne, N. C......................	2,177	1,077	3,254
Philadelphia, Pa.....	1,881	28	1,909
Pittsburg Landing, Tenn.	1,229	2,361	3,590
Poplar Grove, Va......	2,198	4,001	6,199
Port Hudson, La......................	596	3,223	3,819
Raleigh, N. C.....................	619	562	1,181
Richmond, Va..................	842	5,700	6,542
Rock Island, Ill......................	277	19	296
Salisbury, N. C.	94	12,032	12,126
San Antonio, Tex...	324	167	491
Seven Pines, Va......................	150	1,208	1,358
Soldiers' Home, D. C........	5,314	288	5,602
Staunton, Va	233	520	753
Stone River, Tenn...	3,821	2,324	6,145
Vicksburg, Miss......................	3,896	12,704	16,600
Wilmington, N. C.	710	1,398	2,108
Winchester, Va...................... .	2,094	2,365	4,459
Woodlawn, Elmira, N. Y	3,074	16	3,090
Yorktown, Va	748	1,434	2,182
	171,302	147,568	318,870

Of the whole number of interments indicated above, there are about 6,900 known and 1,500 unknown civilians, and 6,100 known and 3,200 unknown Confederates. Of these latter, the greater portion are buried at Woodlawn Cemetery, Elmira, N. Y., and Finn's Point Cemetery, near Salem, N. J. The interments at Mexico City are mainly of those who were killed or died in that vicinity during the Mexican War, and include also such citizens of the United States as may have died in Mexico, and who, under treaty provision, have the right of burial therein. From the foregoing, it will appear that, after making all proper deductions for civilians and Confederates, there are gathered in the various places mentioned the remains of nearly 300,000 men who at one time wore the blue during the late war, and who yielded up their lives in defence of the Government which now so graciously cares for their ashes.

PART II.

CHRONOLOGICAL RECORD OF ENGAGE-
MENTS, BATTLES, ETC., IN THE
UNITED STATES, 1861 TO 1865.

2,261.

CHRONOLOGICAL RECORD.

UNDER the orders of the Surgeon-General of the Army, a work of the greatest importance was undertaken and completed by that Department, viz., " The Medical and Surgical History of the War of the Rebellion," and great credit is due for the magnificent and instructive work to Surgeons-General Wm. A. Hammond and J. K. Barnes, U. S. Army; Surgeon J. H. Brinton, U. S. Volunteers; Assistant-Surgeons (then) J. J. Woodward and George A. Otis, U. S. Army, who were directly connected with the work, as well as the members of the Medical Department, regulars and volunteers, generally.

In this work there is a chronological record of engagements, etc., compiled by the Chief Clerk of the Surgical Division, Mr. Frederick R. Sparks, from official sources where practicable, from Confederate reports, and from Union and Confederate newspapers in other cases, where the statement was not obviously false. As full as the record is, it is not complete. In preparing it for publication here, several minor engagements were added, and others may find omissions as well; nevertheless, this is the completest record in existence at present.

1861.—(156).

Fort Sumter, S. O.

1. April 12th and 13th—Battery E, 1st U. S. Artillery. In saluting the flag before the evacuation on April 15th, Private Daniel Hough was killed and three men wounded by the premature explosion of a gun.

Harper's Ferry, Va.

2. April 18th—Detachment of ordnance men.

Streets of Baltimore, Md.

3. April 19th—6th Massachusetts State Militia and 26th Pennsylvania Volunteers.

Camp Jackson, Mo.

4. May 10th—1st, 3d, and 4th Missouri Reserve Corps and 3d Missouri Volunteers.

4*

St. Louis, Mo., corner Fifth and Walnut Streets.

5. May 10th—5th Missouri U. S. Reserve Corps.

Fairfax Court-house, Va.

6. June 1st—Company B, 2d U. S. Cavalry.

Phillippi, West Va.

7. June 3d—1st West Virginia, 16th Ohio, 7th and 9th Indiana, and 14th Ohio Volunteers.

Great Bethel, Va.

8. June 10th—1st, 2d, 3d, 5th, and 7th New York, 4th Massachusetts Volunteers, and a detachment of 2d U. S. Artillery.

Romney, West Va.

9. June 11th—11th Indiana Volunteers.

Vienna, Va.

10. June 17th—1st Ohio Volunteers.

Booneville, Mo.

11. June 17th—2d Missouri (three months), Batteries H and L, 1st Missouri Light Artillery, Volunteers.

Edward's Ferry, Va.

12. June 17th—1st Pennsylvania Volunteers (300 men).

Independence, Mo.

13. June 17th—Detachment of Missouri Volunteers.

New Creek, West Va.

14. June 17th—Local Militia.

Camp Cole, Mo.

15. June 18th—Union Home Guards (800 men).

Patterson Creek, Va. (also called Kelly's Island).

16. June 26th—11th Indiana Volunteers.

Mathias Point, Va.

17. June 27th—Crews of U. S. Gunboats Pawnee and Freeborn.

Falling Waters (also called Haynesville and Martinsburg), Md.

18. July 2d—1st Wisconsin and 11th Pennsylvania Volunteers, advance of Brig.-General George H. Thomas's command.

Carthage (also called Dry Forks), Mo.

19. July 5th—3d and 5th Missouri (three months), and Battery of Missouri Artillery Volunteers.

Newport News, Va.

20. July 5th—9th New York (one Company).

Middle Creek Fork, West Va.

21. July 6th—3d Ohio Volunteers (one Company).

Great Falls, Va.

22. July 7th—8th New York Volunteers.

Laurel Hill (also named Bealington), West Va.

23. July 8th—14th Ohio and 9th Indiana Volunteers.

1861.]   **Monroe Station, Mo.**

24. July 10th—16th Illinois and 3d Iowa Volunteers and Hannibal Home Guards.

Rich Mountain, West Va.

25. July 11th—8th, 10th, and 13th Indiana and 19th Ohio Volunteers.

Barboursville (also designated Red House), West Va.

26. July 12th—2d Kentucky Volunteers.

Beverly, West Va.

27. July 12th—4th and 9th Ohio Volunteers.

Carrick's Ford, West Va.

28. July 14th—14th Ohio, 9th and 7th Indiana Volunteers.

Millsville or Wentzville (North Mo. R.R.), Mo.

29. July 16th—8th Missouri Volunteers.

Fulton, Missouri.

30. July 17th—3d Missouri Reserves (four hundred men).

Scarytown, West Va.

31. July 17th—2d Kentucky, 12th and 21st Ohio Volunteers, and 1st Ohio Battery.

Martinsburg, Mo.

32. July 17th—1st Missouri Reserves (one Company).

Bunker Hill, Va.

33. July 17th—Detachment of General Patterson's command.

Harrisonville and Parkersville, Mo.

34. July 18th and 19th—Van Horn's Battalion (Missouri) Cass County Home Guards.

Blackburn's Ford, Va.

35. July 18th—1st Massachusetts, 2d and 3d Michigan, 12th New York Volunteers, detachment of 2d U. S. Cavalry, and Battery E, 3d U. S. Artillery.

Bull Run (also Manassas), Va.

36. July 21st—Infantry, Volunteers, or Militia : 2d Maine, 2d New Hampshire, 2d Vermont, 1st, 4th, and 5th Massachusetts, 1st and 2d Rhode Island, 1st, 2d, and 3d Connecticut, 8th, 11th, 12th, 13th, 16th, 18th, 27th, 29th, 31st, 32d, 35th, 38th, and 39th New York Volunteers, 2d, 8th, 14th, 69th, 71st, and 79th New York Militia, 27th Pennsylvania Volunteers, 1st, 2d, and 3d Michigan, 1st and 2d Minnesota, 1st and 2d Ohio; detachment of 2d, 3d, and 8th Regular Infantry, and a battalion of Marines ; Artillery : Batteries D, E. G, and M, 2d, E, 3d Artillery, D, 5th Artillery, and the 2d Rhode Island Battery ; Cavalry : detachments from the 1st and 2d Dragoons.

Forsyth, Mo.

37. July 22d—1st Iowa and 2d Kansas Volunteers, Stanley Dragoons and Totten's Battery.

Ætna, Mo.

38. July 22d—21st Missouri Volunteers.

Blue Mills, Mo.

39. July 24th—5th Missouri Reserves.

Lane's Prairie, near Rolla, Mo.

40. July 26th—Missouri Home Guards.

Harrisonville, Mo.

41. July 26th—Missouri Home Guards and 5th Kansas Cavalry.

Fort Fillmore, New Mexico.

42. July 27th—7th U. S. Infantry and U. S. Mounted Rifles.

Dug Springs, Mo.

43. August 2d—1st Iowa and 3d Missouri Volunteers, and five batteries Missouri Light Artillery.

Mesilla, New Mexico.

44. August 3d—7th U. S. Infantry and U. S. Mounted Rifles.

Athens, Mo.

45. August 5th—Home Guards and 21st Missouri Volunteers.

Point of Rocks, Md.

46. August 5th—28th New York Volunteers.

Hampton, Va.

47. August 7th—20th New York Volunteers.

Lovettsville, Va.

48. August 8th—19th New York Volunteers.

Wilson's Creek, Mo. (also known as Springfield and Oak Hills).

49. August 10th—Cavalry : 6th and 10th Missouri, 2d Kansas Mounted Volunteers, and one Company 1st U. S. Infantry, 1st Iowa, 1st Kansas, 1st, 2d, 3d, and 5th Missouri, detachments of the 1st and 2d Regulars, Missouri Home Guards; Artillery : 1st Missouri Light and Battery F, 2d U. S., commanded by Brig.-General Nathaniel Lyons.

Potosi, Mo.

50. August 10th—Missouri Home Guards.

Grafton, West Va.

51. August 13th—One Company 4th West Virginia Volunteers.

Brunswick, Mo.

52. August 17th—5th Missouri Reserves.

Charlestown (or Bird's Point), Mo.

53. August 19th—22d Illinois Volunteers.

Hawk's Nest, West Va.

54. August 20th—11th Ohio Volunteers.

Lookout Station, Mo.

55. August 20th—Organization not reported ; Union loss, 1 killed and 6 wounded.

Jonesboro, Mo.

56. August 21st—Missouri Home Guards.

Cross Lanes (or Summerville), West Va.

57. August 26th—7th Ohio Volunteers.

Ball's Cross Roads, Va.

58. August 27th—Two companies of the 23d New York Volunteers.

1861.]   **Wayne Court House, West Va.**
59. August 27th—5th West Virginia Volunteers.

Fort Hatteras (Cape Hatteras Inlet), N. C.
60. August 28th and 29th—9th, 20th, and 99th New York Volunteers, and a naval force commanded by Commodore Stringham.

Lexington, Mo.
61. August 29th—Missouri Home Guards.

Munson's Hill, Va.
62. August 31st—Two companies 23d New York Volunteers.

Bennett's Mills, Mo.
63. September 1st—Missouri Home Guards.

Boone Court House, West Va.
64. September 1st—1st Kentucky Volunteers.

Dallas, Mo.
65. September 2d—11th Missouri Volunteers.

Worthington, Marion Co , West Va.
66. September 2d—Organization not reported, see Rebellion Record, Volume III., page 13.

Dry Wood (also known as Fort Scott), Mo.
67. September 2d—5th and 6th Kansas Volunteers, one company 9th Cavalry, and 1st Kansas Battery.

Beher's Mills, Va.,
68. September 2d—13th Massachusetts Volunteers.

Shelbina, Mo.
69. September 4th—3d Iowa Volunteers.

Petersburg, West Va.
70. September 7th—Three companies of the 4th Ohio Volunteers.

Carnifex Ferry, West Va.
71. September 10th—9th, 10th, 12th, 13th, 28th, and 47th Ohio Volunteers.

Lewinsville, Va.
72. September 11th—19th Indiana, 3d Vermont, and 65th New York Volunteers, and 79th New York Militia.

Elk Water, West Va.
73. September 11th—3d Ohio, 15th and 17th Indiana Volunteers.

Black River, near Ironton, Mo.
74. September 12th—Three companies of 1st Indiana Cavalry.

Cheat Mountain, West Va.
75. September 12th and 13th—13th, 14th, 15th, and 17th Indiana, 3d, 6th, 24th, and 25th Ohio, and 2d West Virginia Volunteers.

Lexington, Mo.
76. September 12th to 20th—8th, 25th, and 27th Missouri Volunteers, 13th and 14th Missouri Home Guards, Berry's and Van Horn's Missouri Cavalry, 1st Cavalry and 23d Infantry Illinois Volunteers, Colonel James A. Mulligan, 23d Illinois Volunteers, Commanding.

Booneville, Mo.

77. September 13th—Missouri Home Guards.

Near Pensacola, Fla.

78. September 14th—Rebel privateer Judah destroyed by the crew of U. S. Flagship Colorado.

Pritchard's Mills (also known as Damestown), Va.

79. September 15th—28th Pennsylvania and 13th Massachusetts Volunteers.

Morristown, Mo.

80. September 17th—5th, 6th, and 9th Kansas Cavalry, and 1st Kansas Battery.

Blue Mills, Mo.

81. September 17th—3d Iowa Volunteers.

Barboursville, West Va.

82. September 18th—Kentucky Home Guards.

Papinsville (also Osceola), Mo.

83. September 21st and 22d—5th, 6th, and 9th Kansas Cavalry.

Elliott's Mills (called also Camp Crittenden), Mo.

84. September 22d—7th Iowa Volunteers.

Romney (called also Hanging Rock), West Va.

85. September 23d—4th and 8th Ohio Volunteers.

Chapmansville, West Va.

86. September 25th—1st Kentucky, and 34th Ohio Volunteers.

Lucas Bend, Ky.

87. September 26th—Captain Stewart's Cavalry.

Shanghai, Mo.

88. September 27th—Organizations not known; see Tribune Almanac of 1862, page 45.

Munson's Hill (Camp Advance), Va.

89. September 29th—69th Pennsylvania fire into 71st Pennsylvania Volunteers through mistake.

Greenbrier, West Va.

90. October 3d—Battery G, 4th United States Artillery, Battery "A," 1st Michigan Artillery, 24th, 25th, and 32d Ohio, and 7th, 9th, 13th, 14th, 15th, and 17th Indiana Volunteers.

Alimosa (near Fort Craig), N. M.

91. October 4th—Mink's New Mexico Cavalry, and U. S. Regulars.

Buffalo Hill, Ky.

92. October 4th—Organization not recorded; Union loss, twenty killed; Confederate loss, fifty killed.

Chicamicomico, N. C.

93. October 5th—20th Indiana Volunteers.

Hillsboro, Ky.

94. October 8th—Flemingsburg Home Guards.

1861.]   **Santa Rosa, Fla.**

95. October 9th—6th New York Volunteers, detachments of Companies "A," 1st, and "H," 2d U. S. Artillery, and Companies C and E, 3d U. S. Infantry.

Cameron, Ray Co., Mo.

96. October 12th—Major James' Cavalry.

Upton Hill, Ky.

97. October 12th—39th Indiana Volunteers.

Bayles' Cross Roads, La.

98. October 12th—79th New York Volunteers.

Beckwith's Farm (twelve miles from Bird's Point), Mo.

99. October 13th—Lieutenant Tuff's detachment of Cavalry.

West Glaze (also known as Shanghai, Henrytown, and Monday's Hollow), Mo.

100. October 13th—10th and 6th Missouri Cavalry, and Fremont Battalion Cavalry.

Big River Bridge, near Potosi, Mo.

101. October 15th—Forty men of the 38th Illinois Volunteers.

Linn Creek, Mo.

102. October 15th—6th Missouri Cavalry and 13th Illinois Volunteers.

Bolivar Heights, Va.

103. October 16th—Detachments from 28th Pennsylvania, 3d Wisconsin, and 13th Massachusetts Volunteers.

Warsaw, Mo.

104. October 16th—Organizations not recorded ; see Rebellion Record, Vol. III., page 51.

Fredericktown, Mo. (including skirmish at Ironton).

105. October 17th to 21st—Company A, 1st Missouri Light Artillery, 11th Missouri, and 17th, 20th, 21st, 33d, and 38th Illinois, 1st Indiana, and 8th Wisconsin Volunteers.

Big Hurricane Creek, Mo.

106. October 19th—18th Missouri Volunteers.

Ball's Bluff (also Edward's Ferry, Harrison's Island, and Leesburg), Va.

107. October 21st—15th and 20th Massachusetts, 40th New York, and 71st Pennsylvania Volunteers, and Battery B Rhode Island Artillery.

Wild Cat, Ky.

108. October 21st—33d Indiana, 14th and 17th Ohio Volunteers, 1st Kentucky Cavalry, and 1st Ohio Battery.

Buffalo Mills, Mo.

109. October 22d—Organizations not recorded ; see Tribune Almanac of 1862.

West Liberty, Ky.

110. October 23d—2d Ohio Volunteers, 1st and Loughlin's Ohio Cavalry, and 1st Ohio Artillery.

Hodgeville, Ky.

111. October 23d— Detachment of 6th Indiana Volunteers.

Springfield, Mo. (also known as Zagony's Charge).

112. October 25th—Fremont's Body Guard, White's Prairie Scouts.

Romney, West Va. (also Mill Creek Mills).

113. October 26th—4th and 8th Ohio and 7th West Virginia Volunteers, 2d Regiment Potomac Home Brigade, Maryland Volunteers, and Ringgold (Pa.) Cavalry Battalion.

Saratoga, Ky.

114. October 26th—9th Illinois Volunteers.

Plattsburg, Clinton Co., Mo.

115. October 27th—Organization not recorded; Confederate loss, 8 killed, 12 captured.

Spring Hill, Mo.

116. October 27th—One Company of 7th Missouri Cavalry.

Woodbury and Morgantown, Ky.

117. October 29th—17th Kentucky Infantry and 3d Kentucky Cavalry Volunteers.

Renick, Randolph Co., Mo.

118. November 1st—Organization not recorded; see Rebellion Record, Vol. III., page 268.

Little Santa Fe, Mo.

119. November 6th—4th Missouri and 5th Kansas Cavalry, and Kowald's Missouri Battery.

Belmont, Mo.

120. November 7th—22d, 27th, 30th, and 31st Illinois, and 7th Iowa Volunteers, Battery B, 1st Illinois Artillery, and two companies of the 15th Illinois Cavalry, Brig.-General U. S. Grant commanding.

Galveston Harbor, Texas.

121. November 7th—Burning of the Royal Yacht by the crew of the U. S. Frigate Santee.

Port Royal, S. C.

122. November 7th—U. S. Navy, Commodore S. F. Dupont, U. S. N., commanding.

Piketown, Pike Co. (also called Try Mountain), Ky.

123. November 9th—2d, 21st, 33d, and 59th Ohio and 16th Kentucky Volunteers, commanded by Col. J. W. Sill, 33d Ohio.

Taylor's Ford, Wautauga River, Tenn.

124. November 10th—Loyal citizens; from Confederate newspapers.

Guyandotte, West Va.

125. November 10th—Recruits of the 9th West Virginia Volunteers.

Gauley Bridge, West Va.

126. November 10th—11th Ohio Volunteers and 2d Kentucky Cavalry.

Little Blue, Mo.

127. November 11th—One hundred and ten men of the 7th Kansas Cavalry.

Occoquan Creek, Va.

128. November 12th—Reconnoitring party of the 1st New York Cavalry.

1861.]　　　　　　　　　　**Cypress Bridge, Ky.**

129. November 17th—Organization not recorded; Union loss, 10 killed and 15 wounded.

Palmyra, Mo.

130. November 18th—Detachment of 3d Missouri Cavalry.

Wirt Court House, West Va.

131. November 19th—Detachment of 1st West Virginia Cavalry.

Pensacola, Fort Pickens, Fla.

132. November 23d—Batteries A, F, L, 1st U. S. Artillery, C, H, and K, 2d U. S. Artillery ; Companies C and E, 3d U. S. Infantry, and Companies G and I, 6th New York Volunteers.

Lancaster, Mo.

133. November 24th—21st Missouri Volunteers.

Johnstown, Mo.

134. November 24th—Missouri Home Guard.

Independence, Little Blue, Mo.

135. November 26th—7th Kansas Cavalry.

Drainesville, Va.

136. November 26th—1st Pennsylvania Cavalry.

Hunter's Mills, Va.

137. November 26th—3d Pennsylvania Cavalry.

Black Walnut Creek, near Sedalia, Mo.

138. November 29th—1st Missouri Cavalry.

Morristown, Tenn.

139. December 1st—Organization not recorded.

Salem, Dent Co., Mo.

140. December 3d—Detachment of 10th Missouri Cavalry.

Vienna, Va.

141. December 3d—Detachment of 3d Pennsylvania Cavalry.

Anandale, Va.

142. December 4th—Thirty men of 3d New Jersey Volunteers.

Dunksburg, near Sedalia, Mo.

143. December 4th—Citizens; see New York Herald, December 7, 1861.

Bushy Creek, Ark.

144. December 9th—Union Indians under Opothleyholo.

Dam No. 4, Potomac, Va.

145. December 11th—12th Indiana Volunteers.

Bertrand, Mo.

146. December 11th—2d Illinois Cavalry.

Bagdad, Shelby Co., Ky.

147. December 12th—6th Kentucky Volunteers.

Camp Alleghany (also Buffalo Mountain), W. Va.

148. December 13th—9th and 13th Indiana, 25th and 32d Ohio, and 2d W. Virginia Volunteers, commanded by Brig.-General R. H. Milroy.

Rowlett's Station (also known as Mumfordsville and Woodsonville), Ky.

149. December 17th—32d Indiana Volunteers.

Milford (also Shawnee or Blackwater Mound), Mo.

150. December 18th—27th Ohio, and 8th, 18th, 22d, and 24th Indiana Volunteers, 31st Kansas and 1st Iowa Cavalry, a detachment of U. S. Cavalry, and two batteries of 1st Missouri Light Artillery.

Drainesville, Va.

151. December 20th—1st, 6th, 9th, 10th, and 12th Regiments Pennsylvania Reserve Corps, 1st Pennsylvania Artillery, and 1st Pennsylvania Cavalry.

Hudson, Mo.

152. December 21st—Detachment of 7th Missouri Cavalry.

New Market Bridge, near Newport News, Va.

153. December 22d—20th New York Volunteers.

Wadesburg, Mo.

154. December 24th—Missouri Home Guards.

Sacramento, Ky.

155. December 28th—3d Kentucky Cavalry.

Mount Zion, Mo.

156. December 28th—Birge's Sharpshooters and 3d Missouri Cavalry.

1862.—(564.)

Port Royal, Coosa River. S. C.

157. January 1st—3d Michigan, 47th, 48th, and 79th New York, and 50th Pennsylvania Volunteers.

Hunnewell, Mo.

158. January 3d—Four companies of the 10th Missouri Cavalry.

Huntersville, Va.

159. January 4th—Detachment of the 25th Ohio Volunteers, and 2d West Virginia and 1st Indiana Cavalry.

Bath, Va.

160. January 4th—39th Illinois Volunteers. This includes skirmishes at Great Cacapon Bridge, Alpine Station, and Hancock.

Calhoun, Green Co., Mo.

161. January 4th—Organization not recorded.

Blue Gap, near Romney, Va.

162. January 7th—4th, 5th, 7th, and 8th Ohio, and 14th Indiana Volunteers, and 1st West Virginia Cavalry.

1862.]   Jennie's Creek (also known as Paintsville), Ky.

163. January 7th—Four companies of the 1st West Virginia Cavalry.

Charlestown, Mo.

164. January 8th—10th Iowa Volunteers.

Dry Forks, Cheat River, W. Va.

165. January 8th—One company of the 2d West Virginia Cavalry.

Silver Creek, Randolph Co., Mo.

166. January 8th—Detachments of 1st and 2d Mo., 4th Ohio and 1st Iowa Cavalry. (Also known as *Roan's Tanyard* and *Sugar Creek*.)

Columbus, Mo.

167. January 9th—7th Kansas Cavalry.

Middle Creek and Prestonburg, Ky.

168. January 10th—40th and 42d Ohio, 14th and 22d Kentucky Volunteers, Col. J. A. Garfield commanding.

Mill Springs, Ky.

169. January 19th and 20th—9th Ohio, 2d Minnesota, 4th Kentucky, and 10th Indiana Volunteers, and 1st Kentucky Cavalry, commanded by Brig.-General Geo. H. Thomas. (Also known as *Logan's Crossroads, Fishing Creek, Somerset,* and *Beech Grove.*)

Knob Noster, Mo.

170. January 22d—2d Missouri Cavalry.

Occoquan Bridge, Va.

171. January 29th—Detachments of the 37th New York Volunteers and 1st New Jersey Cavalry.

Bowling Green, Ky.

172. February 1st—One company of the 2d Indiana Cavalry.

Morgan County, Tenn.

173. February 2d—Organization not mentioned; obtained from Confederate sources.

Fort Henry, Tenn.

174. February 6th—U. S. Gunboats Essex, Carondelet, St. Louis, Cincinnati, Conestoga, Tyler, and Lexington.

Linn Creek, Logan County, Va.

175. February 8th—Detachment of 5th West Virginia Volunteers.

Roanoke Island, N. C.

176. February 8th—U.S. Gunboats Southfield, Delaware, Stars and Stripes, Louisiana, Hetzel, Commodore Perry, Underwriter, Valley City, Commodore Barney, Hunchback, Ceres, Putnam, Morse, Lockwood, J. A. Seymour, Granite, Brinker, Whitehead, Shawseen, Picket, Pioneer, Hussar, Vidette, Chasseur, 21st, 23d, 24th, 25th, and 27th Massachusetts, 10th Connecticut, 9th, 51st, and 53d New York, 9th New Jersey, 51st Pennsylvania, and 4th and 5th Rhode Island Volunteers, Brig.-General A. E. Burnside, commanding Army and Commodore L. M. Goldsborough the Navy.

Elizabeth City (known also as Cobb's Point), N. C.

177. February 10th—U. S. Gunboats Delaware, Underwriter, Louisiana, Seymour, Hetzel, Shawseen, Valley City, Putnam, Commodore Perry, Ceres, Morse, Whitehead, and Brinker.

Blooming Gap, Va.

178. February 13th—1st West Virginia Cavalry, and 8th Ohio and 7th West Virginia Volunteers.

Flat Lick Fords, Cumberland River, Ky.

179. February 14th—49th Indiana Volunteers, and 6th Kentucky Cavalry.

Marshfield, Mo

180. February 14th—6th Missouri and 3d Illinois Cavalry.

Fort Donelson (sometimes called Dover), Tenn.

181. February 14th, 15th, and 16th—17th and 25th Kentucky, 11th, 25th, 31st, and 44th Indiana, 2d, 7th, 12th, and 14th Iowa, 1st Nebraska, 58th and 76th Ohio, 8th and 13th Missouri, 8th Wisconsin, 8th, 9th, 11th, 12th, 17th, 18th, 20th, 28th, 29th. 30th, 31st, 41st, 45th, 46th, 48th, 49th, 57th, and 58th Illinois Volunteers, Batteries B and D, 1st, and D and E, 2d Illinois Artillery, four companies Illinois Cavalry, Birge's Sharpshooters, and six gunboats, commanded by Brig.-General U. S. Grant and Commodore A. H. Foote.

Bowling Green, Ky.

182. February 15th—Occupied by troops of Brig.-General D. C. Buell's army.

Sugar Creek (also called Pea Ridge), Mo.

183. February 17th—1st and 6th Missouri and 3d Illinois Cavalry.

Independence, Mo.

184. February 18th—2d Ohio Cavalry.

Valverde (or Fort Craig), New Mexico.

185. February 21st—Detachments of the 1st, 2d, and 5th New Mexico Volunteers, 1st New Mexico and 2d Colorado Cavalry, detachments of 5th, 7th, and 10th U. S. Infantry, and Hall's and McRae's Batteries, commanded by Colonel E. R. S. Canby, U. S. A.

Mason's Neck, Occoquan, Va.

186. February 24th—37th New York Volunteers.

Keytesville, Barry County, Mo.

187. February 26th—6th Missouri Cavalry.

Sykestown, Mo.

188. March 1st—7th Cavalry and 10th Infantry, Illinois Volunteers.

Pittsburg Landing, Tenn.

189. March 2d—U. S. Gunboats Lexington and Tyler and 32d Illinois Volunteers.

New Madrid, Mo.

190. March 3d—5th Iowa, 59th Indiana, 39th and 63d Ohio Infantry; and 2d Michigan and 7th Illinois Cavalry Volunteers.

Occoquan, Va.

191. March 5th—Reconnoitring party of the 63d Pennsylvania Volunteers.

1862.]   Pea Ridge, Ark.

192. March 5th, 6th, 7th, 8th—This includes engagements at *Bentonville* on the
    6th, *Leetown* on the 7th, and *Elkhorn Tavern* on the 8th ; troops engaged
    were 25th, 35th, 36th, 37th, 44th, and 59th Illinois, 2d, 3d, 12th, 15th,
    17th, 24th, and Phelps' Missouri, 8th, 18th, and 22d Indiana, and 4th and
    9th Iowa Volunteers, 3d Iowa, 3d and 15th Illinois, and 1st, 4th, 5th, and
    6th Missouri Cavalry, Batteries B and F 2d Missouri Light Artillery, 2d
    Ohio Battery, 1st Indiana Battery, and Battery A 2d Illinois Artillery,
    Brig.-General Samuel R. Curtis, commanding.

                             Fox Creek, Mo.

193. March 7th—4th Missouri Cavalry.

                         Near Nashville, Tenn.

194. March 8th—1st Wisconsin Volunteers and 4th Ohio Cavalry.

                         Mississippi City, Miss.

195. March 8th—26th Massachusetts Volunteers.

                          Mountain Grove, Mo.

196. March 9th—10th Missouri Cavalry.

                 Hampton Roads, near Newport News, Va.

197. March 9th—Minnesota, Congress, Cumberland, and Monitor, 20th Indiana,
    7th and 11th New York Volunteers, Monitor and Rebel Merrimac.

                          Burke's Station, Va.

198. March 10th—One company 1st New York Cavalry.

                    Jacksboro' Big Creek Gap, Tenn

199. March 10th—2d Tennessee Volunteers.

                             Paris, Tenn.

200. March 11th—Detachments of the 5th Iowa and 1st Nebraska Cavalry, and
    Battery K 1st Missouri Artillery.

                   Lexington, Lafayette County, Mo.

201. March 12th—1st Iowa Cavalry.

                         Near Lebanon, Mo.

202. March 12th—Organizations not stated ; taken from official report of Major-
    General H. W. Halleck.

                           New Madrid, Mo.

203. March 13th—10th and 16th Illinois, 27th, 39th, 43d, and 63d Ohio Volun-
    teers, 3d Michigan Cavalry, 1st U. S. Infantry, and Bissell's Missouri
    Engineers, Brig.-General John Pope, commanding.

                           Newbern, N. C.

204. March 14th—51st New York, 8th, 10th, and 11th Connecticut, 21st, 23d, 24th,
    25th, and 27th Massachusetts, 9th New Jersey, 51st Pennsylvania, 4th
    and 5th Rhode Island Volunteers, Brig.-General A. E. Burnside com-
    manding.

           Pound Gap (also Sounding Gap), Cumberland Mountains, Tenn.

205. March 14th—Detachments of 22d Kentucky, 40th and 42d Ohio Volunteers,
    and 1st Ohio Cavalry.

Acquia Creek Batteries, Va.

206. March 16th—U. S. gunboats Yankee and Anacostia.

Black Jack Forest, Tenn.

207. March 16th—Detachments of 4th Illinois and 5th Ohio Cavalry.

Salem, Ark., also Spring River.

208. March 18th—Detachments of the 6th Missouri and 3d Iowa Cavalry.

Mosquito Inlet, Fla.

209. March 21st—U. S. gunboats Penguin and Henry Andrew.

Independence (or Little Santa Fé), Mo.

210. March 22d—2d Kansas.

Carthage, Mo.

211. March 23d—6th Kansas Cavalry.

Winchester (or Kearnstown), Va.

212. March 23d—1st West Virginia, 84th and 110th Pennsylvania, 5th, 7th, 8th, 29th, 62d, and 67th Ohio, 7th, 13th, and 14th Indiana, and 39th Illinois Volunteers, 1st West Virginia, 1st Ohio, and Company E, 1st U. S. Artillery, 1st Michigan and 1st Ohio Cavalry, Brig.-General James Shields commanding.

Warrensburg (or Briar), Mo.

213. March 26th—Sixty men of the 7th Missouri Militia Cavalry.

Humonsville, Polk County, Mo.

214. March 26th—Company B, 8th Missouri Militia Cavalry.

Apache Cañon, near Santa Fé (or Glorietta), New Mexico.

215. March 26th to 28th—1st and 2d Colorado Cavalry.

Strasburg, Va.

216. March 27th—Portion of Brig.-General Banks' command.

Middleburg, Va.

217. March 28th—28th Pennsylvania Volunteers.

Warrensburg, Mo.

218. March 28th—1st Illinois Cavalry.

Union City, Tenn.

219. March 30th—2d Illinois Cavalry.

Putnam's Ferry, near Doniphan, Mo.

220. April 2d—5th Illinois Cavalry, 21st and 38th Illinois Volunteers, and 16th Ohio Battery, Colonel Carlin's Brigade.

Thoroughfare Gap, Va.

221. April 2d—28th Pennsylvania Volunteers.

Pass Christian, Miss.

222. April 4th—9th Connecticut, and 6th Massachusetts Artillery.

Great Bethel, Va.

223. April 4th—Advance of the 3d Corps, Army of the Potomac.

Crump's Landing (or Adamsville), Tenn.

224. April 4th—5th Ohio Cavalry, 48th, 70th, and 72d Ohio Volunteers.

1862.]   Siege of Yorktown.

225. April 5th to May 3d—2d, 3d, and 4th Corps, Army of the Potomac.

Shiloh (or Pittsburg Landing), Tenn.

226. April 6th and 7th—Army of the District of Western Tennessee, commanded
by Maj.-General U. S. Grant : 1st Division, Maj.-General J. A. McClernand ; 2d Division, Maj.-General C. F. Smith ; 3d Division, Brig.-General
Lewis Wallace ; 4th Division, Brig.-General S. A. Hurlburt ; 5th Division,
Brig.-General W. T. Sherman, and 6th Division, Brig.-General B. M. Prentiss.   Army of the Ohio, commanded by Maj.-General D. C. Buell ; 2d Division, Brig.-General A. McD. McCook ; 4th Division, Brig.-General W.
Nelson ; 5th Division, Brig.-General T. L. Crittenden ; and one brigade of
the 6th Division.   Gunboats Tyler and Lexington.

Reconnoisance on the Corinth Road, Miss.

227. April 8th—3d Brigade, 5th Division, Army of Western Tennessee, and 4th
Illinois Cavalry.

Island No. 10, Tenn.

228. April 8th—Navy commanded by Flag-Officer A. H. Foote, the Army by Maj.-
General John Pope.   The siege commenced March 16, 1862.

Owen's River, Cal.

229. April 9th—2d California Cavalry.

Fort Pulaski, Ga.

230. April 10th—6th and 7th Connecticut, 3d Rhode Island, 46th and 48th New
York, and 8th Maine Volunteers, 15th U. S. Infantry, and crew of U. S.
S. Wabash.

Huntsville, Ala.

231. April 11th—3d Division, Army of the Ohio, Brig.-General O. M. Mitchell
commanding.

Skirmish before Yorktown, Va.

232. April 11th—12th New York, 57th and 63d Pennsylvania Volunteers.

Little Blue River, Mo.

233. April 12th—Organization not recorded.

Monterey, Va.

234. April 12th—75th Ohio Volunteers, and 1st West Virginia Cavalry.

Pollocksville, N. C.

235. April 14th—Organization not recorded ; taken from Confederate sources.

Diamond Grove, Mo.

236. April 14th—6th Kansas Cavalry.

Walkersville, Mo.

237. April 14th—2d Missouri Militia Cavalry.

Montavallo, Mo.

238. April 14th—Two companies of the 1st Iowa Cavalry.

Fort Pillow, Tenn.

239. April 14th—Bombardment by U. S. Navy.

XIII.—5

Pechacho Pass, D. T.

240. April 15th—1st California Cavalry.

Peralto, N. M.

241. April 15th—Organization not specified; official.

Savannah, Tenn.

242. April 16th—Organization not recorded; see Rebellion Record, Volume IV., page 90.

Whitemarsh (or Wilmington Island), Ga.

243. April 16th—8th Michigan Volunteers, and Battery Rhode Island Artillery.

Lee's Mills, Va.

244. April 16th—3d, 4th, and 6th Vermont Volunteers, 3d New York Battery, and Battery of 5th U. S. Artillery.

Holly River, West Va.

245. April 17th—10th West Virginia Volunteers.

Falmouth, near Fredericksburg, Va.

246. April 18th—2d New York Cavalry.

Edisto Island, S. C.

247. April 18th—Crew of U. S. S. Crusader, 3d New Hampshire and 55th Pennsylvania Volunteers.

Forts Jackson and St. Philip, and Capture of New Orleans, La.

248. April 18th to 28th—Fleet of war vessels, commanded by Commodore D. G. Farragut, and Mortar boats, commanded by Commodore D. D. Porter.

Talbot's Ferry, Ark.

249. April 19th—4th Iowa Cavalry.

Camden (also known as South Mills), N. C.

250. April 19th—21st Massachusetts, 51st Pennsylvania, 6th New Hampshire, 9th and 89th New York Volunteers.

Grass Lick, West Va.

251. April 23d—3d Maryland, and Potomac Home Brigade.

Fort Macon, N. C.

252. April 25th—U. S. Gunboats Daylight, State of Georgia, Chippewa, the bark Gemsbok and General Parke's Division.

Turnback Creek, Mo.

253. April 26th · 5th Kansas Cavalry.

Neosho, Mo.

254. April 26th—1st Missouri Cavalry.

Reconnoisance to Lick Creek, Miss.

255. April 26th—Troops commanded by Brig.-General A. J. Smith, army before Corinth, Miss.

Redoubt before Yorktown, Va.

256. April 26th—Three companies of the 1st Massachusetts Volunteers.

Horton's Mills, near Newbern, N. C.

257. April 27th—103d New York Volunteers.

1862.]   **Paint Rock Railroad Bridge.**

258. April 28th—Twenty-two men of the 10th Wisconsin Volunteers (General
     D. C. Buell's command).

Cumberland Mountain, Tenn.

259. April 28th—22d Kentucky, 16th and 42d Ohio Volunteers.

Monterey, Tenn.

260. April 28th—2d Iowa Cavalry.

Bridgeport, Ala.

261. April 29th—3d Division, Army of the Ohio, Brig.-General O. M. Mitchell.

Siege of Corinth, Miss.

262. April 30th—Maj.-General H. W. Halleck's army.

Clark's Hollow, West Va.

263. May 1st—Company C, 23d Ohio Volunteers.

Farmington, Miss.

264. May 3d—10th, 16th, 22d, 27th, 41st and 42d Illinois, 10th and 16th Michi-
     gan Volunteers, Yates' Illinois Sharpshooters, 2d Michigan Cavalry, and
     Battery C, 1st Illinois Artillery.

Licking, Mo.

265. May 4th—5th Missouri Militia Cavalry and 24th Missouri Volunteers.

Cheese Cake Church, Va.

266. May 4th—3d Pennsylvania and 1st and 6th U. S. Cavalry.

Lebanon, Tenn.

267. May 5th—Detachment of the 7th Pennsylvania Cavalry, and 1st, 4th, and 5th
     Kentucky Cavalry.

Lockridge Mills (or Dresden), Ky.

268. May 5th—5th Iowa Cavalry.

Williamsburg, Va.

269. May 5th—3d and 4th Corps Army of the Potomac.

West Point, Va., or Eltham's Landing.

270. May 7th—16th, 31st, and 32d New York, 95th and 96th Pennsylvania, and
     5th Maine Volunteers, 1st Massachusetts and Battery D, 2d U. S. Artil-
     lery.

Somerville Heights, Va.

271. May 7th—13th Indiana Volunteers.

McDowell (or Bull Pasture Mountain), Va.

272. May 8th—25th, 32d, 75th, and 82d Ohio, and 3d West Virginia Volunteers,
     1st West Virginia and 1st Connecticut Cavalry, and 1st Indiana Battery,
     Brig.-General R. H. Milroy commanding.

Glendale, near Corinth, Miss.

273. May 8th—7th Illinois Cavalry.

Elkton Station, near Athens, Ala.

274. May 9th—Company E, 37th Indiana.

Slatersville (or New Kent Court House), Va.

275. May 9th—6th U. S. Cavalry, 98th Pennsylvania, and 2d Rhode Island Volunteers.

Farmington, Miss.

276. May 9th—Two brigades of the Army of the Mississippi.

Fort Pillow, Tenn.

277. May 10th—U. S. Gunboats Cincinnati and Mound City.

Norfolk, Va.

278. May 10th—10th, 20th, and 99th New York, 1st Delaware, 58th Pennsylvania, 20th Indiana, and 16th Massachusetts Volunteers, Battery D, 4th U. S. Artillery, and 1st New York Mounted Rifles.

Bloomfield, Mo.

279. May 11th—1st Wisconsin Cavalry.

Reedy Creek, Cumberland Mountain, West Va.

280. May 13th—Brig.-General B. F. Kelley's command.

Rodgersville, Ala.

281. May 13th—1st Wisconsin and 38th Indiana Volunteers, and Cavalry commanded by Col. Starkweather.

Monterey, Tenn.

282. May 13th—Portion of Brig.-General M. L. Smith's Brigade.

Trenton Bridge, N. C.

283. May 14th—17th, 25th, and 27th Massachusetts Volunteers, Battery B, 3d New York Artillery, and two troops 3d New York Cavalry.

Linden, Va.

284. May 15th—One company of the 28th Pennsylvania Volunteers.

Fort Darling, James River, Va.

285. May 15th—U. S. S. Galena, Port Royal, Naugatuck, Monitor, and Aristook.

Chalk Bluffs, Mo.

286. May 15th—1st Wisconsin Cavalry.

Butler, Bates Co., Mo.

287. May 15th—1st Iowa Cavalry.

Princeton, West Va.

288. May 15th, 16th, and 18th—Kanawha Division, commanded by Brig.-General J. D. Cox.

Russell's House, before Corinth, Miss.

289. May 17th—General M. L. Smith's brigade of the 5th Division, Army of Tennessee.

Searcy Landing, Little Red River, Ark.

290. May 19th—Detachments of 4th Missouri Cavalry, 3d and 17th Missouri Volunteers, Battery B, 1st Missouri Light Artillery.

Clinton, N. C.

291. May 19th—Organizations not recorded.

1862.]   **Phillip's Creek, Miss.**

292. May 21st—Brig.-General Thomas A. Davis' 2d Division Army of Tennessee.

Florida, Monroe Co., Mo.

293. May 22d—Detachment of the 3d Iowa Cavalry.

Near Newbern, N. C.

294. May 22d—Company I, 17th Massachusetts Volunteers.

Lewisburg, Va.

295. May 23d—36th and 44th Ohio Volunteers and 2d West Virginia Cavalry.

Front Royal, Va.

296. May 23d—1st Maryland Volunteers, and detachments of the 29th Pennsylvania, Capt. Mape's Pioneers, and 5th New York Cavalry, and 1st Pennsylvania Artillery.

Buckton Station, Va.

297. May 23d—3d Wisconsin and 27th Indiana Volunteers.

Fort Craig, New Mexico.

298. May 23d—3d United States Cavalry.

Middletown, Va.

299. May 24th—46th Pennsylvania and 28th New York Volunteers, 1st Maine and 1st Vermont Cavalry, and one Battery of New York Artillery ; skirmish on Banks' retreat to Winchester.

Newtown, Va.

300. May 24th—28th New York, 2d Massachusetts, 29th Pennsylvania, 27th Indiana, and 3d Wisconsin Volunteers, and two Batteries of Artillery ; skirmish on Banks' retreat to Winchester.

New Bridge, Va.

301. May 24th—4th Michigan Volunteers.

Chickahominy, Va.

302. May 24th—Davidson's Brigade, Smith's Division, Fourth Corps.

Winchester, Va.

303. May 25th—2d Massachusetts, 29th Pennsylvania, 27th Indiana, 3d Wisconsin, 28th New York, 5th Connecticut, and 46th Pennsylvania Volunteers, Battery M, 1st New York Artillery, 1st Vermont, 1st Michigan and 5th New York Cavalry, Major-General N. P. Banks commanding.

Hanover Court House, Va.

304. May 27th—12th, 13th, 14th, 17th, 25th and 44th New York, 62d and 83d Pennsylvania, 16th Michigan, 9th and 22d Massachusetts Volunteers, 5th Massachusetts, 2d Maine, and Battery F, 5th U. S. Artillery, and 1st U. S. Sharpshooters.

Big Indian Creek, near Searcy, Ark.

305. May 27th—1st Missouri Cavalry.

Osceola, Mo.

306. May 27th—1st Iowa Cavalry.

Charlestown and Harper's Ferry, Va.

307. May 28th—Organization not recorded, report of Brig.-General R. Saxton.

Cache River Bridge, Ark.

308. May 28th—9th Illinois Cavalry.

Wardensville, Va.

309. May 28th—3d Maryland Potomac Home Brigade and 3d Indiana Cavalry.

Sylamore, Ark.

310. May 28th and 29th—10th Missouri and 3d Iowa Cavalry.

Pocataligo, S. C.

311. May 29th—50th Pennsylvania, 79th New York, and 8th Michigan Volunteers, and 1st Massachusetts Cavalry.

Booneville, Miss.

312. May 30th—2d Iowa and 2d Michigan Cavalry.

Tuscumbia Creek, Miss.

313. May 30th—Organizations not recorded.

Evacuation of Corinth, Miss.

314. May 30th—Major-General H. W. Halleck's army takes possession.

Front Royal, Va.

315. May 30th—1st Rhode Island Cavalry, advance of Major-General McDowell's command.

Neosho, Mo.

316. May 31st—10th Illinois Cavalry, and 14th Missouri Militia Cavalry.

Greenville Road, near Washington, N. C.

317. May 31st—3d New York Cavalry.

Seven Pines and Fair Oaks, Va.

318. May 31st and June 1st—2d Corps, Maj.-General E. V. Sumner, 3d Corps, Maj.-General S. P. Heintzelman, and 4th Corps, Maj.-General E. D. Keyes, Army of the Potomac.

Seabrook's Point, S. C.

319. June 1st—Organization not recorded.

Strasburg and Staunton Road, Va.

320. June 1st and 2d—8th West Virginia, and 60th Ohio Volunteers, 1st New Jersey and 1st Pennsylvania Cavalry ; Jackson's retreat.

Legare's Point, S. C.

321. June 3d—28th Massachusetts and 100th Pennsylvania Volunteers.

Fort Pillow (or Fort Wright), Tenn.

322. June 4th—Mississippi Flotilla, Commodore C. H. Davis.

Jasper, Sweden's Cove, Tenn.

323. June 4th—5th Kentucky and 7th Pennsylvania Cavalry, 79th Pennsylvania Volunteers, and 1st Ohio Battery.

Blackland, Miss.

324. June 4th—2d Iowa and 2d Michigan Cavalry.

Tranter's Creek, N. C.

325. June 5th—24th Massachusetts Volunteers, Company I, 3d New York Cavalry, and Marine Artillery.

1862.] **Memphis, Tenn.**

326. June 6th—U. S. Gunboats Benton, Louisville, Carondelet, Cairo, and St. Louis, and Rams Queen of the West, and Monarch.

Harrisonburg, Va.

327. June 6th—1st New Jersey Cavalry, 1st Pennsylvania Rifles, 60th Ohio, and 8th West Virginia Volunteers.

Cross Keys (or Union Church), Va.

328. June 8th—8th, 39th, 41st, 45th, 54th, and 58th New York, 2d, 3d, 5th, and 8th West Virginia, 25th, 32d, 55th, 60th, 73d, 75th, and 82d Ohio, and 1st and 27th Pennsylvania Volunteers, and 1st Ohio Battery.

Baldwin, Miss.

329. June 9th—2d Iowa and 2d Michigan Cavalry.

Port Republic, Va.

330. June 9th—5th, 7th, 29th, and 66th Ohio, 84th and 110th Pennsylvania, 7th Indiana and 1st West Virginia Volunteers, and Batteries E, 4th U. S., and A and L, 1st Ohio Artillery.

James Island, S. C.

331. June 10th—Organizations not given ; from official reports.

Monterey, Owen Co., Ky.

332. June 11th—Captain Blood's Mounted Provost Guards and 13th Indiana Battery.

Waddell's Farm, near Village Creek, Ark.

333. June 12th—Detachment of the 9th Illinois Cavalry.

Old Church, Va.

334. June 13th—5th U. S. Cavalry.

James Island, S. C.

335. June 13th—Organizations not recorded.

Tunstall Station, Va.

336. June 14th—Confederates firing into a railroad train ; Union loss, 4 killed, 8 wounded.

Secessionville (or Fort Johnson), James Island, S. C.

337. June 16th—46th, 47th, and 79th New York, 3d Rhode Island, 3d New Hampshire, 45th, 97th, and 100th Pennsylvania, 6th and 7th Connecticut, 8th Michigan, and 28th Massachusetts Volunteers, 1st New York Engineers, 1st Connecticut, Batteries E, 3d U. S., and I, 3d Rhode Island Artillery, and Company H, 1st Massachusetts Cavalry.

St. Charles, White River, Ark.

338. June 17th—U. S. Gunboats Lexington, Mound City, Conestoga, and St. Louis, 43d and 46th Indiana Volunteers.

Warrensburg, Mo.

339. June 17th—7th Missouri Militia Cavalry.

Smithville, Ark.

340. June 18th—Organizations not stated ; see Rebellion Record, Vol. V., page 29.

Cumberland Gap.

341. June 18th—Occupied by Brig.-General G. W. Morgan's command.

Tallahatchie, Fla.

342. June 18th—From Rebellion Record, Vol. V., page 29.

Williamsburg Road, Va.

343. June 18th—16th Massachusetts Volunteers.

Battle Creek, Tenn.

344. June 21st—2d and 33d Ohio, 10th Wisconsin, and 24th Illinois Volunteers, 4th Ohio and 4th Kentucky Cavalry, and Edgarton's Battery.

Raceland, near Algiers, La.

345. June 22d—8th Vermont Volunteers.

Raytown, Mo.

346. June 23d—7th Missouri Cavalry.

Oak Grove (or King's School House, or The Orchards), Va.

347. June 25th—Hooker's and Kearney's Divisions of the 3d, and Palmer's Brigade of Couch's Division of the 4th, and part of Richardson's Division of the 2d Corps.

Germantown, Tenn.

348. June 25th—56th Ohio Volunteers; guarding a railroad train at the time.

Little Red River, Ark.

349. June 25th—4th Iowa Cavalry.

Vicksburg, Miss.

350. June 26th, 27th, 28th, and 29th—U. S. Fleet, commanded by Commodore D. G. Farragut.

Seven Days' Retreat.

351. June 26th to July 1st—1st, 2d, 3d, 4th, 5th, 6th, and Cavalry Corps, and Engineers, Army of the Potomac, Maj.-General Geo. B. McClellan commanding; this retreat comprises the following battles:

1st.—Mechanicsville (or Ellison's Mills), Va.

352. June 26th—5th Army Corps, and McCall's Division of the 1st Corps, Army of the Potomac.

2d.—Gaines' Mill (or Cold Harbor, or Chickahominy), Va.

353. June 27th and 28th—5th Corps, Army of the Potomac, re-enforced by Meagher's and French's Brigades, 1st Division, 2d Corps.

3d.—Savage's Station, Va.

354. June 29th—2d and Sixth Corps, Army of Potomac, commanded by Generals Sumner and Franklin.

4th.—Peach Orchard (or Allen's Farm), Va.

355. June 29th—Richardson's and Sedgwick's Divisions of the 2d Corps, Army of the Potomac.

5th.—White Oak Swamp (or Glendale, Charles City Cross Roads, Nelson's Farm, Frazier's Farm, Turkey Bend, New Market Cross Roads), Va.

356. June 30th—2d, Sumner's; 3d, Heintzelman's; 4th, Keyes'; 5th, Porter's; 6th, Franklin's; and McCall's Division of the 1st Corps, Army of the Potomac.

6th.—Malvern Hill (or Crew's Farm), Va.

357. July 1st—2d, 3d, 4th, 5th, and 6th Corps, Army of the Potomac.

1862.]   **Williamsbridge, Amite River, La.**

358. June 27th—21st Indiana Volunteers.

Swift Creek Bridge, N. C.

359. June 27th—See Rebellion Record, Vol. V., page 33.

Village Creek (or Stewart's Plantation), Ark.

360. June 27th—9th Illinois Cavalry.

Waddell's Farm, Ark.

361. June 27th—Detachment of 3d Iowa Cavalry, guarding wagon train.

Golding's Farm, Va.

362. June 28th—23d and 49th New York Volunteers and 3d New York Battery.

Willis Church, Va.

363. June 29th—Cavalry advance of Casey's Division, 4th Corps.

Luray, Va.

364. June 30th—Detachment of Cavalry of Brig.-General Crawford's command.

Booneville, Miss.

365. July 1st—2d Iowa and 2d Michigan Cavalry

Morning Sun, Tenn.

366. July 1st—57th Ohio Volunteers.

Russellville, Tenn.

367. July 1st—1st Ohio Cavalry.

Milford, Va.

368. July 2d—1st Maine Cavalry.

Haxals (or Evlington Heights), Va.

369. July 3d—14th Indiana, 7th West Virginia, 4th and 8th Ohio Volunteers.

Grand Haze, White River, Ark.

370. July 4th—13th Illinois Cavalry.

Sperryville, Va.

371. July 5th—1st Maine Cavalry.

Grand Prairie, near Aberdeen, Ark.

372. July 6th—24th Indiana Volunteers.

Bayou Cache (or Cotton Plant, Round Hill, Bayou de View, and Hill's Plantation), Ark.

373. July 7th—11th Wisconsin, 33d Illinois, and 8th Indiana Volunteers, 1st Missouri Light Artillery, 1st Indiana, 5th and 13th Illinois Cavalry.

Black River, Mo.

374. July 8th—5th Kansas Cavalry.

Lotspeach Farm, Mo.

375. July 8th—One company 1st Iowa Cavalry.

Clinton, Mo.

376. July 9th—Organization not recorded.

Hamilton, N. C.

377. July 9th—U. S. gunboats Perry, Ceres, and Shawseen, and 9th New York Volunteers.

5*

Aberdeen, Ark.

378. July 9th—24th, 34th, 43d, and 46th Indiana Volunteers.

Tompkinsville, Ky.

379. July 9th—3d Pennsylvania Cavalry.

Scatterville, Ark.

380. July 10th—Detachment of 1st Wisconsin Cavalry.

Williamsburg, Va.

381. July 11th—Organizations not recorded.

Pleasant Hill, Mo.

382. July 11th—1st Iowa Cavalry and Missouri Militia.

New Hope, Ky.

383. July 11th—33d Ohio Volunteers.

Lebanon, Ky.

384. July 12th—Lebanon Home Guards and 28th Kentucky Volunteers.

Near Culpeper, Va.

385. July 12th—1st Maryland, 1st Vermont, 1st West Virginia, and 5th New York Cavalry.

Fairfax (near Rapidan R.R. Bridge), Va.

386. July 13th—1st Maryland Cavalry.

Murfreesboro', Tenn.

387. July 13th—9th Michigan and 3d Pennsylvania Volunteers, 4th Kentucky and 7th Pennsylvania Cavalry, and 1st Kentucky Battery.

Batesville, Ark.

388. July 14th—4th Iowa Cavalry.

Attempt to Destroy the Rebel Ram Arkansas.

389. July 15th—Carondelet, Queen of the West, Tyler, and Essex, and 4th Wisconsin Volunteers.

Apache Pass, A. T.

390. July 15th—2d California Cavalry.

Fayetteville, Ark.

391. July 15th—Union troops, commanded by Major W. H. Miller, 2d Wisconsin Cavalry.

Near Decatur, Tenn.

392. July 15th—Detachment of 1st Ohio Cavalry.

Cynthiana, Ky.

393. July 17th—18th Kentucky Volunteers, Cynthiana, Newport, Cincinnati, and Bracken County Home Guards, and 7th Kentucky Cavalry; Morgan's raid.

Memphis, Mo.

394. July 18th—2d Missouri Cavalry, and 9th and 11th Missouri S. M.

Guerilla Campaign in Missouri.

395. July 20th to September 20th—Includes all the engagements with Porter's and Pointdexter's Guerillas by Maj.-General Schofield's command.

1862.]   **Turkey Island Bridge, Va.**

396. July 20th—8th Pennsylvania Cavalry.

Pittman's Ferry, Ark.

397. July 20th—13th Illinois Cavalry.

Nashville, Tenn.

398. July 21st—2d Kentucky Volunteers.

Florida (or Bole's Farm), Mo.

399. July 23d—Two companies 3d Iowa Cavalry.

North Anna River, Va.

400. July 23d—2d New York and 3d Indiana Cavalry.

Columbus, Mo.

401. July 23d—7th Missouri Cavalry.

Coldwater, Miss.

402. July 24th—Organizations not stated.

Trinity, Ala.

403. July 24th—Company E, 31st Ohio Volunteers.

Bott's Farm, Monroe Co., Mo.

404. July 24th—3d Iowa Cavalry.

Santa Fé, Mo.

405. July 24th and 25th—3d Iowa Cavalry.

Brownsville, Hatchie River, Tenn.

406. July 25th—Cavalry commanded by Major Wallace.

Orange Court House, Va.

407. July 25th—Reconnoitring expedition from General Gibson's Division.

Courtland Bridge, Ala.

408. July 25th—Two companies each of Kentucky Volunteers and 1st Ohio Cavalry.

Mountain Store and Big Piney, Mo.

409. July 25th and 26th—Three companies 3d Missouri Cavalry, and Battery L, 2d Missouri Artillery.

Patten, Mo.

410. July 26th—Missouri Militia.

Young's Crossroads, N. C.

411. July 26th—9th New Jersey Volunteers and 3d New York Cavalry.

Greenville, Mo.

412. July 26th—3d and 12th Missouri Militia Cavalry.

Buchannon, West Va.

413. July 26th—See "Ohio in the War," Vol. II., page 487.

Brown Springs, Mo.

414. July 27th—2d Iowa Cavalry.

Bayou Bernard, Cherokee Nation.

415. July 28th—1st, 2d, and 3d Kansas Indian Home Guards, and 1st Kansas Battery.

Moore's Mills, Fulton Co., Mo.

416. July 28th—3d Iowa Cavalry, 2d Missouri Cavalry, 9th Missouri Volunteers, and 3d Indiana Battery.

Mount Sterling, Ky.

417. July 29th—18th Kentucky and Home Guards.

Bollinger's Mills, Mo.

418. July 29th—Two companies of the 13th Missouri Volunteers.

Russellville, Ky.

419. July 29th—Russellville Home Guards and 70th Indiana Volunteers.

Brownsville, Tenn.

420. July 29th—One company of the 15th Illinois Cavalry.

Paris, Ky.

421. July 30th—9th Pennsylvania Cavalry.

Coggin's Point, opposite Harrison's Landing, Va.

422. July 31st—Gunboat fleet.

Newark, Mo.

423. August 1st—73 men of the 11th Missouri State Militia.

Ozark (or Forsyth), Mo.

424. August 2d—14th Missouri Militia.

Orange Court House, Va.

425. August 2d—5th New York Cavalry and 1st Vermont Cavalry.

Clear Creek (or Taberville), Mo.

426. August 2d—Four companies 1st Iowa Cavalry.

Coahoma County, Miss.

427. August 2d—11th Wisconsin Volunteers.

Austin, Tunica Co., Miss.

428. August 2d—8th Indiana Volunteers.

Sycamore Church (near Petersburg), Va.

429. August 3d—5th U. S. and 3d Pennsylvania Cavalry.

Chariton Bridge, Dodge Co., Mo.

430. August 3d—6th Missouri Cavalry.

Jonesboro', Ark.

431. August 3d—1st Wisconsin Cavalry.

Languelle Ferry, Ark.

432. August 3d—1st Wisconsin Cavalry.

Sparta, Tenn.

433. August 4th—Detachments of the 4th Kentucky and 7th Indiana Cavalry.

White Oak Swamp Bridge, Va.

434. August 4th—3d Pennsylvania Cavalry.

Baton Rouge, La.

435. August 5th—14th Maine, 6th Michigan, 7th Vermont, 21st Indiana, 30th Massachusetts, 9th Connecticut, and 4th Wisconsin Volunteers, 2d, 4th and 6th Massachusetts Batteries, Brig.-General Thomas Williams commanding.

1862.]   **Malvern Hill, Va.**
436. August 5th—Portion of Hooker's Division, 3d Corps, and Richardson's Division, 2d Corps, and Cavalry, Army of the Potomac.

Montavallo (or Church in the Woods), Mo.
437. August 6th—3d Wisconsin Cavalry.

Beech Creek, Va.
438. August 6th—4th West Virginia Volunteers.

Kirksville, Adair Co., Mo.
439. August 6th—Missouri Militia.

Matapony (or Thornburg), Va.
440. August 6th—Portion of King's Division, commanded by Colonel Cutler.

Tazewell, Tenn.
441. August 6th—16th and 42d Ohio, and 14th and 22d Kentucky Volunteers, and 4th Wisconsin Battery.

Fort Fillmore, New Mexico.
442. August 7th—California troops, commanded by General Canby.

Trenton, Tenn.
443. August 7th—2d Illinois Cavalry.

Panther Creek, Mo.
444. August 8th—1st Missouri Militia Cavalry.

Stockton, Mo.
445. August 9th—Colonel McNiel's command of Missouri State Militia.

Cedar Mountain (or Slaughter Mountain, Southwest Mountain, Cedar Run, and Mitchell's Station), Va.
446. August 9th—2d Corps, Maj.-General N. P. Banks, and 3d Corps, Maj.-General I. McDowell, Army of Virginia, Maj.-General John Pope commanding.

Nueces River, Tex.
447. August 10th—Texas Loyalists.

Grand River, Mo.
448. August 10th to 13th—Includes Lee's Ford, Chariton River, Walnut Creek, Compton Ferry, Switzler's Mills, and Yellow Creek. 9th Missouri Militia, commanded by Colin Odin Guitar.

Taberville, Ark.
449. August 11th—1st Missouri and 3d Wisconsin Cavalry.

Independence, Mo.
450. August 11th—7th Missouri Militia Cavalry.

Salisbury, Tenn.
451. August 11th—11th Illinois Cavalry.

Williamsport, Tenn.
452. August 11th—Troops of Brig.-General Jas. S. Negley's command.

Wyoming Court House, West Va.
453. August — —Detachment of the 37th Ohio Volunteers.

Kinderhook, Tenn.

454. August 11th—Detachments of the 3d Kentucky and 1st Tennessee Cavalry.

Helena, Ark.

455. August 11th to 14th—2d Wisconsin Cavalry.

Gallatin, Tenn.

456. August 12th—2d Indiana, 4th and 5th Kentucky, and 6th Pennsylvania Cavalry; Rebels capture the post; John H. Morgan's raid.

457. August 13th—69th Ohio and 11th Michigan Volunteers drive the rebels from the town, with slight loss.

Clarendon, Ark.

458. August 13th—Brig.-General Hovey's Division, 13th Corps.

Merriweather's Ferry, Obion River, Tenn.

459. August 15th—One company 2d Illinois Cavalry.

Lone Jack, Mo.

460. August 16th—Missouri Militia Cavalry.

Capture of Rebel Steamer Fair Play, near Milliken's Bend, La.

461. August 18th—58th and 76th Ohio Volunteers.

Red Wood, Minn.

462. August 18th—One company 5th Minnesota Volunteers massacred by Indians.

Clarksville, Tenn.

463. August 19th—71st Ohio Volunteers, commanded by Colonel Rodney Mason, who surrendered the post without an engagement.

Rienzi, Miss.

464. August 19th—Organizations not recorded.

White Oak Ridge, near Hickman, Ky.

465. August 19th—2d Illinois Cavalry.

Brandy Station, Va.

466. August 20th—Cavalry of Army of Virginia.

Edgefield Junction, Tenn.

467. August 20th—Detachment of 50th Indiana Volunteers.

Union Mills, Mo.

468. August 20th—1st Missouri and 13th Illinois Cavalry.

Fort Ridgely, Minn.

469. August 20th and 22d—Companies B and C, 5th Minnesota Volunteers, and Renville Rangers; fight with Indians.

Kelley's Ford, Rappahannock River, Va.

470. August 21st—Cavalry of the Army of Virginia.

Pinckney Island, S. C.

471. August 21st—Organizations not recorded.

Courtland, Tenn.

472. August 22d—42d Illinois Volunteers.

1862.]   Crab Orchard, Ky.
473. August 22d—9th Pennsylvania Cavalry.

Catlett's Station, Va.
474. August 23d—Purnell Legion, Maryland ; and 1st Pennsylvania Rifles.

Big Hill, Madison Co., Ky.
475. August 23d—7th Kentucky Cavalry and 3d Tennessee Volunteers.

Skirmishes on the Rappahannock, at Waterloo Bridge, Lee Springs, Freeman's Ford, and Sulphur Springs, Va.
476. August 23d to 25th—Army of Virginia, commanded by Maj.-General Pope.

Dallas, Mo.
477. August 24th—12th Missouri S. M. Cavalry.

Coon Creek (or Lamar), Mo.
478. August 24th—Organizations not recorded ; official.

Fort Donelson, Tenn.
479. August 25th—71st Ohio Volunteers and 5th Iowa Cavalry.

Bloomfield, Mo.
480. August 25th—13th Illinois Cavalry.

New Ulm, Minn.
481. August 25th and 26th—Indian fight; organizations not recorded.

Cumberland Iron Works, Tenn.
482. August 26th—71st Ohio Volunteers and 5th Iowa Cavalry.

Madisonville, Ky.
483. August 26th—Cavalry by Lieut.-Colonel Porter.

Rienzi and Kossuth, Miss.
484. August 26th—2d Iowa and 7th Kansas Cavalry.

Danville, Ky.
485. August 26th—Harrodsburg and Danville, Ky., Home Guards.

Bull Run Bridge, Va.
486. August 27th—11th and 12th Ohio, and 1st, 2d, 3d, and 4th New Jersey Volunteers.

Kettle Run, Va.
487. August 27th—Maj.-General Hooker's Division, 3d Corps, Army of the Potomac.

Fort McCook, near Bridgeport, Ala.
488. August 27th—33d Ohio Volunteers and detachment of Cavalry.

Readyville, Round Hill, Tenn.
489. August 28th—10th Brigade, Army of the Ohio, commanded by Colonel W.
Grose.

Howard County, Mo.
490. August 28th—4th Missouri Militia Cavalry.

Shady Springs, Va.
491. August 28th—2d West Virginia Cavalry.

Groveton and Gainesville, Va.

492. August 28th and 29th—1st Corps, Maj.-General F. Sigel, and 3d Corps, Maj. General I. McDowell, Army of Virginia, Hooker's and Kearney's Divisions of the 3d Corps, and Reynolds' Division of the 1st Corps, and 9th Corps, Maj.-General Reno, Army of the Potomac.

Manchester, Tenn.

493. August 29th—Two companies of 18th Ohio and one company of the 9th Michigan Volunteers.

Bull Run, 2d (or Manassas), Va.

494. August 30th—1st Corps, Maj.-General F. Sigel, and 3d Corps, Maj.-General J. McDowell, Army of Virginia, Hooker's and Kearney's Divisions, 3d Corps, Porter's 5th Corps, and Reynolds' Division, 1st Corps, Army of the Potomac, and 9th Corps, Maj.-General Reno.

Bolivar, Tenn.

495. August 30th—2d and 11th Illinois Cavalry, 9th Indiana Artillery, and 20th and 78th Ohio Volunteers.

McMinnville (or Little Pond), Tenn.

496. August 30th—26th Ohio, 17th and 58th Indiana Volunteers, and 8th Indiana Battery.

Richmond, Ky.

497. August 30th—6th and 7th Kentucky Cavalry, 95th Ohio, 18th Kentucky, 12th, 16th, 55th, 66th, 69th, and 71st Indiana Volunteers, and Batteries D and G, Michigan Artillery.

Weston, West Va.

498. August 31st—Two companies 6th West Virginia Volunteers.

Medon (or Toon's Station, Miss. O. R. R.), Tenn.

499. August 31st—45th Illinois and 7th Missouri Volunteers.

Stevenson, Ala.

500. August 31st—Organizations not recorded.

Yate's Ford, Ky.

501. August 31st—94th Ohio Volunteers.

Chantilly (or Oxhill), Va.

502. September 1st—McDowell's Corps, Army of Virginia, Hooker's and Kearney's Divisions, 3d Corps, Army of the Potomac, and Reno's Corps.

Briton's Lane, near Denmark, Tenn.

503. September 1st—20th and 30th Illinois Volunteers, Battery A, 2d Illinois Artillery, 4th Illinois Cavalry, and Foster's company of Ohio Cavalry.

Morgansville, Ky.

504. September 2d—A force of Union troops, commanded by Colonel Schackleford, 8th Kentucky Cavalry.

Plymouth, N. O.

505. September 2d—Company F, 9th New York, and 1st North Carolina Volunteers.

Vienna, Va.

506. September 2d—1st Minnesota Volunteers.

1862.]   Birch, Coolie (or Acton), Minn.
507. September 2d and 3d—Indian fight.

Hutchinson, Minn.
508. September 3d and 4th—Fight with Indians.

Fort Abercrombie, Dakota Ter.
509. September 3d to 6th—Fight with Indians.

Slaughterville, Ky.
510. September 3d—Lieut.-Colonel Foster's Cavalry.

Geiger Lake, Ky.
511. September 3d—8th Kentucky Cavalry.

Big Creek Gap, Tenn.
512. September 4th—Detachment of the 6th Tennessee Volunteers.

Cacapon Bridge, Va.
513. September 6th—1st New York Cavalry.

Martinsburg, Va.
514. September 6th—Report of Brig.-General Julius White.

Washington, N. C.
515. September 6th—1st North Carolina and 24th Massachusetts Volunteers, and 3d New York Cavalry.

La Grange, Ark.
516. September 6th—1st Missouri Cavalry.

Poolesville, Md.
517. September 7th—3d Indiana and 8th Illinois Cavalry.

Clarksville (or Rickettshill), Tenn.
518. September 7th—11th Illinois, 13th Wisconsin, and 71st Ohio Volunteers, 5th Iowa Cavalry, and two batteries.

Columbia, Tenn.
519. September 9th—42d Illinois Volunteers.

Nolansville, Md.
520. September 9th—3d Indiana and 8th Illinois Cavalry.

Williamsburg, Va.
521. September 9th—5th Pennsylvania Cavalry.

Des Allemands, La.
522. September 9th—21st Indiana and 4th Wisconsin Volunteers.

Cold Water (or Cochran's Cross Roads), Miss.
523. September 10th—Cavalry, commanded by Colonel Grierson, 6th Illinois Cavalry.

Sugar Loaf Mountain, Md.
524. September 10th—6th U. S. Cavalry.

Fayetteville, West Va.
525. September 10th—34th and 37th Ohio and 4th West Virginia Volunteers.

Cotton Hill, West Va.
526. September 11th—34th and 37th Ohio and 4th West Virginia Volunteers.

Bloomfield, Mo.

527. September 11th to 13th—Battery E, 2d Missouri Artillery, 13th Illinois Volunteers, 1st Wisconsin Cavalry, and Missouri Militia.

Charlestown, near Elk River, West Va.

528. September 12th—34th Ohio and 4th West Virginia Volunteers.

Frederick, Md.

529. September 12th—Advance of the Army of the Potomac.

Harper's Ferry, Va.

530. September 12th to 15th—12th New York State Militia, 39th, 111th, 115th, 125th, and 126th New York, 32d, 60th and 87th, Ohio, 9th Vermont, 65th Illinois, 1st and 3d Maryland (Home Brigade), and 15th Indiana Volunteers, Phillip's Battery, 5th New York, Graham's, Pott's, and Rigby's Batteries, and 8th New York, 12th Illinois, and 1st Maryland Cavalry.

Newtonia, Mo.

531. September 13th—3d and 6th Missouri Militia Cavalry.

Ponchatoula, La.

532. September 14th—12th Maine, 26th Massachusetts, and 13th Connecticut Volunteers.

Turner's and Crampton's Gap, South Mountain, Md.

533. September 14th—9th Corps, Maj.-General J. L. Reno, 1st Corps, Maj.-General J. Hooker, and 6th Corps, Maj.-General W. B. Franklin, Army of the Potomac, Maj.-General G. B. McClellan commanding.

Mumfordsville, Ky.

534. September 14th to 16th—18th U. S. Infantry, 28th and 33d Kentucky, 17th, 50th, 60th, 67th, 68th, 74th, 78th, and 89th Indiana Volunteers, and Conkle's Battery, 13th Indiana Artillery, and Louisville Provost Guard.

Shelburne, Mo.

535. September 15th—Missouri Militia.

Boonsboro', Md.

536. September 15th—Cavalry, Army of Potomac.

Durhamville, Tenn.

537. September 17th—Detachment of the 52d Indiana Volunteers.

Florence, Ky.

538. September 17th—Detachment of the 10th Kentucky Cavalry.

Goose Creek and Leesburg Road, Va.

539. September 17th—Reconnoissance of Kilpatrick's Cavalry Brigade.

Antietam (also Sharpsburg), Md.

540. September 17th—1st Corps, Maj.-General J. Hooker, 2d Corps, Maj.-General E. V. Sumner, 5th Corps, Maj.-General Fitz John Porter, 6th Corps, Maj.-General W. B. Franklin, 9th Corps, Maj.-General A. E. Burnside, 12th Corps, Maj.-General Williams, Couch's Division, 4th Corps, and Pleasonton's Division of Cavalry, Army of the Potomac, commanded by Maj.-General G. B. McClellan.

Hickory Grove, Mo.

541. September 19th—6th Kansas Cavalry.

1862.]   Owensburg, Ky.

542. September 19th and 20th—14th Kentucky Cavalry and Spencer (Indiana) County Home Guards.

I-u-k-a, Miss.

543. September 19th and 20th—Stanley's and Hamilton's Divisions, Army of the Mississippi, Maj.-General W. S. Rosecrans commanding.

Blackford's Ford, Sheppardstown, Va.

544. September 20th—Griffin's and Barnes' Brigades, 5th Corps.

Shirley's Ford, Spring River, Mo.

545. September 20th—2d Kansas Indian Home Guards.

Helena, Ark.

546. September 20th—4th Iowa Cavalry.

Williamsport, Md.

547. September 20th—Couch's Division, Army of the Potomac.

Prentis and Bolivar, Miss.

548. September 20th—U. S. Ram, Queen of the West, with transports and 83d Illinois.

Cassville, Mo.

549. September 21st—1st Arkansas Cavalry.

Mumfordsville, Ky.

550. September 21st—Cavalry commanded by Major Foster, 3d Ohio Cavalry.

Shepherdsville, Ky.

551. September 21st—Colonel Granger's command.

Sturgeon, Mo.

552. September 22d—Major Hunt's command.

Ashby's Gap, Va.

553. September 22d—2d Pennsylvania and 1st West Virginia Cavalry.

Yellow Medicine (also Wood Lake), Minn.

554. September 23d—3d, 6th, and 7th Minnesota Volunteers, and Renville Guards.

Wolf Creek Bridge, near Memphis, Miss.

555. September 23d—57th Ohio Volunteers.

Sutton, Va.

556. September 23d—10th West Virginia.

Warrenton Junction, Va.

557. September 26th—Cavalry commanded by Colonel McLean.

Cambridge, Mo.

558. September 26th—9th Missouri Militia Cavalry.

Buffalo, West Va.

559. September 27th—34th Ohio.

Augusta, Ky.

560. September 27th—Kentucky Home Guards.

Blackwater, Va.

561. September 28th—1st New York Mounted Rifles.

Newtonia, Mo.

562. September 30th—1st Brigade, Army of Kansas, and 4th Brigade Missouri State Militia.

Russellville, Ky.

563. September 30th—Union troops, commanded by Colonel Harrison, 17th Kentucky.

Floyd's Fork, Ky.

564. October 1st—4th Indiana Cavalry, 34th Illinois, and 77th Pennsylvania Volunteers, of the Army of the Ohio.

Gallatin, Tenn.

565. October 1st—1st Tennessee Cavalry, commanded by Colonel Stokes.

Shepherdstown, Va.

566. October 1st—8th Illinois, 8th Pennsylvania, and 3d Indiana Cavalry, and Pennington's Battery.

Olive Hill, Ky.

567. October 2d—Carter County Home Guards.

Mount Washington, Ky.

568. October 2d—Advance of the Army of the Ohio.

Baldwin, Miss.

569. October 2d—Cavalry of the Army of the Mississippi.

Reconnoissance to Franklin, on the Blackwater, Va.

570. October 3d—Union gunboats, commanded by Captain Flusser, and troops commanded by General Spear.

Corinth, Miss.

571. October 3d and 4th—McKean's, Davies', Hamilton's, and Stanley's Divisions, Army of the Mississippi, Maj.-General W. S. Rosecrans commanding.

Bardstown, Ky.

572. October 4th—Advance of the Army of the Ohio.

Big Hatchie River (or Metamora), Miss.

573. October 5th—Hurlbut's and Ord's Divisions, Army of the Mississippi, Maj.-General Ord commanding.

Glasgow, Ky.

574. October 5th—20th Kentucky Volunteers.

Madisonville, Ky.

575. October 5th—4th Indiana Cavalry.

Charleston, Va.

576. October 6th—6th U. S. Cavalry.

Liberty and Sibley's Landing, Mo.

577. October 6th—5th Missouri Militia Cavalry.

Springfield to near Texas, Ky.

578. October 6th—Advance of 3d Corps, Army of the Ohio.

La Vergne, Tenn.

579. October 7th—Palmer's Brigade.

1862.]   Perryville (or Chaplin Hill), Ky.

580. October 8th—1st Corps, Maj.-General A. McD. McCook, and 3d Corps, Brig.-
General C. C. Gilbert, Army of the Ohio, commanded by Maj.-General
D. C. Buell.

Lawrenceburg (also called Dog Walk), Ky.

581. October 9th—15th and 19th U. S. Infantry, 1st and 49th Ohio Volunteers,
Battery H, 5th U. S. Artillery, and 9th Kentucky Cavalry.

Aldie, Va.

582. October 9th—Detachment of Cavalry from Maj.-General Sigel's command.

Harrodsburg, Ky.

583. October 10th—Union troops commanded by Lieut.-Colonel Boyle, 9th Kentucky Cavalry.

Upper Missouri River.

584. October 10th—Indian fight.

La Grange (near Helena), Ark.

585. October 11th—Detachment of the 4th Iowa Cavalry.

Cape Fear River, N. C.

586. October 11th—U. S. gunboat Maratanza.

Mouth of Monocacy, Md.

587. October 11th—3d and 4th Maine Volunteers.

Stanford (or Lancaster), Ky.

588. October 14th—Advance of the Army of the Ohio.

Hazel Bottom, Mo.

589. October 14th—Organization not reported.

Apalachicola River, Fla.

590. October 15th—Naval expedition.

Carsville, Va.

591. October 15th—One company of the 7th Pennsylvania Cavalry.

Charleston, Va.

592. October 16th—Reconnoissance of the Army of the Potomac.

Lexington, Ky.

593. October 17th—Detachments of the 3d and 4th Ohio Cavalry.

Thoroughfare Gap, Va.

594. October 17th—Detachment of Cavalry from General Stahel's command.

Helena, Ark.

595. October 18th—Detachment of the 43d Indiana Volunteers.

Haymarket, Va.

596. October 18th—Detachment of the 6th Ohio Cavalry.

Near Nashville, Tenn.

597. October 20th—Union troops, commanded by Colonel Miller.

Anxvois River, Mo.

598. October 20th—10th Missouri Militia Cavalry.

Marshfield, Mo.

599. October 20th—10th Illinois Cavalry.

Lovettsville, Loudon Co., Va.

600. October 21st—Detachment of General Geary's Brigade.

Woodville, Tenn.

601. October 21st—2d Illinois Cavalry.

Fort Cobb, Indian Ter.

602. October 21st—Loyal Indians.

Old Fort Wayne (or Maysville), Ark.

603. October 22d—1st Division, Army of the Frontier.

Hedgeville, Va.

604. October 22d—4th Pennsylvania Cavalry.

Pocotaligo (or Yemassee), S. C.

605. October 22d—47th, 55th, and 76th Pennsylvania, 48th New York, 6th and 7th Connecticut, 3d and 4th New Hampshire, and 3d Rhode Island Volunteers, 1st New York Engineers, 1st Massachusetts Cavalry, and Batteries D and M, 1st, and E, 3d U. S. Artillery.

Waverly, Tenn.

606. October 23d—83d Illinois Volunteers.

Shelby Depot, Tenn.

607. October 23d—Reconnoitring party, commanded by Colonel D. Stuart, 55th Illinois Volunteers.

Point Lick and Big Hill Road, Ky.

608. October 23d—Cavalry commanded by Colonel E. McCook.

Manassas Junction, Va.

609. October 24th—Organizations not recorded.

Catlett's Station, Va.

610. October 24th—Detachment of 3d West Virginia Cavalry.

Grand Prairie, Mo.

611. October 24th—Two battalions Missouri Militia Cavalry.

Blackwater, Va.

612. October 24th—1st New York Mounted Rifles, 39th Illinois, and 62d Ohio Volunteers, and other troops, commanded by Brig.-General Terry.

Morgantown, Ky.

613. October 24th—Organization not recorded.

Pittman's Ferry, Mo.

614. October 27th—23d Iowa and 24th and 25th Missouri Volunteers, 1st Missouri Militia, and 12th Missouri Cavalry.

Labadiesville (or Thibodeauxville, or Georgia Landing), La.

615. October 27th—8th New Hampshire, 12th and 13th Connecticut, and 75th New York Volunteers, 1st Louisiana Cavalry, and 1st Maine Battery, commanded by Brig.-General G. Weitzel.

1862.]   **Cross Hollows (or Oxford Bend), Fayetteville, Ark.**

616. October 28th—One Division of the Army of the frontier, commanded by Brig.-General Herrow.

Clarkson, Mo.

617. October 28th—Detachments commanded by Captain Rodgers, 2d Illinois Artillery.

Williamsburg, Ky.

618. October 28th—7th Kentucky Volunteers.

Butler and Osage (or Island Mounds), Mo.

619. October 29th—1st Kansas Colored Troops (79th U. S. C. Troops).

Aldie, Va.

620. October 31st—1st New Jersey and 2d New York Cavalry, of General Bayard's Cavalry Brigade, Army of the Potomac.

Franklin, Va.

621. October 31st—Organizations not given.

Philomont, Va.

622. November 1st—Cavalry of the Army of the Potomac, commanded by General Pleasonton.

Snicker's Gap, Va.

623. November 2d—Batteries of the Second Corps of the Army of the Potomac.

Bloomfield and Union, Loudoun Co., Va.

624. November 2d and 3d—Cavalry advance of the Army of the Potomac.

Upperville, Va.

625. November 3d—Cavalry advance of the Army of the Potomac.

Rawles' Mills (also Little Creek), Williamston, N. C.

626. November 3d—24th and 44th Massachusetts, and 9th New Jersey Volunteers, and New York and Maine Batteries.

Bayou Teche, fourteen miles from Brashear City, La.

627. November 3d—Union Gunboats Kinsman, Estrella, St. Mary, Calhoun, and Diana, and 21st Indiana Volunteers.

Harrisonville, Cass Co., Mo.

628. November 3d—5th and 6th Missouri Cavalry.

Lamar, Mo.

629. November 5th—8th Missouri and 8th Missouri Militia Cavalry.

Manassas Gap, Va.

630. November 5th—Cavalry Brigade, commanded by General Averill, advance of Army of Potomac.

Barbee's Crossroads and Chester Gap (also Markham), Va.

631. November 5th—Cavalry Brigade, Army of the Potomac, General Pleasonton in command.

New Baltimore, Salem, and Thoroughfare Gap, Va.

632. November 5th—Cavalry Brigade, Army of the Potomac, commanded by General Bayard.

Greenville Road, Ky.

633. November 5th—8th Kentucky Cavalry.

Nashville, Tenn.

634. November 5th—16th and 51st Illinois, 69th Ohio, 14th Michigan and 78th Pennsylvania Volunteers, and 5th Tennessee and 7th Pennsylvania Cavalry.

Leatherwood, Ky.

635. November 6th—Captain Ambrose Powell's command.

Garrettsburg, Ky.

636. November 6th—8th Kentucky Cavalry.

Rhea's Mills, Ark.

637. November 7th—3d Arkansas Indian Home Guard.

Big Beaver Creek, Mo.

638. November 7th—10th Illinois and two companies Missouri Militia Company.

Mariana (also La Grange), Ark.

639. November 7th—3d and 4th Iowa and 9th Illinois Cavalry.

Rappahannock Bridge, Va.

640. November 8th—Cavalry Brigade, Army of the Potomac, General Bayard commanding.

Hudsonville (or Cold Water), Miss.

641. November 8th—7th Kansas and 2d Iowa Cavalry.

Fredericksburg, Va.

642. November 9th—1st Indiana Cavalry.

Moorefield (or South Fork, Potomac), Va.

643. November 9th—1st New York Ringgold and Washington Cavalry, and 23d Illinois Volunteers.

Perry County, near Kentucky River, Ky.

644. November 9th—14th Kentucky Cavalry.

Huntsville, Tenn.

645. November 11th—Tennessee Home Guards.

Newbern (or Bachelor's Creek), N. C.

646. November 11th—Organizations not stated.

Lebanon (or La Grange), Tenn.

647. November 11th—1st Kentucky and 4th Michigan Cavalry.

Lamar and Holly Springs, Miss.

648. November 12th—2d Illinois, 3d Michigan, 2d Iowa, and 7th Kansas Cavalry.

Fayetteville and White Sulphur Springs (also Little Washington), Va.

649. November 15th—1st and 2d Brigades, Sturgis' Division, 9th Corps and Cavalry, Army of the Potomac.

Gloucester, Va.

650. November 17th—104th Pennsylvania Volunteers.

Cove Creek, N. C.

651. November 18th—3d New York Cavalry.

1862.]   **Rural Hills, Tenn**
652. November 18th—8th Kentucky Cavalry.

Bayou Bontecar, near Fort Pike, La.
653. November 21st—31st Massachusetts Volunteers.

Beaver Creek, Texas Co., Mo.
654. November 24th—3d Missouri Cavalry and 21st Iowa Volunteers.

Camp Babcock, Ark.
655. November 25th—3d Kansas Indian Home Guards.

Crawford County, Mo.
656. November 25th— Missouri Enrolled Militia.

Cold Knob Mountains (or Sinking Creek, or Frankfort), Va.
657. November 26th—2d West Virginia Cavalry.

Summerville, Miss.
658. November 26th—7th Illinois Cavalry.

Carthage, Ark.
659. November 27th—2d Kansas Cavalry.

Scrougesville and La Vergne, Tenn.
660. November 27th—5th Brigade, Sill's Division, Army of the Ohio.

Cane Hill, Boston Mountains, and Boonsboro', Ark.
661. November 28th—1st Division, Army of the Frontier, commanded by Brig.-
General Jas. G. Blunt.

Little Bear Creek, Ala.
662. November 28th —Portion of the 2d Division, 16th Corps.

Hartwood Church, Va.
663. November 28th—3d Pennsylvania Cavalry.

Cold Water River, Miss.
664. November 28th—1st Indiana Cavalry.

Waterford and Lumkin's Mills, Miss.
665. November 29th and 30th—Advance Cavalry of General Grant's army.

Reconnoissance to Snicker's Ferry and Berryville, Va.
666. November 30th—1st Cavalry Brigade, Stabel's Division.

Charleston and Berryville, Va.
667. December 1st—2d Division, 12th Corps.

Franklin, Va.
668. December 2d—11th Pennsylvania Cavalry.

King George Court House, Va.
669. December 2d—8th Pennsylvania Cavalry.

Ozark, Mo.
670. December 2d—3d and 9th Missouri Cavalry.

Oakland, Miss.
671. December 3d—1st Indiana Cavalry.

XIII.—6

Oxford, Miss.

672. December 3d—2d Cavalry Brigade, commanded by Col. Hatch

Wireman's Shoals, Big Sandy River, Ky.

673. December 4th—39th Kentucky Volunteers.

Water Valley, Miss.

674. December 4th—1st and 2d Cavalry Brigades, Colonels Hatch and Lee

Coffeeville, Miss.

675. December 5th—1st, 2d, and 3d Cavalry Brigades of General Grant's army, Colonels Hatch, Lee, and Mizner.

Helena, Ark.

676 December 5th—30th Iowa and 29th Wisconsin Volunteers.

Reed's Mountains, Ark.

677. December 5th—2d Kansas Cavalry.

Lebanon, Tenn.

678. December 6th—93d Ohio Volunteers.

Prairie Grove (or Fayetteville and Illinois Creek), Ark.

679. December 7th—1st, 2d, and 3d Divisions of the Army of the Frontier, commanded by Brig.-Generals J. G. Blunt and F. J. Herrow.

Hartsville, Tenn.

680. December 7th—106th and 108th Ohio, 104th Illinois Volunteers, 2d Indiana and 11th Kentucky Cavalry, and 13th Indiana Battery.

Dobbins Ferry (or La Vergne), Tenn.

681. December 9th—35th Indiana, 51st Ohio, 8th and 21st Kentucky Volunteers, and 7th Indiana Battery.

Brentville, Tenn.

682. December 9th—25th Illinois, 8th Kansas, and 81st Indiana Volunteers, and 8th Wisconsin Battery.

Little Bear Creek, Ala.

683. December 12th—Troops commanded by Col. Sweeney, 52d Illinois Volunteers.

Zuni, near Blackwater, Va.

684. December 12th—Brigade commanded by General Terry.

Trenton, N. C.

685. December 12th—3d New York Cavalry; advance of Maj.-General Foster's Troop.

Franklin, Tenn.

686. December 12th—Stanley's Cavalry Division, Army of the Cumberland.

Foster's Expedition to Goldsboro', N. C.

687. December 12th to 18th—Wessell's Brigade of Peck's Division, 1st, 2d, and 3d Brigades, 1st Division, Department of North Carolina.

Fredericksburg, Va.

688. December 13th—2d Corps, Maj.-General Couch, and 9th Corps, Maj.-General Wilcox, Right Grand Division, Maj.-General Sumner; 1st Corps, Maj.-General Reynolds, and 6th Corps, Maj.-General W. F. Smith,

1862.] Left Grand Division, Maj.-General Franklin ; 5th Corps, Maj.-General Butterfield, and 3d Corps, Maj.-General Stoneman, Centre Grand Division, Maj.-General Hooker, Army of the Potomac, Maj.-General A. E. Burnside.

South-West Creek, N. C.

689. December 13th—9th New Jersey and 85th Pennsylvania Volunteers, 3d New York Cavalry, and 3d New York Artillery.

Kingston, N. C.

690. December 14th—Wessell's Brigade of Peck's Division, and 1st, 2d, and 3d Brigades, 1st Division, Department of North Carolina.

Fort Brown Road, Texas.

691. December 14th—Troops not given.

Whitehall, N. C.

692. December 16th—9th New Jersey, 17th, 23d, 24th, and 45th Massachusetts Volunteers, 3d New York Cavalry, and 3d and 23d New York Batteries.

Goldsboro', N. C

693. December 17th—9th New Jersey, 3d, 17th, 25th, 27th, and 43d Massachusetts Volunteers, 3d New York Cavalry, and 3d and 23d New York Batteries.

Lexington, Tenn

694. December 18th—11th Illinois, 5th Ohio, and 2d Tennessee Cavalry.

Jackson, or Salem Cemetery, Tenn.

695. December 18th—11th Illinois and 5th Ohio Cavalry ; 43d and 61st Illinois Volunteers.

Occoquan, Dumfries, Va.

696. December 19th—Wagon train Guard of the 12th Army Corps.

Holly Springs, Miss.

697. December 20th—2d Illinois Cavalry surrendered by Colonel Murphy, 8th Wisconsin Volunteers.

Trenton, Tenn.

698. December 20th—Detachments 7th Tennessee Cavalry, 122d Illinois Volunteers, and Convalescents captured by Forrest.

Davis' Mills, Wolf River, Miss.

699. December 21st—6 companies 25th Indiana Volunteers and 2 companies 5th Ohio Cavalry.

Isle of Wight Court-house, Va.

700. December 22d—Detachment 2d New York Mounted Rifles.

Middleburg, Miss. Central R.R.

701. December 24th—115 men of the 12th Michigan Volunteers.

Glasgow, Ky.

702. December 24th—5 companies of the 2d Michigan Cavalry.

Green's Chapel, Ky

703. December 25th—Detachment of the 4th and 5th Indiana Cavalry.

Bear Wallow, Ky.

704. December 25th—2 battalions of the 12th Kentucky Cavalry.

Bacon Creek, Ky.

705. December 26th—Detachment of the 2d Michigan Cavalry.

Nolensville (or Knob Gap), Tenn.

706. December 26th—2d Brigade, 1st Division, McCook's Corps; advance of the Right Wing, Army of the Cumberland.

Elizabethtown, Ky.

707. December 27th—91st Illinois Volunteers; post captured by Morgan.

Dumfries, Va.

708. December 27th—5th, 7th, and 66th Ohio Volunteers, 6th Maine Battery, 12th Illinois and 1st Maryland Cavalry.

Muldraugh's Hill, Ky.

709. December 28th—6th Indiana Cavalry.

Suffolk, Va.

710. December 28th—Reconnoitring force.

Dripping Springs, near Van Buren, Ark.

711. December 28th—Army of the Frontier.

Elk Fork, Campbell Co., Tenn.

712. December 28th—6th and 10th Kentucky Cavalry.

Occoquan, Va.

713. December 28th—2d and 17th Pennsylvania Cavalry.

Clinton, La.

714. December 28th—Troops not given.

Chickasaw Bayou, Vicksburg, Miss.

715. December 28th and 29th—Brig.-Generals G. W. Morgan's, Frederick Steel's, Morgan L. Smith's, and A. J. Smith's Divisions, Right Wing, Army of the Tennessee, commanded by Maj.-General W. T. Sherman.

Stewart Creek, Tenn.

716. December 29th—3d Kentucky,.in advance of Crittenden's Corps, Left Wing of Army of the Cumberland.

Wautauga Bridge and Carter's Station, Tenn.

717. December 30th—7th Ohio and 9th Pennsylvania Cavalry; Carter's raid into East Tennessee.

Parker's Cross Roads (or Red Mound), Tenn.

718. December 30th—18th, 106th, 119th, and 122d Illinois, 27th, 39th, and 63d Ohio, 50th Indiana, 39th Iowa, and 7th Tennessee Volunteers, and 7th Wisconsin Battery.

Jefferson, Tenn.

719. December 30th—2d Brigade, 1st Division, Thomas' Corps, guarding wagon train.

Stone's River (or Murfreesboro'), Tenn.

720. December 31st to January 2d, 1863—McCook's Corps, right wing, Thomas' Corps, centre, and Crittenden's Corps, left wing, Army of the Cumberland, Maj.-General W. S. Rosecrans commanding.

1863.—(627.)

Galveston, Texas.

721. January 1st—U. S. Gunboats Westfield, Harriet Lane, Owasco, Sachem, Clifton, and Coryphæus, and three companies of 42d Massachusetts Volunteers.

Stewart's Creek, Tenn.

722. January 1st—3d Ohio Cavalry and 10th Ohio Volunteers, guarding wagon train.

La Vergne, Tenn.

723. January 1st—1st Michigan Engineers and Mechanics.

La Grange, Ark.

724. January 3d—Portion of General Washburn's Cavalry Regiment.

Moorefield, W. Va.

725. January 3d—116th Ohio Volunteers.

Middletown, Tenn.

726. January 5th —Cavalry of the Army of the Cumberland.

Hardy County, W. Va.

727. January 5th—Troops not specified.

Springfield, Mo.

728. January 7th and 8th—Missouri Militia, Convalescents, and Citizens.

Ripley, Tenn.

729. January 8th—2d Illinois Cavalry.

Catlett's Station, Va.

730. January 10th—Organizations not specified.

Hatteras and Alabama, off the Coast of Texas.

731. January 11th—U. S. Steamer Hatteras, eight guns.

Fort Hindman, Arkansas Post, Ark.

732. January 11th—13th Corps, Maj.-General J. A. McClernand, 15th Corps, Maj.-General W. T. Sherman, Army of the Mississippi; and Gunboats of the Mississippi Squadron.

Hartsville (also Wood's Fork), Mo.

733. January 11th—21st Iowa and 99th Illinois Volunteers, 3d Iowa and 3d Missouri Cavalry, and Battery L, 2d Missouri Artillery.

Lick Creek, Ark.

734. January 12th—2d Wisconsin Cavalry.

Bayou Teche, La.

735. January 14th—8th Vermont, 16th and 75th New York, 12th Connecticut, 6th Michigan, and 21st Indiana Volunteers, 1st Louisiana Cavalry, 4th and 6th Massachusetts and 1st Maine Batteries, and Gunboats Calhoun, Diana, Kinsman, and Estrella.

Helena and Clarendon Road, Ark.

736. January 15th—2d Wisconsin Cavalry.

Duval's Bluff and Des Arcs, Ark.

737. January 16th—U. S. Gunboat DeKalb and 24th Indiana Volunteers.

Pollocksville and Northeast River, N. C.

738. January 17th—3d New York Cavalry.

Burnt Ordinary, Va.

739. January 19th—5th Pennsylvania Cavalry.

Fish Springs, Tenn.

740. January 23d—From Confederate sources.

Woodbury, Tenn.

741. January 24th—2d Division, Crittenden's Corps.

Construction Train, near Murfreesboro, Tenn.

742. January 25th—Train Guard re-enforced by part of the 10th Michigan Volunteers.

Township, Fla.

743. January 26th—32d U. S. Colored Troops.

Bear River, Washington Ter.

744. January 26th—Four companies of the 2d California Cavalry and one company 3d California Volunteers; Indian fight, 142 men of the command had their feet frozen.

Indian Village, Placquemine Bayou, La.

745. January 27th—1st Louisiana Cavalry.

Pinos Altos, Arizona Ter.

746. January 29th—One company 1st California Volunteers.

Dyersburg, Tenn.

747. January 30th—22d Ohio Volunteers.

Deserted House, near Suffolk (also Cassville and Kelly's Store), Va.

748. January 30th—Portion of Maj. General Peck's forces, commanded by Brig.-General Michael Corcoran and Colonel S. P. Spear.

Rover, Tenn.

749. January 31st—4th Ohio Cavalry.

Middleton, Tenn.

750. January 31st—2d and 3d Tennessee Cavalry.

Off Charleston Bar, S. C.

751. January 31st—U. S. Steamers Mercedita, Keystone State, Augusta, Quaker City, Housatonic, and Memphis.

Fort McAlister, Genesis Point, Ga.

752. February 1st—U. S. Navy.

Franklin, Tenn.

753. February 1st—Troops not specified.

Mingo Swamp, Mo.

754. February 3d—12th Missouri Militia, commanded by Major F. W. Reader

Fort Donelson (or Cumberland Iron Works), Tenn.

755. February 3d—83d Illinois Volunteers, 2d Illinois Artillery, and a battalion of the 5th Iowa Cavalry.

1863.]   Batesville, Ark.
756. February 4th—Brigade of Cavalry, commanded by Col. Geo. E. Waring, Jr.

                              Bear Creek, Johnson Co., Mo.
757. February 5th—40th Missouri Enrolled Militia.

                                  Williamsburg, Va.
758. February 7th—5th Pennsylvania Cavalry.

                                  Independence, Mo.
759. February 3d and 8th—5th Missouri Militia Cavalry.

                                  Lebanon, Tenn.
760. February 8th—Organizations not recorded.

                                  Summerville, Va.
761. February 9th—Cavalry, commanded by Major Knox.

                          Old River, Lake Providence, La.
762. February 10th—Detailed men from 1st Kansas, 17th and 95th Illinois, and
       16th Wisconsin Volunteers, and 3d Louisiana Cavalry.

                                  Gloucester Point, Va.
763. February 10th—Organizations not recorded.

                          Wachita Indian Agency, Texas.
764. February 10th—Loyal Delawares and Shawnees.

                                  Bone Yard, Tenn.
765. February 10th—18th Missouri Volunteers.

                                  Smithfield, Va.
766. February 13th—12th Pennsylvania Cavalry.

                                  Bolivar, Tenn.
767. February 13th—Cavalry.

                                  Brentsville, Va.
768. February 14th—1st Michigan Cavalry.

                          Gordon's Landing, Red River, La.
769. February 14th—U. S. Ram Queen of the West.

                                  Cainsville, Tenn.
770. February 15th—123d Illinois Volunteers and one company of the 5th Ten-
       nessee Cavalry.

                                  Nolensville, Tenn.
771. February 15th—Detachment from 2d Minnesota Volunteers, guarding a
       wagon train.

                                  Arkadelphia, Ark.
772. February 15th—Captain Brown's command.

                                  Romney (near), Va.
773. February 16th—Detachment of the 116th and 122d Ohio Volunteers, guard-
       ing a wagon train.

                                  Milton, Tenn.
774. February 18th—2d Michigan and 3d Ohio Cavalry.

                                  Spring River, Mo.
775. February 19th—One company of the 9th Kansas.

Cold Water, Miss.

776. February 19th—Cavalry commanded by Lieut.-Colonel W. F. Wood, 1st Indiana Cavalry.

Yazoo Pass, Miss.

777. February 20th—5th Illinois Cavalry.

Prairie Station, Miss.

778. February 21st—2d Iowa Cavalry.

Tuscumbia, Ala.

779. February 22d—Cavalry Brigade, commanded by Colonel F. M. Comyn, 10th Missouri Cavalry.

Deer Creek, near Greenville, Miss.

780. February 23d—General Burbridge's Division of the 13th Corps.

Athens, Ky.

781. February 23d—Organizations not specified.

Mississippi River, below Vicksburg.

782. February 24th—U. S. Steamer Indianola.

Hartwood Church, Va.

783. February 25th—Brig.-General Averill's Cavalry Brigade.

Strasburg Road, Va.

784. February 26th—13th Pennsylvania and 1st New York Cavalry.

Near Newbern, N. C.

785. February 27th—Detachment of 3d New York Cavalry, commanded by Captain Jacobs.

Bradyville, Tenn.

786. March 1st—1st Tennessee and 3d and 4th Ohio Cavalry.

Eagleville, Tenn.

787. March 2d—15th, 16th, 18th, and 19th U. S. Infantry.

Petersburg, Chapel Hill, and Harpeth River, Tenn.

788. March 2d and 4th—1st Tennessee Cavalry.

Fort McAlister, Genesis Point, Ga.

789. March 3d—U. S. Navy.

Owen's Valley.

790. March 3d—2d California Cavalry.

Skeet (or Swan's Headquarters), N. C.

791. March 4th—3d New York Cavalry, commanded by Captain Colin Richardson.

Thompson's Station (or Springhill, and Unionville), Tenn.

792. March 4th and 5th—33d and 85th Indiana, 22d Wisconsin, 19th Michigan, and 124th Ohio Volunteers, 18th Ohio Battery, and 2d Michigan, 9th Pennsylvania, and 4th Kentucky Cavalry.

Fairfax Court House, Va.

793. March 8th—Mosby's midnight raid.

Bolivar, Tenn.

794. March 9th—Troops not specified.

1863.]   **Franklin, Tenn.**

795. March 9th—125th Ohio Volunteers.

Covington, Tenn.

796. March 10th—6th and 7th Illinois Cavalry.

Rutherford's Creek, Tenn.

797. March 10th—4th Cavalry Brigade, commanded by Colonel Minty.

Paris, Ky.

798. March 11th—Wagon-train Guard.

Fort Pemberton, Greenwood, Miss.

799. March 13th to April 5th—U. S. Gunboats Chillicothe and DeKalb and troops of the 13th and 17th Corps.

Berwick City, La.

800. March 13th—160th New York Volunteers.

Port Hudson, Mississippi River, La.

801. March 14th—Union Fleet, commanded by Admiral D. G. Farragut, and Union Troops, commanded by Maj.-General N. P. Banks.

Newbern, N. C.

802. March 14th—Troops of the Department of Virginia and North Carolina, commanded by Maj.-General Foster, and Gunboats.

Expedition up Steele's Bayou, Miss.

803. March 16th to 22d—2d Division, 15th Corps, commanded by General Sherman, and Navy commanded by Admiral Porter.

Blackwater, Va.

804. March 17th—11th Pennsylvania Cavalry.

Kelly's Ford, Va.

805. March 17th—1st and 5th U. S.. 3d, 4th, and 16th Pennsylvania, 1st Rhode Island, 6th Ohio, and 4th New York Cavalry, and 6th New York Battery.

Brashear City, La.

806. March 18th—1st Louisiana Cavalry.

Vaught's Hill, near Milton, Tenn.

807. March 20th—105th Ohio, 101st Indiana, 80th and 123d Illinois Volunteers, 1st Tennessee Cavalry, and 9th Indiana Battery.

Salem Pike, near Murfreesboro, Tenn.

808. March 21st—3d Tennessee Cavalry.

Cottage Grove, Tenn.

809. March 21st—Troops not mentioned.

Deer Creek, Miss.

810. March 21st—Engagement during the Expedition up Steele's Bayou.

Blue Springs, Mo.

811. March 22d—1st and 5th Missouri Militia Cavalry ; skirmish with Quantrell's Guerillas.

Mount Sterling, Ky.

812. March 22d—10th Kentucky Cavalry.

6*

Danville, Ky.

813. March 24th—1st Kentucky and 2d Tennessee Cavalry, 18th and 22d Michigan Volunteers, and 1st Indiana Battery.

Ponchatoula, La.

814. March 24th—127th and 165th New York, 9th Connecticut, 14th and 24th Maine, and 6th Michigan Volunteers.

Brentwood, Tenn.

815. March 25th—Detachment of 22d Wisconsin and 9th Michigan Volunteers.

Franklin and Little Harpeth, Tenn.

816. March 25th—4th and 6th Kentucky, 9th Pennsylvania, and 2d Michigan avalry.

Pattersonville, La.

817. March 28th—Gunboat Diana, with detachments of the 12th Connecticut and 160th New York Volunteers on board.

Hurricane Bridge, West Va.

818. March 28th—Four companies of the 13th West Virginia Volunteers.

Amite River, La.

819. March 28th—14th and 24th Maine Volunteers.

Somerville, Tenn.

820. March 29th—6th Illinois Cavalry.

Expedition to Jacksonville, Fla.

821. March 29th—8th Maine and 6th Connecticut Volunteers and 33d U. S. Colored Troops (1st South Carolina) ; skirmish at Baldwin.

Williamsburg, Va.

822. March 29th—5th Pennsylvania Cavalry.

Tahliquah, I. T.

823. March 30th—3d Kansas Indian Home Guards.

Massacre on the Steamer Sam Gaty, at Sibley's Landing, Mo.

824. March 30th—Civilians, Missouri Militia, and Contrabands.

The Island, Mo.

825. March 30th—3d Wisconsin Cavalry.

Dutton's Hill (also Somerset), Ky.

826. March 30th—1st Kentucky and 7th Ohio Cavalry, and 44th and 45th Ohio Mounted Volunteers.

Point Pleasant, West Va.

827. March 30th—One company of the 13th West Virginia Volunteers, commanded by Captain J. D. Carter.

Richmond (or Round Away Bayou), La.

828. March 30th—69th Indiana Volunteers and a detachment of the 2d Illinois Cavalry.

Washington, N. C.

829. March 30th to April 4th—Troops commanded by Maj.-General Foster ; includes skirmish at Rodman's Point, April 4, 1863.

1863.]   **Chalk Bluff, Ark.**

830. April 1st—One company of the 2d Missouri Militia Cavalry.

Broad Run, Va.

831. April 1st—Detachments of the 1st Vermont and 5th New York Cavalry.

Little Rock Road, Ark.

832. April 2d—One company of the 5th Kansas Cavalry.

Woodbury and Snow Hill, Tenn.

833. April 2d and 3d—3d and 4th Ohio Cavalry.

Carroll County, Ark.

834. April 4th—1st Arkansas Cavalry.

Madison, Ark.

835. April 4th—3d Iowa Cavalry.

Black Bayou Expedition, Miss.

836. April 5th to 10th—A division of the 15th Corps, commanded by Maj.-General Frederick Steele.

Bombardment of Fort Sumter, Charleston Harbor (also called Stone Inlet), S. C.

837. April 7th—South Atlantic Squadron, Keokuk, Weehawken, Passaic, Montauk, Patapsco, New Ironsides, Catskill, Nantucket, and Nahant.

St. Francis County, Mo.

838. April 8th—Detachment of Cavalry and one company of the 4th Iowa Cavalry, commanded by Major E. F. Winslow.

Broad River, S. C.

839. April 8th—3d Rhode Island Artillery, on the Gunboat Washington.

East Pascagoula, Miss.

840. April 9th—74th U. S. Colored Troops (2d Louisiana).

Blount's Mills, N. C.

841. April 9th—3d and 17th Massachusetts, 1st Rhode Island, and 3d New York Artillery.

Waverly, Tenn.

842. April 10th—One company of the 5th Iowa Cavalry.

Franklin and Harpeth River, Tenn.

843. April 10th—40th Ohio, guarding the Railroad, and a portion of Granger's Cavalry Division.

Antioch Station, Tenn.

844. April 10th—Detachment of the 10th Michigan Volunteers.

Whittaker's Mills, near Williamsburg, Va.

845. April 11th—5th Pennsylvania Cavalry.

Irish Bend and Bisland (also designated Bayou Teche, Indian Ridge, and Centreville), La.

846. April 12th to 14th—Grover's Division, 19th Corps, at Irish Bend, Emory's and Weitzel's Divisions, 19th Corps, at Bisland.

Siege of Suffolk, Va.

847. April 12th to May 4th—Troops of Department of Virginia and North Carolina, commanded by Maj.-General John J. Peck.

West Branch and Nansemond, Va.

848. April 14th—Gunboats Commodore Barney, West End, Mount Washington, and Stepping Stones.

Spanish Fork Cañon, Utah Territory.

849. April 15th—2d California Cavalry; fight with Indians.

Pikeville, Ky.

850. April 15th—39th Kentucky Mounted Infantry.

Dunbar's Plantation, La.

851. April 15th—2d Illinois Cavalry.

Running the Vicksburg Batteries.

852. April 16th—Ironclads and transports belonging to Commodore Porter's fleet and General Grant's army.

Medalia (also known as South Branch of the Watonwan), Minn.

853. April 16th—Eighteen soldiers of the 7th Minnesota Volunteers; fight with Indians.

South Quay, Va.

854. April 17th—99th and 130th New York Volunteers; skirmish during the siege of Suffolk.

Bear Creek, Cherokee Station, and Lundy's Lane (known also as Hillsborough), Ala.

855. April 17th—10th Missouri and 7th Kansas Cavalry.

Bayou Vermilion, La.

856. April 17th—Division of the 19th Corps, commanded by Brig.-General Grover.

Grierson's Expedition from La Grange, Tenn., to Baton Rouge, La.

857. April 17th to May 2d—6th and 7th Illinois and 2d Iowa Cavalry.

Hernando, Miss.

858. April 18th—2d Brigade, Cavalry Division, commanded by General Smith, and Infantry and Artillery from the 16th Corps.

Sabine Pass, Tex.

859. April 18th—Crews of the Gunboats Cayuga and New London.

Fayetteville, Ark.

860. April 18th—1st Arkansas Volunteers and 1st Arkansas Cavalry.

Battery Huger (Hill's Point), Va.

861. April 18th—Detachments of the 89th New York and 8th Connecticut Volunteers; skirmish during siege of Suffolk.

New Albany, Miss.

862. April 19th—7th Illinois Cavalry; skirmish during Grierson's raid.

Coldwater, Miss.

863. April 19th—Same force as on the 18th at Hernando, Miss.

1863.]   Celina, Ky.

864. April 20th—5th Indiana Cavalry.

Patterson, Mo.

865. April 20th—3d Missouri Militia Cavalry.

McMinnville, Tenn.

866. April 20th—1st Brigade of Cavalry, Army of the Cumberland, Colonel Minty.

Bute La Rose, La.

867. April 20th—Union gunboats Estrella, Clifton, Arizona, and Calhoun.

Palo Alto, Miss.

868. April 21st and 22d—2d Iowa Cavalry ; skirmish during Grierson's raid.

Tompkinsville, Ky.

869. April 22d—Organizations not stated.

Strasburg Road, Va.

870. April 22d—3d West Virginia Cavalry.

Chuckatuck, Va.

871. April 23d—Crew of the Gunboat Commodore Barney.

Tuscumbia, Ala.

872. April 24th—2d Division, 16th Corps.

Beverly, West Va.

873. April 24th—5th West Virginia Cavalry.

White Water, Mo.

874. April 24th—1st Wisconsin Cavalry.

Little Rock Landing (Duck River Shoals), Tenn.

875. April 24th—Ellet's Mississippi Ram fleet.

Greenland Gap, West Va.

876. April 25th—Detachments of the 23d Illinois and 14th West Virginia Volunteers.

Cape Girardeau, Mo.

877. April 26th—1st Wisconsin and 2d Missouri Militia Cavalry, 32d Iowa Volunteers, and Batteries D and L, 1st Missouri Artillery.

Franklin, Tenn.

878. April 27th—Cavalry, commanded by Colonel Watkins.

Streight's Raid from Tuscumbia, Ala., to Rome, Ga.

879. April 27th to May 3d—3d Ohio, 51st and 73d Indiana Volunteers, 80th Illinois Mounted Infantry, and two companies of the 1st Alabama Cavalry ; includes skirmish at *Day's Gap*, April 30th, *Black Warrior Creek*, May 1st, and *Blount's Farm*, May 2d.

Stoneman's Raid, Va.

880. April 27th to May 8th—Cavalry Corps, Army of the Potomac, Maj.-General Stoneman.

Howe's Ford (or Weaver's Store), Ky.

881. April 28th—1st Kentucky Cavalry.

Dover Road, N. C.

832. April 28th—Troops of the District of North Carolina, commanded by Brig.-General Palmer.

Town Creek, Ala.

883. April 28th—Portion of the 16th Corps, commanded by Maj.-General G. M. Dodge.

Union Church, Miss.

884. April 28th—6th Illinois Cavalry; skirmish during Grierson's raid.

Castor River and Bloomfield, Mo.

885. April 29th—1st Wisconsin Cavalry.

Fairmont, West Va.

886. April 29th—Detachments of the 106th New York, 6th West Virginia, and Virginia Militia.

Grand Gulf, Miss.

887. April 29th—Gunboats Louisville, Carondelet, Mound City, Pittsburg, Tuscumbia, Benton, and Lafayette.

Fitzhugh's Crossing (Rappahannock River), Va.

888. April 29th and 30th—1st Corps, Army of the Potomac.

Spottsylvania Court House, Va.

889. April 30th—6th New York Cavalry.

Snyder's Bluff, Miss.

890. April 30th—Portions of the 15th Corps.

Chalk Bluff and St. Francis River, Mo.

891. April 30th and May 1st—3d Missouri and 1st Iowa Cavalry, 2d Missouri Militia, and Battery E, 1st Missouri Light Artillery.

Day's Gap, Sand Mountain, and Black Warrior Creek (also designated Driver's Gap and Crooked Creek), Ala.

892. April 30th and May 1st—Skirmishes of troops on Streight's raid from April 27th to May 3d.

Port Gibson (also known as Thompson's Hill and Magnolia Hills), Miss.

893. May 1st—13th Corps, Maj.-General J. A. McClernand, 3d Division, 17th Corps, Maj.-General J. B. McPherson, commanded by Maj.-General U. S. Grant; includes the skirmishes at Bayou Pierre, and is the first engagement in Grant's campaign against Vicksburg.

Chancellorsville, Va.

894. May 1st to 4th—1st Corps, Maj.-General J. F. Reynolds; 2d Corps, Maj. General D. N. Couch; 3d Corps, Maj.-General D. E. Sickles; 5th Corps, Maj.-General G. G. Meade; 6th Corps, Maj.-General J. Sedgwick; 11th Corps, Maj.-General O. O. Howard; 12th Corps, Maj.-General H. W. Slocum, Army of the Potomac, commanded by Maj.-General Joseph Hooker; includes the battles of the 6th Corps at Fredericksburg, Salem Heights, and Marye's Heights.

1863.]   **La Grange, Ark.**

895. May 1st—3d Iowa Cavalry, commanded by Captain J. Q. A. Huff.

Monticello, Ky.

896. May 1st—2d Tennessee, 1st Kentucky, and 2d and 7th Ohio Cavalry, 45th Ohio and 112th Illinois Mounted Infantry.

South Quay Bridge, Nansemond River, Va.

897. May 1st—99th New York Volunteers; skirmish during siege of Suffolk.

Tickfaw River, Miss.

898. May 1st—7th Illinois Cavalry; skirmish during Grierson's raid.

Rapidan Station, Va.

899. May 1st—Averell's Cavalry Division, Army of the Potomac; skirmish during Stoneman's raid.

Louisa Court House, Va.

900. May 1st—Two companies 1st Maine Cavalry; detachment of Stoneman's raiding forces.

Blount's Farm, Ala.

901. May 2d—51st and 73d Indiana and 80th Illinois Volunteers, 3d Ohio Mounted Infantry, and 1st Alabama Cavalry; skirmish during Streight's raid.

Warrenton Junction, Va.

902. May 3d—1st West Virginia and 5th New York Cavalry.

Nansemond River, Va.

903. May 3d—Maj.-General John J. Peck's troops; skirmish during siege of Suffolk, Va.

Forty Hills (or Hankinson's Ferry), Miss.

904. May 3d—7th Division 17th Corps; skirmish during Grant's Vicksburg campaign.

Shannon Hill, Va.

905. May 4th—5th New York Cavalry; skirmish during Stoneman's raid.

Tunstall Station, Va.

906. May 4th—12th Illinois Cavalry; skirmish during Stoneman's raid.

Siege of Suffolk, Va., Raised.

907. May 4th—Troops of Department of Virginia and North Carolina.

Tupelo, Miss.

908. May 6th—10th Missouri and 7th Kansas Cavalry.

Civiques Ferry, La.

909. May 10th—14th and 24th Maine, and 177th New York Volunteers, and 21st New York Battery.

Horse Shoe Bend (or Greasy Creek), Ky.

910. May 11th—Detachment of Union troops, commanded by Colonel R. T. Jacobs.

Mount Vernon, Ark.

911. May 11th—5th Kansas and 5th Illinois Cavalry, commanded by Colonel Powell Clayton.

Linden, Tenn.
912. May 12th—6th Tennessee Cavalry.

Fourteen Mile Creek, Miss.
913. May 12th—13th Corps, Maj.-General J. A. McClernand, and 15th Corps, Maj.-General W. T. Sherman ; skirmish during General Grant's Vicksburg campaign.

Raymond, Miss.
914. May 12th—17th Corps, Maj.-General J. B. McPherson ; engagement during Grant's Vicksburg campaign.

Ponchatoula, La.
915. May 13th—Colonel Davis's command.

Hall's Ferry, Miss.
916. May 13th—2d Illinois Cavalry ; Grant's campaign against Vicksburg.

South Union, Ky.
917. May 13th—Organizations not specified.

Jackson, Miss.
918. May 14th—17th Corps, Maj.-General J. B. McPherson ; 15th Corps, Maj.-General W. T. Sherman ; engagement during Grant's Vicksburg campaign.

Warrenton Junction, Va.
919. May 14th—Organizations not specified.

Camp Moore, La.
920. May 15th—Expedition commanded by Colonel Davis.

Carsville and Suffolk (known also as Holland House), Va.
921. May 15th and 16th—Expedition commanded by Brig.-General R. S. Foster.

Carthage, Mo.
922. May 16th—7th Missouri Militia Cavalry.

Piedmont Station, Va.
923. May 16th—West Virginia and Pennsylvania Cavalry.

Cripple Creek (or Bradysville), Va.
924. May 16th —Detachment of 5th Tennessee Cavalry ; escort to Brig.-General Palmer.

Champion Hills (also known as Baker's Creek and Edward's Station), Miss.
925. May 16th—Hovey's Division, 13th Corps, Maj.-General J. A. McClernand, and 17th Corps, Maj.-General J. B. McPherson ; engagement during Grant's Vicksburg campaign.

Berry's Ferry, Va.
926. May 16th—Detachment of 1st New York Cavalry, commanded by Lieutenant Vermillion.

Big Black River, Miss.
927. May 17th—Car's and Osterhaus' Divisions, 13th Corps, Maj.-General J. A. McClernand ; engagement during Grant's Vicksburg campaign.

1863.]   **Fayetteville, Va.**

928. May 17th to 20th—12th and 91st Ohio Volunteers, and 2d West Virginia Cavalry.

Sherwood, Mo.

929. May 18th—Detachment of 2d Kansas Artillery and 1st Kansas (20th U. S. Colored Troops) Volunteers.

Attack by Guerillas on the Transport Crescent City, near Island No. 82.

930. May 18th—3d Iowa Volunteers.

Carsville, Va.

931. May 18th—170th New York Volunteers.

Siege of Vicksburg, Miss.

932. May 18th to July 4th—13th Corps, Maj.-General J. A. McClernand ; 15th Corps, Maj.-General W. T. Sherman ; 17th Corps, Maj.-General J. B. McPherson, commanded by Maj.-General U. S. Grant, assisted by the Navy on the Mississippi River under Admiral Porter. Re-enforced later by Lauman's, Smith's, and Kimball's Divisions, of the 16th Corps ; two Divisions of the 9th Corps, Maj.-General J. S. Parke, and a Division from the Department of the Missouri under Maj.-General F. J. Herron ; first assault, May 19th, unsuccessful.

Winchester, Va.

933. May 19th—Detachment of Cavalry from Milroy's command.

Richfield, Clay Co., Mo.

934. May 19th—25th Missouri Volunteers.

Fort Gibson and Fort Blount, Ind. Terr.

935. May 20th—6th Kansas and 3d Wisconsin Cavalry, and 1st, 2d, and 3d Kansas Indian Home Guards.

Second Assault on Fortifications at Vicksburg, Miss.

936. May 20th—Army of the Tennessee.

Glendenin's Raid below Fredericksburg, Va.

937. May 20th to 28th—8th Illinois Cavalry, commanded by Lieut.-Colonel G. R. Glendenin.

Middleton, Tenn.

938. May 21st—4th Michigan, 3d Indiana, 7th Pennsylvania, 3d and 4th Ohio, and 4th U. S. Cavalry, and 39th Indiana Mounted Infantry.

Plain Stores, Port Hudson Plains, La.

939. May 21st—1st Division, Anger's 19th Corps.

Gum Swamp, N. C.

940. May 22d—58th Pennsylvania, and 5th, 25th, 27th, and 46th Massachusetts Volunteers, and Boggs' Battery.

Bachelor's Creek, N. C.

941. May 23d—58th Pennsylvania and 46th Massachusetts Volunteers.

Beaver Dam Lake, near Austin, Miss.

942. May 23d—Mississippi Marine Brigade of Cavalry and Infantry.

Fishing Creek, Hartford, Ky.

943. May 25th—Organizations not given.

Polk's Plantation, near Helena, Ark.

944. May 25th—3d Iowa and 5th Kansas Cavalry.

Franklin, La.

945. May 25th—41st Massachusetts Volunteers and several other regiments, commanded by Colonel Chickering.

Senatobia, Miss.

946. May 25th—3d Illinois Cavalry.

Lake Providence, La.

947. May 27th—47th U. S. Colored Troops.

Florence, Ala.

948. May 27th—Brigade of Cavalry, commanded by Colonel Comyn, 10th Missouri Cavalry.

Siege of Port Hudson, La.

949. May 27th to July 9th—Maj.-Generals Weitzel's, Grover's, Paine's, Anger's, and Dwight's Divisions, 19th Corps; Maj.-General Banks' Army of the Gulf, assisted by the Navy under Admiral Farragut.

Bushy Creek (or Little Black River), Mo.

950. May 28th—13th Illinois Cavalry.

Mechanicsville, Miss.

951. May 29th—Portion of the 17th Corps, commanded by Major-General F. P. Blair, U. S. V.

Greenwich, Va.

952. May 30th—1st Vermont, 5th New York, and 7th Michigan Cavalry.

Rocheport, Mo.

953. June 1st—1st Missouri Enrolled Militia and 9th Missouri Militia Cavalry.

Clinton, La.

954. June 4th—Cavalry, commanded by Colonel B. H. Grierson, 6th Illinois Cavalry.

Mechanicsburg and Sartoria, Miss.

955. June 4th—5th Illinois Cavalry and 8th Wisconsin Volunteers.

Frying Pan, Va.

956. June 4th—Detachment of 5th Michigan Cavalry, commanded by Captain Gray.

Franklin, Tenn.

957. June 4th—35th Indiana Volunteers, 4th, 6th, and 7th Kentucky, 9th Pennsylvania, and 2d Michigan Cavalry.

Bluffton, S. C.

958. June 4th—Troops not specified.

Franklin's Crossing, Rappahannock River, Va.

959. June 5th—26th New Jersey and 5th Vermont Volunteers, 15th and 50th New York Engineers, supported by the 6th Corps.

Murfreesboro, Shelbyville, Tenn.

960. June 6th—2d and 8th Indiana Cavalry.

Shawneetown, Kan.

961. June 6th—Organizations not given.

1863.]   **Berryville, Va.**

962. June 6th—67th Pennsylvania Volunteers.

                        Milliken's Bend (or Ashland), La.

963. June 6th to 8th—5th U. S. Colored Heavy Artillery, 9th Louisiana, 49th U.
    S. Colored Troops, 11th Louisiana, 51st U. S. Colored Troops, 1st Missis-
    sippi and 23d Iowa Volunteers; no quarter was given to the Union troops.

                        Fort Lyons, Va.

964. June 9th—3d New York Artillery; accidental explosion of a magazine.

                        Monticello and Rocky Gap, Ky.

965. June 9th—2d and 7th Ohio and 1st Kentucky Cavalry, 45th Ohio and 2d
    Tennessee Mounted Infantry.

                        Beverly Ford and Brandy Station, Va.

966. June 9th—2d, 3d, and 7th Wisconsin, 2d and 33d Massachusetts, 6th Maine,
    and 86th and 104th New York Volunteers, 1st, 2d, 5th, and 6th U. S., 2d,
    6th, 8th, 9th, and 10th New York, 1st Maryland, 8th Illinois, 3d Indiana,
    1st New Jersey, 1st, 6th, and 17th Pennsylvania, 1st Maine, and 3d West
    Virginia Cavalry.

                        Triune, Tenn.

967. June 9th—General Mitchell's Cavalry Division.

                        Lake Providence, La.

968. June 10th—Organizations not specified.

                        State Creek, near Mt. Sterling, Ky.

969. June 11th—1st Tennessee and 14th Kentucky Cavalry.

                        Port Hudson, La.

970. June 11th—Army of the Gulf; serious engagement during siege of Port
    Hudson, La.

                        Seneca, Md.

971. June 11th—6th Michigan Cavalry.

                        Middletown, Va.

972. June 11th—13th Pennsylvania Cavalry, 87th Pennsylvania Volunteers, and
    Battery L, 5th Artillery.

                        Berryville, Va.

973. June 12th—1st Brigade, Milroy's Division, commanded by Colonel McRey-
    nolds.

                        Winchester, Va.

974. June 13th and 15th—2d, 67th, and 87th Pennsylvania, 18th Connecticut,
    12th West Virginia, 110th, 116th, 122d, and 123d Ohio, and 3d, 5th, and
    6th Maryland Volunteers, 12th and 13th Pennsylvania, 1st New York, and
    1st and 3d West Virginia Cavalry, Battery L, 5th U. S. Artillery, 1st
    West Virginia Battery, Baltimore Battery, and one company 14th Massa-
    chusetts Heavy Artillery, of the 2d Division, 8th Corps.

                        Wilson's Creek, near Boston, Ky.

975. June 13th—Kentucky Provost Guard.

                        Martinsburg, Va.

976. June 14th—106th New York and 126th Ohio Volunteers and West Virginia
    Battery, 3d Brigade, 2d Division, 8th Corps, commanded by Brig.-
    General Tyler.

Second Assault on Fortifications at Port Hudson, La.

977. June 14th—Army of the Gulf.

Richmond, La.

978. June 15th—General Mower's Brigade and Ellet's Mississippi Marine Brigade.

Triplett's Bridge, Fleming Co., Ky.

979. June 16th—10th and 14th Kentucky and 7th and 9th Michigan Cavalry, 15th Michigan Volunteers, and 11th Michigan Battery.

Jornado Del Muerto, New Mexico.

980. June 16th—One company of the 1st New Mexico Cavalry.

Orleans, Ind.

981. June 17th—Home Guards ; Morgan's raid in Indiana and Ohio.

Aldie, Va.

982. June 17th—2d and 4th New York, 6th Ohio, 1st Massachusetts, 1st Maine, and 1st Rhode Island Cavalry.

Westport, Mo.

983. June 17th—Two companies of the 9th Kansas Volunteers.

Capture of the Atlanta.

984. June 17th—U. S. Ironclad Weehawken.

Plaquemine, La.

985. June 18th—Organizations not given.

Blue Island, near Leavenworth, Ind.

986. June 19th—Home Guards, commanded by Major Glendenin.

Middleburg, Va.

987. June 19th—1st Maine, 2d, 4th, and 10th New York, 4th and 16th Pennsylvania, and 6th Ohio Cavalry.

Rocky Crossing, Tallahassee River, Miss.

988. June 20th—9th Illinois Mounted Infantry and 5th Ohio Cavalry.

Greencastle, Penn.

989. June 20th—1st New York Cavalry.

Warm Springs, Fort McRae, New Mexico.

990. June 20th—Detachment of 1st New Mexico Cavalry.

Pawnee Reservation.

991. June 20th—One company of the 2d Nebraska Cavalry.

Jackson Cross Roads, La.

992. June 20th—Detachments of the 6th and 7th Illinois and 2d Rhode Island Cavalry, 52d Massachusetts Volunteers, and a section of Artillery.

Hernando, Miss.

993. June 20th—5th Ohio, 2d Illinois, and 1st Missouri Cavalry.

La Fourche Crossing (or Thibodeaux), La.

994. June 20th and 21st—Detachments of the 23d Connecticut, 176th New York, 26th, 42d, and 47th Massachusetts, and 21st Indiana Volunteers.

Upperville, Va.

995. June 21st—Cavalry Corps, Army of the Potomac.

1863]   Low Creek, W. Va.
996. June 21st—Organizations not given.

Hill's Plantation, Miss.
997. June 22d—Portions of three companies of the 4th Iowa Cavalry.

Cypress Bend, Miss.
998. June 22d—Union Gunboats.

Brashear City, La.
999. June 23d—Detachments of the 176th and 114th New York, 23d Connecticut, 42d Massachusetts, and 21st Indiana Volunteers.

Rosecrans' Campaign from Murfreesboro to Tullahoma, Tenn.
1,000. June 23d to 30th—14th Corps, Maj.-General George H. Thomas; 20th Corps, Maj.-General A. McD. McCook; 21st Corps, Maj.-General T. S. Crittenden; Reserve Corps, Maj.-General G. Granger; and Cavalry Corps, Maj.-General Stanley; Army of the Cumberland, Maj.-General W. S. Rosecrans; includes Middleton, Hoover's Gap, Beech Grove or Liberty, and Guy's Gap.

Middleton, Shelbyville Pike, Tenn.
1,001. June 24th—1st Cavalry Division, Army of the Cumberland.

Hoover's Gap, Tenn.
1,002. June 24th—17th and 72d Indiana, 123d and 98th Illinois Mounted Infantry, and 18th Indiana Battery.

McConnellsburg, Pa
1,003. June 24th—12th Pennsylvania Cavalry.

Chakapoola Station, La.
1,004. June 24th—Five companies of the 9th Connecticut Volunteers.

Liberty Gap (or Beech Grove), Tenn.
1,005. June 25th—20th Corps, Maj.-General Alex. McD. McCook, Army of the Cumberland.

Fort Hill, Vicksburg, Miss.
1,006. June 25th—Siege of Vicksburg.

South Anna, near Hanover Court House, Va.
1,007. June 26th—11th Pennsylvania Cavalry, 2d Massachusetts, and 12th Illinois Volunteers.

Baltimore Cross Roads, Va.
1,008. June 26th—4th Corps, Maj.-Gen. Keyes.

Fairfax, Va.
1,009. June 27th—11th New York Cavalry.

Beaver Creek, Floyd Co., Ky.
1,010. June 27th—39th Kentucky Volunteers.

Guy's Gap and Shelbyville, Tenn.
1,011. June 27th—Cavalry Division, Army of the Cumberland, supported by Maj.-General Granger's Infantry Division.

Donaldsonville, La.

1,012. June 28th—28th Maine Volunteers and Convalescents, assisted by Gunboats.

Fort Hill, Vicksburg, Miss.

1,013. June 28th—Part of siege of Vicksburg.

McConnellsburg, Pa.

1,014. June 29th—1st New York Cavalry.

Westminster, Md.

1,015. June 29th—Detachment of the 1st Delaware Cavalry.

Lake Providence, La.

1,016. June 29th—Organizations not stated.

Sporting Hill, near Harrisburg, Pa.

1,017. June 30th—22d and 37th New York Militia and Lander's Battery.

Hanover, Pa.

1,018. June 30th—3d Division Cavalry Corps, Army of the Potomac.

Bayou Tensas, La.

1,019. June 30th—Mississippi Brigade of Infantry and Cavalry, commanded by Col. C. R. Ellet.

Tullahoma, Tenn.

1,020. July 1st—Occupation by Maj.-General Rosecrans' army.

Gettysburg, Pa.

1,021. July 1st to 3d—1st Corps, Maj.-General J. F. Reynolds ; 2d Corps, Maj.-General W. S. Hancock; 3d Corps, Maj.-General D. E. Sickles ; 5th Corps, Maj.-General George Sykes ; 6th Corps, Maj.-General J. Sedgwick; 11th Corps, Maj.-General O. O. Howard ; 12th Corps, Maj.-General H. W. Slocum ; Cavalry Corps, Maj.-General A. Pleasonton ; Army of the Potomac, commanded by Maj.-General G. E. Meade ; includes Cavalry skirmish at Hunterstown.

Black River, at Messengers and Bridgeport Ferries, Miss.

1,022. July 1st and 2d—Portion of the 17th Corps.

Cabin Creek, Ind. Terr.

1,023. July 1st and 2d—3d Wisconsin, 6th and 9th Kansas, and 2d Colorado Cavalry, 1st Kansas (79th U. S. Colored Troops), and 3d Kansas Indian Home Guards.

Morgan's Raid into Kentucky, Ohio, and Indiana.

1,024. July 1st to 26th—Cavalry, commanded by Brig.-General E. H. Hobson ; includes skirmishes at Burkesville, July 2d ; Columbia, 3d ; Green River Bridge, 4th ; Lebanon, 5th ; Brandenburg, 8th ; Corydon, Md., 9th ; capture of raiders at Buffington Island, Ohio, 19th ; and final capture at New Lisbon on the 26th.

Baltimore Cross Roads, Va.

1,025. July 2d—Portion of 4th Corps, commanded by Maj.-General Keyes.

Elk River, Tenn.

1,026. July 2d—Cavalry, Army of the Cumberland.

Bottom's Bridge, Va.

1,027. July 2d—5th Pennsylvania Cavalry.

Beverly, Va.

1,028. July 2d—10th West Virginia Volunteers, and Battery G, West Virginia Artillery.

Marrowbone (or Burkesville), Ky.

1,029. July 2d—1st and 9th Kentucky Cavalry and 24th Indiana Battery; Morgan's raid.

Springfield Landing, La.

1,030. July 2d—2d Rhode Island Cavalry.

Fairfield, Pa.

1,031. July 3d—6th U. S. Cavalry.

Columbia, Ky.

1,032. July 3d—1st Kentucky and 2d Ohio Cavalry, and 45th Ohio Mounted Volunteers; Morgan's raid.

University Place, Tenn.

1,033. July 4th—6th Kentucky Cavalry.

Green River Bridge (or Tebb's Bend), Ky.

1,034. July 4th—Five companies 25th Michigan Volunteers; Morgan's raid.

Bolton and Birdsong Ferry, Big Black River, Miss.

1,035. July 4th and 5th—Troops commanded by Maj.-General W. T. Sherman.

Vicksburg, Miss.

1,036. July 4th—Vicksburg surrendered.

Helena, Ark.

1,037. July 4th—One Division 16th Corps, commanded by Maj.-General B. M. Prentiss, assisted by Gunboat Tyler.

Monterey Gap and Smithsburg, Md.

1,038. July 4th—3d Cavalry Division, Army of the Potomac.

Fairfield, Pa.

1,039. July 5th—Cavalry, Army of the Potomac.

Lebanon, Ky.

1,040. July 5th—20th Kentucky Volunteers.

Pound Gap Expedition, Tenn.

1,041. July 6th—10th Kentucky and 1st Ohio Cavalry.

Quaker Bridge (also known as Comfort), N. C.

1,042. July 6th—9th New Jersey, 17th, 23d, and 27th Massachusetts, 81st and 158th New York Volunteers, and Belger's and Angel's Battery.

Hagerstown, Md.

1,043. July 6th—3d Cavalry Division, Army of the Potomac.

Williamsport, Md.

1,044. July 6th—3d Cavalry Division, Army of the Potomac.

Jones' Ford, Black River, Miss.

1,045. July 6th—6th Iowa and 48th Illinois Volunteers.

I-u-ka, Miss.

1,046. July 7th and 9th—10th Missouri and 7th Kansas Cavalry.

Boonsboro', Md.

1,047. July 7th and 9th—1st and 3d Divisions, Cavalry Corps, Army of the Potomac.

Grand Pass, Fort Halleck, Ind. Terr.

1,048. July 7th—9th Kansas Volunteers; Indian fight.

Redwood Creek, Cal.

1,049. July 7th—One company, 1st Battalion, California Mountaineers; Indian fight.

Convalescent Corral, near Corinth, Miss.

1,050. July 7th—One company 39th Iowa Volunteers.

Harper's Ferry Bridge, Va.

1,051. July 7th—Potomac Home Brigade and 1st Massachusetts Heavy Artillery.

Brandenburg, Ky.

1,052. July 8th—Indiana Home Guards; Morgan's raid.

Port Hudson, La.

1,053. July 9th—Port Hudson surrendered to Army of the Gulf.

Corydon, Md.

1,054. July 9th—Indiana Home Guards; Morgan's raid.

Jackson, Miss.

1,055. July 9th to 16th—9th Corps, Maj.-General Parke; 13th Corps, Maj.-General E. O. C. Ord; 15th Corps, Maj.-General W. T. Sherman; and a portion of the 16th Corps; includes skirmishes at Rienzi, Bolton Depot, Canton, and Clinton.

Fort Wagner, Morris Island, S. C.

1,056. July 10th to September 6th—Troops of the Department of the South, commanded by Maj.-General Q. A. Gillmore, and U. S. Navy under Admiral Dahlgren.

Assault on Fort Wagner.

1,057. July 10th and 11th—67th Connecticut, 76th Pennsylvania, 9th Maine, 3d New Hampshire, 48th and 100th New York Volunteers.

Union City, Tenn.

1,058. July 10th—4th Missouri Cavalry.

Big Creek, Ark.

1,059. July 10th—Organizations not stated.

Hagerstown, Md.

1,060. July 11th—Cavalry, Army of the Potomac.

Funkstown, Md.

1,061. July 12th—Infantry, Cavalry, and Artillery of the Army of the Potomac.

Vernon, Ind.

1,062. July 12th—Indiana Minute Men; Morgan's raid.

Ashby Gap, Va.

1,063. July 12th—2d Massachusetts Cavalry.

1863.]   **Yazoo City, Miss.**

1,064. July 13th—Maj.-General Herron's Division, assisted by three Gunboats under Admiral Porter.

Jackson, Tenn.

1,065. July 13th—3d Michigan, 3d Iowa, and 1st Tennessee Cavalry, and 9th Illinois Cavalry.

Donaldsonville, or Kock's Plantation, La.

1,066. July 13th—Portions of Wietzel's and Grover's Divisions of the 19th Corps.

Draft Riots, New York City.

1,067. July 13th to 15th—Over 1,000 of the rioters were killed and wounded.

Lawrenceburg, O.

1,068. July 14th—105th Indiana Minute Men firing into each other ; Morgan's raid.

Falling Waters, Md.

1,069. July 14th—3d Cavalry Division, Army of the Potomac.

Elk River, Tenn.

1,070. July 14th—Advance of the 14th Corps, Maj.-General Geo. H. Thomas, Army of the Cumberland.

Shady Spring, W. Va.

1,071. July 14th—2d West Virginia Cavalry.

Near Bolivar Heights, Va.

1,072. July 14th—1st Connecticut Cavalry.

Pulaski, Ala.

1,073. July 15th—3d Ohio and 5th Tennessee Cavalry.

Halltown, Va.

1,074. July 15th—16th Pennsylvania and 1st Maine Cavalry.

Jackson, Miss.

1,075. July 16th—Evacuated by the Confederates. See, 1,055.

Sheppardstown, Va.

1,076. July 16th—1st, 4th, and 16th Pennsylvania, 1st Maine, and 10th New York Cavalry.

Secessionville, James Island, S. C.

1,077. July 16th—Troops commanded by Brig.-General Terry ; skirmish during siege of Fort Wagner.

Honey Springs, Elk Creek, Ind. Terr.

1,078. July 17th—2d, 6th, and 9th Kansas Cavalry, 2d and 3d Kansas Batteries, and 2d and 3d Kansas Indian Home Guards.

Brandon, Miss.

1,079. July 18th—Portion of General Sherman's troops.

Rio Hondo, New Mexico.

1,080. July 18th—One company of the 1st New Mexico Cavalry ; Indian fight.

Second Assault on Fort Wagner, S. C.

1,081. July 18th—54th Massachusetts (Colored), 6th Connecticut, 48th and 100th New York, 3d and 7th New Hampshire, 76th Pennsylvania, 9th Maine, 62d and 67th Ohio Volunteers.

XIII.—7

Wytheville, W. Va.

1,082. July 18th—34th Ohio Volunteers and 1st and 2d West Virginia Cavalry.

Canton, Miss.

1,083. July 18th—2d Wisconsin, 5th Illinois, 3d and 4th Iowa Cavalry, 76th Ohio, 25th and 31st Iowa, and 3d, 13th, and 17th Missouri Volunteers, and a battery of artillery.

Raid, Tar River and Rocky Mount, N. C.

1,084. July 18th to 21st—3d and 12th New York and 1st North Carolina Battery.

Buffington Island (also known as St. George's Creek), O.

1,085. July 19th—1st, 3d, 8th, 9th, 11th, and 12th Kentucky, 8th, 9th, and 12th Michigan, 2d and 7th Ohio, and 5th Indiana Cavalry, 45th Ohio, and 2d Tennessee Mounted Infantry, Militia and Union Gunboats; capture of Morgan's raiders.

Manassas Gap, Va.

1,086. July 21st—1st, 2d, and 5th U. S. Cavalry, Advance Cavalry, Army of the Potomac.

Chester Gap, Va.

1,087. July 21st and 22d—8th New York, 3d Indiana, and 12th Illinois, Advance Cavalry, Army of the Potomac.

Concha's Springs, New Mexico.

1,088. July 22d—One company of New Mexico Cavalry.

Wapping Heights (or Manassas Gap), Va.

1,089. July 23d—3d Corps, Army of the Potomac, Maj.-General French.

Big Mound, Dakota Terr.

1,090. July 24th—1st Minnesota Cavalry, 3d Minnesota Battery, and 6th, 7th, and 10th Minnesota Volunteers; fight with the Sioux Indians.

New Lisbon, O.

1,091. July 26th—Portion of Brig.-General Shackleford's Cavalry; surrender of John Morgan and the remnant of his forces.

Dead Buffalo Lake, Dakota Terr.

1,092. July 26th—1st Minnesota Cavalry, 3d Minnesota Battery, 6th, 7th, and 10th Minnesota Volunteers; fight with the Sioux Indians.

Pattacassey Creek (or Mount Tabor Church), N. C.

1,093. July 26th—Troops of the district, North Carolina.

Marshall, Mo.

1,094. July 28th—4th Missouri Militia Cavalry.

Richmond and Lexington, Ky.

1,095. July 28th—Organizations not stated.

Coldwater, Miss.

1,096. July 28th—Illinois troops.

Stony Lake, Dakota Terr.

1,097. July 28th—1st Minnesota Cavalry, 3d Minnesota Battery, 6th, 7th, and 10th Minnesota Volunteers; fight with the Sioux Indians.

St. Catharine's Creek, near Natchez, Miss.

1,098. July 28th—Detachment of the 72d Illinois Volunteers.

18(3]   **Paris, Ky.**
1,099. July 29th—Troops not specified.

Irvine, Estill Co., Ky.
1,100. July 30th—14th Kentucky Cavalry.

Saline Co., Mo.
1,101. July 30th—1st and 4th Missouri Enrolled Militia.

Missouri River, Dakota Terr.
1,102. July 30th—1st Minnesota Cavalry, 3d Minnesota Battery, and 6th Minnesota Volunteers ; fight with Indians.

Rappahannock Station, Kelly's Ford, and Brandy Station, Va.
1,103. August 1st to 3d—1st Division of Cavalry, Brig.-General Buford.

Jackson, La.
1,104. August 3d—73d, 75th, and 78th U. S. Colored Troops.

Dutch Gap, James River, Va.
1,105. August 5th—U. S. Gunboats Commodore Barney and Cohasset.

Waterford, Va.
1,106. August 7th—Detachments of 1st Connecticut and 6th Michigan Cavalry.

New Madrid, Mo.
1,107. August 7th—One company of the 24th Missouri Volunteers.

Sparta, Tenn.
1,108. August 9th—Cavalry of the Army of the Cumberland.

Grenada, Miss.
1,109. August 13th—3d, 4th, 9th, and 11th Illinois, 3d Michigan, and 2d Iowa Cavalry, and 9th Illinois Volunteers.

Pineville, Mo.
1,110. August 13th—6th Missouri Militia Cavalry.

West Point, White River, Ark.
1,111. August 14th—Union Gunboats Lexington, Cricket, and Mariner, with the 32d Iowa Volunteers.

Pasquotank, N. C.
1,112. August 18th — 1st New York Mounted Rifles and 11th Pennsylvania Cavalry.

Pueblo, Colorado, New Mexico.
1,113. August 18th—Three companies of the 1st New Mexico Cavalry.

Lawrence, Kan.
1,114. August 21st—Plunder and massacre by Quantrell.

Coldwater, Miss.
1,115. August 21st—3d and 4th Iowa and 5th Illinois Cavalry.

Chattanooga, Tenn.
1,116. August 21st—Artillery of Maj.-General Rosecrans' army.

Coyle Tavern, near Fairfax Court House, Va.
1,117. August 24th—2d Massachusetts Cavalry.

King George Co., Va.

1,118. August 24th—3d Division Cavalry Corps, Army of the Potomac.

Waynesville, Mo.

1,119. August 25th—Detachment of the 5th Missouri Militia Cavalry.

Averill's Raid in W. Va.

1,120. August 25th to 30th—Cavalry, passed through Hardy, Pendleton, Highland, Bath, Greenbrier, and Pocahontas Counties.

Brownsville, Ark.

1,121. August 25th and 26th—Davidson's Cavalry Division, Department of Missouri.

Perryville, Ark.

1,122. August 26th—6th Missouri Militia, 3d Wisconsin and 2d Kansas Cavalry, and 2d Indiana Battery.

Rocky Gap, near White Sulphur Springs, Va.

1,123. August 26th—2d and 3d West Virginia and 14th Pennsylvania Cavalry, and 3d and 8th West Virginia Volunteers.

Vinegar Hill, Morris Island, S. C.

1,124. August 26th—Troops commanded by Maj.-General Q. A. Gillmore. See Fort Wayne, July 10th.

Vicksburg, Miss.

1,125. August 27th—5th Heavy Artillery (U. S. Colored Troops).

Clark's Neck, Lawrence Co., Ky.

1,126. August 27th—39th Kentucky Volunteers.

Bayou Metoe, Ark.

1,127. August 27th—Davidson's Cavalry Division, Department of the Missouri.

Maysville, Ala.

1,128. August 28th—4th Kentucky Cavalry.

Bottom's Bridge (or Dry Creek), Va.

1,129. August 29th—1st New York Mounted Rifles and 5th Pennsylvania Cavalry.

Austin, Ark.

1,130. August 31st—Davidson's Cavalry Division, Department of the Missouri.

Bayou Metoe, Ark.

1,131. September 1st—Rice's Division, Department of Arkansas.

Barbee's Cross Roads, Va.

1,132. September 1st—Detachment of 6th Ohio Cavalry.

Devil's Back Bone (known also as Fort Smith and Cotton Gap), Ark.

1,133. September 1st—1st Arkansas Volunteers, 6th Missouri Militia, 2d Kansas Cavalry, and 2d Indiana Battery.

White Stone Hill, Dakota Terr.

1,134. September 3d to 5th—2d Nebraska, 6th Iowa, and one company of the 7th Iowa Cavalry; fight with Indians.

Limestone Station, near Telford, Tenn.

1,135. September 5th—Five companies of the 100th Ohio Volunteers.

1863.]   **Moorefield, W. Va.**

1,136. September 5th—1st West Virginia Volunteers.

Brandy Station, Va.

1,137. September 6th—Cavalry, Army of the Potomac.

Evacuation of Battery Gregg and Fort Wagner, Morris Island, S. C.

1,138. September 7th—Maj.-General Q. A. Gillmore's troops and the U. S. Navy.

Bear Skin Lake, Mo.

1,139. September 7th—2d Missouri Cavalry.

Ashley's Mills, Ark.

1,140. September 7th—Davidson's Cavalry Division, Department of the Missouri.

Atchafalaya River, La.

1,141. September 7th—2d Brigade, 2d Division, 13th Corps.

Baton Rouge, La.

1,142. September 8th—4th Wisconsin Cavalry.

Night Attack on Fort Sumter, S. C.

1,143. September 8th—413 Marines and Sailors, commanded by Commodore Stevens, U. S. Navy.

Bath, Va.

1,144. September 8th—7th Pennsylvania Cavalry.

Sabine Pass, La.

1,145. September 8th—U. S. Navy, escort to the troops of the 19th Corps, commanded by Maj.-General Franklin.

Cumberland Gap, Tenn.

1,146. September 9th—Cavalry Division and Army of the Ohio.

Weber's Falls, Ind. Terr.

1,147. September 9th—2d Colorado Cavalry.

Dardenelle, Ark.

1,148. September 9th—2d Kansas Cavalry and 2d Indiana Battery.

Graysville, Ga.

1,149. September 10th—Cavalry, Army of the Cumberland.

Little Rock, Ark.

1,150. September 10th—Troops of the Department of Arkansas and Cavalry Division of the Department of the Missouri.

Brimstone Creek, Tenn.

1,151. September 10th—11th Kentucky Mounted Volunteers.

Knoxville, Tenn., occupied.

1,152. September 10th—Army of the Ohio, Maj.-General Burnside.

Ringgold, Ga.

1,153. September 11th—Advance of the 21st Corps, Army of the Cumberland.

Dug, Alpine, and Stevens' Gap (also known as Davis' Cross Roads), Ga.

1,154. September 11th—Advance of the Army of the Cumberland.

Moorefield, W. Va.

1,155. September 11th—Troops not mentioned.

Waldron, Ark.

1,156. September 11th—14th Kansas Cavalry.

Sterling's Plantation, La.

1,157. September 12th—Battery " E," 1st Missouri Artillery.

Texas Co., Mo.

1,158. September 12th—5th Missouri Militia Cavalry.

Paris, Tenn.

1,159. September 13th—Troops not stated.

Culpepper, Va.

1,160. September 13th—1st, 2d, and 3d Divisions, Cavalry Corps, Army of the Potomac.

Lett's Tan Yard, near Chickamauga, Ga.

1,161. September 13th—Wilder's Brigade of Mounted Infantry.

Brownsville, Ark.

1,162. September 14th and 16th—5th Kansas Cavalry.

Racoon Ford, Rapidan Station, Va.

1,163. September 14th—Cavalry Corps, Army of the Potomac.

Seneca Station, Buffalo Creek, Ind. Terr.

1,164. September 14th—1st Arkansas Volunteers.

Vidalia, La.

1,165. September 14th—3d Missouri Volunteers.

Hendricks, Miss.

1,166. September 15th—10th Missouri Cavalry.

Smithfield, Va.

1,167. September 15th—Detachments of the 1st New York and 12th Pennsylvania Cavalry.

Racoon Ford, Va.

1,168. September 19th—Reconnoisance by 1st Cavalry Division, Army of the Potomac.

Chickamauga, Ga.

1,169. September 19th and 20th—14th Corps, Maj.-General Geo. H. Thomas; 20th Corps, Maj.-General A. McD. McCook; 21st Corps, Maj.-General T. L. Crittenden ; and Reserve Corps, Maj.-General G. Granger; Army of the Cumberland, Maj.-General W. S. Rosecrans.

Bristol, Tenn.

1,170. September 21st—Foster's Cavalry Brigade, Shackleford's Cavalry Division, of Army of the Ohio.

White's Ford, Va.

1,171. September 21st—Cavalry of the Army of the Potomac.

Johnson Depot, Tenn.

1,172. September 22d—8th Tennessee Volunteers.

Jack's Shop, Madison Court House, Va.

1,173. September 22d—1st Division, Cavalry Corps, Army of the Potomac.

1863.]   Carter's Station, Tenn.

1,174. September 22d—3d Brigade, Cavalry Division, Army of the Ohio.

Blountsville, Tenn.

1,175. September 22d—2d Mounted Brigade, Cavalry Division, Army of the Ohio.

Rockville, Md.

1,176. September 22d—11th New York Cavalry.

Zollicoffer, Tenn.

1,177. September 24th—3d Brigade, Cavalry Division, Army of the Ohio.

Upperville, Va.

1,178. September 25th—1st Maryland Potomac Home Brigade of Cavalry.

Red Bone Church, Mo.

1,179. September 25th—2d Wisconsin Cavalry.

Calhoun (or Haguewood Prairie), Tenn.

1,180. September 26th—Cavalry of the Army of the Ohio.

Moffat's Station, Franklin Co. (also called Haguewood Station), Ark.

1,181. September 27th—Detachment of the 1st Arkansas Volunteers.

McMinnville, Tenn.

1,182. September 28th—Troops not given.

Sterling's Farm, near Morganzia, La.

1,183. September 29th—19th Iowa and 26th Indiana Volunteers.

Swallow's Bluff, Tenn.

1,184. September 30th—7th Kansas and 7th Illinois Cavalry.

Anderson's Gap, Tenn.

1,185. October 1st—21st Kentucky Volunteers.

Anderson's Cross Roads, Tenn.

1,186. October 2d—1st Wisconsin, 2d Indiana, and 1st Tennessee Cavalry, Army of the Cumberland.

Thompson Cove, Tenn.

1,187. October 3d—1st Brigade, 2d Division Cavalry, and Wilder's Brigade of Mounted Infantry.

McMinnville, Tenn.

1,188. October 3d—4th Tennessee Volunteers.

Murfreesboro Road, Tenn.

1,189. October 4th—2d Kentucky Cavalry and Wilder's Brigade of Mounted Infantry.

Newton, La.

1,190. October 4th—Organizations not stated.

Neosho, Mo.

1,191. October 4th—Three companies of the 6th Missouri Militia Cavalry.

Stockade at Stone River, Tenn.

1,192. October 5th—One company of the 19th Michigan Volunteers.

Harper's Ferry, Va.

1,193. October 5th—Troops not stated.

Near Blue Springs, Tenn.

1,194. October 5th—Portion of General Burnside's forces.

New Albany, Miss.

1,195. October 5th—Troops not given.

Glasgow, Ky.

1,196. October 5th—37th Kentucky Mounted Infantry.

Wartrace, Tenn.

1,197. October 5th—5th Iowa Cavalry.

Baxter Springs, near Fort Scott, Ark.

1,198. October 6th—Detachments of the 3d Wisconsin and 14th Kansas Cavalry, and 12th Kansas Volunteers (83d U. S. Colored Troops); the prisoners were robbed and murdered by the rebels, commanded by Quantrell.

Fort Blair, Waldron, Ark.

1,199. October 6th—Detachment of 3d Wisconsin Cavalry.

Como, Miss.

1,200. October 7th—Troops not given.

Shelbyville Pike, near Farmington, Tenn.

1,201. October 7th—1st, 2d, and 4th Ohio, and 2d Kentucky Cavalry, and Wilder's Brigade of Mounted Infantry.

Charlestown, Va.

1,202. October 8th—Troops not given.

Salem, Miss.

1,203. October 8th—Colonels McCrellis' and Phillips' Cavalry Brigades.

Warsaw, Mo.

1,204. October 8th—7th Missouri Militia Cavalry.

Sugar Creek, near Pulaski, Tenn.

1,205. October 9th—3d Brigade, 2d Cavalry Division.

Rapidan, Va.

1,206. October 10th—1st Division Cavalry, Army of the Potomac.

Ingham's Plantation, Miss.

1,207. October 10th—2d Wisconsin Cavalry.

James City, Rappahannock (also called Robertson's Run), Va.

1,208. October 10th—3d Cavalry Division, Army of the Potomac.

Blue Springs, Tenn.

1,209. October 10th—Shackleford's Cavalry Division, and Infantry of the 9th Corps, Army of the Ohio.

Vermilion Bayou, La.

1,210. October 10th—1st Brigade, 1st Division, 19th Corps.

Rheatown, Tenn.

1,211. October 11th—2d Brigade, Cavalry Division, Army of the Ohio.

Henderson's Mill, Tenn.

1,212. October 11th—5th Indiana Cavalry.

1863.]   Collinsville, Tenn.

1,213. October 11th—66th Indiana Volunteers and 13th U. S. Infantry.

Jeffersonton, Va.

1,214. October 12th—2d Cavalry Division, Army of the Potomac.

Ingham's Mills, near Byhalia, Miss.

1,215. October 12th— 2d Brigade of Cavalry of the 16th Corps.

Culpepper White Sulphur Springs (also called Warrenton Springs), Va.

1,216. October 12th and 13th—Cavalry Corps, Army of the Potomac.

Merrill's Crossing to Lamine Crossing (also known as Marshall, Arrow Rock, Blackwater, and Jonesboro'), Mo.

1,217. October 12th and 13th—1st, 4th, and 7th Missouri Militia Cavalry, Enrolled Militia Infantry, and 1st Missouri Militia Battery.

Wyatt, Tallahatchee, Miss.

1,218. October 13th—2d Brigade, Cavalry Division, 16th Corps.

Big Black River, Miss.

1,219. October 13th—Reconnoisance of Infantry and Cavalry commanded by Maj.-General McPherson.

Maysville, Ala.

1,220. October 13th—1st Division Cavalry Corps, Army of the Cumberland.

Blountsville, Tenn.

1,221. October 13th—3d Brigade, Cavalry Division, Army of the Ohio.

Bulltown, Braxton Co., Va.

1,222. October 13th—Detachment of the 6th and 11th West Virginia Volunteers.

Auburn, Va.

1,223. October 14th—Portion of the 1st Division, 2d Corps, Army of the Potomac.

Bristoe Station, Va.

1,224. October 14th—2d Corps, Warren's; portion of Syke's 5th Corps, assisted by 2d Cavalry Division, Army of the Potomac.

Salt Lick, Va.

1,225. October 14th—6th West Virginia Volunteers.

Canton, Miss.

1,226. October 15th—Portion of the 15th and 17th Corps, commanded by Maj.-General McPherson.

McLean's Ford (also known as Liberty Mills), Va.

1,227. October 15th—New Jersey Brigade, 3d Corps, Army of the Potomac.

Hedgeville, Va.

1,228. October 15th—Detachment of 1st New York and 12th Pennsylvania Cavalry and 116th Ohio Volunteers.

Blackburn Ford, Va.

1,229. October 15th—Portion of the 2d Corps, Army of the Potomac.

Brownsville, Miss.

1,230. October 16th to 18th—Portion of the 15th and 17th Corps, Maj.-General McPherson.

7*

Cross Timbers, Mo.

1,231. October 16th—18th Iowa Volunteers.

Destruction of two Blockade Runners in Tampa Bay, Fla.

1,232. October 17th—Union Gunboats Tahonia and Adele.

Clinton, Miss.

1,233. October 17th—Detachment of the Army of the Tennessee, commanded by Maj.-General McPherson.

Rapidan, Va.

1,234. October 17th—1st Division, Cavalry Corps, Army of the Potomac.

Humansville, Mo.

1,235. October 17th—6th Missouri Militia Cavalry.

Charlestown, Va.

1,236. October 18th—9th Maryland Volunteers.

Berrysville, Va.

1,237. October 18th—34th Massachusetts Volunteers and 17th Indiana Battery.

Buckland Mills, Va.

1,238. October 19th—3d Division, Cavalry Corps, Army of the Potomac.

Barton Station, Miss.

1,239. October 20th—Troops of the Army of the Tennessee.

Philadelphia, Tenn.

1,240. October 20th to 22d—45th Ohio Mounted Infantry, 1st, 11th, and 12th Kentucky Cavalry, and 24th Indiana Battery.

Cherokee Station, Ala.

1,241. October 21st—Osterhaus' 1st Division, 15th Corps, Army of the Tennessee.

Opelousas, La.

1,242. October 21st—Franklin's Division of Banks' troops.

Beverly Ford and Rappahannock Crossing, Va.

1,243. October 22d—2d Pennsylvania and 1st Maine Cavalry.

New Madrid Bend, Tenn.

1,244. October 22d—32d Iowa Volunteers.

Supply Train, Tullahoma, Tenn.

1,245. October 23d—70th Indiana Volunteers.

Bealton and Rappahannock Bridge, Va.

1,246. October 24th—1st Division, Cavalry Corps, Army of the Potomac.

Sweetwater, Tenn.

1,247. October 24th—Cavalry, Army of the Ohio.

Colliersville, Tenn.

1,248. October 25th—Troops not given.

Pine Bluff, Ark.

1,249. October 25th—5th Kansas and 1st Indiana Cavalry.

Creek Agency, Ind. Terr.

1,250. October 25th—1st Kansas Indian Home Guards and 2d Indiana Battery.

1863.]   Cane Creek (also Bear Creek, or Tuscumbia), Ala.

1,251. October 26th—1st Division, Osterhaus, 15th Corps.

Philadelphia, Tenn.

1,252. October 26th—Confederate Official Reports.

Vincent's Cross Roads (or Bay Springs, Tishamingo Co.), Miss.

1,253. October 26th—1st Alabama Union Cavalry.

Brown's Ferry, Tenn.

1,254. October 27th—Detachments from 5th, 6th, and 23d Kentucky, 1st, 6th, 41st, 93d, and 124th Ohio, and 26th Indiana Volunteers.

Wauhatchie, Tenn.

1,255. October 27th—11th Corps, and 2d Division, 12th Corps.

Clarksville, Ark.

1,256. October 28th—3d Wisconsin Cavalry.

Leiper's Ferry, Tenn.

1,257. October 28th—11th and 37th Kentucky and 112th Illinois Volunteers.

Cherokee Station, Ala.

1,258. October 29th—1st Division, 15th Corps.

Washington, N. C.

1,259. November 1st—Organizations not given.

Fayetteville, Tenn.

1,260. November 1st—4th Indiana Cavalry.

Brazios de Santiago, Tex.

1,261. November 2d—Troops of the 13th Corps.

Centerville and Pine Factory, Tenn.

1,262. November 3d—A mixed command under Lieut.-Colonel Scully, 10th Tennessee Volunteers.

Grand Coteau (or Bayou Bourbeaux, or Carrion Crow Bayou), La.

1,263. November 3d—3d and 4th Divisions, 13th Corps.

Colliersville, Tenn.

1,264. November 3d—Cavalry Brigade, 16th Corps.

Lawrenceburg, Tenn.

1,265. November 4th—14th Michigan Mounted Infantry.

Moscow, Tenn.

1,266. November 4th—Cavalry Brigade, 16th Corps.

Metly's Ford, Little Tennessee River.

1,267. November 4th—Cavalry of the Army of the Ohio.

Mill Point, Pocahontas Co., W. Va.

1,268. November 5th—14th Pennsylvania and 3d West Virginia Cavalry.

Kincaels, Tenn.

1,269. November 6th—Troops not stated.

Rogersville, Tenn.

1,270. November 6th—7th Ohio Cavalry, 2d Tennessee Mounted Infantry, and 2d Illinois Battery.

Droop Mountain, Va.

1,271. November 6th—14th Pennsylvania, and 2d and 5th West Virginia Cavalry, 8th and 10th West Virginia, and 28th Ohio Volunteers, and Battery B, West Virginia Artillery.

Rappahannock Station, Va.

1,272. November 7th—5th Wisconsin, 5th and 6th Maine, 49th and 119th Pennsylvania, and 121st New York Volunteers, supported by the remainder of the 6th and portion of the 5th Corps, Army of the Potomac.

Kelly's Ford, Va.

1,273. November 7th—1st U. S. Sharpshooters, 40th New York, 1st and 20th Indiana, 3d and 5th Michigan, and 110th Pennsylvania Volunteers, supported by the remainder of the 3d Corps, Army of the Potomac.

Stevensburg, Va.

1,274. November 7th—3d Cavalry Division, Army of the Potomac.

Clarksville, Ark.

1,275. November 8th—3d Wisconsin Cavalry.

Muddy Run, near Culpepper, Va.

1,276. November 8th—1st Division, Cavalry Corps, Army of the Potomac.

Bayou Sara, Miss.

1,277. November 9th—From Confederate Official Reports.

Natchez, Miss.

1,278. November 11th—58th U. S. Colored Troops (6th Mississippi).

Roseville, Ark.

1,279. November 12th—Two companies 2d Kansas Cavalry.

Trinity River, Cal.

1,280. November 13th—Two companies 1st Battalion California Mountaineer Infantry.

Mill Creek Valley, W. Va.

1,281. November 13th—Troops not stated.

Palmyra, Tenn.

1,282. November 13th—Mounted Infantry, commanded by Captain Cutter.

Huff's Ferry, Tenn.

1,283. November 14th—111th Ohio, 107th Illinois, 11th and 13th Kentucky, and 23d Michigan Volunteers, and 24th Michigan Battery.

Rockford, Tenn.

1,284. November 14th—1st Kentucky Cavalry and 45th Ohio Mounted Infantry.

Marysville, Tenn.

1,285. November 14th—11th Kentucky Cavalry.

Loudon Creek, Tenn.

1,286. November 15th—111th Ohio Volunteers.

Lenoirs, Tenn.

1,287. November 15th—Cavalry and Infantry of the Army of the Ohio.

1863.]   Holston River, near Knoxville, Tenn.

1,288. November 15th—11th Kentucky, 45th Ohio, and 37th Kentucky Mounted Infantry.

                        Charles City Cross Roads, Va.

1,289. November 16th—Cavalry expedition, commanded by Colonel West.

                        Campbell Station, Tenn.

1,290. November 16th—9th Corps, 2d Division, 23d Corps, and Cavalry, Army of the Ohio.

                        Siege of Knoxville, Tenn.

1,291. November 17th to December 4th—Army of the Ohio.

                        Willow Creek, Cal.

1,292. November 17th—1st California Battalion Mountaineer Infantry.

                        Mount Jackson, Va.

1,293. November 17th—1st New York Cavalry.

                        Mustang Island, near Aranzas Pass, Tex.

1,294. November 17th—13th and 14th Maine, 34th Iowa, and 8th Indiana Volunteers, and Battery F, 1st Missouri Artillery.

                        Carrion Crow Bayou, La.

1,295. November 18th—6th Missouri Cavalry.

                        Union City, Tenn.

1,296. November 19th—2d Illinois Cavalry.

                        Waterproof, La.

1,297. November 21st—Steamer Welcome.

                        Chattanooga, Tenn.

1,298. November 23d to 25th—4th Corps and 14th Corps, Army of the Cumberland ; 11th Corps and Geary's Division of the 12th Corps ; and 15th Corps, Army of the Tennessee; this includes Orchard Knob on the 23d, Lookout Mountain on the 24th, and Missionary Ridge on the 25th.

                        Barnwell's Island, S. C.

1,299. November 24th—33d U. S. Colored Troops, 1st South Carolina.

                        Greenville, N. C.

1,300. November 25th—12th New York Cavalry, 1st North Carolina Volunteers, and 24th New York Battery.

                        Bonfouca, La.

1,301. November 26th—31st Massachusetts Volunteers and 4th Massachusetts Battery.

                        Sparta, Tenn.

1,302. November 26th—1st Tennessee and 9th Pennsylvania Cavalry.

                        Bersheeba Springs, Tenn.

1,303. November 26th—Alabama and Tennessee Scouts.

                        Warm Springs, N. C.

1,304. November 26th—Troops not given.

                        Kingston, Tenn.

1,305. November 26th—Cavalry, Army of the Ohio.

Operations at Mine Run, Va.

1,306. November 26th to 28th—1st, 2d, 3d, 5th, and 6th Corps, and 1st and 2d Cavalry Divisions, Army of the Potomac; includes engagements at *Raccoonford, Bartlett's Mills, Robertson's Tavern, and New Hope*, and is also known as Locust Grove, Payne's Tavern, and Orange Grove.

Ringgold, Greysville, Pea Vine Creek, and Taylor's Ridge, Ga.

1,307. November 27th—Johnson's Division, 14th Corps; Osterhaus' Division, 15th Corps; and Geary's Division, 12th Corps.

Cleveland, Tenn.

1,308. November 27th—2d Brigade, 2d Cavalry Division, Colonel Eli Long.

Fort Esperanza, Tex.

1,309. November 27th to 29th—8th and 18th Indiana, 33d and 99th Illinois, 23d and 34th Iowa, 13th and 15th Maine Volunteers, 7th Michigan, and Company F, 1st Missouri Battery, portions of 1st and 2d Divisions, 13th Corps.

Louisville, Tenn.

1,310. November 28th—6th Illinois Cavalry.

Fort Sanders, Knoxville, Tenn.

1,311. November 29th—Army of the Ohio; during siege of Knoxville.

Salyersville, Ky.

1,312. November 30th—14th Kentucky Volunteers.

Ripley, Miss.

1,313. December 1st—2d Brigade, Cavalry Division, Army of the Tennessee.

Walker's Ford, Clinch River, W. Va.

1,314. December 2d—5th Indiana and 14th Illinois Cavalry, 21st Ohio Battery, 65th, 116th, and 118th Indiana Volunteers

Salisbury, Tenn.

1,315. December 3d—2d Brigade, Cavalry Division, 16th Corps.

Niobrera, Neb.

1,316. December 4th—One company 7th Iowa Cavalry.

Moscow Station (or Wolf River Bridge), Miss.

1,317. December 4th—Cavalry Division, 16th Corps.

Clinch Mountain, Tenn

1,318. December 6th—Cavalry, Army of the Ohio.

Natchez, Miss.

1,319. December 7th—One company 4th Iowa Cavalry.

Creelsboro', Ky.

1,320. December 7th—13th Kentucky Cavalry.

Celina, Tenn.

1,321. December 7th—13th Kentucky Cavalry.

Princeton, Ark.

1,322. December 8th—Detachment of Cavalry.

Averill's Raid, Southwestern Va.

1,323. December 8th to 21st—2d, 3d, 4th, and 8th West Virginia Mounted Infantry, 14th Pennsylvania, and Dodson's Battalion Cavalry, and Battery G, West Virginia Artillery.

1863.]   Bean's Station, Tenn.
1,324. December 10th—Bond's Brigade of Cavalry, Army of the Ohio.

                                Morristown, Tenn.
1,325. December 10th—Garrard's Brigade of Cavalry, Army of the Ohio.

                                Moresburg, Tenn.
1,326. December 10th—Cavalry, Army of the Ohio.

                                Duval's Bluff, Ark.
1,327. December 12th—8th Missouri Cavalry.

                        Big Sewell and Meadow Bluff, W. Va.
1,328. December 12th—12th Ohio Volunteers.

                                Bean's Station, Tenn.
1,329. December 14th—Cavalry Division, Army of the Ohio.

                                Sangster's Station, Va.
1,330. December 15th—150th New York Volunteers.

                            Blain's Cross Roads, Tenn.
1,331. December 16th—Army of the Ohio.

                                Rodney, Miss.
1,332. December 17th and 24th—1st Mississippi Marine Brigade, Cavalry and
          Infantry.

                                Indian Town, N. C.
1,333. December 18th—36th U. S. Colored Troops, 2d North Carolina, and 5th
          U. S. Colored Troops.

                            Barren Fork, Ind. Terr.
1,334. December 19th—1st and 3d Kansas Indian Home Guards.

                                Cleveland, Tenn.
1,335. December 22d—From Confederate sources.

                                Jacksonport, Ark.
1,336. December 23d—8d Missouri Cavalry.

                        Bolivar and Summerville, Tenn.
1,337. December 24th and 25th—7th Illinois Cavalry.

                                Lafayette, Tenn.
1,338. December 25th—117th Illinois Volunteers.

                        Legarsville, Stone Inlet, S. C.
1,339. December 25th—U. S. Gunboat Marblehead.

                                Port Gibson, Miss.
1,340. December 26th—Mississippi Marine Brigade of Infantry and Cavalry.

                                Colliersville, Tenn.
1,341. December 27th and 28th—Cavalry of the Army of the Tennessee.

                                Charleston, Tenn.
1,342. December 28th—Detachments of Infantry and Cavalry, commanded by
          Colonel Laibold, 2d Missouri Volunteers, and 4th Ohio Cavalry, guarding
          a wagon train.

Talbot's Station and Mossy Creek, Tenn.

1,343. December 29th—1st Brigade, 2d Division, 23d Corps, 1st Tennessee, 1st Wisconsin, and 2d and 4th Indiana Cavalry, and 24th Indiana Battery.

Matagorda Bay, Tex.

1,344. December 29th and 30th—Three companies of the 13th Maine and Gunboat Sciota.

St. Augustine, Fla.

1,345. December 30th—10th Connecticut and 24th Massachusetts Volunteers.

Greenville, N. C.

1,346. December 30th—Detachment of the 12th New York, 23d New York Battery, and 1st North Carolina Volunteers.

Waldron, Ark.

1,347. December 30th—2d Kansas Cavalry.

1864.—(779.)

Rectortown (or Five Points), Va.

1,348. January 1st—1st Maryland Cavalry, Potomac Home Brigade.

Jonesville, Va.

1,349. January 3d—Detachment of the 16th Illinois Cavalry and 22d Ohio Battery.

Fort Sumner, New Mexico.

1,350. January 4th—Company B, 2d California, Apaches, and citizens; fight with the Navajo Indians.

Martin's Creek, Ark.

1,351. January 7th—11th Missouri Cavalry.

Madisonville, La.

1,352. January 7th—Troops not specified.

Petersburg, W. Va.

1,353. January 8th—Troops not specified.

Turman's Ferry, Ky.

1,354. January 9th—39th Kentucky Volunteers.

London Heights, Va.

1,355. January 10th—1st Maryland Potomac Home Brigade.

Strawberry Plains, Tenn.

1,356. January 10th—Cavalry.

Mayfield, Ky.

1,357. January 12th—58th Illinois Volunteers.

Mossy Creek, Tenn.

1,358. January 13th—Cavalry, commanded by Colonel Cook.

Middleton, Tenn.

1,359. January 14th—35th Iowa Volunteers.

1864.]   **Bealton, Va.**
1,360. January 14th—One company 9th Massachusetts Volunteers.

Terrisville, Cosby Creek, Tenn.
1,361. January 14th—Detachments of the 15th Pennsylvania and 10th Ohio Cavalry.

Grand Gulf, Miss.
1,362. January 16th to 18th—Cavalry and Infantry of the Mississippi Marine Brigade.

Dandridge, Tenn.
1,363. January 16th to 17th—Cavalry Division, Army of the Ohio, and Infantry, 4th Corps.

Lewisburg, Ark.
1,364. January 17th—Detachment of 2d Arkansas Cavalry.

Branchville (or Ivy Ford, near Pine Bluff), Ark.
1,365. January 19th—5th Kansas Cavalry.

Island No. 76, Miss.
1,366. January 20th—Battery E, 2d Colored Light Artillery.

Tracy City, Tenn.
1,367. January 20th—Detachment of the 20th Connecticut Volunteers.

Near Dalton, Ga.
1,368. January 21st—28th Kentucky Mounted Infantry and 4th Michigan Cavalry.

Armstrong Ferry, Tenn.
1,369. January 22d—Troops not specified.

Rolling Prairie, Ark.
1,370. January 23d—11th Missouri Cavalry.

Baker Springs, Caddo Gap, Ark.
1,371. January 24th—2d and 6th Kansas Cavalry.

Tazewell, Tenn.
1,372. January 24th—34th Kentucky, 116th and 118th Indiana Volunteers, 11th Tennessee Cavalry, and 11th Michigan Battery.

Athens, Ala.
1,373. January 25th—Troops not stated.

Florence, Ala.
1,374. January 26th—Troops commanded by Colonel A. O. Miller, 72d Indiana Volunteers.

Cameron, Va.
1,375. January 27th—Train on the Orange and Alexandria Railroad.

Fair Gardens (or French Broad and Kelly's Ford, near Seviersville), Tenn.
1,376. January 27th—Cavalry Division, Army of the Ohio.

Scott's Mills Road, near Knoxville, Tenn.
1,377. January 27th—13th Kentucky and 23d Michigan Volunteers.

Tunnell Hill, Ga.
1,378. January 28th—Part of 14th Corps, Army of the Cumberland.

Oregon Mountains.

1,379. January 28th—1st California Cavalry.

Medley, near Williamsport, W. Va.

1,380. January 29th—23d Illinois, 2d Maryland Potomac Home Brigade, 1st and 14th West Virginia Volunteers, and 4th West Virginia and Ringgold's (Pa.) Cavalry.

Cumberland Gap, Tenn.

1,381. January 29th—Troops not stated.

Canon de Chelly.

1,382. January — —Troops commanded by Colonel Kit Carson ; fight with Indians.

Bachelor Creek, Newport Barracks, and Newbern, N. C.

1,383. February 1st, 2d, and 3d—132d New York, 9th Vermont, 17th Massachusetts, and 2d North Carolina Volunteers, 12th New York Cavalry, and 3d New York Artillery.

Smithfield, Va.

1,384. February 1st—Detachments of the 3d Pennsylvania Artillery, 20th New York Cavalry, 99th New York and 21st Connecticut Volunteers, and a detachment of Seamen from the U. S. Steamer Minnesota, on the Gunboat Smith Briggs.

Waldron, Ark.

1,385. February 1st—2d Kansas Cavalry.

New Creek Valley, W. Va.

1,386. February 1st—One company of Infantry.

Expedition up the Yazoo, Miss.

1,387. February 1st to March 8th—11th Illinois, 47th U. S. Colored Troops (8th Louisiana), 3d U. S. Colored Cavalry (1st Mississippi), and a portion of Rear-Admiral Porter's Fleet.

Lebanon, Ala.

1,388. February 3d—Detachment from the Army of the Cumberland.

Liverpool Heights, Miss.

1,389. February 3d—11th Illinois Volunteers and 47th U. S. Colored Troops (8th Louisiana).

Patterson Creek, W. Va.

1,390. February 3d—Troops not given.

Springfield, W. Va.

1,391. February 3d—Cavalry, commanded by Lieut.-Colonel Thompson.

Expedition from Vicksburg to Meridian, Miss.

1,392. February 3d to March 5th—Veatch's and A. J. Smith's Divisions, 16th Corps ; Leggett's and Crocker's Divisions, 17th Corps, with 5th and 11th Illinois, 4th Iowa, 10th Missouri, and Foster's Ohio Battalion of Cavalry.

Rolling Prairie, Mo.

1,393. February 4th—8th Missouri Militia Cavalry.

Hot Springs, Ark.

1,394. February 4th—3d Missouri Cavalry.

1864.]

Champion Hills, Baker's Creek, Raymond, and Bolton Depot, Miss.

1,395. February 4th—10th Missouri, 4th Iowa, 5th and 11th Illinois, and Foster's Battalion Ohio Cavalry, and a portion of the 17th Corps; part of expedition to Meridian, Miss.; also designated *Big Black River*.

Moorefield, W. Va.

1,396. February 4th—Portion of the troops of the Department of West Virginia, commanded by Colonel J. A. Mulligan, 23d Illinois Volunteers.

Clinton and Jackson, Miss.

1,397. February 5th—Cavalry and a portion of the 17th Corps; expedition to Meridian.

Quallatown (or Deep Creek), N. C.

1,398. February 5th—Detachment of the 14th Illinois Cavalry.

Cape Girardeau, Mo.

1,399. February 5th—2d Missouri Militia Cavalry.

Wyatt's, Miss.

1,400. February 5th—114th Illinois Volunteers.

Bolivar, Tenn.

1,401. February 6th—Detachment of the 7th Indiana Cavalry.

Morton's Ford, Va.

1,402. February 6th—Reconnoissance by a part of the 2d Corps, Army of the Potomac.

Barnett's Ford, Va.

1,403. February 7th—1st Cavalry Division, Army of the Potomac.

Vidalia, La.

1,404. February 7th—6th U. S. Colored Heavy Artillery, 2d Mississippi, 64th U. S. Colored Troops, 7th Louisiana, and 30th Missouri Volunteers.

Morton, Miss.

1,405. February 8th—Cavalry of Maj.-General Sherman's forces; expedition to Meridian.

Donaldsonville, La.

1,406. February 8th—4th Wisconsin Cavalry.

Near Point Washington, Fla.

1,407. February 9th—Detachment of the 7th Vermont Volunteers.

Morgan's Mills, Spring River, White Co., Ark.

1,408. February 9th—Detachment of the 11th Missouri and 1st Nebraska Cavalry, and 4th Arkansas Infantry.

Barber's Place, South Fork, St. Mary's River, Fla.

1,409. February 9th and 10th—40th Massachusetts Mounted Volunteers and Independent Battalion Massachusetts Cavalry.

Smith's Raids from Germantown, Tenn.

1,410. February 10th to 25th—4th Missouri, 2d New Jersey, 7th Indiana, 19th Pennsylvania, 2d Iowa, 2d, 3d, 6th, 7th, and 9th Illinois, 3d Tennessee, 4th U. S., and 5th Kentucky Cavalry, 72d Indiana Mounted Infantry and other regiments composing Smith's and Grierson's Divisions of Cavalry; co-operation with Sherman's expedition to Meridian.

Rock House, Wayne Co., W. Va.

1,411. February 12th—14th Kentucky Infantry.

Caddo Gap and Scott's Farm, Ark.

1,412. February 12th—2d Kansas Cavalry.

Lake City, Fla.

1,413. February 12th—40th Massachusetts Volunteers and Independent Battalion Massachusetts Cavalry.

Decatur, Miss.

1,414. February 12th—One regiment of the 16th Corps, guarding a wagon train; expedition to Meridian.

Chunky Station, Miss.

1,415. February 12th—20th, 29th, 31st, 45th, and 124th Illinois Volunteers, 17th Corps; expedition to Meridian.

Vicksburg, Miss.

1,416. February 13th—52d U. S. Colored Troops and 2d Mississippi.

Tunnell Hill, Miss.

1,417. February 13th—Cavalry advance of General Sherman's forces; expedition to Meridian.

Ross Landing, Grand Lake, Ark.

1,418. February 14th—51st U. S. Colored Troops and 1st Mississippi.

Meridian, Miss.

1,419. February 14th—Occupation by Maj.-General Sherman's forces; expedition to Meridian.

Gainesville, Fla.

1,420. February 14th—40th Massachusetts Volunteers.

Brentsville, Va.

1,421. February 14th—13th Pennsylvania Cavalry.

Waterproof, La.

1,422. February 14th and 15th—49th U. S. Colored Troops, 11th Louisiana, and Gunboat Forest Rose.

Lauderdale Springs, Miss.

1,423. February 16th—32d Wisconsin Volunteers and an Indiana regiment; expedition to Meridian.

Marion, Miss.

1,424. February 17th—Portion of the 17th Corps; expedition to Meridian.

Loss of the Housatonic.

1,425. February 17th—Charleston Harbor, S. C.

Grosse Tete Bayou, La.

1,426. February 19th—4th Wisconsin Cavalry.

Waugh's Farm, near Batesville, Independence Co., Ark.

1,427. February 19th—11th Missouri Cavalry and 4th Arkansas Infantry.

Holston River, Tenn.

1,428. February 20th—4th Tennessee Volunteers.

1864.]   Olustee (also Ocean Pond and Silver Lake), Fla.

1,429. February 20th—47th, 48th, and 115th New York, 7th Connecticut, 7th New
Hampshire, and 40th Massachusetts Volunteers, 1st Massachusetts Cav-
alry, 54th Massachusetts Colored Troops, 1st North Carolina Colored
Troops, 8th U. S. Colored Troops, 1st and 3d U.S. Artillery, and 3d Rhode
Island Artillery.

Prairie Station, Miss.

1,430. February 20th—Smith's raid in Mississippi.

West Point, Miss.

1,431. February 21st—Smith's raid in Mississippi.

Powell's River Bridge, Tenn.

1,432. February 22d—Two companies of the 34th Kentucky Infantry.

Cumberland Gap, Tenn.

1,433. February 22d—One company of the 91st Indiana Volunteers.

Mulberry Gap (or Wyerman's Mills), Tenn.

1,434. February 22d—9th Tennessee Cavalry.

Ocalona and Mount Ivy (or Ivy Kills), Miss.

1,435. February 22d—Brig.-General W. S. Smith's and B. F. Grierson's Cavalry
Division.

Drainsville, Va.

1,436. February 22d—Detachment of 2d Massachusetts Cavalry.

Luna Landing, Ark.

1.437. February 22d—1st Mississippi Marine Brigade (Missouri Volunteers).

Willmarsh Island, S. C.

1,438. February 22d—85th Pennsylvania and 4th New Hampshire Volunteers.

Johnson's Mills, White Co., Tenn.

1,439. February 22d—Detachment of the 5th Tennessee Cavalry ; prisoners
killed by Champ Ferguson's Guerillas.

Calfkiller Creek, Tenn.

1,440. February 23d—5th Tennessee Cavalry.

Buzzard Roost and Tunnell Hill, Rocky Face Ridge, Ga.

1,441. February 25th to 27th—4th and 14th Corps and Cavalry Corps, Army of the
Cumberland.

Near Canton, Miss.

1,442. February 27th and 28th—Foraging detachments, one of the 3d Iowa and
another of the 32d Iowa Volunteers.

Kilpatrick's Raid from Stevensburg to Richmond, Va.

1,443. February 28th to March 4th—Division of Cavalry, Army of the Potomac.

Dukedom, Ky.

1,444. February 28th—7th Tennessee Cavalry.

Near Yazoo City, Miss.

1,445. February 28th—3d U. S. Colored Cavalry and 1st Mississippi.

Newbern, N. C.

1,446. February 29th—Troops not given.

Taylorsville, South Anna River, Va.
1,447. February 29th—6th New York Cavalry ; Kilpatrick's raid.

Stanardsville and Burton's Ford, Rapidan, Va.
1,448. March 1st—1st, 2d, 5th, and 6th U. S., 6th Pennsylvania, 1st New York, and 1st New Jersey Cavalry.

Brook's Turnpike, Richmond Fortifications, Va.
1,449. March 1st—Cavalry, Army of the Potomac ; Kilpatrick's raid.

Atlee's, Bidnella Cross Roads, Va.
1,450. March 1st—Cavalry, Army of the Potomac ; Kilpatrick's raid.

Near Walkertown, Va.
1,451. March 2d—2d New York Cavalry ; Kilpatrick's raid.

Harrisonburg, La.
1,452. March 2d—Mississippi Squadron, Rear-Admiral Porter.

Tunstall Station, Va.
1,453. March 3d—7th Michigan and 1st Vermont Cavalry ; Kilpatrick's raid.

Rodney, Miss.
1,454. March 4th—Cavalry and Infantry, Mississippi Marine Brigade.

Panther Springs, Tenn.
1,455. March 5th—One company 3d Tennessee.

Yazoo City, Miss.
1,456. March 5th—3d U. S. Colored Cavalry (1st Mississippi), 47th U. S. Colored Troops (8th Louisiana), and 11th Illinois Volunteers ; expedition up Yazoo River.

Coleman's, Miss.
1,457. March 5th—Mississippi Marine Brigade.

Flint Creek, Ark.
1,458. March 6th—14th Kansas Cavalry.

Decatur, Ala.
1,459. March 7th—Troops of the Army of the Tennessee, commanded by General Dodge.

Suffolk, Va.
1,460. March 9th—2d U. S. Colored Cavalry.

Cabletown, Va.
1,461. March 10th—1st New York Veteran Cavalry.

Carrolton Store, Va.
1,462. March 13th—1st New York Mounted Rifles and 11th Pennsylvania Cavalry.

Cheek's Cross Roads, Tenn.
1,463. March 14th—Cavalry, commanded by Colonel Garrard, 7th Ohio Cavalry.

Fort de Russy, La.
1,464. March 14th—Detachments of the 16th and 17th Army Corps, and Mississippi Squadron.

Clarendon, Ark.
1,465. March 15th—8th Missouri Cavalry.

1864.]   **Fort Pillow, Tenn.**

1,466. March 16th—Troops not stated.

Manchester, Tenn.

1,467. March 17th—5th Tennessee Cavalry.

Monticello, Ark.

1,468. March 18th—7th Missouri Cavalry.

Calfkiller River, Tenn.

1,469. March 18th—5th Tennessee Cavalry.

Bersheba Springs, Tenn.

1,470. March 20th—5th Tennessee Cavalry.

Henderson Hills (or Bayou Rapides), La.

1,471. March 21st—Detachment 16th Corps and Cavalry 19th Corps.

Union City, Ky.

1,472. March 24th—7th Tennessee Cavalry.

Fort Anderson, Paducah, Ky

1,473. March 25th—16th Kentucky Cavalry, 122d Illinois Infantry, and 8th U. S. Colored Heavy Artillery (1st Kentucky).

Longview, Ark.

1,474. March 26th—5th Kansas and 7th Missouri Cavalry, and 28th Wisconsin Volunteers.

Danville, Ark.

1,475. March 26th—2d Kansas Cavalry.

Arkadelphia, Ark.

1,476. March 28th—Advance Cavalry, 7th Corps.

Charleston, Ill.

1,477. March 28th—Portion 54th Illinois Volunteers attacked by a mob of Copperheads while assembling from veteran furlough.

Bolivar, Tenn.

1,478. March 29th—6th Tennessee Cavalry.

Mount Elba, Ark.

1,479. March 30th—7th Missouri and 5th Kansas Cavalry, and 28th Wisconsin Volunteers.

Grosse Tete Bayou, La.

1,480. March 30th—Detachment of 118th Illinois Volunteers.

Natchitoches, La.

1,481. March 31st—Cavalry 19th Corps; Red River expedition.

Roach's, or Brook's, Plantation, near Snydersville, Miss.

1,482. March 31st—3d U. S. Colored Cavalry (1st Mississippi).

Near the Rappahannock, Va.

1,483. April 1st—Patrol of 1st Connecticut Cavalry.

Fitzhugh's Woods, Augusta, Ark.

1,484. April 1st—3d Minnesota Volunteers and 8th Missouri Cavalry.

Antoine, Ark.

1,485. April 2d—13th Illinois and 1st Iowa Cavalry; Steele's expedition in cooperation with Banks' expedition.

Spoonville, Terre Noire Creek, Ark.

1,486. April 2d—29th Iowa, 50th Indiana, and 9th Wisconsin Volunteers, and 1st Missouri Cavalry; Steele's expedition.

Crump's Hill (also Pine Woods), La.

1,487. April 2d—14th New York, 2d Louisiana, 2d Illinois, and 16th Missouri Cavalry, and 5th U. S. Colored Artillery; Banks' Red River expedition.

Cleveland, Tenn.

1,488. April 2d—1st Wisconsin Cavalry.

Pensacola, Fla.

1,489. April 2d—One company 14th New York Cavalry.

Okalona, Ark.

1,490. April 3d—1st Missouri and 13th Illinois Cavalry, and 27th Wisconsin, 40th Iowa, 77th Ohio, and 43d Illinois Volunteers, of 1st and 3d Divisions, 7th Corps; Steele's expedition.

Campti, La.

1,491. April 4th—2d and 18th New York and 3d Rhode Island Cavalry, 35th Iowa and 5th Minnesota Volunteers; Banks' Red River expedition.

Elkin's Ford, Little Missouri River, Ark.

1,492. April 4th to 6th—43d Indiana, 29th and 36th Iowa Volunteers, Battery E, 2d Missouri Artillery, and 1st Iowa Cavalry; Steele's expedition.

Roseville, Ark.

1,493. April 5th—75 men of the 2d and 6th Kansas Cavalry.

Stone's Farm, Ark.

1,494. April 5th—20 men of the 6th Kansas Cavalry, 11 of whom were captured and killed by guerillas.

Quicksand Creek, Ky.

1,495. April 6th—Company I, 14th Kentucky Volunteers.

Wilson's Farm, La.

1,496. April 7th—Advance Cavalry, 19th Corps; Banks' Red River expedition.

Harney Lake Valley, Or.

1,497. April 7th—1st Oregon Cavalry.

Plain's Store, near Port Hudson, La.

1,498. April 7th—Detachment of the 118th Illinois and 21st New York Battery, and 3d Illinois Cavalry.

Pembescott Bayou, near Osceola, Ark.

1,499. April 8th—Battery I, 2d Missouri Light Artillery.

Wolf River, Tenn.

1,500. April 8th—Cavalry, commanded by General Grierson.

Sabine Cross Roads (also known as Mansfield and Pleasant Grove), La.

1,501. April 8th—Cavalry Division, 3d and 4th Divisions, 13th Corps; 1st Division, 19th Corps, Army of the Department of the Gulf, under Banks.

1864.]   **Pleasant Hills, La.**

1,502. April 9th—Cavalry Division, 1st and 3d Divisions, 16th Corps; 1st Division, 19th Corps; Banks' Red River expedition.

Prairie D'Ann, Ark.

1,503. April 10th to 13th—1st Arkansas, 18th, 29th, 33d, 36th, and 40th Iowa, 50th Indiana, 43d Illinois, 27th Wisconsin, and 12th Kansas Volunteers, 2d and 3d Missouri, 13th Illinois, 2d, 6th, and 14th Kansas and 1st Iowa Cavalry, Battery A, 3d Illinois, and 2d Indiana Artillery; Steele's expedition.

Little Cacapon, Va.

1,504. April 10th—Company K, 54th Pennsylvania Volunteers.

Fort Pillow, Tenn.

1,505. April 12th—11th U. S. Colored Troops (6th U. S. Colored Heavy Artillery and 1st Alabama), Battery F, 2d U. S. Colored Light Artillery, and Bradford's Battalion of 13th Tennessee Cavalry, about 600 men.

Fremont's Orchard, near Denver, Col. Terr.

1,506. April 12th—Two companies of the 1st Colorado Cavalry.

Pleasant Hill (or Blair's Landing), La.

1,507. April 12th—Ironclads Osage and Lexington, and troops of 17th Corps on transports; Red River expedition.

Indian Bay, Ark.

1,508. April 13th—56th U. S. Colored Troops (3d Arkansas).

Florence, Ala.

1,509. April 13th—Detachment of the 9th Ohio Cavalry.

Cleveland, Tenn.

1,510. April 13th—1st Wisconsin Cavalry.

Moscow, Ark.

1,511. April 13th—18th Iowa Volunteers, 2d Indiana Battery, and 6th Kansas Cavalry; Steele's raid in Arkansas.

Paintsville, Ky.

1,512. April 13th—Kentucky Volunteers, commanded by Colonel Gallup, 14th Kentucky.

Smithfield (or Cherry Grove), Va.

1,513. April 14th—9th New Jersey, 23d and 25th Massachusetts, and 118th New York Volunteers.

Half Mount, Magoffin Co., Ky.

1,514. April 14th—Kentucky Volunteers, commanded by Colonel Gallup, 14th Kentucky.

Dutch Mills, Ark.

1,515. April 14th—6th Kansas Cavalry; Steele's raid.

Bristoe Station, Va.

1,516. April 15th—13th Pennsylvania Cavalry.

Liberty Post-Office, Ark.

1,517. April 15th—29th Iowa, 50th Indiana, and 9th Wisconsin Volunteers; Steele's campaign.

XIII.—8

Occupation of Camden, Ark.

1,518. April 15th and 16th—Advance of 17th Corps; Steele's campaign.

King's River, Carroll Co., Ark.

1,519. April 16th—2d Arkansas Cavalry.

Scullyville, Ind. Terr.

1,520. April 16th—3d Kansas Indian Home Guards.

Plymouth, N. C.

1,521. April 17th to 20th—85th New York, 103d Pennsylvania, and 16th Connecticut, assisted by the Navy, under Lieut.-Commander Flusser; includes engagements at Forts Gray, Wessells, and Williams.

Decatur, Ala.

1,522. April 17th—25th Wisconsin Volunteers.

Poison Springs, eight miles from Camden, Ark.

1,523. April 18th—Forage Train, 18th Iowa Volunteers, 79th U. S. Colored Troops (2d Kansas), and 6th Kansas Cavalry; Steele's campaign.

Boyken's Mills, S. C.

1,524. April 18th—54th Massachusetts U. S. Colored Troops.

Pound Gap, Ky.

1,525. April 19th—45th Kentucky Volunteers.

Natchitoches, La.

1,526. April 19th—4th Brigade, Cavalry Division, 19th Corps; Banks' expedition.

Waterproof, La.

1,527. April 20th—63d U. S. Colored Troops (9th Louisiana).

Cotton Plant, Cache River, Ark.

1,528. April 21st—8th Missouri Cavalry.

Red Bone, Miss.

1,529. April 21st—2d Wisconsin Cavalry.

Near Tunica Bend, Red River, La.

1,530. April 22d—Three companies of the 3d Rhode Island Cavalry on transports.

Swan Lake, Ark.

1,531. April 23d—5th Kansas Cavalry.

Moneti's Bluff, Cana River, La.

1,532. April 23d—Cavalry Division and 3d Brigade, 1st Division, 19th Corps, and 3d Division, 13th Corps; Banks' Red River expedition.

Cloutersville, La.

1,533. April 23d and 24th—Portions of 13th, 17th, and 19th Corps; Red River expedition.

Nickajack Trace, Ga.

1,534. April 23d—Detachment of the 92d Illinois Volunteers.

Jacksonport, Ark.

1,535. April 24th—1st Nebraska Cavalry.

Wautauga Bridge (or Carter's Station), Tenn.

1,536. April 25th and 26th—10th Michigan Cavalry.

1864.]   **Marks' Mills, Ark.**

1,537. April 25th—36th Iowa, 77th Ohio, and 43d Indiana Volunteers, Battery E, 2d Missouri Light Artillery, and 1st Indiana and 7th Missouri Cavalry; Steele's campaign in Arkansas.

Red River, La.

1,538. April 26th—U. S. Gunboats Cricket and Fort Hindman.

Moro Creek, Ark.

1,539. April 26th—33d and 40th Iowa Volunteers, and 5th Kansas, 2d and 4th Missouri, and 1st Iowa Cavalry; Steele's campaign.

Alexandria, La.

1,540. April 26th—14th New York and 6th Missouri Cavalry; Red River expedition.

Offetts Knob, Mo.

1,541. April 28th—1st Missouri Militia Cavalry.

Princeton, Ark.

1,542. April 29th—40th Iowa and 43d Illinois Volunteers, 3d Illinois Battery, and 6th Kansas Cavalry.

Snia Hills, Mo.

1,543. April 29th—2d Colorado Cavalry.

Jenkins' Ferry, Saline River, Ark.

1,544. April 30th—77th Ohio, 4th, 18th, 29th, 33d, 36th, and 40th Iowa, 1st Arkansas, 12th Kansas, 9th and 27th Wisconsin, and 43d Illinois Volunteers; 79th (1st Kansas) and 83d (2d Kansas) U. S. Colored Troops, Battery A, 3d Illinois and 2d Indiana Battery, and 1st Iowa, 2d, 6th, and 14th Kansas, 1st and 2d Missouri, and 13th Illinois Cavalry, 3d Division of the 17th Corps; Banks' expedition.

Jacksonville, Fla.

1,545. May 1st—7th U. S. Colored Troops.

Hudnot's Plantation, La.

1,546. May 1st—Cavalry of the 19th Corps.

Ashwood Landing, La.

1,547. May 1st to 4th—64th U. S. Colored Troops.

Clinton, La.

1,548. May 1st—Troops not stated.

Near Alexandria, La.

1,549. May 1st to 8th—Portions of the Cavalry of the 13th and 19th Corps; Banks' Red River expedition.

Memphis, Tenn.

1,550. May 2d—7th Kansas Cavalry.

Governor Moore's Plantation, La.

1,551. May 2d—83d Ohio Volunteers and 3d Rhode Island Cavalry.

Cedar Bluffs, Col. Terr.

1,552. May 3d—One company of the 1st Colorado Cavalry.

Bolivar, Tenn.

1,553. May 3d—Cavalry, commanded by General S. D. Sturgis.

Red Clay, Ga.

1,554. May 3d—1st Cavalry Division, Army of the Cumberland.

Baton Rouge, La.

1,555. May 3d—4th Wisconsin Cavalry.

Transport City Belle, near Snaggy Point, Red River, La.

1,556. May 3d—120th Ohio Volunteers and 73d U. S. Colored Troops.

Richland, Ark.

1,557. May 3d—2d Arkansas Cavalry.

Doubtful Cañon, Arizona Terr.

1,558. May 4th—Detachment of 5th California Volunteers and 1st California Cavalry.

Yazoo City Expedition, Miss.

1,559. May 4th to 13th—3d U. S. Colored Cavalry, 11th, 72d, and 76th Illinois Volunteers, 5th Illinois Cavalry, and 7th Ohio Battery.

Kautz's Cavalry Raid from Suffolk to City Point, Va.

1,560. May 4th to 12th—5th and 16th Pennsylvania, 3d New York, and 1st District of Columbia Cavalry, and 8th New York Battery.

Ram Albemarle, Roanoke River, N. C.

1,561. May 5th—U. S. Gunboats Ceres, Commodore Hull, Mattabesett, Sassacus, Seymour, Wydusing, Miami, and Whitehead.

Dunn's Bayou, Red River, La.

1,562. May 5th—U. S. Steamer Covington, Gunboat Signal, and Transport Warner, with the 56th Ohio Volunteers on board.

Wall Bridge, Va.

1,563. May 5th—Cavalry Division, Army of the James ; Kautz's raid.

Craig's Meeting House, Va.

1,564. May 5th—3d Division, Cavalry, Army of the Potomac.

Wilderness, Va.

1,565. May 5th to 7th—2d Corps, 5th Corps, 6th Corps, 9th Corps, and Cavalry Corps, Army of the Potomac.

Rocky Face Ridge, Ga.

1,566. May 5th to 9th—4th, 14th, and 20th Corps, Army of the Cumberland ; 15th and 16th Corps, Army of the Tennessee ; 23d Corps, Army of the Ohio.

Campaign in Northern Georgia, from Chattanooga to Atlanta.

1,567. May 5th to September 8th—Armies of the Cumberland, Tennessee, and Ohio.

James River, near City Point, Va.

1,568. May 6th—Gunboat Commodore Jones.

Princeton, W. Va.

1,569. May 6th—Advance of General Crook's command.

Richmond and Petersburg Railroad, near Port Walthal and Chester Station, Va.

1,570. May 6th and 7th—Portion of the 10th and 18th Corps, Army of the James.

Benton, Miss.

1,571. May 7th—11th, 72d, and 76th Illinois Volunteers, and 7th Ohio Battery.

Bayou La Mourie, La.

1,572. May 7th—Portion of the 16th Corps ; Banks' Red River expedition.

Tunnell Hill, Ga.

1,573. May 7th—4th Corps and Cavalry, Army of the Cumberland.

Mill Creek and Dug Gaps, Ga.

1,574. May 7th—20th Corps, Army of the Cumberland.

Stoney Creek Station, Weldon Railroad, Va.

1,575. May 7th—5th and 11th Pennsylvania, 3d New York, and 1st District Columbia Cavalry, and 8th New York Battery ; Kautz's raid.

Todd's Tavern, Va.

1,576. May 8th—2d Division, Cavalry Corps, Army of the Potomac.

Spottsylvania Court House, Va.

1,577. May 8th to 18th—2d, 5th, 6th, 9th, and Cavalry Corps, Army of the Potomac ; includes engagements at Laurel Hill and Ny River.

Jeffersonville (or Abb's Valley), Va.

1,578. May 8th—Cavalry of the Army of West Virginia.

Buzzard Roost Gap, Ga.

1,579. May 8th—4th Corps and Cavalry, Army of the Cumberland.

Snake Creek Gap, Ga.

1,580. May 8th—15th Corps, Army of the Tennessee.

Dalton, Ga.

1,581. May 9th—23d Corps, Army of the Ohio.

Sheridan's Cavalry Raid, Va.

1,582. May 9th to 13th—1st and 2d Divisions, Cavalry Corps, Army of the Potomac.

Jarrett's Station, Weldon Railroad, Va.

1,583. May 9th—11th Pennsylvania Cavalry and 8th New York Battery ; Kautz's raid.

White's Bridge, Nottaway Creek, Va.

1,584. May 9th—3d New York and 1st District of Columbia Cavalry, and 8th New York Battery ; Kautz's raid.

Varnell's Station, Ga.

1,585. May 9th—1st Cavalry Division, Army of the Cumberland.

Childsbury, Va.

1,586. May 9th—6th Ohio and 1st New Jersey ; Sheridan's raid.

Swift Creek (or Arrowfield Church), Va.

1,587. May 9th and 10th—10th and 18th Corps, Army of the James.

Cloyd's Mountain and New River Bridge, Va.

1,588. May 9th and 10th—12th, 23d, 34th, and 36th Ohio, 9th, 11th, 14th, and 15th West Virginia Volunteers, and 3d and 4th Pennsylvania Reserves, Army of West Virginia.

Cove Mountain (or Grassy Lick), near Wytheville, Va.

1,589. May 9th and 10th—14th Pennsylvania, 1st, 2d, and 3d West Virginia, and 34th Ohio Mounted Volunteers.

Beaver Dam Station, North Anna, Va.

1,590. May 9th—1st Division, Cavalry Corps, Army of the Potomac; Sheridan's raid.

Ground Squirrel Church Bridge, South Anna, Va.

1,591. May 10th—1st Division, Cavalry Corps, Army of the Potomac; Sheridan's raid.

Dardanelle, Ark.

1,592. May 10th—6th Kansas Cavalry.

Ashland, Va.

1,593. May 11th—1st Massachusetts Cavalry ; Sheridan's raid.

Yellow Tavern, near Richmond, Va.

1,594. May 11th—1st and 3d Divisions, Cavalry Corps, Army of the Potomac; Sheridan's raid.

Smith's Station, Ind. Terr.

1,595. May 12th—1st Nebraska Battalion Cavalry.

Vaughn, Miss.

1,596. May 12th—11th, 72d, and 76th Illinois Volunteers; expedition to Yazoo City.

Fort Darling, Drury's Bluff, Va.

1,597. May 12th to 16th—10th and 18th Corps, Army of Virginia and North Carolina; includes engagements at Wierbottom Church, Proctor's and Palmer's Creeks.

Kautz's Raid on the Petersburg and Lynchburg Railroad, Va.

1,598. May 12th to 17th—Cavalry of the Army of the James.

Meadow Bridge, Chickahominy River, Va.

1,599. May 12th—1st and 3d Divisions, Cavalry Corps, Army of the Potomac; Sheridan's raid.

Resaca (or Sugar Valley, or Oostenaula), Ga.

1,600. May 13th to 16th—4th, 14th, and 20th Corps, Cavalry, Army of the Cumberland; 15th and 16th Corps, Army of the Tennessee, and 23d Corps, Army of the Ohio.

Pulaski, Tenn.

1,601. May 13th—111th U. S. Colored Troops (3d Alabama).

Tilton, Tenn.

1,602. May 13th—1st Division, Cavalry of the Army of the Cumberland.

Point Lookout, Va.

1,603. May 13th—Detachment of the 36th U. S. Colored Troops and Seamen from the Potomac Flotilla.

1864.]

Mansura (or Avoyelle's Prairie, Morreausville, Marksville), La.

1,604. May 14th to 16th—3d Division, 16th Corps, and portion of Cavalry Division, 19th Corps; Red River expedition.

Rood's Hill, Va.

1,605. May 14th—Portion of the Army of West Virginia.

Mount Pleasant Landing, La.

1,606. May 15th—67th U. S. Colored Troops.

New Market, Va.

1,607. May 15th—Portion of the Army of West Virginia.

Ley's Ferry, Ga.

1,608. May 15th—Portion of the 16th Corps, Army of the Tennessee.

Tanner's Bridge, near Rome, Ga.

1,609. May 15th—2d Cavalry Division, Army of the Cumberland.

Rome Cross Roads, Ga.

1,610. May 16th—16th Corps, Army of the Tennessee.

Ashepoo River, S. C.

1,611. May 16th—34th U. S. Colored Troops.

Pond Creek, Pike Co., Ky.

1,612. May 16th—39th Kentucky Volunteers.

Clear Creek, Mo.

1,613. May 16th—Two companies of the 15th Kansas Cavalry.

Fredericksburg Road, Va.

1,614. May 16th to 20th—Tyler's Division, 5th Corps, Army of the Potomac.

Smoky Hill, Col.

1,615. May 16th—One company 1st Colored Cavalry and McLain's Colorado Battery.

Bermuda Hundred, Va.

1,616. May 16th to 30th—10th and 18th Corps, Army of the James.

Belcher's Mills, Va.

1,617. May 16th—3d New York, 5th and 11th Pennsylvania, and 1st District Columbia Cavalry; Kautz's raid.

Adairsville, Ga.

1,618. May 17th to 18th—4th Corps, Army of the Cumberland; includes engagements at Graves House and Calhoun.

Madison Station, Ala.

1,619. May 17th—3d Division, 15th Corps, Army of the Tennessee.

Rome, Ga.

1,620. May 18th—2d Division, 14th Corps, and Cavalry, Army of the Cumberland.

Kingston, Ga.

1,621. May 18th—2d Cavalry Division, Army of the Cumberland.

Bayou De Glaize (also known as Old Oaks, Yellow Bayou, Simmsport, and Calhoun Station), La.

1,622. May 18th—1st and 3d Divisions, 16th Corps; portion of 17th Corps, and Cavalry, 19th Corps; Red River expedition.

Crooked River, Oregon.

1,623. May 18th—1st Oregon Cavalry.

Fayetteville, Ark.

1,624. May 19th—6th Kansas Cavalry.

Welaka and Saunders, Fla.

1,625. May 19th—Detachment of 17th Connecticut Volunteers.

Cassville, Ga.

1,626. May 19th to 22d—20th Corps, Army of the Cumberland.

Downer's Bridge, Va.

1,627. May 20th—5th New York Cavalry.

Milford Station, Va.

1,628. May 20th—1st Cavalry Division, Army of the Potomac.

Snia Hills, Mo.

1,629. May 21st—2d Colorado Cavalry.

Mount Pleasant, Miss.

1,630. May 21st—4th Missouri Cavalry.

Old River, La.

1,631. May 22d—6th Missouri Cavalry.

North Anna River (or Jericksford and Taylor's Bridge), Va.

1,632. May 23d to 27th—2d, 5th, and 9th Corps, Army of the Potomac.

Capture of Steamtug Columbine at Horse Landing, St. John's River, Fla.

1,633. May 23d—35th U. S. Colored Troops and Sailors on the Columbine.

Holly Springs, Miss.

1,634. May 24th—4th Missouri Cavalry.

Kingston, Ga.

1,635. May 24th—50th Ohio and 14th Kentucky Volunteers, and 2d Kentucky Cavalry.

Wilson's Wharf Landing, Va.

1,636. May 24th—1st District of Columbia and 10th U. S. Colored Troops, and Battery B, U. S. Colored Artillery.

Nashville, Tenn.

1,637. May 24th—15th U. S. Colored Troops.

Dallas (also designated New Hope Church, Burned Hickory, Pumpkin Vine Creek, and Altoona Hills), Ga.

1,638. May 25th to June 4th—4th, 14th, 20th Corps, and Cavalry, Army of the Cumberland ; 23d Corps, Army of the Ohio ; 15th, 16th, and 17th Corps, Army of the Tennessee.

Cassville Station, Ga.

1,639. May 25th—1st and 11th Kentucky Cavalry.

Burned Church, Ga.

1,640. May 26th—Cavalry of the 1st Division, Army of the Cumberland.

Lane's Prairie, Morris Co., Mo.

1,641. May 26th—Two companies 2d Wisconsin Cavalry.

1864.]   Torpedo Explosion on Bachelor's Creek, N. C.

1,642. May 26th—132d and 158th New York and 58th Pennsylvania Volunteers.

Decatur, Courtland Road, Ala.

1,643. May 26th and 27th—1st, 3d, and 4th Ohio Cavalry, Cavalry Corps, and 3d Brigade, 4th Division, 16th Corps.

San Carlos River, Cal.

1,644. May 27th—Company K, 5th California Infantry.

Hanoverton, Pamunkey River, Va.

1,645. May 27th—1st and 2d Divisions, Cavalry Corps, Army of the Potomac.

Hawe's Shop, Tocopotomy Creek (or Salem Church), Va.

1,646. May 28th—1st and 2d Divisions, Cavalry, Army of the Potomac.

Little Rock, Ark.

1,647. May 28th—57th U. S. Colored Troops.

Pleasant Hill, Mo.

1,648. May 28th—2d Colorado Cavalry.

Jacksonville, Fla.

1,649. May 28th—7th U. S. Colored Troops.

Moulton, Ala.

1,650. May 28th and 29th—1st, 3d, and 4th Ohio Cavalry, Army of the Cumberland.

Tocopotomy, Va.

1,651. May 29th to 31st—2d and 5th Corps, Army of the Potomac.

Hanover Court House, Va.

1,652. May 30th—3d Division, Cavalry Corps, Army of the Potomac.

Ashland, Va.

1,653. May 30th—3d Division, Cavalry Corps, Army of the Potomac.

Old Church, Va.

1,654. May 30th—1st Division, Cavalry Corps, Army of the Potomac.

Cold Harbor, Va.

1,655. June 1st to 12th—2d, 5th, 6th, 9th, and Cavalry Corps, Army of the Potomac, and 18th Corps, Army of the James.

Bermuda Hundred, Va.

1,656. June 2d—10th Corps, Army of Virginia and North Carolina.

Engagements at Gaines' Mills, Salem Church, and Hawe's Shop, Va.

1,657. June 2d—Cavalry of the Army of the Potomac.

Searcy, Ark.

1,658. June 3d—Detachment of the 3d Missouri Cavalry.

Panther Gap, W. Va.

1,659. June 3d—General Hayes' Brigade, 2d Division, Army of West Virginia.

Ackworth, Ga.

1,660. June 3d and 4th—Cavalry of the 2d Division, Army of the Cumberland.

Piedmont (or Mount Crawford), Va.

1,661. June 5th—Cavalry and Infantry of the Army of West Virginia.

8*

Buffalo Gap, W. Va.

1,662. June 6th—General Hayes' Brigade of the 2d Division, Army of West Virginia.

Lake Chicot (or Old River Lake), Ditch Bayou, Columbia, Fish Bayou, Ark.

1,663. June 6th—16th Corps.

Greenland Gap Road, near Moorefield, W. Va.

1,664. June 6th—22d Pennsylvania Cavalry.

Ripley, Miss.

1,665. June 7th—Cavalry advance of Maj.-General Sturgis' command; engagement during expedition to Guntown, June 5th to 10th.

1,666. Error.

Point of Rocks, Md.

1,667. June 9th—2d U. S. Colored Cavalry.

Kenesaw Mountain (also designated Lost Mountain, Nose's Creek, Marietta, and Big Shanty), Ga.

1,668. June 9th to 30th—4th, 14th, and 20th Corps, Army of the Cumberland; 15th, 16th, and 17th Corps, Army of the Tennessee; 23d Corps, Army of the Ohio.

Mount Stirling, Ky.

1,669. June 9th—Cavalry of the Division of Kentucky.

Lafayette, Tenn.

1,670. June 9th—7th Kansas Cavalry.

Frankfort, Ky.

1,671. June 10th—Enrolled Militia and citizens; Morgan's raid.

Lexington, W. Va.

1,672. June 10th and 11th—2d Division, Army of West Virginia.

Cane Creek, Ala.

1,673. June 10th—106th Ohio Volunteers; skirmish with Guerillas.

Lexington, Ky.

1,674. June 10th—4th Kentucky Cavalry.

Princeton, Ky.

1,675. June 10th—Troops not stated.

Petersburg, Va.

1,676. June 10th—Cavalry, commanded by General Kautz, and portion of the 10th Army Corps of the Army of the James.

Brice's Cross Roads, near Guntown, Miss.

1,677. June 10th—4th Missouri, 2d New Jersey, 19th Pennsylvania, 7th and 9th Illinois, 7th Indiana, 3d and 4th Iowa, and 10th Kansas Cavalry; 9th Minnesota, 81st, 95th, 108th, 113th, 114th, and 120th Illinois, 72d and 95th Ohio, and 93d Indiana Volunteers; 1st Illinois, 6th Indiana, and Company F, 2d Illinois Batteries; 59th (1st Tennessee) and 55th (1st Alabama) U. S. Colored Troops, and Battery F, 2d U. S. Colored Artillery.

1864.]   **Corinth, Miss.**

1,678. June 10th—2d New Jersey Cavalry; engagement during Guntown expedition.

Cynthiana, Ky.

1,679. June 10th—168th Ohio (100 days' men); Morgan's raid.

Keller's Bridge, Licking River, Ky.

1,680. June 10th—171st Ohio (100 days' men); Morgan's raid.

Old Church, Va.

1,681. June 10th and 11th—3d Division, Cavalry Corps, Army of the Potomac.

Wilson's Landing, Va.

1,682. June 11th—1st U. S. Colored Cavalry.

Cynthiana, Ky.

1,683. June 11th—Cavalry of the Division of Kentucky; Morgan's raid.

Ripley, Miss.

1,684. June 11th—3d and 4th Iowa, 2d New Jersey, and 4th Missouri Cavalry.

Trevellian Station, Central Railroad, Va.

1,685. June 11th and 12th—1st and 2d Divisions, Cavalry Corps, Army of the Potomac.

McAfee's Cross Roads, La.

1,686. June 12th—Cavalry, Army of the Cumberland.

Kingsville, Mo.

1,687. June 12th—Scouting party, 1st Missouri Militia Cavalry.

White Oak Swamp Bridge, Charles City Cross Roads (or Riddle's Shop), Va.

1,688. June 13th—3d Division, Cavalry Corps, and 2d Division, 5th Corps, Army of the Potomac.

White Post, W. Va.

1,689. June 13th—6th West Virginia Cavalry.

Pine Mountain, Ga.

1,690. June 14th—During Kenesaw Mountain.

Lexington, Lafayette Co., Mo.

1,691. June 14th—Detachment 1st Missouri Militia Cavalry.

Buchanan, near Lexington, Va.

1,692. June 14th—Advance of Army of West Virginia.

Samaria Church, Malvern Hill, Va.

1,693. June 15th—3d Division, Cavalry Corps, Army of the Potomac.

Moscow, Tenn.

1,694. June 15th—55th U. S. Colored Troops (1st Alabama).

Baylor's Farm, Va.

1,695. June 15th—3d Division, 10th Corps, Army of the James.

Siege of Petersburg, Va.

1,696. June 15th to April 2d, 1865. (See next.)

Petersburg, Va.

1,697. June 15th to 19th—10th and 18th Corps, Army of the James; 2d, 5th, 6th, and 9th Corps, Army of the Potomac.

West Point, Ark.

1,698. June 16th—9th Iowa Cavalry.

Otter Creek, near Liberty, Va.

1,699. June 16th—Advance of Army of West Virginia.

Wierbottom Creek, Va.

1,700. June 16th—2d Division, 10th Corps, Army of the James; siege of Petersburg, Va.

Golgotha, Ga.

1,701. June 16th—20th Corps; Kenesaw Mountain.

Walthal, Va.

1,702. June 16th—1st Division, 10th Corps, Army of the James; siege of Petersburg.

Pierson's Farm, Va.

1,703. June 16th—36th U. S. Colored Troops.

Nose's Creek, Ga.

1,704. June 17th—During Kenesaw Mountain.

Lynchburg, Va.

1,705. June 17th to 18th—1st and 2d Divisions, Averill's and Duffie's Cavalry, Army of West Virginia.

Pine Knob, Ga.

1,706. June 19th—During Kenesaw Mountain.

Kearsage and Alabama, off Cherbourg, France.

1,707. June 19th—U. S. Steamer Kearsage.

White House, Va.

1,708. June 20th—Brigade of Union troops, commanded by Brig.-General Abercrombie.

Liberty, Va.

1,709. June 20th—2d Division, Cavalry, Army of West Virginia.

Powder Spring, Ga.

1,710. June 20th—Cavalry, Army of the Cumberland.

Lattamore's Mills, Noonday Creek, Ga.

1,711. June 20th—Cavalry of the Army of the Cumberland.

Trenches in front of Petersburg, Va.

1,712. June 20th to 30th—5th and 9th Corps, Army of the Potomac, and 10th and 18th Corps, Army of the James.

Salem, Va.

1,713. June 21st—2d Division. Cavalry, Army of West Virginia.

Pine Bluff, Ark.

1,714. June 21st—27th Wisconsin.

Naval Engagement on the James River, near Dutch Gap.

1,715. June 21st—Forces not given.

White House Landing, Va.

1,716. June 21st—Portions of the 1st and 2d Divisions, Cavalry Corps, Army of the Potomac.

1864.]   **Buford's Gap, Va.**

1,717. June 21st—23d Ohio Volunteers.

White River, Ark.

1,718. June 22d—Three companies of the 12th Iowa and U. S. Steamer Lexington.

Wilson's Raid on the Weldon Railroad, Va.

1,719. June 22d to 30th—Cavalry of the Army of the James, and 3d Division, Cavalry, Army of the Potomac.

Culp's House, Ga.

1,720. June 22d—Part of Kenesaw Mountain.

Ream's Station, Va.

1,721. June 22d—Kautz's Cavalry, Army of the James, and 3d Division, Cavalry, Army of the Potomac ; Wilson's raid.

Weldon Railroad (or William's Farm, Davis' Farm, Jerusalem Plank Road), Va.

1,722. June 22d and 23d—2d and 6th Corps, and 1st Division, 5th Corps, Army of the Potomac.

Nottoway Court House, Va.

1,723. June 23d—3d Division, Cavalry, Army of the Potomac ; Wilson's raid.

Collinsville, Miss.

1,724. June 23d—Train on the Charlestown and Mississippi Railroad.

Jones' Bridge, Va.

1,725. June 23d—1st and 2d Divisions, Cavalry Corps, Army of the Potomac, and 28th U. S. Colored Troops.

Samaria Church, Va.

1,726. June 24th—1st and 2d Divisions, Cavalry Corps, Army of the Potomac.

White River, Ark.

1,727. June 24th—U. S. Steamer Queen City and Gunboats.

Staunton Bridge, Va.

1,728. June 24th—3d Division, Cavalry Corps, Army of the Potomac, and Kautz's Cavalry, Army of the James ; Wilson's raid.

La Fayette, Macon Co., Tenn.

1,729. June 24th—Troops not mentioned.

Point Pleasant, La.

1,730. June 25th—64th U. S. Colored Troops.

Clarendon, St. Charles River (or Pikesville, St. Charles), Ark.

1,731. June 25th to 29th—11th Missouri, 9th Iowa, and 3d Michigan Cavalry, 126th Illinois Volunteers, and Battery D, 2d Missouri Artillery.

Kenesaw Mountain (General Assault).

1,732. June 27th—Army of the Military Division of the Mississippi. (See Kenesaw Mountain, June 9th.)

Charlestown, W. Va.

1,733. June 27th—1st Division, Army of West Virginia.

Stoney Creek, Va.

1,734. June 28th—Cavalry, with Wilson on his raid on the Weldon Railroad.

Ream's Station, Va.

1,735. June 29th—Cavalry, with Wilson on his raid.

La Fayette, Ga.

1,736. June — —4th and 6th Kentucky Cavalry.

Front of Petersburg, Va.

1,737. July 1st to 31st—2d, 5th, and 9th Corps, Army of the Potomac, and 10th and 18th Corps, Army of the James.

Pine Bluff, Ark.

1,738. July 2d—64th U. S. Colored Troops.

Saulsbury, Miss.

1,739. July 2d—3d Iowa Cavalry.

Fort Johnson, James' Island, S. O.

1,740. July 2d—Troops of the Department of the South.

Nickajack Creek (or Smyrna and Vining Station).

1,741. July 2d to 5th—Army of the Cumberland and Army of the Tennessee.

Platte City, Mo.

1,742. July 3d—9th Missouri Militia Cavalry.

North Mountain, Va.

1,743. July 3d—Outpost of the 135th Ohio National Guards.

Expedition from Vicksburg to Jackson, Miss.

1,744. July 3d to 9th—Troops of 1st Division, 17th Corps.

Leetown, Va.

1,745. July 3d—1st New York Cavalry and 10th West Virginia Volunteers.

Hammack's Mills, North River, W. Va.

1,746. July 3d—153d Ohio National Guards.

Searcy, Ark.

1,747. July 4th—Detachment of 3d Arkansas Cavalry.

Vicksburg, Miss.

1,748. July 4th—48th U. S. Colored Troops (10th Louisiana).

Clay Co., Mo.

1,749. July 4th—9th Missouri Militia Cavalry.

Clinton, Miss.

1,750. July 4th—2d Wisconsin Cavalry, during expedition to Jackson.

Point of Rocks, Md.

1,751. July 4th—Maryland Potomac Home Brigade.

Coleman's Plantation, near Port Gibson, Miss.

1,752. July 4th and 5th—52d U. S. Colored Troops (2d Mississippi) and Mississippi Marine Brigade.

Bolivar and Maryland Heights, Va.

1,753. July 4th to 7th—Reserve Division of the Army of West Virginia.

1864.]

Smith's Expedition from La Grange, Tenn., to Tupelo, Miss.

1,754. July 5th to 18th—1st and 3d Divisions, 16th Corps, Cavalry Brigade, and one Brigade U. S. Colored Troops.

John's Island, S. C.

1,755. July 5th to 7th—Troops of the Department of the South.

Hagerstown, Pleasant Valley, Md.

1,756. July 5th—1st Maryland Cavalry, Potomac Home Brigade.

Jackson, Miss.

1,757. July 5th and 6th—2d Wisconsin, 5th and 11th Illinois, and 3d U. S. Colored Cavalry, 46th, 76th, and 79th Illinois Volunteers; expedition to Jackson.

Little Blue, Mo

1,758. July 6th—2d Colorado Cavalry.

Mount Zion Church, Va.

1,759. July 6th—2d Massachusetts Cavalry.

Chattahoochee River, Ga.

1,760. July 6th to 10th—Armies of the Ohio, Tennessee, and Cumberland.

Hagar's Mountain and Middleton, Md.

1,761. July 7th—8th Illinois Cavalry and Alexander's Baltimore Battery.

Clinton, Miss.

1,762. July 7th—11th Illinois and 2d Wisconsin Cavalry and Battery of 2d Illinois Artillery; return of expedition to Jackson, Miss.

Solomon's Gap, Frederick City, Md.

1,763. July 7th—8th Illinois Cavalry, 3d Maryland Potomac Home Brigade, and Alexander's Baltimore Battery.

Ripley, Miss.

1,764. July 7th—2d Iowa Cavalry; Smith's expedition to Tupelo, Miss.

Monocacy, Md.

1,765. July 9th—1st and 2d Brigades, 3d Division, 6th Corps, and detachment of 8th Corps.

Rousseau's Raid in Alabama and Georgia.

1,766. July 11th to 22d—8th Indiana, 5th Iowa, 9th Ohio, 2d Kentucky, and 4th Tennessee Cavalry, and Battery E, 1st Michigan Artillery.

Pontotoc, Miss.

1,767. July 11th—8th Wisconsin, 5th Minnesota, and 11th Missouri Volunteers, and 2d Iowa Cavalry; Smith's expedition to Tupelo.

Fort Stevens, Washington, D. C.

1,768. July 12th—1st and 2d Divisions, 6th Corps; 22d Corps, convalescents, Marines, Home Guards, and citizens.

Petit Jean, Arkansas River, Ark.

1,769. July 12th—One company of the 3d Arkansas Cavalry.

Lee's Mills, near Ream's Station, Va.

1,770. July 12th—2d Division, Cavalry Corps, Army of the Potomac.

Tupelo, Miss.

1,771. July 13th to 15th—1st and 3d Divisions, 16th Corps, Cavalry, and a Brigade of Colored Troops; includes the engagements at Harrisburg, July 13th, and Old Town Creek, July 15th.

Ozark, Mo.

1,772. July 14th and 15th—14th Kansas Cavalry.

Ten Islands, Coosa River (or Jackson's Ford), Ala.

1,773. July 14th—8th Indiana and 5th Iowa Cavalry; Rousseau's raid.

Farr's Mills, Montgomery Co., Ark.

1,774. July 14th—A battalion of the 4th Arkansas Cavalry.

Stone's Ferry, Tallapoosa River, Ala.

1,775. July 15th—Engagement during Rousseau's raid.

Grand Gulf, Port Gibson, Miss.

1,776. July 16th and 17th—72d and 76th Illinois Volunteers, 2d Wisconsin Cavalry, and 53d U. S. Colored Troops.

Snicker's Gap, Va.

1,777. July 17th—Army of West Virginia.

Fredericksburg, Mo.

1,778. July 17th—2d Colorado Cavalry.

Auburn, Ga.

1,779. July 18th—9th Ohio and 4th Tennessee Cavalry; Rousseau's raid.

Chewa Station, Montgomery and West Point Railroad, Ga.

1,780. July 18th—8th Indiana, 5th Iowa, and 4th Tennessee Cavalry.

Snicker's Ferry, Island Ford, Shenandoah River, Va.

1,781. July 18th—Army of West Virginia and portion of the 6th Corps.

Ashby's Gap, Va.

1,782. July 18th—Cavalry of the Army of West Virginia.

Darksville, Va.

1,783. July 19th—Portion of the Army of West Virginia.

Winchester (or Stevenson's Depot and Carter's Farm), Va.

1,784. July 20th—2d Cavalry Division, Army of West Virginia.

Peach Tree Creek, Ga.

1,785. July 20th—Army of the Cumberland.

Deep Bottom, Va.

1,786. July 21st—1st Division, 10th Corps, Army of the James.

Henderson, Ky.

1,787. July 21st—Troops not given.

Atlanta (Hood's First Sortie), Ga.

1,788. July 22d—Army of the Tennessee.

Vidalia, La.

1,789. July 22d—6th U. S. Colored Heavy Artillery (2d Mississippi).

Kernstown, Va.

1,790. July 23d—Cavalry of the Army of West Virginia.

1864.]   **Winchester, Va.**

1,791. July 24th—Portion of the Army of West Virginia.

Steamer Clara Bell, Carrolton Landing, Carolina Bend, Miss.

1,792. July 24th—6th Michigan Artillery.

Courtland, Ala.

1,793. July 25th—18th Michigan and 32d Wisconsin Volunteers.

Wallace's Ferry, Big Creek, Ark.

1,794. July 26th—15th Illinois Cavalry, Company E, 2d U. S. Colored Artillery, and 60th (1st Iowa) and 56th (3d Arkansas) U. S. Colored Troops.

Des Arc, Ark.

1,795. July 26th—11th Missouri Cavalry.

Stoneman's Raid to Macon, Ga.

1,796. July 26th to 31st—Stoneman's and Garrard's Cavalry Division, Army of the Cumberland.

McCook's Raid to Lovejoy Station, Ga.

1,797. July 26th to 31st—1st Wisconsin, 5th and 8th Iowa, 2d and 8th Indiana, 1st and 4th Tennessee, and 4th Kentucky Cavalry.

St. Mary's Trestle, Fla.

1,798. July 26th—75th Ohio Mounted Infantry.

Mazzard Prairie, Fort Smith, Ark.

1,799. July 27th—Two hundred men of the 6th Kansas Cavalry.

Deep Bottom, New Market and Malvern Hill, Va.

1,800. July 27th and 28th—1st Division, 10th Corps, Cavalry, Army of the James; 2d Corps and 1st and 2d Divisions, Cavalry Corps, Army of the Potomac.

Whiteside, Black Creek, Fla.

1,801. July 27th—35th U. S. Colored Troops (1st North Carolina).

Tah-kah-o-kuty, Dak. Terr.

1,802. July 28th—8th Minnesota Mounted Infantry, 6th and 7th Iowa, and Dakota and Brackett's Minnesota Cavalry; Indian fight.

Atchafalaya River, La.

1,803. July 28th—Portion of the 19th Corps.

West Point, Ark.

1,804. July 28th—11th Missouri Cavalry.

Ezra Chapel, Atlanta, Ga. (2d sortie).

1,805. July 28th—Army of the Tennessee.

Campbelltown, Ga.

1,806. July 28th—Portion of McCook's Cavalry; McCook's raid.

Flatshoals, Ga.

1,807. July 28th—Portion of Garrard's Cavalry; Stoneman's raid.

Siege of Atlanta, Ga.

1,808. July 28th to September 2d—Armies of the Cumberland, Tennessee, and Ohio.

Fort Smith, Ark.

1,809. July 29th to 31st—Troops not given.

Lovejoy Station, Ga.

1,810. July 29th to 30th—Cavalry of the Army of the Cumberland; McCook's raid.

Clear Springs, Md.

1,811. July 29th—12th and 14th Pennsylvania Cavalry.

Mine Explosion at Petersburg, Va.

1,812. July 30th—9th Corps, supported by the 18th Corps, with 2d and 5th Corps in reserve.

Newnan, Ga.

1,813. July 30th—Cavalry Army of the Cumberland; McCook's raid.

Chambersburg, Pa.

1,814. July 30th –Burned by Confederates.

Macon, Ga.

1,815. July 30th—Cavalry of the Army of the Cumberland; Stoneman's raid.

Lee's Mills, Va.

1,816. July 30th— Davis's Brigade, 2d Cavalry Division, Army of the Potomac.

Lebanon, Ky.

1,817. July 30th— One Company of the 12th Ohio Cavalry.

Hillsboro (or Sunshine Church), Ga.

1,818. July 31st—Cavalry, Army of the Cumberland; Stoneman's raid.

Rolla, Mo.

1,819. August 1st—5th Missouri Militia Cavalry.

Trenches before Petersburg, Va.

1,820. August 1st to 31st—2d, 5th, and 9th Corps Army of the Potomac, and 18th Corps, Army of the James.

Cumberland (or Plock's Mills), Md.

1,821. August 1st—-Command of Brig.-General B. F. Kelly.

Green Springs Depot, W. Va., near Old Town, Md.

1,822. August 2d—153d Ohio Volunteers.

Osceola, Ark.

1,823. August 2d—2d, 3d Militia, and 1st and 6th Missouri Cavalry.

Elkshute, Mo.

1,824. August 3d—Troops commanded by Colonel J. L. Burris.

New Creek, Va.

1,825. August 4th—Troops not mentioned.

Forts Gaines and Morgan, Mobile Harbor, Ala.

1,826. August 5th to 23d—U. S. Steamships Brooklyn, Octorora, Hartford, Ossippee, Itasca, Oneida, Galena, Metacomet, Richmond, Port Royal, Lackawanna, Seminole, Monongahela, and Tecumseh, commanded by Admiral Farragut, and 13th Army Corps.

Utoy Creek, Ga.

1,827. August 5th and 6th—Armies of the Cumberland, Tennessee, and Ohio.

1864.]   Cowskin, Mo.
1,828. August 5th to 7th—8th Missouri Militia Cavalry.

Decatur, Ga.
1,829. August 5th—2d Cavalry Division, Army of the Cumberland.

Donaldsonville, La.
1,830. August 5th—11th New York Cavalry.

Cabin Point, Va.
1,831. August 5th—1st U. S. Colored Cavalry.

Plaquemine (or Indian City Village), La.
1,832. August 6th—4th Wisconsin Cavalry and 11th (14th Rhode Island) Heavy
       Artillery.

Moorefield, Va.
1,833. August 7th—14th Pennsylvania, 8th Ohio, 1st and 3d West Virginia, and
       1st New York Cavalry.

Tallahatchie River, Miss.
1,834. August 7th to 9th—Cavalry and Infantry, 16th Corps.

Fort Gaines, Ala.
1,835. August 8th—U. S. fleet, commanded by Admiral Farragut (Mobile Harbor).

Two Hills, Bad Lands, Little Missouri River, Dak. Ter.
1,836. August 8th—8th Minnesota Volunteers, and 2d Minnesota, 6th and 7th
       Iowa, Brackett's Battalion Minnesota, and 1st Battalion Dakota Cavalry.

Explosion of Ammunition at City Point, Va.
1,837. August 9th—Loss, 70 killed and 130 wounded.

U. S. Steamer Empress, Miss.
1,838. August 10th—Loss, 6 killed and 12 wounded.

Berryville Pike, Va.
1,839. August 10th—Reserve Brigade and 1st Cavalry Division, Army of the
       Potomac.

Sulphur Springs Bridge and White Post, Va.
1,840. August 11th—1st and 3d Divisions and Reserve Brigade, Cavalry, Army of
       the Potomac.

Van Buren, Crawford County, Ark.
1,841. August 11th—2d and 6th Kansas Cavalry.

Abbeville and Oxford, Miss.
1,842. August 12th—Cavalry and Infantry of the 16th Corps.

Little Blue, Dak. Ter.
1,843. August 12th—Detachment of the 7th Iowa Cavalry.

Near Snicker's Gap, Va.
1,844. August 13th—144th and 149th Ohio Volunteers; guarding a supply train.

Gravel Hill, Va.
1,845. August 14th—2d Cavalry Division, Army of the Potomac.

Strawberry Plains, Deep Bottom Run, Va.
1,846. August 14th to 18th—2d Cavalry Division and 2d Corps, Army of the
       Potomac, and 10th Corps, Army of the James.

Hurricane Creek, Miss.

1,847. August 14th—Cavalry and Infantry of the 16th Corps.

Dalton, Ga.

1,848. August 14th to 16th—2d Missouri Volunteers, and 14th U. S. Colored Troops.

Fisher's Hill, near Strassburg, Va.

1,849. August 15th—1st Cavalry Division and 6th and 8th Corps, Army of the Potomac.

Smoky Hill Crossing, Kan.

1,850. August 16th—Detachments of 7th Iowa and U. S. Cavalry.

Crooked Run, Front Royal, Va.

1,851. August 16th—1st and 2d Brigades, 1st Cavalry Division, Army of the Potomac.

Gainesville, Fla.

1,852. August 17th—75th Ohio Mounted Infantry.

Cleveland, Tenn.

1,853. August 17th—6th Ohio Heavy Artillery.

Winchester, Va.

1,854. August 17th—3d Cavalry Division Army of the Potomac, and the New Jersey Brigade, 6th Corps.

Decatur, Ala.

1,855. August 18th—2d Cavalry Division Army of the Cumberland, and 1st U. S. Colored Artillery.

Six Mile House, Weldon R. R., Va.

1,856. August 18th, 19th, and 21st—Kautz's Cavalry, and 2d Cavalry Division, 5th and 9th Corps, Army of the Potomac.

Fairburn, Ga.

1,857. August 18th—Cavalry of the Army of the Cumberland.

Snicker's Gap Pike, Va.

1,858. August 19th—Detachment of the 5th Michigan Cavalry; prisoners and wounded put to death by Mosby's guerillas.

Blockhouse No. 4, Nashville and Chattanooga R. R., Tenn.

1,859. August — —One Company of the 115th Ohio Volunteers.

Martinsburg, Va.

1,860. August 19th—One Company of Cavalry of Averell's command.

Kilpatrick's Raid on the Atlanta Railroad.

1,861. August 18th to 22d—Cavalry, Army of the Cumberland.

Red Oak, Ga.

1,862. August 19th—Cavalry, Army of the Cumberland; Kilpatrick's raid.

Jonesboro, Ga.

1,863. August 19th and 20th—2d Division Cavalry, Army of the Cumberland; Kilpatrick's raid.

Pine Bluff, Tennessee River, Tenn.

1,864. August 19th—Detachment of Company B, 83d Illinois Mounted Infantry; killed and mutilated by guerillas.

1864.]   **Lovejoy Station, Ga.**

1,865. August 20th—Cavalry, Army of the Cumberland; Kilpatrick's raid.

Summit Point, Va.

1,866. August 21st—1st and 3d Divisions Cavalry Corps, and 6th Corps; includes engagement of 6th Division at Berryville, 3d Division at Summit, and 6th Corps at Flowing Springs.

Duvall's Bluff, Ark.

1,867. August 21st—11th Missouri Cavalry.

Memphis, Tenn.

1,868. August 21st—Detachment of 8th Iowa, 108th and 113th Illinois, 39th, 40th and 41st Wisconsin Volunteers, 61st (2d Tennessee) U. S. Colored troops, 3d and 4th Iowa Cavalry, and Battery G, 1st Missouri Light Artillery.

College Hill (or Oxford Hill and Hurricane Creek), Miss.

1,869. August 21st and 22d—4th Iowa and 11th and 21st Missouri Volunteers, and 3d Iowa and 12th Missouri Cavalry, of the 16th Corps.

Canton, Ky.

1,870. August 22d—Troops not given.

Rodgersville, Tenn.

1,871. August 22d—Troops not given.

Fort Morgan, Ala.

1,872. August 23d—Naval forces under Admiral Farragut, Mobile Harbor.

Abbeville, Miss.

1,873. August 23d—10th Missouri, 14th Iowa, 5th and 7th Minnesota, and 8th Wisconsin Volunteers.

Bermuda Hundred, Va.

1,874. August 24th and 25th—10th Corps, Army of the James.

Fort Smith, Ark.

1,875. August 24th—16th U. S. Colored troops.

Jones' Hay Station and Ashley Station, Long Prairie, Ark.

1,876. August 24th—9th Iowa, and 8th and 11th Missouri Cavalry.

Halltown, Va.

1,877. August 24th—Portion of the 8th Corps, Army of the Shenandoah.

Smithfield and Shepherdstown (or Kearneysville), Va.

1,878. August 25th—1st and 3d Divisions Cavalry, Army of the Potomac.

Ream's Station, Va.

1,879. August 25th—2d Corps, and 2d Cavalry Division, Army of the Potomac.

Conee Creek, Clinton, La.

1,880. August 25th—Portion of the Cavalry of the Department of the Gulf.

Sacramento Mountain, New Mex.

1,881. August 25th—1st New Mexico Cavalry.

Bull Bayou, Ark.

1,882. August 26th—9th Kansas and 3d Wisconsin Cavalry.

Halltown, Va.

1,883. August 26th and 27th—1st and 2d Divisions, 8th Corps, Army of West Virginia.

Owensboro', Ky

1,884. August 27th—108th U. S. Colored troops.

Holly Springs, Miss.

1,885. August 27th and 28th—14th Iowa Volunteers, 11th U. S. Colored troops (1st Alabama Artillery), and 10th Missouri Cavalry.

Fort Cotton Wood, Nev. Ter.

1,886. August 28th—7th Iowa Cavalry ; fight with Indians.

Howard County, Mo.

1,887. August 28th—Company E, 4th Missouri Militia Cavalry.

Ghent, Ky.

1,888. August 29th—117th U. S. Colored troops.

Smithfield, Va.

1,889. August 29th—1st Division Cavalry Corps, and 3d Division, 6th Corps, Army of the Potomac.

Wormley's Gap, Va.

1,890. August 29th—Detachment commanded by Captain Blazer, 96th Ohio.

Arthur's Swamp, Va.

1,891. August 29th and 30th—2d Cavalry Division, Army of the Potomac.

Blockhouse No. 5, Nashville and Chattanooga R. R., Tenn.

1,892. August 31st—115th Ohio Volunteers.

Jonesboro', Ga.

1,893. August 31st to September 1st—Cavalry and Davis's Division 14th Corps, Army of the Cumberland ; 15th, 16th, and 17th Corps, Army of the Tennessee.

Rousseau's Pursuit of Wheeler in Tennessee.

1,894. September 1st to 8th—1st and 4th Tennessee, 2d Michigan, 1st Wisconsin, 8th Iowa, 2d and 8th Indiana, and 6th Kentucky Cavalry.

Trenches before Petersburg.

1,895. September 1st to October 30th—Army of the Potomac.

Lavergne, Tenn.

1,896. September 1st—Rousseau in pursuit of Wheeler.

Occupation of Atlanta, Ga.

1,897. September 2d—20th Corps, Army of the Cumberland.

Franklin, Tenn.

1,898. September 2d—Rousseau in pursuit of Wheeler.

Lovejoy Station, Ga.

1,899. September 2d to 6th—23d Corps, Army of the Ohio, and 4th Corps, Army of the Cumberland.

Big Shanty, Ga.

1,900. September 2d—9th Ohio Cavalry, on a railroad train.

1864.]   **Murfreesboro, Tenn.**

1,901. September 3d—100th U. S. Colored troops.

Berryville, Va.

1,902. September 3d and 4th—1st Cavalry Division, Army of the Potomac, 8th Corps, Army of Western Virginia, and 19th Corps.

Darkesville, Va.

1,903. September 3d—3d Cavalry Division, Army of the Potomac.

Greenville, Tenn.

1,904. September 4th—9th and 13th Tennessee and 10th Michigan Cavalry.

Campbellville, Tenn.

1,905. September 5th—Rousseau's Cavalry in pursuit of Wheeler.

Searcy, Ark.

1,906. September 6th—Detachment of the 9th Iowa Cavalry.

Readyville, Tenn.

1,907. September 7th—Detachment of 9th Pennsylvania Cavalry.

Dutch Gap, Va.

1,908. September 7th—4th U. S. Colored troops.

Capture of Fort Hell, Jerusalem Plank Road, Va.

1,909. September 10th—99th Pennsylvania, 2d U. S. Sharpshooters, and 20th Indiana Volunteers.

Lock's Ford, Opequan, Va.

1,910. September 13th—2d Brigade, 3d Division Cavalry Corps, Army of the Middle Military Division.

Near Pine Bluff, Ark.

1,911. September — —Two Companies of the 1st Indiana Cavalry.

Fort Gibson, Indian Territory.

1,912. September 16th and 18th—79th U. S. Colored troops (1st Kansas) and 2d Kansas Cavalry.

Sycamore Church, Va.

1,913. September 16th—1st District of Columbia and 13th Pennsylvania Cavalry.

Fairfax Station, Va.

1,914. September 17th—13th and 16th New York Cavalry.

Belcher's Mills, Va.

1,915. September 17th—Kautz's Cavalry of the Army of the James and 2d Cavalry Division, Army of the Potomac.

Doniphan and Black River, Mo.

1,916. September 17th to 20th—One Company of the 3d Missouri Militia Cavalry.

Martinsburg, Va.

1,917. September 18th—2d Cavalry Division, Army of West Virginia.

Fort Cottonwood, Nev. Ter.

1,918. September 18th—7th Iowa Cavalry.

Opequan, Winchester (or Belle Grove), Va.

1,919. September 19th—8th Corps and 2d Cavalry Division, Army of West Virginia; 6th Corps and 1st and 3d Cavalry Division, Army of the Potomac; 1st and 2d Divisions 19th Corps, Army of the Middle Military Division.

Cabin Creek, Indian Territory.

1,920. September 19th—2d, 6th, and 14th Kansas Cavalry and 1st and 2d Kansas Indian Home Guards.

Front Royal Pike, Va.

1,921. September 21st—3d Division Cavalry Corps, Army of the Potomac.

Fisher's Hill (or Woodstock), Va.

1,922. September 22d—6th Corps, 1st and 2d Cavalry Divisions, Army of the Potomac, 8th Corps, Army of West Virginia, and 1st and 2d Divisions 19th Corps.

Athens, Ala.

1,923. September 23d—106th, 110th, and 114th U. S. Colored troops, 3d Tennessee Cavalry, and 18th Michigan, and 102d Ohio Volunteers.

Rockport, Mo.

1,924. September 23d—3d Missouri Militia Cavalry.

Blackwater, Mo.

1,925. September 23d—One Battalion of the 1st Missouri Militia Cavalry.

Luray, Va.

1,926. September 24th—1st Division Cavalry Corps, Army of the Potomac.

Fayette, Mo.

1,927. September 24th—9th Missouri Militia Cavalry.

Bull's Gap, Tenn.

1,928. September 24th—Cavalry and Mounted Infantry.

Price's Invasion of Missouri.

1,929. September 24th to October 28th—Missouri Militia Cavalry, and Cavalry of General A. J. Smith's command, Kansas Militia, and Cavalry of the Army of the Border.

Sulphur Branch, Trestle, Ala.

1,930. September 25th—111th U. S. Colored troops (3d Tennessee) and 9th Indiana Cavalry.

Johnsonville, Tenn.

1,931. September 25th—13th U. S. Colored troops.

Henderson, Ky.

1,932. September 25th—118th U. S. Colored troops.

Vache Grass, Ark.

1,933. September 26th—14th Kansas Cavalry.

Fort Davidson, Pilot Knob (or Ironton), Mo.

1,934. September 26th and 27th—47th and 50th Missouri and 14th Iowa Volunteers, 2d and 3d Missouri Cavalry, and Battery H 2d Missouri Light Artillery, Price's Invasion of Missouri.

1864.] **Brown's Gap, Va.**

✦ 1,935. September 26th—1st Cavalry Division, Army of the Potomac, and 2d Cavalry Division Army of West Virginia.

Richland, Tenn.

1,936. September 26th—111th U. S. Colored troops (3d Alabama).

Weyer's Cave, Va.

1,937. September 27th—2d Division Cavalry Army of West Virginia.

Pulaski, Tenn.

1,938. September 27th—Cavalry commanded by General Rousseau.

Massacre on North Missouri R.R.

1,939. September 27th—Furloughed Soldiers.

Massacre at Centralia, Mo.

1,940. September 27th—Three Companies 39th Missouri Volunteers, Price's invasion of Missouri.

Carter's Station, Watauga River, Ark.

1,941. September 27th—Cavalry and Mounted Infantry, commanded by General Ammen.

Mariana, Fla.

1,942. September 27th—82d U. S. Colored Troops, 7th Vermont Volunteers, and 2d Maine Cavalry.

Fort Rice, Dak. Ter.

1,943. September 27th—Detachment of 6th Iowa Cavalry ; fight with Indians.

Clarksville, Ark.

1,944. September 28th—3d Wisconsin Cavalry.

Waynesboro, Va.

1,945. September 28th—3d Division Cavalry Corps, Army of the Potomac.

New Market Heights (or Chapin's Farm, Laurel Hill, Forts Harrison and Gilmore), Va.

1,946. September 28th to 30th—10th and 18th Corps and Cavalry, Army of the James.

Fort Sedgwick, Jerusalem Plank Road, Va. ,

1,947. September 28th—3d Division, 9th Corps.

Centreville, Tenn.

1,948. September 29th—2d Tennessee Mounted Infantry

Leesburg and Harrison, Mo.

1,949. September 29th and 30th—2d Missouri Militia Cavalry, Battery H, 2d Missouri Light Artillery, and 14th Iowa Volunteers; Price's invasion of Missouri.

Preble's Farm, Poplar Springs Church, Va.

1,950. September 30th to October 1st—1st Division, 5th Corps, and 2d Division, 9th Corps.

Arthur's Swamp, Va.

1,951. September 30th to October 1st—2d Cavalry Division, Army of the Potomac.

Athens, Ala.

1,952. October 1st and 2d—73d Indiana Volunteers.

XIII.—9

Huntsville, Ala.

1,953. October 1st—Detachments of the 12th and 13th Indiana Cavalry.

Franklin, Mo.

1,954. October 1st—Enrolled Missouri Militia.

Reconnoissance on Charles City Cross Roads, Va.

1,955. October 1st—Spear's Cavalry Brigade and Terry's Brigade, 10th Corps, Army of the James.

Yellow Tavern, Weldon R. R., Va.

1,956. October 1st to 5th—3d Division, 2d Corps, Army of the Potomac.

Sweetwater, Noses, and Powder Spring Creeks, Ga.

1,957. October 1st to 3d.—Kilpatrick's Cavalry, Army of the Cumberland.

Waynesboro, Va.

1,958. October 2d—Portions of 1st Division, and 3d Division, Cavalry Corps, Army of the Potomac.

Saltville, Va.

1,959. October 2d—11th and 13th Kentucky, 12th Ohio, 11th Michigan, and 5th and 6th U. S. Colored Cavalry, and 26th, 30th, 35th, 37th, 39th, 40th, and 45th Kentucky Mounted Infantry.

Gladesville, Pound Gap, Va.

1,960. October 2d—1st Kentucky Cavalry, and 3d Kentucky Mounted Infantry.

Near Memphis, Tenn.

1,961. October 4th—One company 7th Indiana Cavalry

Jackson, La.

1,962. October 5th—23d Wisconsin Volunteers, 1st Texas, and 1st Louisiana Cavalry, and 2d and 4th Massachusetts Battery.

Allatoona, Ga.

1,963. October 5th—7th, 12th, 50th, 57th, and 93d Illinois, 39th Iowa, 4th Minnesota, and 18th Wisconsin Volunteers, and 12th Wisconsin Battery.

Fort Adams, La.

1,964. October 5th—2d Wisconsin, and 3d U. S. Colored Cavalry.

Florence, Ala.

1,965. October 6th—60th Illinois Volunteers, and 3d and 6th Tennessee Cavalry.

North Shenandoah, Va.

1,966. October — —8th Ohio Cavalry.

Prince's Place, Osage River, Cole Co., Mo.

1,967. October 6th—1st, 7th, and 9th Missouri Militia Cavalry. Price's invasion of Missouri.

Woodville, Miss.

1,968. October 6th—Troops not specified.

New Market, Va.

1,969. October 7th—3d Cavalry Division, Army of the Potomac.

Darbytown Roads, near New Market Heights, Va.

1,970. October 7th—10th Corps and Cavalry, Army of the James.

1864.]   **Moreau Bottom, near Jefferson City, Mo.**

1,971. October 7th—Missouri Militia, Cavalry, Artillery, and Infantry.   Price's invasion of Missouri.

Reconnoissance to the Boydtown Plank Road, Va.

1,972. October 8th—5th and 9th Corps, Army of the Potomac.

Tom's Brook (or Fisher's Hill), Strasburg, Woodstock, Va.

1,973. October 9th—1st and 3d Divisions Cavalry, Army of the Potomac.

California, Mo.

1,974. October 9th to 11th—4th and 7th Missouri Militia Cavalry, and Batteries H and L, 2d Missouri Artillery.

Boonsville, Mo.

1,975. October 9th to 11th—1st, 4th, 5th, 6th, and 7th Missouri Militia Cavalry, 15th Missouri, and 17th Illinois Cavalry, and Battery H, 2d Missouri Light Artillery.   Price's invasion of Missouri.

South Tunnel, Tenn.

1,976. October 10th—40th U. S. Colored Troops.

East Point, Miss.

1,977. October 10th—61st U. S. Colored Troops (2d Tennessee).

Fort Donelson, Tenn.

1,978. October 11th—Portion of 4th U. S. Colored Heavy Artillery.

Stony Creek Station, Va.

1.979. October 11th—13th Pennsylvania Cavalry.

Narrows, Ga.

1,980. October 11th—Garrard's Cavalry Division, Army of the Cumberland.

Greenville, Tenn.

1,981. October 12th—Troops not given.

Resaca, Ga.

1,982. October 12th—Garrison, commanded by Colonel Weaver.

Reconnoissance to Strasburg, Va.

1,983. October 13th—1st and 2d Divisions, 19th Corps ; and 1st and 2d Divisions, Army of West Virginia.

Tilton, Ga.

1,984. October 13th—Troops not specified.

Dalton, Ga.

1,985. October 13th – Troops commanded by Colonel Johnson.

Buzzard Roost Blockhouse, Ga.

1,986. October 13th—One company of the 115th Illinois Volunteers.

Reconnoissance, Darbytown Road, Va.

1,987. October 13th—1st and 3d Divisions Tenth Corps and Cavalry, Army of the James.

Bayou Biddell, La.

1,988. October 15th—52d U. S. Colored troops. 2d Mississippi.

Glasgow, Mo.

1,989. October 15th—43d Missouri Volunteers, detachments of the 17th Illinois, 9th Missouri Militia, and 13th Missouri Cavalry, and 62d U. S. Colored troops (1st Missouri); Price's invasion of Missouri.

Snake Creek Gap, Ga.

1,990. October 15th—Portion of the Army of the Tennessee.

Sedalia, Mo.

1,991. October 15th—1st and 7th Missouri Militia Cavalry; Price's invasion of Missouri.

Ship's Gap, Taylor's Ridge, Ga.

1,992. October 16th—1st Division, 15th Corps.

Cedar Run Church, Va.

1,993. October 17th—Detachment of 1st Connecticut Cavalry.

Pierce's Point, Blackwater, Fla.

1,994. October 18th—19th Iowa Volunteers, and 2d Maine and 1st Florida Cavalry.

Lexington, Mo.

1,995. October 19th—3d Wisconsin. and 5th, 11th, 15th, and 16th Kansas Cavalry; Price's invasion of Missouri.

Cedar Creek (or Middletown), Va.

1,996. October 19th—1st and 3d Divisions Cavalry, and 6th Corps, Army of the Potomac; 8th Corps and Cavalry, Army of West Virginia; and 1st and 2d Division 19th Corps.

Fort Leavenworth, Kan.

1,997. October 20th to 26th—Troops not given.

Little River, Tenn.

1,998. October 20th—Cavalry and portion of 15th Corps.

Harrodsburg, Ky.

1,999. October 21st—5th U. S. Colored Cavalry.

Little Blue, Mo.

2,000. October 21st—2d Colorado, 3d Wisconsin, 5th, 11th, 15th, and 16th Kansas Cavalry and one Brigade of Kansas Militia, 2d and 5th Missouri Militia, and two Battalions of the 2d Missouri Artillery; two engagements; Price's invasion of Missouri.

Independence, Mo.

2,001. October 22d—2d Colorado, 5th, 7th, 11th, 15th, and 16th Kansas Cavalry and Kansas Militia, 1st, 2d, 4th, 6th, 7th. 8th, and 9th Missouri Militia Cavalry, 13th Missouri, 3d Iowa and 17th Illinois Cavalry; two engagements; Price's invasion of Missouri.

White River, Ark.

2,002. October 22d—53d U. S. Colored troops.

Gunboat attack on the Union Batteries, on the James River, Va.

2,003. October 22d—Confederate loss 11 wounded.

Hurricane Creek, Miss.

2,004. October 23d—1st Iowa and 9th Kansas Cavalry.

1864.]   **Princeton, Ark.**

2,005. October 23d—3d Missouri Cavalry.

Westport, Big Blue, Mo.

2,006. October 23d—Missouri Militia Cavalry, Cavalry of General A. J. Smith's command, and Cavalry and Kansas Militia of the Army of the Border; Price's invasion of Missouri.

Cold Water Grove, Osage, Mo.

2,007. October 24th—Kansas Cavalry of the Army of the Border.

Mine Creek, Maria des Cygnes and Little Osage River, Kan.

2,008. October 25th—Cavalry of Generals Pleasonton's and Curtis' armies; pursuit of Price's forces.

Milton, Blackwater, Fla.

2,009. October 26th—19th Iowa Volunteers and 2d Maine Cavalry.

Decatur, Ala.

2,010. October 26th to 29th—18th Michigan, 102d Ohio, and 68th Indiana Volunteers, and 14th U. S. Colored troops.

Hatche's Run, South Side R. R. (or Boydtown Road, Vaughn Road, and Burgess Farm), Va.

2,011. October 27th—2d Cavalry Division, 2d and 3d Division 2d Corps, 5th and 9th Corps, Army of the Potomac.

Fair Oaks (near Richmond), Va.

2,012. October 27th to 28th—10th and 18th Corps and Cavalry, Army of the James.

Newtonia, Mo.

2,013. October 28th and 30th—Cavalry of the Army of the Border; pursuit of Price's forces.

Fort Haiman, Tenn.

2,014. October 28th—Union Gunboats.

Destruction of the Rebel Ram Albemarle.

2,015. October 28th—Thirteen men, commanded by Lieutenant W. B. Cushing, U. S. Navy.

Fayetteville, Ark.

2,016. October 28th—1st Arkansas Cavalry.

Morristown, Tenn.

2,017. October 28th—Cavalry commanded by General Gillem.

Beverly, W. Va.

2,018. October 29th—8th Ohio Cavalry.

Muscle Shoals, Racoon Ford, Ala.

2,019. October 30th—1st Brigade, 1st Cavalry Division, Army of the Cumberland.

Near Brownsville, Ala.

2,020. October 30th—7th Iowa and 11th Missouri Cavalry.

Ladija, Terrapin Creek, Ala.

2,021. October 30th—Garrard's Cavalry Division, Army of the Cumberland.

Plymouth, N. C.

2,022. October 31st—U. S. steamers Commodore Hill, Shamrock, Otsego, Wyalusing, and Tacony.

Black River, La.

2,023. November 1st—6th U. S. Colored Heavy Artillery.

Union Station, Tenn.

2,024. November 1st to 4th—10th Missouri Cavalry.

Vera Cruz, Ark.

2,025. November 3d—One company of 46th Missouri Volunteers.

Johnsonville, Tenn.

2,026. November 4th and 5th—11th Tennessee Cavalry, 43d Wisconsin Volunteers, and 12th U. S. Colored troops.

Big Pigeon River, Tenn.

2,027. November 5th and 6th—3d North Carolina Mounted Infantry.

Fort Sedgwick, Va.

2,028. November 5th—2d Corps, Army of the Potomac.

Atlanta, Ga.

2,029. November 8th—2d Division, 20th Corps, Army of the Cumberland.

Shoal Creek, Ala.

2,030. November 9th—5th Division, Cavalry, Army of the Cumberland.

Newtown, Ninevah, and Cedar Springs, Va.

2,031. November 12th—1st and 3d Divisions, Cavalry, Army of the Potomac ; and 2d Cavalry Division, Army of West Virginia.

Bull's Gap, Morristown, Tenn.

2,032. November 13th—8th, 9th, and 13th Tennessee Cavalry.

Cow Creek, Ark.

2,033. November 14th to 28th—54th U. S. Colored troops (2d Arkansas), and 3d Kansas Indian Home Guards.

Clinton and Liberty Creek, La.

2,034. November 15th—Expedition commanded by General A. L. Lee.

Lovejoy Station, Jonesboro', Ga.

2,035. November 16th—1st Brigade 3d Division, Cavalry, Army of the Cumberland.

Bear Creek Station, Ga.

2,036. November 16th—2d Brigade 3d Division, Cavalry, Army of the Cumberland.

Chester Station, Bermuda Hundred, Va.

2,037. November 17th—209th Pennsylvania Volunteers.

Aberdeen and Butler Creek, Ala.

2,038. November 17th—2d Iowa Cavalry.

Myerstown, Va.

2,039. November 18th—Detachment 91st Ohio Volunteers.

1864.]   **Bayou La Fouche (or Ash Bayou), La.**

2,040. November 19th—11th Wisconsin Volunteers, and 93d U. S. Colored troops.

Macon, Ga.

2,041. November 20th—10th Ohio and 9th Pennsylvania Cavalry, 92d Illinois Mounted Infantry, and 10th Wisconsin Battery, Army of the Cumberland.

Liberty and Jackson, La.

2,042. November 21st—4th Wisconsin Cavalry and 1st Wisconsin Battery.

Rolling Fork, Miss.

2,043. November 22d—3d U. S. Colored Cavalry (1st Mississippi).

Griswoldville, Ga.

2,044. November 22d—Walcott's Brigade, 1st Division, 15th Corps, and 1st Brigade, 3d Cavalry Division, Army of the Tennessee.

Clinton, Ga.

2,045. November 22d—Advance of the 15th Corps.

Rood's Hill, Va.

2,046. November 22d—1st and 3d Divisions Cavalry Corps, Army of the Potomac, and 2d Cavalry Division, Army of West Virginia.

Lawrenceburg, Tenn.

2,047. November 22d—5th Cavalry Division, Military Division of the Mississippi.

Bent's Old Fork, Texas.

2,048. November 24th—1st California Cavalry.

Campbellville and Lynnville, Tenn.

2,049. November 24th—5th Cavalry Division, Military Division of the Missouri.

Columbia, Duck Run, Tenn.

2,050. November 24th to 28th—Capron's Brigade 1st Cavalry Division, and 4th and 23d Corps, General Thomas' army.

Ball's Ferry, Oconee River, Ga.

2,051. November 24th and 25th—1st Alabama Cavalry, advance of the Army of the Tennessee.

Pawnee Forks, Kansas.

2,052. November 25th—One Company 1st Colorado Cavalry.

St. Vrain's Old Fort, New Mexico.

2,053. November 25th—One Company of 1st New Mexico Cavalry.

Madison Station, Ala.

2,054. November 26th—101st U. S. Colored troops.

Sandersville (or Buffalo Creek), Ga.

2,055. November 26th—3d Brigade 1st Division, 20th Corps.

Sylvan Grove, Ga.

2,056. November 26th—8th Indiana and 2d Kentucky Cavalry.

Big Black River Bridge, Mississippi Central R. R.

2,057. November 27th—Cavalry and Artillery, commanded by Colonel Osband, 3d U. S. Colored Cavalry.

Waynesboro, Thomas' Station, and Buck Head Creek (or Reynolds' Plantation, Jones' Plantation, and Brown's Cross Roads), Ga.

2,058. November 27th to 29th—3d Cavalry Division, Army Military Division of the Mississippi.

Fort Kelly, New Creek, W. Va.

2,059. November 28th—From Confederate reports.

Spring Hill (or Mount Carmel), Tenn.

2,060. November 29th—4th Corps and Cavalry.

Big Sandy, Col. Ter.

2,061. November 29th—1st and 3d Colorado Cavalry.

Franklin, Tenn.

2,062. November 30th—4th Corps, Army of the Cumberland, 23d Corps, Army of the Ohio.

Honey Hill, Broad River (or Grahamsville), S. C.

2,063. November 30th—25th Ohio, 56th and 155th New York Volunteers, and 26th, 32d, 35th, and 102d U. S. Colored troops, and 54th and 55th Massachusetts Colored troops, Army of the South.

Bermuda Hundred, Va.

2,064. November 30th to December 4th—Pickets of the 20th Colored troops.

Stoney Creek Station and Duvall's Mills, Weldon R. R., Va.

2,065. December 1st—2d Cavalry Division, Army of the Potomac.

Twelve miles from Yazoo City, Miss.

2,066. December 1st—Detachment of the 2d Wisconsin Cavalry.

Trenches before Petersburg, Va.

2,067. December 1st to 31st—Army of the Potomac.

Skirmishing in front of Nashville, Tenn.

2,068. December 1st to 14th—4th Corps, Army of the Cumberland, 23d Corps, Army of the Ohio, 1st and 3d Divisions 16th Corps, Army of the Tennessee, and Cavalry.

Millen Grove, Ga.

2,069. December 1st—5th Kentucky and 8th Indiana Cavalry of Sherman's army.

Rocky Creek Church, Ga.

2,070. December 2d—3d Kentucky and 5th Ohio Cavalry ; advance of Sherman's army.

——, Mississippi.

2,071. December 2d—2d New York Cavalry.

Block House No. 2, Mill Creek, Chattanooga, Tenn.

2,072. December 2d and 3d—Detachment of 115th Ohio Volunteers, 44th and two Companies 14th U. S. Colored troops.

Thomas' Station, Ga.

2,073. December 3d—92d Illinois Mounted Infantry.

Coosaw River, S. C.

2,074. December 4th—25th Ohio Volunteers.

1864.]   **Block House No. 7, Overall's Creek, Tenn.**

2,075. December 4th—Troops commanded by General Milroy.

Waynesboro' and Brier Creek, Ga.

2,076. December 4th—3d Cavalry Division, Army Military Division of the Mississippi.

Statesboro, Ga.

2,077. December 4th—Foragers of the 15th Corps.

Murfreesboro (or Cedars), Tenn.

2,078. December 5th to 8th—Troops commanded by General Rousseau.

Deveaux Neck (or Tillafinney River, Mason's Bridge, and Gregory's Farm), S. C.

2,079. December 6th to 9th—26th, 33d, 34th, and 102d U. S. Colored troops, 54th and 55th Massachusetts Colored troops, 56th and 155th New York, and 25th and 107th Ohio Volunteers, and 3d Rhode Island Artillery ; also a Naval Brigade.

White Post, Va.

2,080. December 6th—50 men of the 21st New York Cavalry.

Ebenezer Creek, Cypress Swamp, Ga.

2,081. December 7th—9th Michigan and 9th Ohio Cavalry, rear guard of left wing of Sherman's Army.

Ogeechee River (or Jenk's Bridge, Eden Station, and Poole's Station), Ga.

2,082. December 7th to 9th—15th and 17th Corps, right wing of the Army of the Military Division of the Mississippi.

Weldon R. R. Expedition.

2,083. December 7th to 11th—2d Division Cavalry Corps, 5th Corps, and 3d Division 2d Corps, Army of the Potomac.

Reconnoissance to Hatcher's Run, Va.

2,084. December 8th and 9th—3d and 13th Pennsylvania and 6th Ohio Cavalry, and 1st Division, 2d Corps.

Raid to Gordonsville, Va.

2,085. December 8th to 28th—1st and 3d Divisions Cavalry, Army of the Potomac.

Expedition into Western N. C.

2,086. December 9th to January 14th, 1865—3d North Carolina Volunteers.

Fort Lyons (or Sand Creek), Ind. Ter.

2,087. December 9th—1st Colorado Cavalry, commanded by Colonel J. M. Chivington ; massacre of 500 Indians.

Cuyler's Plantation, Monteith Swamp, Ga.

2,088. December 9th—14th Corps of the left wing of the Army Military Division of the Mississippi.

Expedition to Hamilton, N. C.

2,089. December 9th to 12th—27th Massachusetts and 9th New Jersey Volunteers, North Carolina Cavalry, and 3d New York Artillery ; skirmish at Foster's Bridge on the 10th, and Butler's Bridge on the 12th.

9*

Bellefield and Hicksford, Va.

2,090. December 9th—2d Division, Cavalry Corps, Army of the Potomac; skirmish during the Weldon R. R. expedition.

Siege of Savannah, Ga.

2,091. December 10th to 21st—14th and 20th Corps, left wing; 15th and 17th Corps, right wing; Army Military Division of the Mississippi.

Elkton, Ky.

2,092. December 12th—1st Cavalry Division, commanded by Brigadier-General McCook.

Stoneman's Raid from Bean's Station, Tenn., to Saltville, Va.

2,093. December 12th to 21st—Cavalry of the Army of the Ohio.

Kingsport, Tenn.

2,094. December 13th—8th, 9th, and 13th Tennessee Cavalry; Stoneman's raid.

Fort McAllister, Ga.

2,095. December 13th—2d Division, 15th Corps, Sherman's army.

Bristol, Tenn.

2,096. December 14th—Cavalry commanded by General Burbridge; Stoneman's raid.

Memphis, Tenn.

2,097. December 14th—4th Iowa Cavalry.

Abingdon, Va.

2,098. December 15th—Cavalry commanded by General Burbridge; Stoneman's raid.

Murfreesboro, Tenn.

2,099. December 15th—Troops commanded by General Rousseau.

Glade Springs.

2,100. December 15th—12th Kentucky Cavalry; Stoneman's raid.

Nashville (or Brentwood), Overton's Hills, Tenn.

2,101. December 15th and 16th—4th Corps, Army of the Cumberland; 23d Corps, Army of the Ohio; 1st and 3d Divisions, 16th Corps, Army of the Tennessee; Detachments of Colored troops, Convalescents, Recruits, etc., and Cavalry Corps.

Hopkinsville, Ky.

2,102. December 16th—2d and 3d Brigades, McCook's 1st Cavalry Division.

Marion and Wytheville, Va.

2,103. December 16th—8th, 9th, and 13th Tennessee Cavalry; Stoneman's raid.

Millwood, Va.

2,104. December 17th—Scouting party, 14th Pennsylvania Cavalry.

Hollow Tree Gap, Tenn.

2,105. December 17th—5th and 7th Divisions, Cavalry, General Thomas' army.

Franklin, Tenn.

2,106. December 17th—6th Division, Cavalry, Thomas' army.

1864.]   Mitchell's Creek, Fla.

2,107. December 17th—82d U. S. Colored troops.

Pine Barren Creek, Ala.

2,108. December 17th to 19th—82d and 97th U. S. Colored troops.

Marion, Va.

2,109. December 18th—Cavalry of the Army of the Ohio ; Stoneman's raid.

Franklin Creek, Miss.

2,110. December 18th—Troops of the 3d Corps.

Rutherford Creek, Tenn.

2,111. December 19th—Cavalry of General Thomas' army.

Saltville, Va.

2,112. December 20th—Gillem's and Burbridge's Cavalry, commanded by General Stoneman.

Lacey's Springs, Va.

2,113. December 20th—3d Division of Cavalry, Army of the Potomac.

Madison Court House.

2,114. December 20th—Michigan Cavalry Brigade, 1st Cavalry Division, Army of the Potomac.

Lynnville, Tenn.

2,115. December 23d—Cavalry of General Thomas' army.

Jack's Shop, near Gordonsville, Va.

2,116. December 23d—1st Cavalry Division, Army of the Potomac, and 2d Cavalry Division, Army of West Virginia.

Buford's Station, Tenn.

2,117. December 23d—Cavalry of General Thomas' army.

Elizabethtown, Ky.

2,118. December 24th—1st Wisconsin Cavalry.

Mocassin Gap, Va.

2,119. December 24th—8th Tennessee Cavalry ; Stoneman's raid.

Murfreesboro, Tenn.

2,120. December 24th—12th U. S. Colored troops.

Fort Fisher, N. C.

2,121. December 25th—North Atlantic Squadron, commanded by Rear-Admiral Porter, and troops of 10th Corps, Army of the James.

Pulaski, Lamb's Ferry, Anthony's Hill, and Sugar Creek, Tenn.

2,122. December 25th—Cavalry of General Thomas' army.

Verona, Miss.

2,123. December 25th—7th Indiana Cavalry.

Decatur, Ala.

2,124. December 27th and 28th—Maj.-General Steadman's Provisional Division.

Egypt Station, Miss.

2,125. December 28th—7th Indiana, 4th and 11th Illinois, 4th and 10th Missouri, 2d Wisconsin, 2d New Jersey, 1st Mississippi, and 3d U. S. Colored Cavalry.

Pond Spring, Ala.

2,126. December 29th—15th Pennsylvania, and Detachments of 2d Tennessee and 10th, 12th, and 13th Indiana Cavalry.

1865.—(135.)

Franklin, Miss.

2,127. January 2d—4th and 11th Illinois and 3d U. S. Colored Cavalry.

Nauvoo, Ala.

2,128. January 2d—15th Pennsylvania, and Detachments of 2d Tennessee, and 10th, 12th, and 13th Indiana Cavalry ; Capture and destruction of Hood's Supply and Pontoon Train.

Thorn Hill, Ala.

2,129. January 3d—15th Pennsylvania, and Detachments of the 10th, 12th, and 13th Indiana, and 2d Tennessee Cavalry.

Smithfield, Ky.

2,130. January 5th—6th U. S. Colored Troops.

Julesburg, Ind. Ter.

2,131. January 7th—One company af the 7th Iowa Cavalry ; Indian fight.

Scottsboro, Ala.

2,132. January 8th—54 men of the 101st U. S. Colored troops.

Ivy Ford, Ark.

2,133. January 8th—79th U. S. Colored troops.

Beverly, W. Va.

2,134. January 11th—34th Ohio Volunteers and 8th Ohio Cavalry.

Fort Fisher, N. C.

2,135. January 13th to 15th—2d Division, and 2d Brigade 1st Division, 24th Corps, and 3d Division, 25th Corps, Army of the James, sailors and marines of the Atlantic Blockading Squadron.

1865.]   Red Hill, Ala.

2,136. January 14th—15th Pennsylvania Cavalry.

Dardanelle, Ark.

2,137. January 14th—2d Kansas Cavalry and Iowa Cavalry.

Pocotaligo, S. C.

2,138. January 14th to 16th—17th Corps, Army of the Tennessee.

Explosion of the Magazine at Fort Fisher.

2,139. January 16th—Troops of the Army of the James.

Ten Miles from Columbus, Ky.

2,140. January 18th—Tennessee Cavalry.

Half Moon Battery, Sugar Loaf Hill, N. C.

2,141. January 19th—Portion of the 24th and 25th Corps, Army of the James.

Fort Brady (or Fort Burnham, or Bogg's Mills), Va.

2,142. January 24th—U. S. Colored Troops and Heavy Artillery, Army of the James.

Combahee River, S. C.

2,143. January 25th—15th and 17th Corps, Army of the Tennessee.

Powhatan, Va.

2,144. January 25th—1st U. S. Colored Cavalry.

Simpsonville, Ky.

2,145. January 25th—5th U. S. Colored Cavalry.

Expedition into Western North Carolina.

2,146. January 29th to February 11th—3d North Carolina.

River's Bridge, Salkahatchie, S. C.

2,147. February 3d to 9th—17th and 15th Corps, Army of the Tennessee; includes skirmishes at Hickory Hill, Owen Cross Roads, Lowtonville, Duck Creek, and Whiphy Swamp.

Dabney's Mills (also known as Rowanty Creek and Vaughn Road), Hatcher's Run, Va.

2,148. February 5th to 7th—2d Cavalry Division, 3d and 5th Corps, and 1st Division, 6th Corps, Army of the Potomac.

Dunn's Lake, Volusia Co., Fla.

2,149. February 5th—Detachment of the 17th Connecticut Volunteers.

Mud Springs, Ind. Ter.

2,150. February 8th—11th Ohio and 7th Iowa Cavalry ; Indian fight.

Wiliston, S. C.

2,151. February 8th—Cavalry commanded by General Kilpatrick.

Binnaker's Bridge, South Edisto River, S. C.

2,152. February 9th—17th Corps, Army of the Tennessee.

Rush Creek, Ind. Ter.

2,153. February 9th—11th Ohio and 7th Iowa Cavalry ; Indian fight.

James' Island, S. C.

2,154. February 10th—Schimmelfennigs Division of Troops of the Department of the South.

Blackville, S. C.

2,155. February 11th—3d Cavalry Division, Army Military Division of the Mississippi.

Sugar Loaf Battery, Federal Point, N. C.

2,156. February 11th—2d Division and 1st Brigade 1st Division, 24th Corps, and 3d Division, 25th Corps, Army of the James.

Aiken, S. C.

2,157. February 11th—3d Cavalry Division, Sherman's army.

Orangeburg, North Edisto River, S. C.

2,158. February 12th—17th Corps, Army of the Tennessee.

Gunter's Bridge, S. C.

2,159. February 14th—3d Cavalry Division, Sherman's army.

Congaree Creek, S. C.

2,160. February 15th—15th Corps, Army of the Tennessee.

Cedar Keys, Fla.

2,161. February 16th—2d U. S. Colored troops.

Columbia, S. C.

2,162. February 16th and 17th—15th Corps, Army of the Tennessee.

Fort Jones, Ky.

2,163. February 18th—12th U. S. Colored Heavy Artillery.

Ashby Gap, Va.

2,164. February 18th—Detachment 14th Pennsylvania Cavalry.

Charleston, S. C.

2,165. February 18th—Troops of the Department of the South.

Fort Anderson, N. C.

2,166. February 18th—Navy, troops of the 24th Corps, Army of the James, and 23d Corps, Army of the Ohio.

Fort Meyers, Fla.

2,167. February 20th—Troops not specified.

Town Creek, N. C.

2,168. February 20th—3d Division, 23d Corps, Army of the Ohio.

Wilmington, N. C.

2,169. February 22d—2d and 3d Divisions, 23d Corps. Army of the Ohio, and a portion of the 24th Corps, Army of the James.

1865.]   **Douglass Landing, Pine Bluff, Ark.**

2,170. February 22d—13th Illinois Cavalry.

Mount Clio, S. C.

2,171. February 26th—Detachment of Mounted Men commanded by Captain Duncan.

Lynch Creek, S. C.

2,172. February 26th—Advance of the 15th Corps.

Chattanooga, Tenn.

2,173. February — —16th U. S. Colored troops.

Sheridan's Raid in Va.

2,174. February 27th to March 25th—1st and 3d Division Cavalry Corps, Army of the Potomac.

Mount Crawford, Va.

2,175. February 29th—3d Brigade 3d Division Cavalry, Army of the Potomac; Sheridan's raid.

Waynesboro, Va.

2,176. March 2d—3d Division Cavalry Corps, Army of the Potomac; Sheridan's raid.

Clinton, La.

2,177. March — —4th Wisconsin Cavalry.

Chesterfield, S. C.

2,178. March 2d—Advance of the 20th Corps.

Cheraw, S. C.

2,179. March 2d and 3d—Advance of 17th Corps.

Florence, S. C.

2,180. March 3d—Detachment of Mounted Infantry from Sherman's army.

Olive Branch, La.

2,181. March 6th—4th Wisconsin Cavalry.

Natural Bridge, Fla.

2,182. March 6th—2d and 99th U. S. Colored troops, and other troops, commanded by General Newton.

North Fork, Shenandoah, Va.

2,183. March 6th—Portion of Sheridan's Cavalry, commanded by Colonel Thompson, 1st N. H. Cavalry.

Rockingham, N. C.

2,184. March 7th—Kilpatrick's Cavalry Division, Sherman's army.

Wilcox's Bridge, Wise's Fork, N. C.

2,185. March 8th to 10th—1st and 2d Divisions of the District of Beaufort, and 1st Division 23d Corps, Army of the Ohio.

Monroe's Cross Roads, N. C.

2,186. March 10th—Kilpatrick's Cavalry Division.

Clear Lake, Ark.

2,187. March 11th—3d Wisconsin Cavalry.

Silver Run, Fayetteville, N. C.

2,188. March 13th—Advance of the 14th and 17th Corps.

Kinston, N. C.

2,189. March 14th—Maj.-General Schofield's command ; occupation of.

South Anna River, Va.

2,190. March 15th—5th U. S. Cavalry.

Taylor's Hole Creek, N. C.

2,191. March 15th—Kilpatrick's Cavalry.

Ashland, Va.

2,192. March 15th—2d Brigade, 3d Division, Cavalry, Army of the Potomac ; Sheridan's raid.

Averysboro (or Smith's Farm), N. C.

2,193. March 16th—20th Corps and Kilpatrick's Cavalry Division, Sherman's army.

Boyd's Station, Ala.

2,194. March 18th—101st U. S. Colored Troops.

Bentonville, N. C.

2,195. March 19th to 21st—14th and 20th Corps, left wing, 15th and 17th Corps, right wing, and Cavalry Division, Sherman's army.

Stoneman's Raid, Southwestern Va. and N. C.

2,196. March 20th to April 6th—Palmer's, Brown's, and Miller's Brigades of Cavalry.

Goldsboro, N. C.

2,197. March 21st—Occupied by General Schofield's command.

Hamilton, Va.

2,198. March 21st—12th Pennsylvania Cavalry.

Wilson's Raid, Chickasaw, Ala., to Macon, Ga.

2,199. March 22d to April 24th—1st and 2d Brigades 1st Division, 1st and 2d Brigades 2d Division, 1st and 2d Brigades 4th Division, Cavalry Corps, Military Division of the Mississippi.

Sumterville, S. C.

2,200. March 23d—Troops not specified.

Rerock, Arizona Ter.

2,201. March 24th—1st New Mexico Cavalry.

Coxe's Bridge, N. C.

2,202. March 24th—Provisional Corps, commanded by General Terry.

Fort Steadman (in front of Petersburg), Va.

2,203. March 25th—1st and 3d Divisions, 9th Corps, Army of the Potomac.

1865.]   Petersburg, Va.

2,204. March 25th—2d and 6th Corps, Army of the Potomac.

Pine Barren Creek (or Bluff Spring), Ala.

2,205. March 25th—Cavalry advance of General Steele's column.

Siege of Mobile, Ala.

2,206. March 26th to April 9th—Army of the Military Division of the West Mississippi, Maj.-General E. R. S. Canby.

Spanish Fort, Ala.

2,207. March 26th to April 8th—13th and 16th Corps, Army of the Military Division of the West Mississippi, and Navy.

Quaker Road, Gravelly Run, Va.

2,208. March 29th—1st Division (Griffin), and 5th Corps, Army of the Potomac.

Boydton and White Oak Roads, Va.

2,209. March 31st—5th and 2d Corps, Army of the Potomac.

Dinwiddie Court House, Va.

2,210. March 31st—1st, 2d, and 3d Divisions, Cavalry Corps, Army of the Potomac.

Montavallo and Six Mile Creek, Ala.

2,211. March 31st—4th Division, Cavalry; Wilson's raid.

Five Forks, Va.

2,212. April 1st—Division of Cavalry, Army of the James, 1st, 2d, and 3d Divisions Cavalry Corps, and 5th Corps, Army of the Potomac.

Boone, N. C.

2,213. April 1st—Stoneman's raid.

Trion, Ala.

2,214. April 1st—1st Brigade, 1st Division Cavalry Corps, Military Division of the Mississippi; Wilson's raid.

Mount Pleasant, Ala.

2,215. April 1st—Cavalry of General Canby's forces.

Centreville, Ala.

2,216. April 1st—2d Brigade, 1st Divisions Cavalry Corps, Military Division of the Mississippi; Wilson's raid.

Bogler's Creek and Plantersville (or Ebenezer Church and Maplesville), Ala.

2,217. April 1st—2d and 4th Divisions, Cavalry, Military Division of the Mississippi; Wilson's raid.

Selma, Ala.

2,218. April 2d—2d Division Cavalry, Military Division of the Mississippi; Wilson's raid.

Scottsville, Ala.

2,219. April 2d—2d Brigade, 1st Division, Cavalry, Military Division of the Mississippi; Wilson's raid.

Fall of Petersburg, Va.

2,220. April 2d—2d, 6th, and 9th Corps, Army of the Potomac, 24th Corps, Army of the James.

Namozin Church and Willicomack, Va.

2,221. April 3d—3d Division, Cavalry, Army of the Potomac.

Richmond, Va.

2,222. April 3d—Occupied by General Weitzel's troops.

Salem, N. C.

2,223. April 3d—Cavalry, commanded by Colonel Palmer; Stoneman's raid.

Wytheville, Va.

2,224. April 3d—15th Pennsylvania Cavalry; Stoneman's raid.

Northport, Ala.

2,225. April 3d—1st Brigade, 1st Division, Cavalry, Military Division of the Mississippi; Wilson's raid.

Deep River Bridge, N. C.

2,226. April 4th—Stoneman's raid.

Tuscaloosa, Ala.

2,227. April 4th—1st Brigade 1st Division Cavalry, Military Division of the Mississippi; Wilson's raid.

Amelia Springs (or Jettersville), Va.

2,228. April 5th—2d Division, Cavalry Corps, Army of the Potomac.

Sailor's Creek (or Harper's Farm and Deatonsville), Va.

2,229. April 6th—Cavalry Corps, 2d and 6th Corps, Army of the Potomac.

Sipsey Swamp, Ala.

2,230. April 6th—1st Brigade Cavalry, 1st Division, Military Division of 'the Mississippi; Wilson's raid.

High Bridge, Appomattox River, Va.

2,231. April 6th—Portion of the 24th Corps.

Farmville, Va.

2,232. April 7th—2d Corps, Army of the Potomac.

Appomattox Court House (or Clover Hill), Va.

2,233. April 8th and 9th—Cavalry, Army of the Potomac; 24th Corps, and one division 25th Corps.

Fort Blakeley, Ala.

2,234. April 9th—13th and 16th Corps, Military Division of West Mississippi; siege of Mobile.

1865]   **Lee's Surrender.**

2,235. April 9th—Armies of the Potomac and James.

Sumterville, S. C.

2,236. April 9th—Troops of the Department of the South.

Neuses River, N. C.

2,237. April 10th—Advance of Sherman's army.

Lowndesboro, Ala.

2,238. April 10th—2d Brigade 1st Division Cavalry, Military Division of the Mississippi ; Wilson's raid.

Montgomery, Ala.

2,239. April 12th to 13th—2d Brigade 1st Division Cavalry, Military Division of the Mississippi ; Wilson's raid.

Grant's Creek, Salisbury, N. C.

2,240. April 12th – Stoneman's raid.

Whistler's Station, Ala.

2,241. April 13th—3d Division 13th Corps, Army of the West Mississippi.

South Fork, John Day's River, Oregon.

2,242. April 16th—One company 1st Oregon Cavalry.

Fort Taylor, West Point, Ga.

2,243. April 16th—2d Brigade 1st Division Cavalry, Military Division of the Mississippi ; Wilson's raid.

Columbus, Ga.

2,244. April 16th—4th Division, Cavalry, Military Division of the Mississippi ; Wilson's raid.

Berryville, Va.

2,245. April 17th—General Hancock's command ; surrender of Mosby's command.

Boykin's Mills (or Bradford's Springs), S. C.

2,246. April 18th—Troops of the Department of the South.

Swift Creek, S. C.

2,247. April 19th—Troops of the Department of the South.

Dallas, N. C.

2,248. April 19th—Stoneman's raid.

Catawba River, N. C.

2,249. April 19th—Stoneman's raid.

Tobosofkee, Ga.

2,250. April 20th—17th Indiana Mounted Infantry ; Wilson's raid.

Macon, Ga.

2,251. April 20th—2d Division, Wilson's Cavalry Corps ; Wilson's raid.

Talladega, Ala.

2,252. April 22d—1st Brigade 1st Division Cavalry, Military Division of the Mississippi ; Wilson's raid.

Mumford's Station, Blue Mount, Ala.

2,253. April 23d—1st Brigade 1st Division Cavalry, Military Division of the Mississippi ; Wilson's raid.

Suwano Gap, N. C.

2,254. April 23d—Gillem's Cavalry Command.

Johnston's Surrender.

2,255. April 26th—Armies of the Tennessee, Georgia, and Ohio.

Taylor's Surrender.

2,256. May 4th— ————————————

Irwinsville, Ga.

2,257. May 10th—1st Wisconsin and 4th Michigan Cavalry ; capture of Jefferson Davis.

Sam Jones' Surrender at Tallahassee, Fla.

2,258. May 10th—Detachments of Wilson's Cavalry.

Jeff Thompson's Surrender at Chalk Bluff, Ark.

2,259. May 11th—General Dodge's forces.

Palmetto Ranch, Texas.

2,260. May 13th—62d U. S. Colored Troops, 34th Indiana Volunteers, and 2d Texas Cavalry.

Kirby Smith's Surrender.

2,261. May 26th—Maj.-General Canby's command.

LOSS IN ENGAGEMENTS, ETC.,

WHERE THE TOTAL WAS FIVE HUNDRED OR MORE ON THE SIDE OF THE UNION TROOPS—(149).

ALTHOUGH the losses here given are generally based on official medical returns, the figures must not be taken as perfectly reliable, for in many instances the returns were based on estimates, and the totals of losses were, by later and more reliable returns, sometimes considerably reduced. Confederate losses are generally based on estimates.

No.	Date	Name	Union Loss				Confederate Loss.—Total.
			Killed.	Wounded.	Missing.	Total.	
	1861.						
2,262	July 21st	Bull Run, Va.	481	1,011	1,460	2,952	1,752
2,263	Aug. 10th	Wilson's Creek, Mo.	223	721	291	1,235	1,095
2,264	Sept. 12th to 20th	Lexington, Mo.	42	108	1,624	1,774	100
2,265	Oct. 21st	Ball's Bluff, Va.	223	226	445	894	302
2,266	Nov. 7th	Belmont, Mo.	90	173	235	498	966
	1862.						
2,267	Feb. 14th to 16th	Fort Donelson, Tenn.	446	1,735	150	2,331	15,067
2,268	March 6th to 8th	Pea Ridge, Ark.	203	972	174	1,349	5,2 0
2,269	March 14th	Newbern, N. C.	91	466	.....	557	583
2,270	March 23d	Winchester, Va.	103	440	24	567	691
2,271	April 6th and 7th	Shiloh, Tenn.	1,735	7,882	3,956	13,573	10,699
2,272	May 5th	Williamsburg, Va.	456	1,460	372	2,228	1,000
2,273	May 23d	Front Royal, Va.	32	122	750	904	.....
2,274	May 25th	Winchester, Va.	38	155	711	904	.....
2,275	May 31st to June 1st	Seven Pines and Fair Oaks, Va.	890	3,627	1,222	5,739	7,997
2,276	June 8th	Cross Keys, Va.	125	500	.....	625	287

LOSS AT ENGAGEMENTS—(Continued).

No.	Date	Name	Killed	Wounded	Missing	Total	Confederate Loss.—Total.
	1862.						
2,277	June 9th	Fort Republic, Va	67	361	574	1,002	657
2,278	June 16th	Secessionville, James Island, S. C	85	472	128	685	204
2,279	June 25th	Oak Grove, Va	51	401	64	516	541
2,280	June 26th to July 1st	Seven days' retreat; includes Mechanicsville, Gaines' Mills, Chickahominy, Peach Orchard, Savage Station, Charles City Cross Roads, and Malvern Hill	1,582	7,709	5,958	15,249	17,583
2,281	July 13th	Murfreesboro, Tenn	33	62	800	895	150
2,282	Aug. 8th	Cedar Mountain, Va	450	660	290	1,400	1,307
2,283	July 20th to Sept. 20th	Guerilla campaign in Missouri; includes with Porter's and Poindexter's Guerillas	77	156	347	580	2,866
2,284	Aug. 28th and 29th	Groveton and Gainesville, Va					7,000
2,285	Aug. 30th	Bull Run, Va, (2d)	800	4,000	3,000	7,800	3,700
2,286	Aug. 30th	Richmond, Ky	200	700	4,000	4,900	750
2,287	Sept. 1st	Chantilly, Va				1,300	800
2,288	Sept. 12th to 16th	Harper's Ferry, Va	80	120	11,583	11,783	500
2,289	Sept. 14th	Turner's and Crampton's Gaps, South Mountain, Md	443	1,806	76	2,325	4,343
2,290	Sept. 14th to 16th	Mumfordsville, Ky	50		3,566	3,616	714
2,291	Sept. 17th	Antietam, Md	2,010	9,416	1,043	12,469	25,899
2,292	Sept. 19th to 20th	I-u-ka, Miss	144	598	40	782	1,516
2,293	Oct. 3d and 4th	Corinth, Miss	315	1,812	232	2,359	14,221
2,294	Oct. 5th	Big Hatchie River, Miss			500	2,500	400
2,295	Oct. 8th	Perryville, Ky	916	2,943	489	4,348	7,000
2,296	Dec. 7th	Prairie Grove, Ark	167	798	183	1,148	1,500

No.	Date	Engagement					
2,297	Dec. 7th	Hartsville, Tenn	55		1,800	1,855	149
2,298	Dec. 12th to 18th	Foster's expedition to Goldsboro', N. C	90	478	9	577	739
2,299	Dec. 13th	Fredericksburg, Va	1,180	9,028	2,145	12,353	4,576
2,300	Dec. 20th	Holly Springs, Miss			1,000	1,000	
2,301	Dec. 27th	Elizabethtown, Ky			500	500	
2,302	Dec. 28th and 29th	Chickasaw Bayou, Vicksburg, Miss	191	982	756	1,929	207
2,303	Dec. 31, 1862, to Jan. 2, 1863	Stone's River, Tenn	1,533	7,245	2,800	11,578	25,560
	1863.						
2,304	Jan. 1st	Galveston, Texas			600	600	50
2,305	Jan. 11th	Fort Hindman, Arkansas Post, Ark	129	831	17	977	5,500
2,306	March 4th and 5th	Thompson's Station, Tenn	100	300	1,306	1,706	600
2,307	April 27th to May 3d	Streight's raid from Tuscumbia, Ala., to Rome, Ga.	12	69	1,466	1,547	
2,308	May 1st	Port Gibson, Miss	130	718	5	853	1,650
2,309	May 1st to 4th	Chancellorsville, Va	1,512	9,518	5,000	16,080	12,281
2,310	May 16th	Champion Hills, Miss	436	1,842	189	2,457	4,300
2,311	May 18th to July 4th	Siege of Vicksburg, Miss	545	3,688	303	4,536	31,277
2,312	May 27th to July 9th	Siege of Port Hudson, La	500	2,500		3,000	7,208
2,313	June 6th to 8th	Milliken's Bend, La	154	223	115	492	725
2,314	June 9th	Beverly Ford and Brandy Station, Va				500	700
2,315	June 13th to 15th	Winchester, Va			3,000	3,000	850
2,316	June 23d to 30th	Rosecrans' campaign from Murfreesboro' to Tullahoma, Tenn	85	462	13	560	1,634
2,317	July 1st to 3d	Gettysburg, Pa	2,884	13,709	6,643	23,186	31,621
2,318	July 9th to 16th	Jackson, Miss	100	800	100	1,000	1,339
2,319	July 18th	Second assault on Fort Wagner, S. C				1,500	174
2,320	Sept. 19th to 20th	Chickamauga, Ga	1,644	9,262	4,945	15,851	17,804
2,321	Nov. 3d	Grand Coteau, La	26	124	576	726	445
2,322	Nov. 6th	Rogersville, Tenn	5	12	650	667	30
2,323	Nov. 23d to 25th	Chattanooga, Tenn.; includes Orchard Knob, Lookout Mountain, and Missionary Ridge	757	4,529	320	5,616	8,684
2,324	Nov. 26th to 28th	Operations at Mine Run, Va	100	400		500	500
2,325	Dec. 14th	Bean's Station, Tenn				700	900
	1864.						
2,326	Feb. 20th	Olustee, Fla	193	1,175	460	1,828	500
2,327	April 8th	Sabine Cross Roads, La	200	900	1,800	2,900	1,500
2,328	April 9th	Pleasant Hills, La	100	700	300	1,100	2,000

LOSS AT ENGAGEMENTS—(Continued).

No.	Date	Name	Killed	Wounded	Missing	Total	Confederate Loss.—Total.
	1864.						
2,329	April 12th	Fort Pillow, Tenn	350	60	164	574	80
2,330	April 17th to 20th	Plymouth, N. C	20	80	1,500	1,600	500
2,331	April 30th	Jenkins' Ferry, Saline River, Ark	200	955		1,155	1,100
2,332	May 5th to 7th	Wilderness, Va	5,597	21,463	10,677	37,737	11,400
2,333	May 5th to 9th	Rocky Face Ridge, Ga.; includes Tunnel Hill, Mill Creek Gap, Buzzard Roost, Snake Creek Gap, and near Dalton	200	637		837	600
2,334	May 8th to 18th	Spotsylvania Court House, Va.; includes engagements on the Fredericksburg Road, Laurel Hill, and Nye River	4,177	19,687	2,577	26,461	9,000
2,335	May 9th to 10th	Swift Creek, Va	90	490		490	500
2,336	May 9th to 10th	Cloyd's Mountain and New River Bridge, Va	196	585	34	745	900
2,337	May 12th to 16th	Fort Darling, Drury's Bluff, Va	432	2,380	210	3,012	2,500
2,338	May 13th to 16th	Resaca, Ga	600	2,147		2,747	2,800
2,339	May 15th	New Market, Va	120	560	240	920	405
2,340	May 16th to 30th	Bermuda Hundred, Va	200	1,009		1,300	3,000
2,341	May 23d to 27th	North Anna River, Va	223	1,460	290	1,973	2,000
2,342	May 25th to June 4th	Dallas, Ga				2,400	3,000
2,343	June 1st to 12th	Cold Harbor, Va	1,905	10,570	2,456	14,931	1,700
2,344	June 5th	Piedmont, Va	130	650		780	2,970
2,345	June 9th to 30th	Kenesaw Mountain, Ga.; includes Pine Mountain, Pine Knob, Golgotha, Culp's House, general assault, June 27th; McAfee's Cross Roads, Lattemore's Mills, and Powder Springs	1,370	6,500	800	8,670	4,600
2,346	June 10th	Brice's Cross Roads, near Guntown, Miss	223	394	1,623	2,240	606

No.	Date	Engagement					
2,347	June 10th	Kellar's Bridge, Licking River, Ky.	13	54	700	767	
2,348	June 11th and 12th	Trevellian Station, Central Railroad, Va.	85	490	160	735	370
2,349	June 15th to 19th	Petersburg, Va.; includes Baylor's Farm, Walthal, and Weir Bottom Church.	1,298	7,474	1,814	10,586	
2,350	June 17th and 18th	Lynchburg, Va.	100	500	400	700	200
2,351	June 20th to 30th	Trenches in front of Petersburg, Va.	112	506	800	1,418	
2,352	June 22d to 30th	Wilson's raid on the Weldon Railroad, Va.	76	265	700	1,041	
2,353	June 22d and 23d	Weldon Railroad, Va.	604	2,494	2,217	5,315	200
2,354	June 27th	Kenesaw Mountain, general assault. See No. 2,345.					503
2,355	July 1st to 31st	Front of Petersburg, Va.; losses at the Crater and Deep Bottom not included.				3,000	630
2,356	July 6th to 10th	Chattahoochee River, Ga.	419	2,076	1,200	3,695	600
2,357	July 9th	Monocacy, Md.	80	450	200	730	400
2,358	July 13th to 15th	Tupelo, Miss.; includes Harrisburg and Old Town Creek.	90	579	1,290	1,959	700
2,359	July 20th	Peach Tree Creek, Ga.	85	563		648	4,706
2,360	July 22d	Atlanta, Ga.; Hood's first sortie.	300	1,410		1,710	8,499
2,361	July 24th	Winchester, Va.	500	2,141	1,000	3,641	660
2,362	July 26th to 31st	Stoneman's raid to Macon, Ga.		100	1,100	1,200	
2,363	July 26th to 31st	McCook's raid to Lovejoy Station, Ga.		100	900	1,000	
2,364	July 28th	Ezra Chapel, Atlanta, Ga.; second sortie.	100	600		700	4,642
2,365	July 30th	Mine explosion at Petersburg, Va.	419	1,679	1,910	4,008	1,200
2,366	Aug. 1st to 31st	Trenches before Petersburg, Va.	87	484		571	
2,367	Aug. 14th to 18th	Strawberry Plains, Deep Bottom Run, Va.	400	1,755	1,400	3,555	1,100
2,368	Aug. 18th, 19th, and 21st	Six Mile House, Weldon Railroad, Va.	212	1,155	3,176	4,543	4,000
2,369	Aug. 21st	Summit Point, Va.			600	600	400
2,370	Aug. 25th	Ream's Station, Va.	127	546	1,769	2,442	1,500
2,371	Aug. 31st to Sept. 1st	Jonesboro', Ga.		1,149		1,149	2,000
2,372	May 5th to Sept. 8th	Campaign in Northern Georgia, from Chattanooga, Tenn., to Atlanta, Ga.	5,284	26,129	5,786	37,199	
2,373	Sept. 1st to Oct. 30th	Trenches before Petersburg, Va.	170	822	812	1,804	1,000
2,374	Sept. 19th	Apequan, Winchester, Va.	653	3,719	618	4,990	5,500
2,375	Sept. 23d	Athens, Ala.			950	950	30
2,376	Sept. 24th to Oct. 28th	Price's invasion of Missouri; includes a number of engagements.	170	336		506	
2,377	Sept. 28th to 30th	New Market Heights, Va.	400	2,029		2,429	2,000
2,378	Sept. 30th to Oct. 1st	Preble's Farm, Poplar Springs Church, Va.	141	788	1,756	2,685	900
2,379	Oct. 5th	Allatoona, Ga.	142	252	212	706	1,142

XIII.—10

LOSS AT ENGAGEMENTS—(Continued).

No.	Date	Name	Killed	Wounded	Missing	Total	Loss.—Total. Confederate
	1864.						
2,380	Oct. 19th	Cedar Creek, Va.	588	3,516	1,891	5,995	4,200
2,381	Oct. 27th	Hatcher's Run, South Side Railroad, Va.	156	1,047	699	1,902	1,000
2,382	Oct. 27th and 28th	Fair Oaks, near Richmond, Va.	120	733	400	1,303	451
2,383	Nov. 28th	Fort Kelly, New Creek, West Va.	...	...	700	700	5
2,384	Nov. 30th	Franklin, Tenn.	189	1,033	1,104	2,326	6,252
2,385	Nov. 30th	Honey Hill, Broad River, S. C.	66	645	...	711	...
2,386	Dec. 6th to 9th	Deveaux's Neck, S. C.	39	390	200	629	400
2,387	Dec. 15th and 16th	Nashville, Tenn.	400	1,740	...	2,140	15,000
	1865.						
2,388	Jan. 11th	Beverly, West Va.	5	20	583	608	...
2,389	Jan. 13th to 15th	Fort Fisher, N. C.	184	749	22	955	2,483
2,390	Feb. 5th to 7th	Dabney's Mills, Hatcher's Run, Va.	232	1,062	186	1,480	1,200
2,391	March 8th to 10th	Wilcox's Bridge, Wise's Fork, N. C	80	421	600	1,101	1,500
2,392	March 16th	Averysboro', N. C.	77	477	...	554	865
2,393	March 19th to 21st	Bentonville, N. C.	191	1,168	287	1,646	2,825
2,394	March 25th	Fort Steadman, in front of Petersburg, Va.	68	337	506	911	2,651
2,395	March 25th	Petersburg, Va.	103	864	209	1,176	834
2,396	March 26th to April 8th	Spanish Fort, Ala.	100	695	...	795	552
2,397	March 22d to April 24th	Wilson's raid from Chickasaw, Ala., to Macon, Ga.; includes a number of engagements	99	598	28	725	8,020
2,398	March 31st	Boydton and White Oak Roads, Va.	177	1,134	556	1,867	1,235
2,399	April 1st	Five Forks, Va.	124	706	54	884	8,500
2,400	April 2d	Fall of Petersburg, Va.	296	2,565	500	3,361	3,000
2,401	April 6th	Sailor's Creek, Va.	166	1,014	...	1,180	7,000

2,402	April 6th	High Bridge, Appomatox River, Va	10			1,041	....
2,403	April 7th	Farmville, Va				655	....
2,404	April 9th	Fort Blakely, Ala	113	516	31	629	2,900
2,405	April 9th	Surrender of Lee					26,000
2,406	April 26th	Johnston surrendered					29,924
2,407	May 4th	Taylor surrendered					10,000
2,408	May 10th	Sam Jones surrendered					8,000
2,409	May 11th	Jeff Thompson surrendered					7,454
2,410	May 26th	Kirby Smith surrendered					20,000

TABULAR STATEMENT OF THE NUMBER OF ENGAGEMENTS IN THE SEVERAL STATES AND TERRITORIES DURING EACH YEAR OF THE WAR.

STATES AND TERRITORIES	1861	1862	1863	1864	1865	TOTAL
New York	..	..	1	..	..	1
Pennsylvania	..	.9	8	1	..	9
Maryland	.3	..	10	8	..	30
District of Columbia	..	..	..	1	..	1
West Virginia	29	114	17	19	.1	80
Virginia	30	40	116	205	28	519
North Carolina	2	27	18	10	28	85
South Carolina	2	10	17	9	22	60
Georgia	..	8	8	92	6	108
Florida	.3	3	4	17	5	32
Alabama	..	10	12	32	24	78
Mississippi	..	43	76	67	1	186
Louisiana	1	11	54	50	2	118
Texas	1	2	8	1	2	14
Arkansas	1	40	40	78	6	167
Tennessee	2	42	124	89	1	298
Kentucky	14	82	30	31	4	138
Ohio	..	..	3	..	..	3
Indiana	..	..	4	..	..	4
Illinois	..	..	1	1	..	1
Missouri	65	95	43	41	..	244
Minnesota	..	5	1	..	..	6
California	..	1	4	.1	..	6
Kansas	..	..	4	5	1	7
Oregon	..	..	2	3	..	4
Nevada	..	..	..	2	..	2
Washington Terr.	..	..	1	..	1	1
Utah	.3	.5	.1	..	..	19
New Mexico	..	..	7	.4	.3	9
Nebraska	..	..	2	..	..	2
Colorado	..	.2	.9	3	..	4
Indian Territory	..	2	5	3	.1	17
Dakota	..	1	1	4	..	11
Arizona	..	..	1	1	..	4
Idaho	..	..	1	..	..	1
	156	564	627	779	135	2,261

INDEX TO CHRONOLOGICAL LIST OF ENGAGEMENTS AND BATTLES.

By the numbers following each name the reader will be enabled to refer to every occurrence of it in the foregoing lists, both in the chronological register and list of losses.

Courtland Bridge, Ala., 408.
Courtland Road, Ala., 1,643.
Cosby Creek, Tenn., 1,361.
Cotton Plantation, Ark., 373, 1,528.
Cotton Hill, W. Va., 526.
Cotton Gap, Ark., 1,133.
Cottage Grove, Tenn., 809.
Cove Creek, N. C., 651.
Cove Mountain, Va., 1,589.
Covington, Tenn., 796.
Cow Skin, Mo., 1,828.
Cow Creek, Kan., 2,033.
Coyle Tavern, Va., 1,117.
Cox's Bridge, N. C., 2,202.
Cross Lanes, W. Va., 57.
Cross Keys, Va., 328, 2,276.
Cross Hollows, Ark., 616.
Cross Timbers, Mo., 1,231.
Crump's Landing, Tenn., 224.
Crump's Hill, La., 1,487.
Crab Orchard, Ky., 473.
Crawford County, Mo., 656.
Crawford County, Ark., 1,841.
Craig's Meeting House, Va., 1,564.
Crampton's Gap, Md., 533, 2,289.
Crew's Farm, Va., 357.
Creek Agency, I. T., 1,250.
Creelsboro', Ky., 1,320.
Crooked Creek, Ala., 892.
Crooked River, Oregon, 1,623.
Crooked Run, Va., 1,851.
Cripple Creek, Tenn., 924.
Culpepper, Va., 385, 1,160, 1,216, 1,276.
Culp's House, Ga., 1,720.
Cumberland, Md., 1,821.
Cumberland River, Ky., 179.
Cumberland Mountains, Tenn., 205, 259.
Cumberland Mountains, W. Va., 280.
Cumberland Gap, Tenn., 341, 1,146, 1,381, 1,433.
Cumberland Iron Works, Tenn., 482, 755.
Cuyler's Plantation, Ga., 2,088.
Cypress Bridge, Ky., 129.
Cypress Bend, Mississippi River, 998.
Cypress Swamp, Ga., 2,081.
Cynthiana, Ky., 393, 1,679, 1,683.

Dabney's Mills, Va., 2,148, 2,390.
Dallas, Mo., 65, 477.

Dallas, Ga., 1,638, 2,342.
Dallas, N. C., 2,248.
Dalton, Ga., 1,368, 1,581, 1,848, 1,985, 2,333.
Dam No. 4, Potomac, Va., 145.
Dandridge, Tenn., 1,363.
Danville, Ky., 485, 813.
Danville, Ark., 1,148, 1,475.
Darbytown Roads, Va., 1,970, 1,987.
Dardanelle, Ark., 1,592, 2,137.
Darkesville, Va., 1,783, 1,903.
Darnestown, Md., 79.
Davis' Farm, Va., 1,722.
Davis' Mills, Miss., 699.
Davis's Cross Roads, Ga., 1,154.
Day's Gap, Ala., 879, 891.
Decatur, Ga., 1,829.
Decatur, Tenn., near, 392.
Decatur, Miss., 1,414.
Decatur, Ala., 1,459, 1,522, 1,643, 1,855, 2,010, 2,124.
Deer Creek, Miss., 780, 810.
Denmark, Tenn., 503.
Dent Co., Mo., 140.
Des Allemando, La., 522.
Des Arks, Ark., 737, 1,795.
Dead Buffalo Lake, D. T., 1,092.
Deatonsville, Va., 2,229.
Denver, C. T., 1,506.
Deep Bottom, Va., 1,786, 1,800.
Deep Bottom Run, Va., 1,846, 2,367.
Deep Creek, 1,398.
Deep River Bridge, N. C., 2,226.
Deserted House, Va., 748.
Devil's Back Bone, Ark., 1,133.
Deveaux Neck, S. C., 2,079, 2,386.
Diamond Grove, Mo., 236.
Dinwiddie Court House, Va., 2,210.
Ditch Bayou, Ark., 1,663.
Dobbin's Ferry, Tenn., 681.
Dodge Co., Mo., 436.
Dog Walk, Ky., 581.
Donaldsonville, La., 1,012, 1,066, 1,406, 1,830.
Donaphan, Mo., 220, 1,916.
Doubtful Cañon, A. T., 1,558.
Douglass Landing, Ark., 2,170.
Dover, Tenn., 181.
Dover Road, N. C., 882.
Downer's Bridge, Va., 1,627.

Floyd's Fork, Ky., 564.

Floyd Co., Ky., 1,010.

Fort Abercrombie, D. T., 509.

Fort Adams, La., 1,964.

Fort Anderson, Ky., 1,473.

Fort Anderson, N. C., 2,166.

Fort Blair, Ark., 1,199.

Fort Blakely, Ala., 2,234, 2,404.

Fort Blunt, I. T., 935.

Fort Brady, Va., 2,142.

Fort Burnham, Va., 2,142.

Fort Cobb, I. T., 602.

Fort Craig, N. M., 91, 185, 298.

Fort Cottonwood, Nev., 1,886, 1,918.

Fort Darling, Va., 285, 1,597, 2,337.

Fort Davidson, Mo., 1,934.

Fort De Russy, La., 1.464.

Fort Donelson, Tenn., 181, 479, 755, 1,978, 2,267.

Fort Esperanza, Texas, 1,309.

Fort Fillmore, N. M., 42, 442.

Fort Fisher, N. C., 2,121, 2,135, 2,139, 2,389.

Fort Gaines, Mobile Harbor, Ala., 1,826, 1,835.

Fort Gibson, I. T., 935, 1,912.

Fort Gilmore, Va., 1,946.

Fort Halleck, I. T., 1,048.

Fort Harrison, Va., 1,946.

Fort Hatt ras, N. C., 60.

Fort Heiman, Tenn., 2,014.

Fort Hell, Va., 1,909.

Fort Henry, Tenn., 174.

Fort Hill, Vicksburg, Miss., 1,006, 1,013.

Fort Hindman, Ark., 732, 2,305.

Forts Jackson and St. Philip, La., 248.

Fort Johnson, S. C., 337, 1,740.

Fort Jones, N. C., 2,163.

Fort Kelly, W. Va., 2,059, 2,383.

Fort Leavenworth, Kas., 1,997.

Fort Lyon, I. T., 2,087.

Fort Lyons, Va., 964.

Fort McAllister, Ga., 752, 789, 2,095.

Fort McCook, Ala., 488.

Fort McRae, N. M., 990.

Fort Macon, N. C., 252.

Fort Morgan, Ala., 1,826, 1,872.

Fort Myers, Fla., 2,167.

Fort Pemberton, Miss., 799.

Fort Pickens, Fla., 132.

Fort Pika, La., 653.

Fort Pillow, Tenn., 239, 277, 322, 1,466, 1,505. 2,329.

Fort Pulaski, Ga., 230.

Fort Rice, D. T., 1,943.

Fort Ridgley, Minn., 469.

Fort Sanders, Tenn., 1,311.

Fort Scott, Mo., 67.

Fort Scott, Ark., 1,198.

Fort Sedgwick, Va., 1,947, 2,028.

Fort Smith, Ark., 1,133, 1,799, 1,809, 1,875.

Fort Steadman, Va., 2,203, 2,394.

Fort Stevens, D. C., 1,768.

Fort Sumner, N. M., 1,350.

Fort Sumter, S. C., 1,837, 1,143.

Fort Taylor, Ga., 2,243.

Fort Wagner, S. C., 1,056, 1,057, 1,081, 1,138, 2,319.

Fort Wright, Tenn., 322.

Fort Brown Road, Texas, 691.

Forsyth, Mo., 37, 424.

Forty Hills, Miss., 904.

Forster's Bridge, N. C., 2,089.

Forster's expedition, N. C., 687, 2,298.

Fourteen Mile Creek, Miss., 913.

Fox Creek, Mo., 193.

Frankfort, Va., 657.

Frankfort, Ky., 1,671.

Franklin, Tenn., 686, 753, 795, 816, 843, 878, 957, 1,898. 2,062, 2,106, 2,384.

Franklin, Mo., 1,954.

Franklin, Miss., 2,127.

Franklin, Va., 570, 621, 668.

Franklin, La., 945.

Franklin's Crossing, Va., 959.

Franklin Co., Ark., 1,181.

Franklin Creek, Miss., 2,110.

Frazier's Farm, Va., 356.

Frederick, Md., 529.

Frederick City, Md., 1,763.

Fredericksburg, Mo., 1,778.

Fredericksburg, Va., 246, 642, 688, 894, 937, 2,299.

Fredericksburg Road., Va., 1,614.

Fredericktown, Mo., 105.

Freeman's Ford, Va., 476.

Fremont's Orchard, C. T., 1,506.

French Broad, Va., 1,376.

Front Royal, Va., 296, 315, 1,851, 2,273.

Thompson's Station, Tenn., 792, 2,206.
Thornburg, Va., 440.
Thornhill, Ala., 2,129.
Thoroughfare Gap, Va., 221, 594, 632.
Tickfaw River, Miss., 898.
Tillafinney River, S. C., 2,079.
Tilton, Tenn., 1,602.
Tilton, Ga., 1,984.
Tishamingo Co., Miss., 1,253.
Tobosofkee, Ga., 2,250.
Todd's Tavern, Va., 1,576.
Tompkinsville, Ky., 379, 869.
Tom's Brook, Va., 1,973.
Toon's Station, Tenn., 499.
Totspotomy, Va., 1,651.
Totspotomy Creek, Va., 1,646.
Town Creek, Ala., 883.
Town Creek, N. C., 2,168.
Township, Fla., 743.
Tracy City, Tenn., 1,367.
Trautner's Creek, N. C., 325.
Trenton, Tenn., 443, 698.
Trenton, N. C., 685.
Trenton Bridge, N. C., 283.
Trevellian Station, Va., 1,685, 2,348.
Trinity, Ala., 403.
Trinity River, Cal., 1,280.
Trion, Ala., 2,214.
Triplett's Bridge, Ky., 979.
Triune, Tenn., 967.
Try Mountain, Ky., 123.
Tullahoma, Tenn., 1.000, 1,020, 1,245.
Tunica Bend, La., 1,530.
Tunica Co., Miss., 428.
Tunnell Hill, Ga., 1,378, 1,441, 1,573, 2,333.
Tunnell Hill, Miss., 1,417.
Tunstall Station, Va., 336, 906, 1,453.
Tupelo, Miss., 908, 1,754, 1,771, 2,358.
Turkey Bend, Va., 356.
Turkey Island Bridge, Va., 396.
Turman's Ferry, Ky., 1,354.
Turnback Creek, Mo., 253.
Turner's and Crampton's Gaps, Md., 533, 2,289.
Tuscumbia, Ala, 779. 872, 879, 1,251.
Tuscumbia Creek, Miss., 313.
Tuscaloosa, Ala., 2,227.
Two Hills, Bad Lands, D. T., 1,836.

Union, Va., 624.
Union City, Tenn., 219, 1,058, 1,296.
Union City, Ky., 1,472.
Union Church, Va., 328.
Union Church, Miss., 884.
Union Mills, Mo., 468.
Unionville, Tenn., 792.
Union Station, Tenn., 2,024.
University Place, Tenn., 1,033.
Upper Missouri River, Ark., 534.
Upperville, Ga., 625, 995, 1,178.
Upton Hill, Ky., 97.
Utoy Creek, Ga., 1,827.

Vache Grasse, Ark., 1,933.
Valverde, N. M., 185.
Van Buren, Ark., 711, 1,841.
Varnell's Station, Ga., 1,585.
Vaughn, Miss., 1,596.
Vaughn Road, Va., 2,011, 2,148.
Vaught's Hill, Tenn., 887.
Vera Cruz, Ark., 2,025.
Vermillion Bayou, La., 1,210.
Vernon, Md., 1,062.
Verona, Miss., 2,223.
Vicksburg, Miss., 250, 715, 782. 893, 932, 936, 1,006, 1,013, 1,036, 1,125, 1,392, 1,416, 1,744, 1,748. 2,302, 2,311.
Vidalia, La., 1,165, 1,404, 1,789.
Vienna, Va., 10, 141, 506.
Village Creek, Ark., 333, 360.
Vincent's Cross Roads, Miss., 1,253.
Vinegar Hill, S. C., 1,124.
Vining Station, Ga., 1,741.
Volusia Co., Fla., 2,149.

Wachita, Indian Agency, Tex., 764.
Wadesburg, Mo., 154.
Waddel's Farm, Ark., 333, 361.
Waldron, Ark., 1,156, 1,199, 1,347, 1,385.
Wallace's Ferry. Ark., 1,794.
Wall Bridge, Va., 1,563.
Walkerville, Mo., 237.
Walker's Ford, W. Va.. 1,314.
Walkeretown, Va., 1,451.
Walthal, Va., 1,702.
Wapping Heights, Va., 1,089.
Wardensville, Va., 309.
Warm Springs, N. M., 990.
Warm Springs, N. C., 1,304.

Warrensburg, Mo., 213, 218, 339.
Warrenton Junction, Va., 557, 902, 919.
Warrenton Springs, Va., 1,216.
Warsaw, Mo., 104, 1,204.
Wartrace, Tenn., 1,197.
Washington, N. C., 317, 515, 829, 1,259.
Washington, D. C., 1,768.
Watauga River, Ark., 1,941.
Wautauga River, Tenn., 124.
Wautauga Bridge. Tenn., 717, 1,536.
Waterford, Miss., 665.
Waterford, Va., 1,106.
Waterloo Bridge, Va., 476.
Waterproof, La., 1,297, 1,422, 1,527.
Water Valley, Miss., 674. ,
Waugh's Farm, Ark., 1.427.
Wauhatchie, Tenn., 1,255.
Waverly, Tenn., 606, 842.
Wayne Co., W. Va., 1,411.
Wayne Court House, W. Va., 59.
Waynesville, Mo., 1.119.
Waynesboro', Va., 1,945, 1,958, 2,176.
Waynesboro', Ga.. 2,058, 2,076.
Weaver's Store, Ky., 881.
Weber's Falls, I. T., 1,147.
Welaka, Fla., 1,625.
Weldon Railroad, Va., 1,575, 1,583, 1,722,1,856,1,956,2,065,2,083,2,353.
Wentzville, Mo., 29.
Western North Carolina, expedition into, 2,086, 2,146.
Westminster, Md., 1,015.
Westport, Mo., 983. 2,006.
Weston, W. Va., 498.
West Branch, Va., 848.
West Glaze, Mo., 100.
West Liberty, Ky., 110.
West Point, Va., 270.
West Point, Ark., 1,111, 1,698, 1,804.
West Point, Miss., 1,431.
West Point, Ga., 2,243.
West Virginia, Averill's raid, 1,120, 1,323.
Weyer's Cave, Va., 1,937.
Whipley Swamp, S. C., 2,147.
Whistler's Station, Ala., 2,241.
Whitemarsh, Ga., 243.
White's Bridge, Va., 1,584.
White's Ford, Va., 1,171.
Whiteside, Fla., 1,801.

Whittaker's Mills, Va., 845.
White Co., Ark., 1,408.
White Co., Tenn., 1,439.
Whitehall, N. C., 692.
White House, Va., 1,708, 1,716.
White Oak Swamp, Va., 356.
White Oak Swamp Bridge, Va., 434, 1,688.
White Oak Bridge, Ky., 465.
White Oak Road, Va., 2,209, 2,398.
White Post, W. Va., 1,689, 1,840, 2,080.
White River, Ark., 338, 370, 1,111, 1,718, 1,727, 2,002.
White Stone Hill, D. T., 1,134.
White Sulphur Springs, Va., 649, 1,123, 1,216.
White Water, Mo., 874.
Wier Bottom Church, Va., 1,597, 1,700.
Wilcox's Bridge, N. C., 2,185, 2,391.
Wild Cat, Ky., 108.
Wilderness, Va., 1,565, 2,332.
Wiliston, S. C., 2,151.
Willis Church, Va., 163.
Williamsburg, Va., 269, 381, 521, 758, 822, 845, 2,272.
Williamsburg, Ky., 618.
Williamsburg Road, Va., 343.
Williams' Bridge, La., 358.
Williams' Farm, Va., 1,722.
Williamsport, Tenn., 452.
Williamsport, Md., 547, 1,044.
Williamsport, W. Va., 1,380.
Williamston, N. C., 626.
Willicomack, Va., 2,221.
Willmarsh Island, S. C., 1,438.
Willow Creek, Cal., 1,292.
Wilmington Island, Ga., 243.
Wilmington, N. C., 2,169.
Wilson's Creek, Mo., 49, 2,263.
Wilson's Creek, Ky., 975.
Wilson's Farm, La., 1,496.
Wilson's Landing, Va., 1,682.
Wilson's Wharf Landing, Va., 1,636.
Wilson's raid on Weldon Railroad, Va., 1,719, 2,352.
Wilson's raid in Alabama and Georgia, 2,199, 2,397.
Winchester, Va., 212, 303, 933, 974, 1,784, 1,791, 1,854, 1,919, 2,270, 2,274, 2,315, 2,361, 2,374.

PART III.

RECORD OF THE GENERAL OFFICERS OF
THE ARMIES OF THE UNITED STATES
DURING THE WAR OF THE
REBELLION.

GENERAL OFFICERS.

This list of general officers is compiled from official army registers of regulars and volunteers, and from the General Orders of the War Department. In the regular army, several officers who were appointed after, but had served during the rebellion, are included to round off the lists. Where the general officers obtained the full, the brevet rank is omitted. The list of general officers deceased includes only those who died while in the service, and those of the regular army to December 31, 1865.

General United States Army.

Full Rank.—1.

1. Lieut.-General Ulysses S. Grant, appointed July 25, 1866.

Lieutenant-Generals United States Army.

Full Rank.—2.

2. Ulysses S. Grant, Major-General U. S Army, from March 2, 1864; promoted General July 25, 1866.
3. William T. Sherman, Major-General U. S. Army, from July 25, 1866.

By Brevet.—1.

4. Major-General Winfield Scott, from March 29, 1847; retired Nov. 1, 1861.

Major-Generals United States Army.

Full Rank.—11.

5. Winfield Scott, Brig.-General U. S. Army, from June 25, 1841; retired Nov. 1, 1861.
6. George B. McClellan, U. S. Army, from May 14, 1861; resigned Nov. 8, 1864.
7. John C. Fremont, late   "   "   May 14, 1861;   "   June 4, 1864.
8. Henry W. Halleck, late   "   "   Aug. 19, 1861.

9. John E. Wool, Brig.-General. U. S. Army, from May 16, 1862; retired Aug. 1, 1863.

10. Ulysses S. Grant, Major-General of Volunteers, from July 4, 1863 ; promoted to Lieut.-General March 2, 1864.

11. William T. Sherman, Major-General of Volunteers, from Aug. 12, 1864 ; promoted to Lieut.-General July 25, 1866.

12. George G. Meade, Major-General of Volunteers, from Aug. 18, 1864.

13. Philip H. Sheridan,   "   "   " Nov. 8, 1864.

14. George H. Thomas,   "   "   " Dec. 15, 1864.

15. Winfield S. Hancock.   "   "   " July 26, 1866.

By Brevet.—152.

16. Brig.-General Irvin McDowell, U. S. Army.............from March 13, 1865.

17.   "   William S. Rosecrans, U. S. Army........ "   "   "

18.   "   Philip St. G. Cook,   ,"   .... "   "   "

19.   "   John Pope, U. S. Army................. "   "   "

20.   "   Joseph Hooker, "   .... "   "   "

21.   "   John M. Schofield, U. S. Army........... "   "   "

22.   "   Oliver O. Howard,   "   .... "   "   "

23.   "   Alfred H. Terry,   "   .... "   "   "

24.   "   Edward O. C. Ord,   "   .... "   "   "

25.   "   Edward R. S. Canby,   "   .... "   "   "

26.   "   Edwin V. Sumner,   "   .... " May   31, 1862.

27.   "   William S. Harney,   "   .... " March 13, 1865.

28.   "   Robert Anderson,   "   .... " Feb.   3, "

29.   "   Lovell H. Rousseau,   "   .... " March 28, 1867.

30.   "   Lorenzo Thomas, Adjutant-General ...... " March 13, 1865.

31. Colonel Edward D. Townsend, Asst. Adjutant-General, "   "   "

32.   "   William A. Nichols,   "   "   "   "   "

33. Lieut.-Colonel Seth Williams,   "   "   "   "   "

34.   "   James B. Fry,   "   "   "   "   "

35.   "   Geo. L. Hartsuff,   "   "   "   "   "

36. Major William D. Whipple,   "   "   "   "   "

37. Colonel Randolph B. Marcy, Inspector-General.......... "   "   "

38.   "   Delos B. Sackett,   "   .... "   "   "

39.   "   Edmund Schriver,   "   .... "   "   "

40.   "   James A. Hardie,   "   .... "   "   "

41. Major Absalom Baird, Asst. Inspector-General .... "   "   "

42. Brig.-General Joseph Holt, Judge Advocate-General.... "   "   "

43.   "   John A. Rawlins, Chief of Staff .... " April   9, 1865.

44.   "   Montgomery C. Meigs, Q'rmaster-General, " July   5, 1864.

45. Colonel Charles Thomas, Asst. Quartermaster-General.. " March 13, 1865.

46.   "   Thomas Swords,   "   "   "   "   "

47.   "   Geo. H. Crossman,   "   "   "   "   "

48. Lieut.-Col. David H. Vinton, "   "   "   "   "

49. Major Robert Allen, Quartermaster U. S. Army .... "   "   "

50.   "   James L. Donaldson,   "   "   .... "   "   "

51.   "   Daniel H. Rucker,   "   "   .... "   "   "

52.   "   Rufus Ingalls,   "   "   .... "   "   "

53.   "   Langdon C. Easton,   "   "   .... "   "   "

54. Major Stewart Van Vliet, Quartermaster U. S. Army....from March 13, 1865.
55. Captain Robert O. Tyler, Asst. Q'rmaster U. S. Army....   "   "   "
56.   "   Alvan C. Gillem,   "   "   "   ....   "   April 12, 1865.
57. Col. Geo. Gibson, Commissary-Gen. of Subsistence, retired,   "   May   30, 1848.
58. Brig.-General Amos B. Eaton, Commissary-General of
        Subsistence....................................   "   March 13, 1865.
59. Colonel Alexander Shiras, Asst. Commissary-General of
        Subsistence....................................   "   "   "
60. Lieut.-Colonel M. D. L. Simpson, Asst. Commissary-
        General of Subsistence ....   "   "   "
61. Lieut.-Colonel Henry F. Clarke, Asst. Commissary-Gen-
        eral of Subsistence..............................   "   "   "
62. Major Amos Beckwith, Commissary of Subsistence......   "   "   "
63. Captain John P. Hawkins   "   "   ......   "   "   "
64.   "   John W. Turner,   "   "   ......   "   "   "
65. Brig.-Gen. Joseph K. Barnes, Surgeon-General, U. S. A.,   "   "   "
66. Colonel Benjamin W. Brice, Paymaster-General,   "   "   "   "
67. Brig.-Gen. Joseph G. Totten, Chief of Engineers, retired,   "   April 21, 1864.
68.   "   Richard Delafield,   "   "   U. S. A.,   "   March 13, 1865.
69. Colonel Thomas J. Cram, Corps of Engineers,   "   "   Jan.   13, 1866.
70.   "   John G. Barnard,   "   "   "   "   March 13, 1865.
71. Lieut.-Colonel Daniel P. Woodbury, Corps of Engineers,
        U. S. Army.......... ....   "   Aug.   15, 1864.
72. Lieut.-Col. Geo. W. Cullum, Corps of Engineers, U. S. A.,   "   March 13, 1865.
73.   "   Henry W. Berham,   "   "   "   "   "   "
74.   "   Andrew A. Humphreys, Corps of Engineers,
        U. S. Army............................   "   "   "
75.   "   Zealous B. Tower, Corps of Engineers, U. S. A.,   "   "   "
76.   "   Horatio G. Wright,   "   "   "   "   "   "
77.   "   John Newton,   "   "   "   "   "   "
78. Major W. F. Smith,   "   "   "   "   "   "
79.   "   John G. Foster,   "   "   "   "   "   "
80.   "   Quincy A. Gilmore,   "   "   "   "   "   "
81.   "   John G. Parke,   "   "   "   "   "   "
82.   "   Gouverneur K. Warren,   "   .   "   "   "   "   "
83.   "   Amiel W. Whipple,   "   "   "   "   May   7, 1863.
84. Captain Godfrey Weitzel,   "   "   "   "   March 13, 1865.
85.   "   James H. Wilson,   "   "   "   "   "   "
86. Brig.-Gen. Jas. W. Ripley, Chief of Ordnance, retired..   "   "   "
87.   "   George D. Ramsey,   "   "   "   ...   "   "   "
88.   "   Alex. B. Dyer,   "   "   U. S. A..   "   "   "
89. Major Washington L. Elliott, 1st Regiment of Cavalry,
        U. S. Army................................ ....   "   "   "
90. Colonel Thos. J. Wood, 2d Regiment of Cavalry, U. S. A.,   "   "   "
91. Major John W. Davidson, 2d Regiment of Cavalry,   "   "   "   "
92.   "   Alfred Pleasonton, 2d   "   "   "   "   "   "
93.   "   Frank Wheaton,   2d   "   "   "   "   "   "
94. Captain Wesley Merritt,   2d   "   "   "   "   "   "
95. Lieut.-Col. George Stoneman, 3d   "   "   "   "   "   "
96. Major Kenner Garrard,   3d   "   "   "   "   "   "
    11*

97. Captain Gordon Granger,	3d Regt. of Cav., U. S. A., from March 13, 1865.
98. " Wm. W. Averell,	3d	"	"	"	"	"	"
99. " Alfred Gibbs,	3d	"	"	"	"	"	"
100. Major Richard W. Johnson,	4th	"	"	"	"	"	"
101. Captain Eli Long,	4th	"	"	"	"	"	"
102. Colonel Wm. H. Emory,	5th	"	"	"	"	"	"
103. Lieut.-Col. Andrew J. Smith,	5th	"	"	"	"	"	"
104. Major Eugene A. Carr,	5th	"	"	"	"	"	"
105. " David S. Stanley,	5th	"	"	"	"	"	"
106. Captain John B. McIntosh,	5th	"	"	"	"	"	"
107. " Geo. A. Custer,	5th	"	"	"	"	"	"
108. Colonel David Hunter,	6th	"	"	"	"	"	"
109. Lieut.-Col. Sam'l D. Sturgis,	6th	"	"	"	"	"	"
110. Major James H. Carleton,	6th	"	"	"	"	"	"
111. Captain August V. Kautz,	6th	"	"	"	"	"	"
112. Colonel Edward Hatch,	9th	"	"	"	"	March 2, 1867.
113. " Benj. H. Grierson,	10th	"	"	"	"	"	"
114. Major James B. Ricketts,	1st Regt. of Artill'y, U.S.A.,	"	March 13, 1865.
115. " John M. Brannon,	1st	"	"	"	"	"	"
116. Captain Jefferson C. Davis,	1st	"	"	"	"	"	"
117. " Judson Kilpatrick,	1st	"	"	"	"	"	"
118. Colonel Wm. W. Morris,	2d	"	"	"	"	"	"
119. " Wm. F. Barry,	2d	"	"	"	"	"	"
120. Lieut.-Col. Wm. H. French,	2d	"	"	"	"	"	"
121. Colonel Thos. W. Sherman,	3d	"	"	"	"	"	"
122. Lieut.-Col. Henry J. Hunt,	3d	"	"	"	"	"	"
123. Major Albion P. Howe,	4th	"	"	"	"	"	"
124. Captain John Gibbon,	4th	"	"	"	"	"	"
125. Col. Harvey Brown, retired,	5th	"	"	"	"	Aug. 2, 1866.
126. Major. Geo. W. Getty,	5th	"	"	"	"	March 13, 1865.
127. Captain Truman Seymour,	5th	"	"	"	"	"	"
128. " Charles Griffin,	5th	"	"	"	"	"	"
129. " Romeyn B. Ayres,	5th	"	"	"	"	"	"
130. " Richard Arnold,	5th	"	"	"	"	"	"
131. " Adelbert Ames,	5th	"	"	"	"	"	"
132. " Emory Upton,	5th	"	"	"	"	"	"
133. Colonel Robert C. Buchanan,	1st Regt. of Inf'y, U. S. A.,	"	"	"
134. Captain Joseph A. Mower,	1st	"	"	"	"	"	"
135. Lt.-Col. Sam'l W. Crawford,	2d	"	"	"	"	"	"
136. Major John C. Robinson,	2d	"	"	"	"	"	"
137. Colonel William Hoffman,	3d	"	"	"	"	"	"
138. Lieut.-Col. Frederick Steele,	3d	"	"	"	"	"	"
139. Major Cuvier Grover,	3d	"	"	"	"	"	"
140. " George Crook,	3d	"	"	"	"	"	"
141. Capt. Alex. McD. McCook,	3d	"	"	"	"	"	"
142. Colonel Silas Casey,	4th	"	"	"	"	"	"
143. " Daniel Butterfield,	5th	"	"	"	"	"	"
144. Lieut.-Colonel George Sykes,	5th	"	"	"	"	"	"
145. Capt. Alfred T. A. Torbert,	5th	"	"	"	"	"	"
146. Major David A. Russell,	8th	"	"	"	"	Sept. 19, 1864.

147. Captain William B. Hazen,	8th	Regt. of Inf'y, U. S. A., from March 13, 1865.
148. Colonel John H. King,	9th	"	"	"	"	"	"	"
149. Captain Samuel S. Carroll,	10th	"	"	"	"	"	"	"
150. Colonel Wm. S. Ketchum,	11th	"	"	"	"	"	"	"
151. Lt.-Col. Rob't S. Granger,	11th	"	"	"	"	"	"	"
152. Captain Alex. S. Webb,	11th	"	"	"	"	"	"	"
153. Colonel Wm. B. Franklin,	12th	"	"	"	"	"	"	"
154. Col. Christopher C. Augur,	12th	"	"	"	"	"	"	"
155. Major Wm. P. Carlin,	16th	"	"	"	"	"	"	"
156. Colonel S. P. Heintzelman,	17th	"	"	"	"	"	"	"
157. Lt.-Col. Abner Doubleday,	17th	"	"	"	"	"	"	"
158. Major Chas. R. Woods,	18th	"	"	"	"	"	"	"
159. Captain Francis Fessenden,	19th	"	"	"	"	"	"	"
160. Colonel Joseph J. Reynolds,	26th	"	"	"	"	March	2, 1867.
161. " John E. Smith,	27th	"	"	"	"	"	"
162. " Charles H. Smith,	28th	"	"	"	"	"	"
163. " Orlando B. Willcox,	28th	"	"	"	"	"	"
164. Col. Galusha Pennypacker,	34th	"	"	"	"	"	"
165. Colonel Nelson A. Miles,	40th	"	"	"	"	"	"
166. " Daniel E. Sickles,	42d	"	"	"	"	"	"
167. " Wager Swayne,	45th	"	"	"	"	"	"

Major-Generals U. S. Volunteers.

Full Rank.—128.

168. John A. Dix, of New York, from May 16, 1861; resigned Nov. 30, 1865.

169. Nathaniel P. Banks, of Massachusetts, from May 16, 1861; mustered out Aug. 24, 1865.

170. Benjamin F. Butler, of Massachusetts, from May 16, 1861; resigned Nov. 30, 1865.

171. Brig.-General David Hunter, U. S. Vols., from Aug. 13, 1861; mustered out Jan. 15, 1866.

172. Edwin D. Morgan, of New York, from Sept. 28, 1861; resigned Jan. 1, 1863.

173. Ethan A. Hitchcock, of Missouri, from Feb. 10, 1862; mustered out Oct. 1, 1867.

174. Brig.-General Ulysses S. Grant, U. S. Vols., from Feb. 16, 1862; promoted Major-General U. S. A., July 4, 1863.

175. Brig.-General Irvin McDowell, U. S. A., from March 14, 1862; mustered out Sept. 1, 1866.

176. Brig.-General Ambrose E. Burnside, U. S. Vols., from March 18, 1862; resigned April 15, 1865.

177. Brig.-General William S. Rosecrans, U. S. A., from March 21, 1862; mustered out Jan. 15, 1866.

178. Brig.-General Don Carlos Buell, U. S. Vols., from March 21, 1862; mustered out May 23, 1864.

179. Brig.-General John Pope, U. S. Vols., from March 21, 1862; mustered out Sept. 1, 1866.

180. Brig.-General Samuel R. Curtis, U. S. Vols., from March 21, 1862; mustered out April 30, 1866.

181. Brig.-General Franz Sigel, U. S. Vols., from March 21, 1862; resigned May 4, 1865.

182. Brig.-General John A. McClernand, U. S. Vols., from March 21, 1862; resigned Nov. 30, 1864.
183. Brig.-General Charles F. Smith, U. S. Vols., from March 21, 1862; died April 25, 1862.
184. Brig. General Lewis Wallace, U. S. Vols., from March 21, 1862; resigned Nov. 30, 1865.
185. Brig.-General Ormsby M. Mitchell, U. S. Vols., from April 11, 1862; died Oct. 30, 1862.
186. Cassius M. Clay, of Kentucky, from April 11, 1862; resigned March 11, 1863.
187. Brig.-General George H. Thomas, U. S. Vols., from April 25, 1862; promoted Major-General U. S. A. Dec. 15, 1864.
188. George C. Cadwalader, of Pennsylvania, from April 25. 1862; resigned July 5, 1865; Major-General of State Volunteers or Militia.
189. Brig.-General Wm. T. Sherman, U. S. Vols., from May 1, 1862; promoted Major-General U. S. A. Aug. 12, 1864
190. Brig.-General Edward O. C. Ord, U. S. Vols., from May 2, 1862; mustered out Sept. 1, 1866.
191. Brig.-General Edwin V. Sumner, U. S. A., from July 4, 1862; died March 21, 1863.
192. Brig.-General Samuel P. Heintzelman, U. S. Vols., from May 5, 1862; mustered out Aug. 24, 1865.
193. Brig.-General Erasmus D. Keyes, U. S. Vols., from May 5, 1862; resigned May 6, 1864.
194. Brig.-General Joseph Hooker, U. S. Vols., from May 5, 1862; mustered out Sept. 1, 1866.
195. Brig.-General Silas Casey, U. S. Vols., from May 31, 1862; mustered out Aug. 24, 1865.
196. Brig.-General Philip Kearney, U. S. Vols., from July 4, 1862; killed Sept. 1, 1862.
197. Brig.-General Fitz John Porter, U. S. Vols., from July 4, 1862; out of service Jan. 21, 1863.
198. Brig.-General Wm. B. Franklin, U. S. Vols., from July 4, 1862; resigned Nov. 10, 1865.
199. Brig.-General Darius N. Couch, U. S. Vols., from July 4, 1862; resigned May 26, 1865.
200. Brig.-General Israel B. Richardson, U. S. Vols., from July 4, 1862; died of wounds Nov. 3, 1862.
201. Brig.-General Henry W. Slocum, U. S. Vols., from July 4, 1862; resigned Sept. 28, 1865.
202. Brig.-General John J. Peck, U. S. Vols., from July 4, 1862; mustered out Aug. 24, 1865.
203. Brig.-General John Sedgwick, U. S. Vols., from July 4, 1862; killed May 9, 1864.
204. Brig.-General George W. Morell, U. S. Vols., from July 4, 1862; expired by constitutional limitation March 4, 1863
205. Brig.-General William F. Smith, U. S. Vols., from July 4, 1862; expired by constitutional limitation March 4, 1863; reappointed from March 9, 1864; resigned Nov. 4, 1865.
206. Brig.-General Alex. McD. McCook, U. S. Vols., from July 17, 1862; resigned Oct. 21, 1865.

207. Brig.-General William Nelson, U. S. Vols., from July 17, 1862; died Sept. 29, 1862.

208. Brig.-General Thomas L. Crittenden, U. S. Vols., from July 17, 1862; resigned December 13, 1864.

209. Brig.-General Jos. K. F. Mansfield, U. S. A., from July 18, 1862; died of wounds Sept. 18, 1862.

210. Brig.-General Isaac I. Stevens, U. S. Vols., from July 18, 1862; killed Sept. 1, 1862.

211. Brig.-General Horatio G. Wright, U. S. Vols., from July 18, 1862; expired by constitutional limitation March 4, 1863; reappointed from May 12, 1864; mustered out Sept. 1, 1866.

212. Brig.-General John G. Foster, U. S. Vols., from July 18, 1862; mustered out Sept. 1, 1866.

213. Brig.-General Jesse L. Reno, U. S. Vols., from July 18, 1862; died of wounds Sept. 14, 1862.

214. Brig.-General John G. Parke, U. S. Vols., from July 18, 1862; mustered out Jan. 15, 1865.

215. Brig.-General Christopher C. Augur, U. S. Vols., from Aug. 9, 1862; mustered out Sept. 1, 1866.

216. Brig.-General Robert C. Schenck, U. S. Vols., from Aug. 30, 1862; resigned Dec. 5, 1863.

217. Brig.-General Stephen A. Hurlbut, U. S. Vols., from Sept. 17, 1862; mustered out June 20, 1865.

218. Brig.-General Schuyler Hamilton, U. S. Vols., from Sept. 17, 1862; resigned Feb. 27, 1863.

219. Brig.-General Gordon Granger, U. S. Vols., from Sept. 17, 1862; mustered out Jan. 15, 1866.

220. Brig.-General Charles S. Hamilton, U. S. Vols., from Sept. 18, 1862; resigned April 13, 1863.

221. Brig.-General Jacob Dolson Cox, U. S. Vols., from Oct. 6, 1862; expired by constitutional limitation March 4, 1863; reappointed from Dec. 7, 1864; resigned Jan. 1, 1866.

222. Brig.-General Lovell H. Rousseau, U. S. Vols., from Oct. 8, 1862; resigned Nov. 30, 1865.

223. Brig.-General James B. McPherson, U. S. Vols., from Oct. 8, 1862; killed July 22, 1864.

224. Brig.-General Thomas A. Morris, U. S. Volunteers, from Oct. 25, 1862; declined.

225. Brig.-General Benjamin M. Prentiss, U. S. Volunteers, from Nov. 29, 1862; resigned Oct. 8, 1863.

226. Brig.-General George Stoneman, U. S. Volunteers, from Nov. 29, 1862; mustered out Sept. 1, 1866.

227. Brig.-General John F. Reynolds, U. S. Volunteers, from Nov. 29, 1862; killed July 1, 1863.

228. Brig.-General George G. Meade, U. S. Volunteers, from Nov. 29, 1862; promoted Major-General U. S. A., Aug. 18, 1864.

229. Brig.-General Oliver O. Howard, U. S. Volunteers, from Nov. 29, 1862; mustered out Jan. 1, 1869.

230. Brig.-General Daniel E. Sickles, U. S. Volunteers, from Nov. 29, 1862; mustered out Jan. 1, 1868.

231. Brig.-General Robert H. Milroy, U. S. Volunteers, from Nov. 29, 1862; resigned July 26, 1865.

232. Brig.-General Daniel Butterfield, U. S. Volunteers, from Nov. 29, 1862; mustered out Aug. 24, 1865.

233. Brig.-General Winfield S. Hancock, U. S. Volunteers, from Nov. 29, 1862; promoted Major-General U. S. A., June 26, 1866.

234. Brig.-General George Sykes, U. S. Volunteers, from Nov. 29, 1862; mustered out Jan. 15, 1866.

235. Brig.-General William H. French, U. S. Volunteers, from Nov. 29, 1862; mustered out May 6, 1864.

236. Brig.-General David S. Stanley, U. S. Volunteers, from Nov. 29, 1862; mustered out Feb. 1, 1866.

237. Brig.-General James S. Negley, U. S. Volunteers, from Nov. 29, 1862; resigned Jan. 19, 1865.

238. Brig.-General John M. Palmer, U. S. Volunteers, from Nov. 29, 1862; resigned Sept. 1, 1866.

239. Brig.-General Frederick Steele, U. S. Volunteers, from Nov. 29, 1862; mustered out March 1, 1867.

240. Brig.-General Abner Doubleday, U. S. Volunteers, from Nov. 29, 1862; mustered out Aug. 24, 1865.

241. Brig.-General Napoleon J. T. Dana, U. S. Volunteers, from Nov. 29, 1862; resigned May 27, 1865.

242. Brig.-Gen. Hiram G. Berry, U.S.Vols., from Nov. 29, 1862; killed May 2, 1863.

243. Brig.-General Richard J. Oglesby, U. S. Voluntᵘers, from Nov. 29, 1862; resigned May 26, 1864.

244. Brig.-General John A. Logan, U. S. Volunteers, from Nov. 29, 1862; resigned Aug. 17, 1865.

245. Brig.-General James G. Blunt, U. S. Volunteers, from Nov. 29, 1862; mustered out July 29, 1865.

246. Brig.-General George L. Hartsuff, U. S. Volunteers, from Nov. 29, 1862; mustered out Aug. 24, 1865.

247. Brig.-General Cadwalader C. Washburn, U. S. Volunteers, from Nov. 29, 1862; resigned May 25, 1865.

248. Brig.-General Francis J. Herron, U. S. Volunteers, from Nov. 29, 1862; resigned June 7, 1865.

249. Brig.-General Frank P. Blair, U. S. Volunteers, from Nov. 29, 1862; resigned Nov. 1, 1865.

250. Brig.-General Joseph J. Reynolds, U. S. Volunteers, from Nov. 29, 1862; mustered out Sept. 1, 1866.

251. Brig.-General Philip H. Sheridan, U. S. Volunteers, from Dec. 31, 1862; promoted Major-General U. S. A. Nov. 8, 1864.

252. Brig -General John M. Schofield, U. S. Volunteers, from Nov. 29, 1862; expired by constitutional limitation March 4, 1863; reappointed from Nov. 29, 1862; mustered out Sept. 1, 1866.

253. Brig.-General N. B. Buford, U. S. Volunteers, from Nov. 29, 1862; commission expired March 4, 1863.

254. Brig.-General Julius H. Stahel, U. S. Volunteers, from March 14, 1863; resigned Feb. 8, 1865.

255. Brig.-General Carl Schurz, U. S. Volunteers, from March 14, 1863; resigned May 6, 1865.

256. Brig-General John Newton, U. S. Volunteers, from March 30, 1863 ; commission expired April 18, 1864.

257. Brig.-General Amiel W. Whipple, U. S. Volunteers, from May 3, 1863 ; died of wounds May 7, 1863.

258. Brig.-General Gouverneur K. Warren, U. S. Volunteers, from May 3, 1863 ; resigned May 27, 1865.

259. Brig.-General David D. Birney, U. S. Volunteers, from May 23, 1863 ; died Oct. 18, 1864.

260. Brig.-General Wm. T. H. Brooks, U. S. Volunteers, from June 10, 1863 ; commission expired April 18, 1864.

261. Brig.-General Alfred Pleasonton, U. S. Volunteers, from June 22, 1863 ; mustered out Jan. 15, 1866.

262. Brig.-General John Buford, U. S. Volunteers, from July 1, 1863 ; died Dec. 16, 1863.

263. Brig.-General Andrew A. Humphreys, U. S. Volunteers, from July 8, 1863 ; mustered out Sept. 1, 1866.

264. Brig.-General Quincy A. Gilmore, U. S. Volunteers, from July 10, 1863 ; resigned Dec. 5, 1865.

265. Brig.-General George C. Strong, U. S. Volunteers, from July 18, 1863 ; died of wounds July 30, 1863.

266. Brig.-General James A. Garfield, U. S. Volunteers, from Sept. 19, 1863 ; resigned Dec. 5, 1863.

267. Brig.-General James B. Steedman, U. S. Volunteers, from April 20, 1864 ; resigned Aug. 18, 1866.

268. Brig.-General Edward R. S. Canby, U. S. Volunteers, from May 7, 1864 ; mustered out Sept. 1, 1866.

269. Brig.-General Andrew J. Smith, U. S. Volunteers, from May 12, 1864 ; mustered out Jan. 15, 1866.

270. Brig.-General Grenville M. Dodge, U. S. Volunteers, from June 7, 1864 ; resigned May 30, 1866.

271. Brig.-General John Gibbon, U. S. Volunteers, from June 7, 1864 ; mustered out Jan. 15, 1866.

272. Brig.-General Peter J. Osterhaus, U. S. Volunteers, from July 23, 1864 ; mustered out Jan. 15, 1866.

273. Brig.-General Joseph A. Mower, U. S. Volunteers, from Aug. 12, 1864 ; mustered out Feb. 1, 1866.

274. Brig.-General George Crook, U. S. Volunteers, from October 21, 1864 ; mustered out Jan. 15, 1866.

275. Brig.-General Godfrey Weitzel, U. S. Volunteers, from Nov. 17, 1864 ; mustered out March 1, 1866.

276. Brig.-General William B. Hazen, U. S. Volunteers, from Dec. 13, 1864 ; mustered out Jan. 15, 1866.

277. Brig.-General Alfred H. Terry, U. S. Volunteers, from Jan. 15, 1865 ; mustered out Sept. 1, 1866.

278. Brig.-General Thomas J. Wood, U. S. Volunteers, from Jan. 27, 1865 ; mustered out Sept. 1, 1866.

279. Brig.-General Wesley Merritt, U. S. Volunteers, from April 1, 1865 ; mustered out Feb 1, 1866.

280. Brig.-General Charles Griffin, U. S. Volunteers, from April 2, 1865 ; mustered out Jan. 15, 1866.

281. Brig.-General George A. Custer, U. S. Vols., from April 15, 1865 ; mustered out Feb. 1, 1866.

282. Brig.-General Henry E. Davies, U. S. Volunteers, from May 4, 1865 ; re-signed Jan. 1, 1866.

283. Brig.-General James H. Wilson, U. S. Volunteers, from May 6, 1865 ; mus-tered out Jan. 8, 1866.

284. Brig.-General Francis C. Barlow, U. S. Volunteers, from May 25, 1865 ; re-signed Nov. 16, 1865.

285. Brig.-General Gersham Mott, U. S. Volunteers, from May 26, 1865 ; resigned Feb. 20, 1866.

286. Brig.-General Benjamin H. Grierson, U. S. Volunteers, from May 27, 1865 ; mustered out April 30, 1866.

287. Brig.-General Judson Kilpatrick, U. S. Volunteers, from June 18, 1865 ; re-signed Jan. 1, 1866.

288. Brig.-General Wager Swayne, U. S. Volunteers, from June 20, 1865 ; mus-tered out Aug. 22, 1867.

289. Brig.-General M. D. Leggett, U. S. Volunteers, from Aug. 21, 1865 ; resigned Sept. 28, 1865.

290. Brig.-General Wm. H. Emory, U. S. Volunteers, from Sept. 25, 1865 ; mus-tered out Jan. 15, 1866.

291. Brig.-General Robert B. Potter, U. S. Volunteers, from Sept. 29, 1865 ; mus-tered out January 15, 1866.

292. Brig.-General Nelson A. Miles, U. S. Volunteers, from Oct. 21, 1865 ; mustered out Sept. 1, 1866.

293. Brig.-General Alvan C. Gillem, U. S. Volunteers, from Nov. 9, 1865 ; mus-tered out Sept. 1, 1866.

294. Brig.-General Francis Fessenden, U. S. Volunteers, from Nov. 9, 1865 ; mus-tered out Sept. 1, 1866.

295. Brig.-General Giles A. Smith, U. S. Volunteers, from Nov. 24, 1865 ; mus-tered out Feb. 1, 1866.

By Brevet.—288.

296.	Brig.-General	S. K. Zook,	U. S. Volunteers	....	from July	2, 1864.
297.	"	Jas. S. Wadsworth,	"	....	" May	6, "
298.	"	John C. Robinson,	"	....	" June	27, "
299.	"	Henry J. Hunt,	"	....	" July	6, "
300.	"	James B. Ricketts,	"	....	" Aug.	1, "
301.	"	Robert O. Tyler,	"	....	" "	1, "
302	"	Joseph J. Bartlett,	"	....	" "	1, "
303.	"	John R. Brooke,	"	....	" "	1, "
304.	"	Orlando B. Willcox,	"	....	" "	1, "
305.	"	S. W. Crawford,	"	....	" "	1, "
306.	"	Geo. W. Getty,	"	....	" "	1, "
307.	"	Romeyn B. Ayres,	"	....	" "	1, "
308.	"	D. McM. Gregg,	"	....	" "	1, "
309.	"	Alex. S. Webb,	"	....	" "	1, "
310.	"	Jefferson C. Davis,	"	....	" "	8, "
311.	"	L. Cutler,	"	....	" "	19, "
312.	"	T. E. S. Ransom,	"	....	" Sept.	1, "
313.	"	William F. Barry,	"	....	" "	1, "

314.	Brig.-General	Absalom Baird,	U. S.	Volunteers	....	from Sept.	1, 1864.
315.	"	Alfred T. A. Torbert,	'	....	"	"	9, "
316.	"	David A. Russell,	"	....	"	"	19, "
317.	"	John W. Turner,	"	....	"	Oct.	1, "
318.	"	John M. Corse,	"	....	"	"	5, "
319.	"	Cuvier Grover,	"	....	"	"	19, "
320.	"	Frank Wheaton,	"	....	"	"	19, "
321.	"	Lewis A. Grant,	"	....	"	"	19, "
322.	"	Emory Upton,	"	....	"	"	19, "
323.	"	Thomas W. Egan,	"	....	"	"	27, "
324.	"	George J. Stannard,	"	....	"	"	28, "
325.	"	August V. Kautz,	"	....	"	"	28, "
326.	"	Charles R. Woods,	"	....	"	Nov.	22, "
327.	"	Thomas H. Ruger,	"	....	"	"	30, "
328.	"	Emerson Opdyke,	"	....	"	"	30, "
329.	"	Edward Ferrero,	"	....	"	Dec.	2, "
330.	"	John McArthur,	"	....	"	"	15, "
331.	"	Edward Hatch,	"	....	"	"	15, "
332.	"	Kenner Garrard,	"	....	"	"	15, "
333.	"	Richard W. Johnson,	"	....	"	"	16, "
334.	"	A. S. Williams,	"	....	"	Jan.	12, 1865.
335.	"	Rufus Saxton,	"	....	"	"	12, "
336.	"	John W. Geary,	"	....	"	"	12, "
337.	"	John E. Smith,	"	....	"	"	12, "
338.	"	Adalbert Ames,	"	....	"	"	15, "
339.	"	Charles J. Paine,	"	....	"	"	15, "
340.	"	John M. Brannon,	"	....	"	"	23, "
341.	"	Nathan Kimball,	"	....	"	Feb.	1, "
342.	"	John B. Sanborn,	"	....	"	"	10, "
343.	"	William T. Ward,	"	....	"	"	24, "
344.	"	John A. Rawlins,	"	....	"	"	24, "
345.	"	H. W. Birge,	"	....	"	"	25, "
346.	"	Charles Cruft,	"	....	"	March	5, "
347.	"	James W. McMillan,	"	....	"	"	5, "
348.	"	Alfred Sully,	"	....	"	"	8, "
349.	"	C. C. Andrews,	"	....	"	"	9, "
350.	"	Eugene A. Carr,	"	....	"	"	11, "
351.	"	Daniel H. Rucker,	"	....	"	"	13, "
352.	"	Frederick Salomon,	"	... .	"	"	"
353.	"	Thos. W. Sherman,	"	....	"	"	"
354.	"	Innis N. Palmer.	"	....	"	"	"
355.	"	John P. Hatch,	"	....	"	"	"
356.	"	John W. Davidson,	"	....	"	"	"
357.	"	Marsena R. Patrick,	"	....	"	"	"
358.	"	Truman Seymour,	"	....	"	"	"
359.	"	George S. Greene,	"	....	"	"	"
360.	"	Samuel P. Carter,	"	....	"	"	"
361.	"	Wash'ton L. Elliott,	"	....	"	"	"
362.	"	N. J. Jackson,	"	....	"	"	"
363.	"	Robert S. Granger,	"	....	"	"	"

364.	Brig.-General	M. K. Lawler,	U. S. Volunteers	....	from March 13, 1865.		
365.	"	Charles K. Graham,	"	....	"	"	"
366.	"	Samuel Beatty,	"	....	"	"	"
367.	"	Joseph D. Webster,	"	....	"	"	"
368.	"	Edward E. Potter,	"	....	"	"	"
369.	"	Hugh Ewing,	"	....	"	"	"
370.	"	Joseph B. Carr,	"	....	"	"	"
371.	"	Robert Allen,	"	....	"	"	"
372.	"	Rufus Ingalls,	"	....	"	"	"
373.	"	Walter C. Whitacker,	"	....	"	"	"
374.	"	Manning F. Force,	"	....	"	"	"
375.	"	John W. Fuller,	"	....	"	"	"
376.	"	John F. Miller,	"	....	"	"	"
377.	"	Edward M. McCook,	"	....	"	"	"
378.	"	Samuel S. Carroll,	"	....	"	"	"
379.	"	Joseph Hayes,	"	... .	"	"	"
380.	"	Geo. H. Chapman,	"	....	"	"	"
381.	"	Joseph A. Cooper,	"	....	"	"	"
382.	"	Charles C. Walcut,	"	....	"	"	"
383.	"	Wm. W. Belknap,	"	....	"	"	"
384.	"	Thomas C. Devin,	"	....	"	"	"
385.	"	Eli Long,	"	....	"	"	"
386.	"	Alfred Gibbs,	"	....	"	"	"
387.	"	N. Martin Curtis,	"	....	"	"	"
388.	"	Alexander Asboth,	"	....	"	"	"
389.	"	John R. Kenly,	"	....	"	"	"
390.	"	James Barnes,	"	....	"	"	"
391.	"	William F. Bartlett,	"	....	"	"	"
392.	"	Henry A. Barnum,	"	....	"	"	"
393.	"	George L. Beal,	"	....	"	"	"
394.	"	Henry W. Benham,	"	....	"	"	"
395.	"	William Birney,	"	....	"	"	"
396.	"	James Bowen,	"	....	"	"	"
397.	"	Mason Brayman,	"	....	"	"	"
398.	"	James S. Brisbin,	"	....	"	"	"
399.	"	R. P. Buckland,	"	....	"	"	"
400.	"	Robert A. Cameron,	"	....	"	"	"
401.	"	James H. Carleton,	"	....	"	"	"
402.	"	Morgan H. Chrysler,	"	..... .	"	"	"
403.	"	Patrick E. Connor,	"	....	"	"	"
404.	"	Abram Duryea,	"	....	"	"	"
405.	"	Isaac H. Dewall,	"	....	"	"	"
406.	"	Thomas Ewing, Jr.,	"	....	"	"	"
407.	"	Jas. D. Fessenden,	"	... .	"	"	"
408.	"	Clinton B. Fisk,	"	....	"	"	"
409.	"	Alvan C. Gillem,	"	....	"	"	"
410.	"	Walter Q. Gresham,	"	....	"	"	"
411.	"	Cyrus Hamlin,	"	....	"	"	"
412.	"	Rutherf'd B. Hayes,	"	....	"	"	"
413.	"	Edward W. Hinks,	"	....	"	"	"

414.	Brig.-General	Benjamin F. Kelly,	U. S.	Volunteers	from	March 13, 1865.
415.	"	John H. Ketchum,	"	"	"	"
416.	"	Jacob G. Lanman,	"	"	"	"
417.	"	John H. Martindale,	"	"	"	"
418.	"	John B. McIntosh,	"	"	"	"
419.	"	Thos. J. McKean,	"	"	"	"
420.	"	Thos. H. Neill,	"	"	"	"
421.	"	John Newton,	"	"	"	"
422.	"	John M. Oliver,	"	"	"	"
423.	"	Galusha Pennypacker,	"	"	"	"
424.	"	Byron R. Pierce,	"	"	"	"
425.	"	B. F. Potts,	"	"	"	"
426.	"	William H. Powell,	"	"	"	"
427.	"	Elliot W. Rice,	"	"	"	"
428.	"	Benjamin S. Roberts,	"	"	"	"
429.	"	James S. Robinson,	"	"	"	"
430.	"	James R. Slack,	"	"	"	"
431.	"	Green Clay Smith,	"	"	"	"
432.	"	Thomas Kelby Smith,	"	"	"	"
433.	"	J. W. Sprague,	"	"	"	"
434.	"	John D. Stevenson,	"	"	"	"
435.	"	John M. Thayer,	"	"	"	"
436.	"	William B. Tibbitts,	"	"	"	"
437.	"	Davis Tillson,	"	"	"	"
438.	"	Erastus B. Tyler,	"	"	"	"
439.	"	Daniel Ullman,	"	"	"	"
440.	"	Stewart Van Vliet,	"	"	"	"
441.	"	Julius White,	"	"	"	"
442.	"	Seth Williams,	"	"	"	"
443.	"	Wm. B. Woods,	"	"	"	"
444.	"	Joseph Bailey,	"	"	"	"
445.	"	Cyrus Bussey,	"	"	"	"
446.	"	Thomas L. Kane,	"	"	"	"
447.	"	John G. Mitchell,	"	"	"	"
448.	"	Wm. H. Morris,	"	"	"	"
449.	"	Halbert E. Paine,	"	"	"	"
450.	"	Henry G. Thomas,	"	"	"	"
451.	"	Napoleon B. Buford,	"	"	"	"
452.	"	Charles E. Hovey,	"	"	"	"
453.	"	Hector Tyndale,	"	"	"	"
454.	"	Horatio P. Van Cleve,	"	"	"	"
455.	"	James A. Williamson,	"	"	"	"
456.	"	James D. Morgan,	"	"	March 19, 1865.	
457.	"	Wm. P. Carlin,	"	"	19,	"
458.	"	John F. Hartranft,	"	"	25,	"
459.	"	James C. Veatch,	"	"	26,	"
460.	"	Wm. P. Benton,	"	"	26,	"
461.	"	Geo. L. Andrews,	"	"	26,	"
462.	"	Thos. J. Lucas,	"	"	26,	"
463.	"	James J. Gilbert,	"	"	26,	"

464. Brig.-General Joshua L. Chamberlain, U. S. Volunteers, from March 29, 1865.
465.   "   Robert S. Foster,   "   "   "   31,   "
466.   "   Ronald S. Mackenzie,   "   "   "   31,   "
467.   "   Henry Baxter,   "   " April 1,   "
468.   "   S. G. Griffin,   "   "   "   2,   "
469.   "   Thos. O. Osborn,   "   "   "   2,   "
470.   "   T. M. Harris,   "   "   "   2,   "
471.   "   Chas. Devens,   "   "   "   3,   "
472.   "   Oliver Edwards,   "   "   "   5,   "
473.   "   Joseph E. Hamblin,   "   "   "   5,   "
474.   "   Thomas A. Smyth,   "   "   "   7,   "
475.   "   George H. Gordon,   "   "   "   9,   "
476.   "   Philip R. De Trobriand,   "   "   "   9,   "
477.   "   Wm. A. Pile,   "   "   "   9,   "
478.   "   John McNeil,   "   "   "   12,   "
479.   "   Elias S. Dennis,   "   "   "   13,   "
480.   "   John T. Croxton,   "   "   "   27,   "
481.   "   Lewis B. Parsons,   "   "   "   30,   "
482.   "   Alex. Hays,   "   " May   5,   "
483.   "   Orris S. Ferry,   "   "   "   23,   "
484.   "   John H. King,   "   "   "   31,   "
485.   "   Wm. Vandever,   "   " June   7,   "
486.   "   Zealous B. Tower,   "   "   "   12,   "
487.   "   Chas. C. Doolittle,   "   "   "   13,   "
488.   "   Aug. L. Chetlain,   "   "   "   18,   "
489.   "   John P. Hawkins,   "   "   "   30,   "
490.   "   Thomas A. Davies,   "   " July 11,   "
491.   "   Albion P. Howe,   "   "   "   13,   "
492.   "   Alex. Shaler,   "   "   "   27,   "
493.   "   Adin B. Underwood,   "   " Aug. 13,   "
494.   "   Salomon Meredith,   "   "   "   14,   "
495.   "   Wm. Grose,   "   "   "   15,   "
496.   "   John C. Caldwell,   "   "   "   19,   "
497.   "   Richard Arnold,   "   "   "   22,   "
498.   "   John Cook,   "   "   "   24,   "
499.   "   Fitz Henry Warren,   "   "   "   24,   "
500.   "   Joseph R. Hawley,   "   " Sept. 28,   "
501.   "   August Willich,   "   " Oct. 21,   "
502.   "   Wm. T. Clark,   "   " Nov. 21,   "
503.   "   Richard H. Jackson,   "   "   "   24,   "
504.   "   Henry H. Sibley,   "   "   "   29,   "
505.   "   R. K. Scott,   "   " Dec.   5,   "
506.   "   Jos. R. West,   "   " Jan.   4, 1866.
507. Colonel Cyrus B. Comstock, Additional Aide-de-Camp.. " March 26, 1865.
508.   "   Daniel C. McCallum,   "   "   ... "   "   13,   "
509. Lieut.-Col. J. Burnham Kingsman, Additional Aide-de-
         Camp .... "   "   13,   "
510. Major Wm. H. Ludlow, Additional Aide-de Camp...... "   "   13,   "
511. Lieut.-Col. Martin T. McMahon, Asst. Adjutant-Gen... "   "   13,   "
512.   "   Chas. G. Loring, Asst. Inspector-General... " July 17,   "

513. Colonel James L. Donaldson, Chief Quartermaster Department of Cumberland................................from June 20, 1865.
514. Colonel Charles H. Smith, 1st Maine Cavalry Vols...... " March 13, "
515. " Daniel Chaplin, 1st " Heavy Art. Vols... " Aug. 17, 1864.
516. " H. M. Plaisted, 11th " Infantry " .. " March 13, 1865·
517. " Geo. H. Nye, 20th " " " .. " " 13, "
518. " Wm. Wells, 1st Vermont Cavalry " .. " " 13, "
519. " Geo. A. Macy, 20th Mass. Infantry " .. " April 9, "
520. " Oliver P. Gooding, 31st " " " .. " March 13, "
521. " Henry L. Abbott, 1st Conn. Heavy Art. " .. " " 13, "
522. " James J. Byrne, 18th N. Y. Cavalry Vols..... " " 13, "
523. " John C. Tidball, 4th " Artillery Vols.... " April 2, "
524. " Elisha G. Marshall,14th " " .... " March 13, "
525. " Fred'k Winthrop, 5th " Vet. Inf. Vols.... " April 1, "
526. " James McQuade, 14th " Infantry Vols.... " March 13, "
527. " Benj. F. Baker, 43d " " ... " " 13, "
528. " John H. Gleeson, 63d " " .... " " 13, "
529. " Nelson Cross, 67th " " .... " " 13, "
530. " Adrian R. Root, 94th " " .... " " 13, "
531. Lieut.-Col. Robert Avery, 102d " " .... " " 13, "
532. Colonel Lewis T. Barney, 106th " " .... " " 13, "
533. " Charles J. Powers, 108th " " .... " " 13, "
534. " Isaac S. Catlin, 109th " " .... " " 13, "
535. " George H. Sharpe, 120th " " .... " " 13, "
536. " James Wood, Jr., 136th " " .... " " 13, "
537. " James Jourdan, 158th " " .... " " 13, "
538. " E. L. Molineux, 159th " " .... " " 13, "
539. " James P. McIvor, 170th " " .... " " 13, "
540. " Lewis M. Peck, 173d " " .... " " 13, "
541. " John Ramsay, 8th N. J. " .... " " 13, "
542. " Robert McAllister, 11th " " .... " " 13, "
543. " Geo. W. Mindil, 33d " " .... " " 13, "
544. " Wm. J. Sewell, 38th " " .... " " 13, "
545. " John I. Gregg, 6th Penn. Cavalry Vols..... " " 13, "
546. " Richard Coulter, 11th " Vet. Inf. Vols.... " April 6, "
547. " Edgar M. Gregory, 91st Penn. Infantry Vols... " Aug. 9, 1866.
548. " Henry R. Guss, 97th " " .. " March 13, 1865.
549. " Chas. H. T. Collis, 114th " " .. " " 13, "
550. " St. Clair Mulholland, 116th Penn. Infantry Vols., " " 13, "
551. " James Gwyn, 118th " " " April 1, "
552. " Henry J. Madill, 141st " " " March 13, "
553. " A. L. Pearson, 155th " " " May 1, "
554. " Horatio G. Sickel, 198th " " " March 13, "
555. " A. W. Dennison, 8th Maryland Inf. Vols.... " " 31, "
556. " Henry Capehart, 1st W. Va. Cavalry Vols... " June 17, "
557. " Nicholas L. Anderson, 6th Ohio Inf. Vols ... " March 13, "
558. " Alvin C. Voris, 67th " " .... " Nov. 15, "
559. " Marshall F. Moore, 69th " " .... " March 13, "
560. " W. L. McMillan, 95th " " .... " " 13, "
561. " J. Warren Keifer, 110th " " .... " April 9, "

562.	Colonel Chas. W. Hill,	128th Ohio Inf. Vols....from March 13, 1865.
563.	" Willard Warner,	180th " " .... " " 13, "
564.	" Henry B. Banning,	195th " " ... " " 13, "
565.	" R. H. G. Minty,	4th Mich. Cavalry Vols., " " 13, "
566.	" Russell A. Alger,	5th " " " June 11, "
567.	" Luther S. Trowbridge,	10th " " " March 13, "
568.	" Wm. L. Stoughton,	11th " Inf. Vols..... " " 13, "
569.	" Henry A. Morrow,	24th " " .... " " 13, "
570.	" John P. C. Shanks,	7th Indiana Inf. Vols.. " " 13, "
571.	" Henry D. Washburn,	18th " " .. " July 26, "
572.	" Benjamin J. Spooner,	51st " " .. " March 13, "
573.	" Edwin S. McCook,	31st Illinois " .. " " 13, "
574.	" Benj. Dornblazer,	46th " " .. " " 13, "
575.	" Smith D. Atkins,	92d " " .. " " 13, "
576.	" Herman H. Heath,	7th Iowa Cavalry Vols.. " " 13, "
577.	" John Ely,	26th Regt. Vet. Reserve Corps, " April 15, "
578.	Lt.-Col. Benj. P. Runkle, 26th " " " Nov. 9, "
579.	Col. Henry E. Maynadier, 5th U. S. Volunteer Infantry, " March 13, "
580.	Colonel George W. Cole, 2d " Colored Cavalry, " " 13, "
581.	" H. W. Barry,	8th " " Heavy Art., " " 13, "
582.	" Sam'l A. Duncan, 4th " " Infantry... " " 13, "
583.	" Jos. B. Kiddoo, 22d " " " " Sept. 4, "

Brigadier-Generals U. S. Army.

Full Rank.—36.

584. John E. Wool, from June 25, 1841 ; promoted Major-General May 16, 1862.

585. William S. Harney, from June 14, 1858 ; retired Aug. 1, 1863.

586. Edwin V. Sumner, Colonel 1st U. S. Cavalry, from March 16, 1861 ; died March 21, 1863.

587. Joseph K. F. Mansfield, Colonel and Brevet Brig.-General, Inspector-General, from May 14, 1861 ; died of wounds Sept. 18, 1862.

588. Irvin McDowell, Brevet Major and Asst. Adjutant-General, from May 14, 1861.

589. Robert Anderson, Major 1st U. S. Artillery, from May 15, 1861 ; retired Oct. 27, 1863.

590. Montgomery C. Meigs, Colonel 11th U. S. Infantry, as Quartermaster-General, from May 15, 1861.

591. William S. Rosecrans, from May 16, 1861 ; resigned March 28, 1867.

592. Lorenzo Thomas, Colonel and Adjutant-General, as Adjutant-General, from Aug. 3, 1861.

593. James W. Ripley, Lieut.-Colonel of Ordnance, as Chief of Ordnance Department, from Aug. 3, 1861 ; retired Sept. 15, 1863.

594. Philip St. G. Cook, Colonel 2d U. S. Cavalry, from Nov. 12, 1861.

595. William A. Hammond, Asst. Surgeon U. S. A., as Surgeon-General, from April 25, 1862 ; out of service Aug. 18, 1864 , and retired Aug. 27, 1879.

596. John Pope, Captain Corps Top. Engs., Major-General of Volunteers, from July 14, 1862.

597. Joseph Hooker, Major-General of Volunteers, from Sept. 20, 1862.

598. Joseph P. Taylor, Colonel and Commissary-General, as Commissary-General of Subsistence, from Feb. 9, 1863 ; died June 29, 1864.

599. Joseph G. Totten, Colonel Corps of Engineers, as Chief of Corps of Engineers, from March 3, 1863 ; died April 22, 1864.

600. George G. Meade, Major Corps of Engineers, Major-General of Volunteers, from July 3, 1863 ; promoted Major-General Aug. 18, 1864.

601. William T. Sherman, Colonel 13th U. S. Infantry, Major-General of Volunteers, from July 4, 1863 ; promoted Major-General Aug. 14, 1864.

602. James B. McPherson, Captain Corps of Engineers, Major-General of Volunteers, from Aug. 1, 1863 ; killed July 22, 1864.

603. George D. Ramsey, Colonel Ordnance Department, as Chief of Ordnance Department, from Sept. 15, 1863 ; retired Sept. 12, 1864.

604. George H. Thomas, Colonel 5th U. S. Cavalry, Major General of Volunteers, from Oct. 27, 1863 ; promoted Major-General Dec. 15, 1864.

605. James B. Fry, Major and Asst. Adjutant-General U. S. A., as Provost Marshal-General, from April 21, 1864 ; commission expired Aug. 27, 1866.

606. Richard Delafield, Colonel Corps of Engineers, as Chief of Corps of Engineers, from April 22, 1864.

607. Joseph Holt, Colonel and Judge Advocate-General, as Judge Advocate-General, from June 22, 1864.

608. Amos B. Eaton, Colonel and Asst. Commissary-General, as Commissary-General of Subsistence, from June 29, 1864.

609. Winfield S. Hancock, Major and Quartermaster U. S. A., Major-General of Volunteers, from Aug. 12, 1864 ; promoted Major-General July 26, 1866.

610. Joseph K. Barnes, Colonel and Medical Inspector, as Surgeon-General. from Aug. 22, 1864.

611. Alexander B. Dyer, Major Ordnance Department, as Chief of Ordnance, from Sept. 12, 1864.

612. Philip H. Sheridan, Captain 13th U. S. Infantry, Major-General of Volunteers, from Sept. 20, 1864 ; promoted Major-General Nov. 8, 1864.

613. John M. Schofield, Captain 1st U. S. Artillery, Major-General of Volunteers, from Nov. 30, 1864.

614. Oliver O. Howard, Major-General of Volunteers, from Dec. 21, 1864.

615. Alfred H. Terry, Major-General of Volunteers, from Jan 15, 1865.

616. John A. Rawlins, Brig.-General of Volunteers, as Chief of Staff, from March 3, 1865.

617. Edward O. C. Ord, Lieut.-Colonel 1st U. S. Artillery, Major-General of Volunteers, from July 26, 1866.

618. Edward R. S. Canby, Colonel 19th U. S. Infantry, Major-General of Volunteers, from July 28, 1866.

619. Lovell H. Rousseau, late Major General of Volunteers, from March 28, 1867.

By Brevet.—187.

620. Lt.-Col. Richard C. Drum, Asst. Adj.-Gen. U. S. A., from March 13, 1865.
621. " John C. Kelton, " " " " 13, "
622. Major Robert Williams, " " " " 13, "
623. " Chauncey McKeever, " " " " 13, "
624. " George D. Ruggles, " " " " 13. "
625. " Thomas M. Vincent, " " " " 13, "
626. " Samuel Breck, " " " " 13, "
627. " Oliver D. Greene, " " " " 13, "
628. " Louis H. Pelouze, " " " " 13, "

629. Major Theodore S. Bowers,   Asst. Adj.-Gen. U. S. A., from April 9, 1865.
630. Colonel Sylvester Churchill, Inspector-General   "   "   Feb. 23, 1847.
631. Lt.-Col. Nelson H. Davis, Asst.   "   "   "   March 13, 1865.
632. Major   James Totten,   "   "   "   "   "   13,   "
633. Colonel Wm. McK. Dunn, "   Judge Advocate-General,   "   "   13,   "
634. Lt.-Col. Edwin B. Babbitt, Deputy Q'rmaster-General,   "   "   13,   "
635.   "   Osborn Cross,   "   "   "   "   13,   "
636.   "   Robert E. Cleary,   "   "   "   "   13,   "
637. Major   Morris S. Miller, Quartermaster U. S. A.,   "   "   13,   "
638.   "   Ralph W. Kirkham,   "   "   "   "   13,   "
639.   "   John C. McFerran,   "   "   "   "   13,   "
640.   "   Frederick Myers,   "   "   "   "   13,   "
641.   "   Tredwell Moore,   "   "   "   "   13,   "
642. Captain Rufus Saxton, Assistant Q'rmaster U. S. A.,   "   April   9,   "
643.   "   Samuel B. Holabird,   "   "   "   March 13,   "
644.   "   Judson D. Bingham,   "   "   "   April   9,   "
645.   "   Alexander J. Perry,   "   "   "   March 13,   "
646.   "   William Myers,   "   "   "   "   13,   "
647.   "   Charles G. Sawtelle,   "   "   "   "   13,   "
648.   "   James J. Dana,   "   "   "   "   13,   "
649.   "   Benjamin C. Card,   "   "   "   "   13,   "
650.   "   Joseph A. Potter,   "   "   "   "   13,   "
651.   "   Charles H. Tompkins,   "   "   "   "   13,   " }
652.   "   George B. Dandy,   "   "   "   "   13,   "
653.   "   James A. Ekin,   "   "   "   "   13,   "
654. Colonel Charles L. Kilburn, Asst. Commissary General
         of Subsistence ....   "   "   13,   "
655. Major   Wm. W. Burns, Com'ry of Subsistence U. S. A.,   "   "   13,   "
656.   "   Thomas J. Haines,   "   "   "   "   13,   "
657.   "   Michael R. Morgan,   "   "   "   April   3,   "
658.   "   George Bell,   "   "   "   "   9,   "
659. Captain Michael P. Small,   "   "   "   "   9,   "
660.   "   John W. Barriger,   "   "   "   March 13,   "
661.   "   Thomas Wilson,   "   "   "   "   13,   "
662. Colonel Clement Finley, Surgeon-Gen. U. S. A., retired,   "   "   13,   "
663.   "   Charles H. Crane, Asst. Surgeon-Gen. U. S. A.   "   "   13,   "
664. Lt.-Col. Rich'd S. Satterlee, Chief Med. Purveyor   "   "   Sept.   2, 1864.
665.   "   Chas. McDougall, Asst.   "   "   "   March 13, 1865.
666. Major   Robert C. Wood, Surgeon U. S. A.,   "   "   13,   "
667.   "   Charles S. Trippler,   "   "   "   "   13,   "
668.   "   Jos. J. B. Wright,   "   "   "   "   13,   "
669.   "   John M. Cuyler,   "   "   "   April   9,   "
670.   "   Madison Mills,   "   "   "   March 13,   "
671. Colonel Nathan W. Brown, Asst. Paymaster-General,
         U. S. A................. ....   "   Oct.   15, 1867.
672. Lt.-Col. Hiram Leonard, Deputy Paymaster-General,
         U. S. A................ ....   "   March 13, 1865.
673.   "   Cary H. Fry, Deputy Paymaster-Gen. U. S. A.,   "   Oct.   15, 1867.
674. Major   Thomas J. Leslie, Paymaster U. S. A.,   "   March 13, 1865.
675.   "   Benjamin Alvord,   "   "   "   April   9,   "

676.	Major	Henry Prince, Paymaster U. S. A.,		from March 13, 1865.
677.	"	Joseph H. Eaton, " "		" " 13, "
678.	"	George P. Ihrie, " "		" " 2, "
679.	Colonel	Sylvanus Thayer, Corps of Engineers, U. S. A.,		" May 31, 1863.
680.	"	René E. De Russy, " "		" March 13, 1865.
681.	"	Hartman Bache, " "		" " 13, "
682.	"	Henry Brewerton, " "		" " 13, "
683.	Lt.-Col.	James H. Simpson, " "		" " 13, "
684.	"	Israel C. Woodruff, " "		" " 13, "
685.	"	George Thorn, " "		" " 13, "
686.	Major	James St. Clair Morton, " "		" June 17, 1864.
687.	"	Barton S. Alexander, " "		" March 13, 1865.
688.	"	Frederick E. Prime, " "		" " 13, "
689.	"	William F. Reynolds, " "		" " 13, "
690.	"	James C. Douane, " "		" " 13, "
691.	"	Nathaniel Michler, " "		" April 2, "
692.	"	Henry L. Abbott, " "		" March 13, "
693.	"	Cyrus B. Comstock, " "		" " 13, "
694.	Captain	Orlando M. Poe, " "		" " 13, "
695.	"	Miles D. McAllister, " "		" April 9, "
696.	"	Chauncey B. Reese, " "		" March 13, "
697.	"	Orville E. Babcock, " "		" " 13, "
698.	"	John C. Palfrey, " "		" " 26, "
699.	"	Ronald S. Mackenzie, " "		" " 13, "
700.	Colonel	Henry K. Craig, Ordnance Dep'tment U. S. A.,		" " 13, "
701.	"	Wm. A. Thornton, " "		" " 13, "
702.	"	William Maynadier, " "		" " 13, "
703.	"	Robert H. K. Whiteley, " "		" " 13, "
704.	Lt.-Col.	Peter V. Hagner, " "		" " 13, "
705.	"	Frank D. Callender, " "		" April 9, "
706.	Major	Thomas J. Rodman, " "		" March 13, "
707.	"	Charles P. Kingsbury, " "		" " 13, "
708.	Captain	Horace Porter, " "		" " 13, "
709.	Colonel	Albert J. Meyer, Chief Signal Officer "		" " 13, "
710.	"	George A. H. Blake, 1st Regt. U. S. Cav.,		" " 13, "
711.	Lieut.-Colonel	Wm. N. Grier, 1st " "		" " 13, "
712.	"	Innis N. Palmer, 2d " "		" " 13, "
713.	Major	Nelson B. Sweitzer, 2d " "		" " 13, "
714.	Capt.	Theophilus F. Rodenbough, 2d " "		" " 13, "
715.	Second Lieut.	Eli S. Parker, 2d " "		" " 2, 1867.
716.	Colonel	John S. Simonson, 3d " "		" " 13, 1865.
717.	Lieut.-Colonel	Charles F. Ruff, 3d " "		" " 13, "
718.	Major	Benjamin S. Roberts, 3d " "		" " 13, "
719.	"	Thomas Duncan, 3d " "		" " 13, "
720.	Captain	Andrew J. Alexander, 3d " "		" April 16, "
721.	Colonel	Lawrence P. Graham, 4th " "		" March 13, "
722.	Major	John P. Hatch, 4th " "		" " 13, "
723.	Capt.	Napoleon B. McLaughlin, 4th " "		" " 13, "
724.	First Lieut.	Edward M. McCook, 4th " "		" " 13, "
725.	Captain	Wm. W. Lowe, 5th " "		" " 13, "

XIII.—13

726. Captain Louis D. Watkins,	5th	Regt. U. S. Cav.,	from March 13, 1865.			
727. Colonel James Oakes,	6th	"	"	"	"	30, "
728. Captain John I. Gregg,	6th	"	"	"	"	13, "
729. Lieut.-Colonel Thomas C. Devin,	8th	"	"	"	"	2, 1867.
730. Colonel Justin Dimick,	1st	"	U. S. Art'y,	"	"	13, 1865.
731. " Israel B. Vogdes,	1st	"	"	"	April	9, "
732. Lieut.-Col. Joseph A. Haskin,	1st	"	"	"	March 13, 1865.	
733. Captain Wm. M. Graham,	1st	"	"	"	"	13, "
734. " Richard H. Jackson,	1st	"	"	"	"	13, "
735. Colonel John L. Gardner,	2d	"	"	"	"	13, "
736. Lieut.-Colonel Lewis G. Arnold,	2d	"	"	"	"	13, "
737. Major Edward G. Beckwith,	2d	"	"	"	"	13, "
738. Captain James M. Robertson,	2d	"	"	"	"	13, "
739. " John C. Tidball,	2d	"	"	"	"	13, "
740. Colonel Wm. Gates,	3d	"	"	"	"	13, "
741. Lieut.-Colonel Martin Burke,	3d	"	"	"	"	13, "
742. Major G. A. De Russy,	3d	"	"	"	"	13, "
743. First Lieut. Martin D. Hardin,	3d	"	"	"	"	13, "
744. Colonel Charles S. Merchant,	4th	"	"	"	"	13, "
745. " Horace Brooks,	4th	"	"	"	"	13, "
746. Lieut.-Colonel Joseph Roberts,	4th	"	"	"	"	13, "
747. Captain Charles H. Morgan,	4th	"	"	"	"	13, "
748. First Lieut. Chas. L. Fitzhugh,	4th	"	"	"	"	13, "
749. Colonel Henry S. Burton,	5th	"	"	"	"	13, "
750. Lieut.-Colonel Bennett H. Hill,	5th	"	"	"	Jan.	31, "
751. Major Wm. Hays	5th	"	"	"	March 13, "	
752. Colonel Carlos A. Waite,	1st	"	U. S. Inf'y,	"	"	13, "
753. Lieut.-Colonel Seth Eastman,	1st	"	"	"	Aug.	9, 1866.
754. Colonel Sidney Burbank,	2d	"	"	"	March 13, 1865.	
755. Col. Benjamin L. E. Bonneville,	3d	"	"	"	"	13, "
756. Captain Wm. H. Penrose,	3d	"	"	"	April	9, "
757. Lieut.-Col. Adam J. Slemmer,	4th	"	"	"	March 13, "	
758. Major Frederick T. Dent,	4th	"	"	"	"	13, "
759. Second Lieut. Adam Badeau,	4th	"	"	"	"	2, 1867.
760. Colonel Gustavus Loomis,	5th	"	"	"	"	13. 1865.
761. Major Elisha G. Marshall,	5th	"	"	"	"	13, "
762. Colonel Washington Seawell,	6th	"	"	"	"	13, "
763. " Hannibal Day,	6th	"	"	"	"	13, "
764. " James D. Greene,	6th	"	"	"	"	13, "
765. Lieut.-Colonel Henry B. Clitz,	6th	"	"	"	"	13, "
766. Colonel John J. Abercrombie,	7th	"	"	"	"	13, "
767. Major Joseph R. Smith,	7th	"	"	"	April	9, "
768. Colonel John Garland,	8th	"	"	"	Aug.	20, 1847.
769. " Pitcairn Morrison,	8th	"	"	"	March 13, 1865.	
770. " Albemarle Cady,	8th	"	"	"	"	13, "
771. " James V. Bomford,	8th	"	"	"	"	13, "
772. Major Alfred Sully,	8th	"	"	"	"	13, "
773. Captain James M. Warner,	8th	"	"	"	April	9, "
774. Colonel George Wright,	9th	"	"	"	Dec.	10. 1864.
775. Lieut.-Col. Frederick Townsend,	9th	"	"	"	March 13, 1865.	

776. Colonel Edmund B. Alexander, 10th Regt. U. S. Inf'y, from Oct. 18, 1865.
777. Lieut.-Colonel Wm. H. Sidell, 10th " " " March 13, "
778. Colonel Erasmus D. Keyes, 11th " " " May 31, 1862.
779. Major Thomas H. Neill, 11th " " " March 13, 1865.
780. Captain Henry G. Thomas, 11th " " " " " 13, "
781. Colonel Isaac V. D. Reeves, 13th " " " " " 13, "
782. " Gabriel R. Paul, 14th " " " Feb. 23, "
783. " Charles S. Lovell, 14th " " " March 13, "
784. Lieut.-Col. Henry D. Wallen, 14th " " " " " 13, "
785. Major Lewis C. Hunt, 14th " " " " " 13, "
786. Captain David B. McKibben, 14th. " " " " " 13, "
787. Colonel Fitz John Porter, 15th " " " June 27, 1862.
788. " Oliver L. Shepherd, 15th " " " March 13, 1865.
789. Lieut.-Col. Julius Hayden, 15th " " " " " 13, "
790. " Samuel K. Dawson, 15th " " " " " 13, "
791. Colonel Caleb. C. Sibley, 16th " " " " " 13, "
792. Major Thomas G. Pitcher, 16th " " " " " 13, "
793. " John S. Mason, 17th " " " " " 13, "
794. Colonel Henry B. Carrington, 18th " " " April 9, "
795. Lieut.-Col. Henry W. Wessels, 18th " " " March 13, "
796. Captain James W. Forsyth, 18th " " " April 9, "
797. Major Joseph H. Potter, 19th " " " March 13, "
798. Lieut.-Col. Luther P. Bradley, 27th " " " " " 2, 1867.
799. " George P. Buell, 29th " " " " " 2, "
800. Colonel John D. Stevenson, 30th " " " " " 2, "
801. " Phil. R. De Trobriand, 31st " " " " " 2, "
802. " Thos. L. Crittenden, 32d " " " " " 2, "
803. " Thomas H. Ruger, 33d " " " " " 2, "
804. Lieut.-Col. John R. Brooke, 37th " " " " " 2, "
805. " Edward W. Hinks, 40th " " " " " 2, "
806. " Joseph B. Kiddoo, 43d " " " " " 2, "

Brigadier-Generals U. S. Volunteers.

Full Rank.—561.

807. Colonel David Hunter, 3d U. S. Cavalry, from May 17, 1861 ; promoted to Major-General Aug. 13, 1861.
808. Colonel Samuel P. Heintzelman, 17th U. S. Infantry, from May 17, 1861 ; promoted to Major-General July 4, 1862.
809. Colonel Erasmus D. Keyes, 11th U. S. Infantry, from May 17, 1861 ; promoted to Major-General July 4th, 1862.
810. Colonel Andrew Porter, 16th U. S. Infantry, from May 17, 1861 ; mustered out April 4, 1864.
811. Colonel Fitz John Porter, 15th U. S. Infantry, from May 17, 1861 ; promoted to Major-General July 4, 1862.
812. Colonel William B. Franklin, 12th U. S. Infantry, from May 17, 1861 ; promoted to Major-General July 4, 1862.
813. Colonel William T. Sherman, 13th U. S. Infantry, from May 17, 1861 ; promoted to Major-General May 1, 1862.

814. Colonel Charles P. Stone, 14th U. S. Infantry, from May 17, 1861 ; mustered out April 4, 1864.

815. Lieut.-Colonel Don Carlos Buell, Assist. Adjutant-General, from May 17, 1861 ; promoted to Major-General March 21, 1862.

816. Lieut.-Colonel Thomas W. Sherman, 5th U. S. Artillery, from May 17, 1861 ; mustered out April 30, 1866.

817. Major James Oakes, 2d U. S. Cavalry, from May 17, 1861 ; declined.

818. Captain Nathaniel Lyon, 2d U. S. Infantry, from May 17, 1861 ; killed in action Aug. 10, 1861.

819. Captain John Pope, Topographical Engineers U. S. A., from May 17, 1861 ; promoted to Major-General March 21, 1862.

820. George A. McCall, of Pennsylvania, from May 17, 1861 ; resigned March 31, 1863.

821. William R. Montgomery, of New Jersey, Colonel 1st New Jersey Volunteers, from May 17, 1861 ; resigned April 4, 1864.

822. Philip Kearney, of New Jersey, from May 17, 1861 ; promoted to Major-General July 4, 1862.

823. Joseph Hooker, of California, from May 17, 1861 ; promoted to Major-General July 4, 1862.

824. John W. Phelps, of Vermont, Colonel 1st Connecticut Volunteers, from May 17, 1861 ; resigned Aug. 21, 1862.

825. Ulysses S. Grant, of Illinois, Colonel 21st Illinois Volunteers, from May 17, 1861 ; promoted to Major-General Feb. 16, 1862.

826. Joseph J. Reynolds, of Indiana, Colonel 10th Indiana Volunteers, from May 17, 1861 ; resigned Jan. 23, 1862; reappointed ; promoted Major-General Nov. 29, 1862.

827. Samuel R. Curtis, of Iowa, Colonel 2d Iowa Infantry, from May 17, 1861 ; promoted Major-General March 21, 1862.

828. Charles S. Hamilton, of Wisconsin, Colonel 3d Wisconsin Volunteers, from May 17, 1861 ; promoted Major-General Sept. 19, 1862.

829. Darius N. Couch, of Massachusetts, Colonel 7th Massachusetts Volunteers, from May 17, 1861 ; promoted Major-General July 4, 1862.

830. Rufus King, of Wisconsin, Brig.-General Wisconsin State Volunteers or Militia, from May 17, 1861 ; resigned Oct. 20, 1863.

831. Jacob Dolson Cox, of Ohio, Brig.-General Ohio State Volunteers or Militia, from May 17, 1861 ; promoted Major-General Oct. 6, 1862 ; not confirmed ; promoted Major-General Dec. 7, 1864.

832. Stephen A. Hurlbut, of Illinois, from May 17, 1861 ; promoted Major-General Sept. 17, 1862.

833. Franz Sigel, of Missouri, Colonel Missouri Volunteers, from May 17, 1861 ; promoted Major-General March 21, 1862.

834. Robert C. Schenck, of Ohio, from May 17, 1861 ; promoted Major-General Aug. 30, 1862.

835. Benjamin M. Prentiss, of Illinois, Colonel 10th Illinois Volunteers, from May 17, 1861 ; promoted Major-General Nov. 29, 1862.

836. Frederick W. Lander, of Massachusetts, from May 17, 1861 ; died March 2, 1862.

837. Edward D. Baker, of Oregon, from May 17, 1861 : declined.

838. Benjamin F. Kelly, of Virginia, Colonel West Virginia Volunteers, from May 17, 1861 ; resigned June 1, 1865.

839. John A. McClernand, of Illinois, from May 17, 1861 ; promoted Major-General March 21, 1862.

840. Alpheus S. Williams, of Michigan, from May 17, 1861 : mustered out Jan. 15, 1866.

841. Israel B. Richardson, of Michigan, Colonel 2d Michigan Volunteers, from May 17, 1861 ; promoted Major-General July 4, 1862.

842. William Sprague, of Rhode Island, from May 17, 1861 ; declined.

843. James Cooper, of Maryland, from May 17, 1861 ; died March 28, 1863.

844. Captain James B. Ricketts, 1st U. S. Artillery, from July 21, 1861 ; mustered out April 30, 1866.

845. Orlando B. Wilcox, of Michigan, Colonel 1st Michigan Volunteers, from July 21, 1861 ; mustered out Jan. 15, 1866.

846. Michael Corcoran, of New York, Colonel 69th New York State Militia, from July 21, 1861 ; died Dec. 22, 1863.

847. Ambrose E. Burnside, of Rhode Island, Colonel Rhode Island Volunteers, from Aug. 6, 1861 ; promoted to Major-General March 18, 1862.

848. Henry H. Lockwood, of Delaware, Colonel 1st Delaware Volunteers, from Aug. 8, 1861 ; mustered out Aug. 24, 1865.

849. Louis Blenker, of New York, Colonel 8th New York Volunteers, from Aug. 9, 1861 ; discharged March 31, 1863.

850. Henry W. Slocum, of New York, Colonel 27th New York Volunteers, from Aug. 9, 1861 ; promoted Major-General July 4, 1862.

851. James S. Wadsworth, of New York, from Aug. 9, 1861 ; killed May 6, 1864.

852. John J. Peck, of New York, from Aug. 9, 1861 ; promoted Major-General July 4, 1862.

853. Ormsby M. Mitchell, of New York, from Aug. 9, 1861 ; promoted Major-General April 11, 1862.

854. George Morell, of New York, from Aug. 9, 1861 ; mustered out Dec. 15, 1864.

855. John H. Martindale, of New York, from Aug. 9, 1861 ; resigned Sept. 13, 1864.

856. Major Samuel D. Sturgis, 4th U. S. Cavalry, from Aug. 10, 1861 ; mustered out Aug. 24, 1865.

857. Major George Stoneman, 1st U. S. Cavalry, from Aug. 13, 1861 ; promoted Major-General Nov. 29, 1862.

858. Major Henry W. Benham, Corps of Engineers, from Aug. 13, 1861 ; mustered out January 15, 1866.

859. Captain W. F. Smith, Topographical Engineers, U. S. A., and Colonel 3d Vermont Volunteer Infantry, from Aug. 13, 1861 ; promoted Major-General July 4, 1862.

860. James W. Denver, of California, from Aug. 14, 1861 ; resigned March 5, 1863.

861. Colonel George H. Thomas, 2d U. S. Cavalry, from Aug. 17, 1861 ; promoted Major-General April 25, 1862.

862. Egbert L. Viele, of New York, from Aug. 17. 1861 ; resigned Oct. 20, 1863.

863. James Shields, of California, from Aug. 19, 1861 ; resigned March 28, 1863.

864. Lieut.-Colonel John F. Reynolds, 14th U. S. Infantry, from Aug. 20, 1861 ; promoted Major-General Nov. 29, 1862.

865. Major William F. Barry, 5th U. S. Infantry, from Aug. 20, 1861 ; mustered out Jan. 15, 1866.

866. Colonel John J. Abercrombie, 6th U. S. Infantry, from Aug. 31, 1861 ; mustered out June 24, 1864.

867. Colonel John Sedgwick, 4th U. S. Cavalry, from Aug. 31, 1861; promoted Major-General July 4, 1862.

868. Lieut.-Colonel Charles F. Smith, 10th U. S. Infantry, from Aug. 31, 1861; promoted Major-General March 21, 1862.

869. Lieut.-Colonel Silas Casey, 9th U. S. Infantry, from Aug. 31, 1861; promoted Major-General May 31, 1862.

870. Major Lawrence P. Graham, 2d U. S. Cavalry, from Aug. 31, 1861; mustered out Aug. 24, 1865.

871. Captain George G. Meade, Topographical Engineers, from Aug. 31, 1861; promoted Major-General Nov. 29, 1862.

872. Charles J. Biddle, of Pennsylvania, Colonel 13th Pennsylvania Reserves, from Aug. 31, 1861; declined.

873. Abram Duryee, of New York, Colonel 5th New York Volunteers, from Aug. 31, 1861; resigned Jan. 5, 1863.

874. Major Justus McKinstry, Quartermaster U. S. Army, from Sept. 2, 1861; commission expired July 17, 1862.

875. Captain Alexander McD. McCook, 3d U. S. Infantry, and Colonel 1st Ohio Volunteer Infantry, from Sept. 3, 1861; promoted Major-General July 17, 1862.

876. Oliver O. Howard, of Maine, Colonel 3d Maine Volunteers, from Sept. 3, 1861; promoted Major-General Nov. 29, 1862.

877. Eleazer Paine, of Illinois, Colonel 9th Illinois Volunteers, from Sept. 3, 1861; resigned April 5, 1865.

878. Daniel E. Sickles, of New York, Colonel 70th New York Volunteers, from Sept. 3, 1861; negatived by the Senate March 20, 1862; reappointed from Sept. 3, 1861; promoted Major-General Nov. 29, 1862.

879. Charles D. Jamison, of Maine, Colonel 2d Maine Volunteers, from Sept. 3, 1861; died Nov. 6, 1862.

880. Ebenezer Dumont, of Indiana, Colonel 7th Indiana Volunteers, from Sept. 3, 1861; resigned Feb 28, 1863.

881. Robert H. Milroy, of Indiana, Colonel 9th Indiana Volunteers, from Sept. 3, 1861; promoted Major-General Nov. 29, 1862.

882. Lewis Wallace, of Indiana, Colonel 11th Indiana Volunteers, from Sept. 3, 1861; promoted Major-General March 21, 1862.

883. William A. Richardson, of Illinois, from Sept. 3, 1861; declined.

884. Charles M. Thurston, of Maryland, from Sept. 7, 1861; resigned April 17, 1862.

885. Willis A. Gorman, of Minnesota, Colonel 1st Minnesota Volunteers, from Sept. 7, 1861; mustered out May 4, 1864.

886. Daniel Butterfield, of New York, Colonel 12th New York State Militia, and Lieut.-Colonel 12th U. S. Infantry, from Sept. 7, 1861; promoted Major-General Nov. 29, 1862.

887. Major Horatio G. Wright, Corps of Engineers, from Sept. 14, 1861; promoted Major-General July 18, 1862.

888. Captain Edward O. C. Ord, 3d U. S. Artillery, from Sept. 14, 1861; promoted Major-General May 2, 1862.

889. Lieut. William Nelson, U. S. Navy, from Sept. 16, 1861; promoted Major-General July 17, 1862.

890. W. T. Ward, of Kentucky, from Sept. 18, 1861; mustered out Aug. 24, 1865.

891. John B. S. Todd, of Dakota Territory, from Sept. 19, 1861; commission expired July 17, 1862.

892. Colonel Randolph B. Marcy, Inspector-General, from Sept. 23, 1861; commission expired July 17, 1862; reappointed from Sept. 23, 1861; commission expired March 4, 1863.

893. Major John G. Barnard, Corps of Engineers, from Sept. 23, 1861; mustered out Jan. 15, 1866.

894. Major Innis N. Palmer, 5th U. S. Cavalry, from Sept. 23, 1861; mustered out Jan. 15, 1866.

895. Major Seth Williams, Asst. Adjutant-General, from Sept. 23, 1861; died March 23, 1866.

896. Major Stewart Van Vliet, Quartermaster, from Sept. 23, 1861; commission expired July 17, 1862; reappointed March 13, 1865; mustered out Sept. 1, 1866.

897. Major John Newton, Corps of Engineers, from Sept. 23, 1861; promoted Major-General March 30, 1863.

898. Captain Winfield S. Hancock, Asst. Quartermaster, from Sept. 23, 1861; promoted Major-General Nov. 29, 1862.

899. Thomas L. Crittenden, of Kentucky, from Sept. 27, 1861; promoted to Major-General July 17, 1862.

900. Colonel George Wright, 9th U. S. Infantry, from Sept. 28, 1861; died July 30, 1865.

901. Major Thomas Williams, 5th U. S. Artillery, from Sept. 28, 1861; killed Aug. 5, 1862.

902. Major George Sykes, 14th U. S. Infantry, from Sept. 28, 1861; promoted Major-General Nov. 29, 1862.

903. Major William W. Burns, Commissary of Subsistence, from Sept. 28, 1861; resigned March 20, 1863.

904. Captain William H. French, 1st U. S. Artillery, from Sept. 28, 1861; promoted Major-General Nov. 29, 1862.

905. Captain William T. H. Brooks, 3d U. S. Infantry, from Sept. 28, 1861; resigned July 14, 1864.

906. Captain John M. Brannan, 1st U. S. Artillery, from Sept. 28, 1861; mustered out May 31, 1866.

907. Captain John P. Hatch, 3d U. S. Cavalry, from Sept. 28, 1861; mustered out Jan. 15, 1866.

908. Captain David S. Stanley, 4th U. S. Cavalry, from Sept. 28, 1861; promoted Major-General Nov. 29, 1862.

909. Isaac I. Stevens, of Washington Territory, Colonel 79th New York Volunteers, from Sept. 28, 1861; promoted Major-General July 18, 1862.

910. William K. Strong, of New York, from Sept. 28, 1861; resigned Oct. 20, 1863.

911. Alban Schoepf, of Maryland, from Sept. 30, 1861; mustered out Jan. 15, 1866.

912. Lovell H. Rousseau, of Kentucky, Colonel 5th Kentucky Volunteers, from Oct. 1, 1861; promoted Major-General Oct. 8, 1862.

913. Melancthon S. Wade, of Ohio, from Oct. 1, 1861; resigned March 18, 1862.

914. James S. Negley, of Pennsylvania, Colonel 48th Pennsylvania Volunteers, from Oct. 1, 1861; promoted Major-General Nov. 29, 1862.

915. Lieut.-Colonel Thomas J. Wood, 4th U. S. Cavalry, from Oct. 11, 1861; promoted Major-General Jan. 27, 1865.

916. Captain Richard W. Johnson, 5th U. S. Cavalry, from Oct. 11, 1861; mustered out January 15, 1866.

917. Adolph von Steinwehr, of New York, Colonel 29th New York Volunteers, from Oct. 12, 1861; resigned July 3, 1865.

918. Captain Joseph B. Plummer, 1st U. S. Infantry, and Colonel 11th Missouri Volunteers, from Oct. 22, 1861; died Aug. 9, 1862.

919. Captain John G. Foster, Corps of Engineers, from Oct. 23, 1861; promoted Major-General July 18, 1862.

920. Major George W. Cullom, Corps of Engineers, Colonel and Additional Aide-de-Camp, from Nov. 12, 1861; commission expired July 17, 1862; reappointed from Nov. 1, 1861; mustered out Sept. 1, 1876.

921. Jeremiah T. Boyle, of Kentucky, from Nov. 4, 1861; resigned Jan. 26, 1864.

922. Major Christopher C. Augur, 13th U. S. Infantry, from Nov. 12, 1861; promoted Major-General Aug. 9, 1862.

923. Captain Jesse L. Reno, Ordnance Department, from Nov. 12, 1861; promoted Major-General July 18, 1862.

924. Schuyler Hamilton, of New York, Colonel and Aide-de-Camp, from Nov. 12, 1861; promoted Major-General Sept. 17, 1862.

925. Julius H. Stahel, of New York, Colonel 8th New York Volunteer Infantry, from Nov. 12, 1861; promoted Major-General March 14, 1863.

926. George W. Morgan, of Ohio, from Nov. 12, 1861; resigned June 8, 1863.

927. Captain John M. Schofield, 1st U. S. Artillery, and Major 1st Missouri Volunteers; Brig.-General Missouri Militia, from Nov. 21, 1861; promoted Major-General May 12, 1863.

928. Thomas J. McKean, Additional Paymaster, from Nov. 21, 1861; mustered out Aug. 24, 1865.

929. Major Zealous B. Power, Corps of Engineers, from Nov. 23, 1861; mustered out Jan. 15, 1866.

930. Captain John G. Parke, Corps of Topographical Engineers, from Nov. 23, 1861; promoted Major-General July 18, 1862.

931. Captain Jefferson C. Davis, 1st U. S. Artillery, and Colonel 22d Indiana Volunteers, from Dec. 18, 1861; mustered out Sept. 1, 1866.

932. John M. Palmer, of Illinois, Colonel 14th Illinois Volunteers, from Dec. 20, 1861; promoted Major-General Nov. 29, 1862.

933. William H. Keim, of Pennsylvania, from Dec. 20, 1861; died May 18, 1862.

934. James A. Garfield, of Ohio, Colonel 42d Ohio Volunteers, from Jan. 11, 1862; promoted Major-General Sept. 19, 1863.

935. Major Lewis G. Arnold, 1st U. S. Artillery, from Jan. 24, 1862; commission expired Feb. 8, 1864.

936. Major Frederick Steele, 11th U. S. Infantry, and Colonel 8th Iowa Volunteers, from Jan. 29, 1862; promoted Major-General Nov. 29, 1862.

937. Lieut.-Colonel W. S. Ketchum, 10th U. S. Infantry, from Feb. 3, 1862; mustered out April 30, 1866.

938. Major Abner Doubleday, 17th U. S. Infantry, from Feb. 3, 1862; promoted Major-General Nov. 29, 1862.

939. Major John W. Davidson, 2d U. S. Cavalry, from Feb. 3, 1862; mustered out Jan. 15, 1866.

940. Napoleon J. T. Dana, of Minnesota, Colonel 1st Minnesota Volunteers, from Feb. 3, 1862; promoted Major-General Nov. 29, 1862.

941. David D. Birney, of Pennsylvania, Colonel 23d Pennsylvania Volunteers, from Feb. 3, 1862; promoted Major-General May 23, 1863.

942. Thomas Francis Meagher, of New York, from Feb. 3, 1862; resigned May 15, 1865.

943. Henry M. Naglee, of California, from Feb. 4, 1862; mustered out April 4, 1864.

944. Andrew Johnson, of Tennessee, from March 4, 1862; resigned March 3, 1865.

945. James G. Spears, of Tennessee, Lieut.-Colonel 1st Tennessee Volunteers, from March 5, 1862; out of service Aug. 30, 1864.

946. Captain Eugene A. Carr, 4th U. S. Cavalry and Colonel 3d Illinois Cavalry Volunteers, from March 7, 1862; mustered out Jan. 15, 1866.

947. Thomas A. Davies, of New York, Colonel 16th New York Volunteers, from March 7, 1862; mustered out Aug. 24, 1865.

948. Daniel Tyler, of Connecticut, Colonel 1st Connecticut Volunteers and Brig.-General State Volunteers or Militia, from March 13, 1862; resigned April 6, 1864.

949. Lieut.-Colonel William H. Emory, 6th U. S. Cavalry, from March 17, 1862; promoted Major-General Sept. 25, 1865.

950. Major Andrew J. Smith, 1st U. S. Cavalry and Colonel 2d California Cavalry Volunteers, from March 17, 1862; promoted Major-General May 12, 1864.

951. Marsena R. Patrick, of New York, Inspector-General New York State Militia, from March 17, 1862; resigned June 12, 1865.

952. Isaac F. Quinby, of New York, late Colonel 13th New York Volunteers, from March 17, 1862; resigned Dec. 31, 1863.

953. Hiram G. Berry, of Maine, Colonel 4th Maine Volunteers, from March 17, 1862; promoted Major-General Nov. 29, 1862.

954. Orris S. Ferry, of Connecticut, Colonel 5th Connecticut Volunteers, from March 17, 1862; resigned June 15, 1865.

955. Major Daniel P. Woodbury, Corps of Engineers, Lieut.-Colonel, and Additional Aide-de-Camp, from March 19, 1862; died Aug. 15, 1864.

956. Captain Henry M. Judah, 4th U. S. Infantry and Colonel 4th California Volunteers, from March 21, 1862; mustered out Aug. 24, 1865.

957. Richard J. Oglesby, of Illinois, Colonel 8th Illinois Volunteers, from March 21, 1862; promoted Major-General Nov. 29, 1862.

958. John Cooke, of Illinois, Colonel 7th Illinois Volunteers, from March 21, 1862; mustered out Aug. 24, 1865.

959. William H. L. Wallace, of Illinois, Colonel 11th Illinois Volunteers, from March 21, 1862; died of wounds April 10, 1862.

960. John McArthur, of Illinois, Colonel 12th Illinois Volunteers, from March 21, 1862; mustered out Aug. 24, 1865.

961. Robert L. McCook, of Ohio, Colonel 9th Ohio Volunteers, from March 21, 1862, killed Aug. 6, 1862.

962. Jacob G. Lauman, of Iowa, Colonel 7th Iowa Volunteers, from March 21, 1862; mustered out Aug. 24, 1865.

963. Horatio P. Van Cleve, of Minnesota, Colonel 2d Minnesota Volunteers, from March 21, 1862; mustered out Aug. 24, 1865.

964. John A. Logan, of Illinois, Colonel 31st Illinois Volunteers, from March 21, 1862; promoted Major-General Nov. 29, 1862.

12*

965. Speed S. Fry, of Kentucky, Colonel 4th Kentucky Volunteers, from March 21, 1862 ; mustered out Aug. 24, 1865.

966. Alexander Asboth, of Missouri, Colonel 2d Missouri Volunteers, from March 21, 1862 ; mustered out Aug. 24, 1865.

967. James Craig, of Missouri, from March 21, 1862 ; resigned May 14, 1863.

968. Mahlon D. Manson, of Indiana, Colonel 10th Indiana Volunteers, from March 24, 1862 ; resigned Dec. 21, 1864.

969. Captain Gordon Granger, 3d U. S. Cavalry and Colonel 2d Michigan Cavalry Vols., from March 26, 1862 ; promoted Major-General Sept. 17, 1862.

970. Colonel Edward R. S. Canby, 19th U. S. Infantry, from March 31, 1862 ; promoted Major-General May 7, 1864.

971. Grenville M. Dodge, of Iowa, Colonel 4th Iowa Volunteers, from March 31, 1862 ; promoted Major-General June 7, 1864.

972. Robert B. Mitchell, of Kansas, Colonel 2d Kansas Volunteers, from April 8, 1862 ; mustered out Jan. 15, 1866.

973. James G. Blunt, of Kansas, from April 8, 1862 ; promoted Major-General Nov. 29, 1862.

974. Francis E. Patterson, of Pennsylvania, Colonel 115th Pennsylvania Volunteers, from April 11, 1862 ; died Nov. 6, 1862.

975. Major Amiel W. Whipple, Topographical Engineers, from April 14, 1862 ; promoted Major-General May 3, 1863.

976. Captain Cuvier Grover, 10th U. S. Infantry, from April 14, 1862 ; mustered out Aug. 24, 1865.

977. Captain George L. Hartsuff, Asst. Adjutant-General, from April 15, 1862 ; promoted Major-General Nov. 29, 1862.

978. Captain Rufus Saxton, Asst. Quartermaster, from April 15, 1862 ; mustered out Jan. 15, 1866.

979. Benjamin Alvord, Paymaster U. S. A., from April 15, 1862 ; resigned Aug. 8, 1865.

980. Napoleon B. Buford, of Illinois, Colonel 27th Illinois Volunteers, from April 15, 1862 ; promoted Major-General, commission as such expired by Constitutional limitation ; mustered out as Brigadier-General, Aug. 24, 1865.

981. William S. Smith, of Ohio, Colonel 13th Ohio Volunteers, from April 15, 1862 ; resigned July 15, 1864.

982. Nathan Kimball, of Indiana, Colonel 14th Indiana Volunteers, from April 15, 1862 ; mustered out Aug. 24, 1865.

983. Charles Devens, of Massachusetts, Colonel 15th Massachusetts Volunteers, from April 15, 1862 ; mustered out Jan. 15, 1866.

984. James H. Van Allen, of New York, Colonel 3d N. Y. Cavalry Volunteers, from April 15, 1862 ; resigned July 14, 1863.

985. Carl Schurz, of Missouri, from April 15, 1862 ; promoted Major-General March 14, 1863.

986. Major Samuel W. Crawford, 13th U. S. Infantry, from April 25, 1862 ; mustered out Jan. 15, 1866.

987. Major Henry W. Wessells, 6th U. S. Infantry and Colonel 8th Kansas Volunteers, from April 25, 1862 ; mustered out Jan. 15, 1866.

988. Milo S. Hascall, of Indiana, Colonel 17th Indiana Volunteers, from April 25, 1862 ; resigned Oct. 27, 1864.

989. Leonard F. Ross, of Illinois, Colonel 17th Illinois Volunteers, from April 25, 1862 ; resigned July 22, 1863.

990. John W. Geary, of Pennsylvania, Colonel 28th Pennsylvania Volunteers, from April 25, 1862 ; mustered out Jan. 15, 1866.

991. Alfred H. Terry, of Connecticut, Colonel 7th Connecticut Volunteers, from April 25, 1862 ; promoted Major-General Jan. 15, 1865.

992. Major Andrew A. Humphreys, Topographical Engineers, Colonel and Additional Aide-de-Camp, from April 28, 1862 ; promoted Major-General July 8, 1863.

993. Major James H. Carleton, 6th U. S. Cavalry and Colonel 1st California Volunteers, from April 28, 1862 ; mustered out April 30, 1866.

994. Major Absalom Baird, Asst. Inspector-General, from April 28, 1862 ; mustered out Sept. 1, 1866.

995. Captain John C. Robinson, 5th U. S. Infantry and Colonel 1st Michigan Volunteers, from April 28, 1862 ; mustered out Aug. 24, 1865.

996. Captain Truman Seymour, 5th U. S. Artillery, from April 28, 1862, mustered out Aug. 24, 1865.

997. Captain Quincy A. Gillmore, Corps of Engineers, from April 28, 1862 ; promoted Major-General July 10, 1863.

998. Captain George D. Bayard, 4th U. S. Cavalry and Colonel 1st Pennsylvania Cavalry Volunteers, from April 28, 1862; died of wounds Dec. 14, 1862.

999. Paymaster Henry Prince, U. S. A., from April 28, 1862 ; mustered out April 30, 1866.

1,000. Abraham Piatt, of Ohio, Colonel 13th Ohio Volunteers, from April 28, 1862; resigned Feb. 17, 1863.

1,001. Thomas T. Crittenden, of Indiana, Colonel 6th Indiana Volunteers, from April 28, 1862 ; resigned May 5, 1863.

1,002. Max Weber, of New York, Colonel 20th N. Y. Volunteers, from April 28, 1862 ; resigned May 13, 1865.

1,003. Pleasant A. Hackleman, of Indiana, Colonel 16th Indiana Volunteers, from April 28, 1862; killed Oct. 3, 1862.

1,004. Jeremiah C. Sullivan, of Indiana, Colonel 13th Indiana Volunteers, from April 28, 1862 ; resigned May 11, 1865.

1,005. Alvin P. Hovey, of Indiana, Colonel 24th Indiana Volunteers, from April 28, 1862 ; resigned Oct. 7, 1865.

1,006. James C. Veatch, of Indiana, Colonel 25th Indiana Volunteers, from April 28, 1862 ; mustered out Aug. 24, 1865.

1,007. William P. Benton, of Indiana, Colonel 8th Indiana Volunteers, from April 28, 1862 ; resigned July 24, 1865.

1,008. Henry Bohlen, of Pennsylvania, Colonel 75th Pennsylvania Volunteers, from April 28, 1862 ; killed Aug. 22, 1862.

1,009. John C. Caldwell, of Maine, Colonel 11th Maine Volunteers, from April 28, 1862 ; mustered out Jan. 16, 1866.

1,010. Isaac P. Rodman, of Rhode Island, Colonel 4th Rhode Island Volunteers, from April 28,1862 ; died of wounds Sept. 30, 1862.

1,011. Neal Dow, of Maine, Colonel 13th Maine Volunteers, from April 28, 1862 ; resigned Nov. 30, 1864.

1,012. George S. Green, of New York, Colonel 60th N. Y. Volunteers, from April 28, 1862 ; mustered out April 30, 1866.

1,013. Samuel P. Carter, of Tennessee, Colonel 2d Tennessee Volunteers, from May 1, 1862 ; mustered out Jan. 15, 1866.

1,014. Captain John Gibbon, 4th U. S. Artillery, from May 2, 1862; promoted Major-General June 7, 1864.

1,015. George W. Taylor, of New Jersey, Colonel 3d New Jersey Volunteers, from May 9, 1862; died of wounds Aug. 31, 1862.

1,016. Erastus B. Tyler, of Ohio, Colonel 7th Ohio Volunteers, from May 14, 1862; mustered out Aug. 24, 1865.

1,017. Captain James B. McPherson, Corps of Engineers, Colonel and Additiona' Aide-de-Camp, from May 15, 1862; promoted Major-General Oct. 8, 1862.

1,018. Captain Charles Griffin, 5th U. S. Artillery, from June 9, 1862; promoted Major-General April 2, 1865.

1,019. George H. Gordon, of Massachusetts, Colonel 2d Massachusetts Volunteers, from June 9, 1862; mustered out Aug. 24, 1865.

1,020. James M. Tuttle, of Iowa, Colonel 2d Iowa Volunteers, from June 9, 1862; resigned June 14, 1864.

1,021. Julius White, of Illinois, Colonel 37th Illinois Volunteers, from June 9, 1862; resigned Nov. 19, 1864.

1,022. Peter J. Osterhaus, of Missouri, Colonel 12th Missouri Volunteers, from June 9, 1862; promoted Major-General July 23, 1864.

1,023. Stephen G. Burbridge, of Kentucky, Colonel 26th Kentucky Volunteers, from June 9, 1862; resigned Dec. 1, 1865.

1,024. Major Washington L. Elliott, 1st U. S. Cavalry, and Colonel 2d Iowa Cavalry, from June 11, 1862 ; mustered out March 1, 1866.

1,025. Captain Albion P. Howe, 4th U. S. Artillery, from June 11, 1862; mustered out Jan. 15, 1866.

1,026. Green Clay Smith, of Kentucky, Colonel 4th Kentucky Cavalry, from June 11, 1862; resigned Dec. 1, 1863.

1,027. William B. Campbell, of Tennessee, from June 30, 1862 ; resigned Jan. 26, 1863.

1,028. Captain Philip H. Sheridan, 13th U. S. Infantry and Colonel 2d Michigan Cavalry Volunteers, from July 1, 1862; promoted Major-General Dec. 31, 1862.

1,029. Major Benjamin S. Roberts, 3d U. S. Cavalry, from July 16, 1862 : mustered out Jan. 15, 1866.

1,030. Major Alfred Pleasanton, 2d U. S. Cavalry, from July 16, 1862; promoted Major-General June 22, 1863.

1,031. Jacob Ammen, of Ohio, Colonel 24th Ohio Volunteers, from July 16, 1862; resigned Jan. 4, 1865.

1,032. Joshua W. Sill, of Ohio, Colonel 33d Ohio Volunteers, from July 16, 1862; killed Dec. 31, 1862.

1,033. Catharinus P. Buckingham, of Ohio, from July 16, 1862 ; resigned Feb. 11, 1863.

1,034. Fitz Henry Warren, of Iowa, Colonel 1st Iowa Cavalry, from July 16, 1862; mustered out Aug. 24, 1865.

1,035. Morgan L. Smith, of Missouri, Colonel 8th Missouri Volunteers, from July 16, 1862; resigned July 12, 1865.

1,036. Charles Cruft, of Indiana, Colonel 31st Indiana Volunteers, from July 16, 1862 ; mustered out Aug. 24, 1865.

1,037. Frederick Salomon, of Wisconsin, Colonel 9th Wisconsin Volunteers, from July 16, 1862 ; mustered out Aug. 24, 1865.

1,038. James S. Jackson, of Kentucky, Colonel 3d Kentucky Cavalry, from July 16, 1862 ; killed Oct. 8, 1862.

1,039. Cadwalader C. Washburn, of Wisconsin, Colonel 2d Wisconsin Cavalry, from July 16, 1862; promoted Major-General Nov. 29, 1862.

1,040. Francis J. Herron, of Iowa, Lieut.-Colonel 9th Iowa Cavalry, from July 16, 1862 ; promoted Major-General Nov. 29, 1862.

1,041. John Cochran, of New York, Colonel 65th New York Volunteers, from July 17, 1862 ; resigned Feb. 25, 1863.

1,042. John B. Turchin, of Illinois, Colonel 19th Illinois Volunteers, from July 17, 1862; resigned Oct. 4th, 1864.

1,043. Henry S. Briggs, of Massachusetts, Colonel 10th Massachusetts Volunteers, from July 17, 1862; mustered out Dec. 4, 1865.

1,044. Conrad Feger Jackson, of Pennsylvania, Colonel 9th Pennsylvania Volunteers, from July 17, 1862 ; killed Dec. 13, 1862.

1,045. James D. Morgan of Illinois, Colonel 10th Illinois Volunteers, from July 17, 1862 ; mustered out Aug. 24, 1865.

1,046. August Willich, of Indiana, Colonel 32d Indiana Volunteers, from July 17, 1862; mustered out Jan. 15, 1866.

1,047. Henry D. Terry, of Michigan, Colonel 5th Michigan Volunteers, from July 17, 1862 ; resigned Feb. 7, 1865.

1,048. James B. Steedman, of Ohio, Colonel 14th Ohio Volunteers, from July 17, 1862 ; promoted to Major-General April 20, 1864.

1,049. George F. Shepley, of Maine, from July 18, 1862 ; resigned July 1, 1865.

1,050. Thomas H. Hicks, of Maryland, from July 22, 1862 ; declined.

1,051. Major John Buford, Asst. Inspector-General, from July 27, 1862; promoted Major-General July 1, 1863.

1,052. Frank P. Blair, of Missouri, Colonel 1st Missouri Artillery, from Aug. 7, 1862; promoted Major-General Nov. 29, 1862.

1,053. Richard Busteed, of New York, from Aug 7, 1862; commission expired March 4, 1863.

1,054. John R. Kenly, of Maryland, Colonel 1st Maryland Volunteers, from Aug. 22, 1862 ; mustered out Aug. 24, 1865.

1,055. John B. Slough, of Colorado, Colonel 1st Colorado Volunteers, from Aug. 25, 1862 ; mustered out Aug. 24, 1865.

1,056. First Lieut. Godfrey Weitzel, Corps of Engineers, from Aug. 29, 1862 ; promoted Major-General Nov. 17, 1864.

1,057. Lieut.-Colonel Gabriel R. Paul, 8th U. S. Infantry and Colonel 4th New Mexico Volunteers, from Sept. 5, 1862 ; commission expired March 4, 1863 ; reappointed from April 18, 1863 ; mustered out Sept. 1, 1866.

1,058. Charles E. Hovey, of Illinois, Colonel 33d Illinois Volunteers, from Sept. 5, 1862 ; commission expired March 4, 1863.

1,059. Colonel Herman Haupt, Additional Aide-de-Camp, from Sept. 5, 1862 ; declined.

1,060. Captain George Crook, 4th U. S. Infantry and Colonel 36th Ohio Volunteers, from Sept. 7, 1862 ; promoted Major-General Oct. 21, 1864.

1,061. Joseph B. Carr, of New York, Colonel 2d New York Volunteers, from Sept. 7, 1862 ; commission expired March 4, 1863 ; reappointed from March 30, 1863; mustered out Aug. 24, 1865.

1,062. Thomas L. Kane, of Pennsylvania, Colonel 1st Pennsylvania Rifles, from Sept. 7, 1863 ; resigned Nov. 7, 1863.

1,063. Nelson Taylor, of New York, Colonel 72d New York Volunteers, from Sept. 7, 1862 ; resigned Jan. 19, 1863.

1,064. Gersham Mott, of New Jersey, Colonel 6th New Jersey Volunteers, from Sept. 7, 1862 ; promoted Major-General May 26, 1865.

1,065. Captain Charles C. Gilbert, 1st U. S. Infantry, from Sept. 9, 1862 ; commission expired March 4, 1863 ; not confirmed.

1,066. Captain William R. Terrill, 5th U. S. Artillery, from Sept. 9, 1862 ; killed Oct. 8, 1862.

1,067. Calvin E. Pratt, of New York, Colonel 31st New York Volunteers, from Sept. 10, 1862 ; resigned April 25, 1863.

1,068. James Nagle, of Pennsylvania, Colonel 48th Pennsylvania Volunteers, from Sept. 10, 1862 ; commission expired March 4, 1863 ; reappointed March 13, 1863 ; resigned May 9, 1863.

1,069. Edward Ferrero, of New York, Colonel 51st New York Volunteers, from Sept. 10, 1862 ; commission expired March 4, 1863 ; reappointed from May 6, 1863 ; mustered out Aug. 24, 1865.

1,070. Major Henry J. Hunt, 5th U. S. Artillery, Colonel and Additional Aide-de-Camp, from Sept. 15, 1862 : mustered out April 30, 1866.

1,071. Captain Francis L. Vinton, 13th U. S. Infantry and Colonel 43d New York Volunteers, from Sept. 19, 1862 ; commission expired March 4, 1863 ; reappointed from March 13, 1863 ; resigned May 5, 1863.

1,072. Gustavus A. Smith, of Illinois, Colonel 35th Illinois Volunteers, from Sept. 19, 1862 ; commission expired March 4, 1863.

1,073. Francis C. Barlow, of New York, Colonel 61st New York Volunteers, from Sept. 19, 1862 ; promoted Major-General May 25, 1865.

1,074. Thomas A. Morris, of Indiana, Brig.-General Indiana State Volunteers or Militia, from Sept. 20, 1862 ; declined.

1,075. Mason Brayman, of Illinois, Colonel 29th Illinois Volunteers, from Sept. 24, 1862 ; mustered out Aug. 24, 1865.

1,076. N. J. Jackson, of Maine, Colonel 5th Maine Volunteers, from Sept. 24, 1862 : mustered out Aug. 24, 1865.

1,077. Captain George W. Getty, 5th U. S. Artillery, Lieut.-Colonel and Additional Aide de-Camp, from Sept. 25, 1862 ; mustered out Oct. 9, 1866.

1,078. Major Alfred Sully, 8th U. S. Infantry and Colonel 1st Minnesota Volunteers, from Sept. 26, 1862 ; mustered out April 30, 1866.

1,079. Captain Gouverneur K. Warren, Topographical Engineers, and Colonel 5th New York Volunteers, from Sept. 26, 1862 ; promoted Major-General May 3, 1863.

1,080. Captain Wm. W. Averell, 3d U. S. Cavalry, and Colonel 3d Pennsylvania Cavalry, from Sept. 26, 1862 ; resigned May 18, 1865.

1,081. Robert Cowden, of Massachusetts, Colonel 1st Massachusetts Volunteers, from Sept. 26, 1862 ; commission expired March 4, 1863.

1,082. Alexander Hays, of Pennsylvania, Colonel 63d Pennsylvania Volunteers, from Sept. 29, 1862 ; killed May 5, 1864.

1,083. Henry H. Sibley, of Minnesota, from Sept. 29, 1862 ; commission expired March 4, 1863 ; reappointed from March 20, 1863 ; mustered out April 30, 1866.

1,084. Francis B. Spinola, of New York, from Oct. 1, 1862 ; resigned June 8, 1865.

1,085. John H. H. Ward, of New York, Colonel 38th New York Volunteers, from Oct. 4, 1862 ; mustered out July 18, 1864.

1,086. Joseph J. Bartlett, of New York, Colonel 27th New York Volunteers, from Oct. 4, 1862; commission expired March 4, 1863; reappointed from March 30, 1863; mustered out Jan. 15, 1866.

1,087. Solomon Meredith, of Indiana, Colonel 19th Indiana Volunteers, from Oct. 6, 1862; mustered out May 22, 1865.

1,088. James Bowen, of New York, from Oct. 11, 1862; resigned July 27, 1864.

1,089. Colonel Gustave P. Cluseret, Additional Aide-de-Camp, from Oct. 14, 1862; resigned March 2, 1863.

1,090. Eliakim P. Scammon, of Ohio, Colonel 23d Ohio Volunteers, from Oct. 15, 1862; mustered out Aug. 24, 1865.

1,091. Major Robert S. Granger, 5th U. S. Infantry, from Oct. 20, 1862; mustered out Aug. 24, 1865.

1,092. Joseph R. West, of California, Colonel 1st California Volunteers, from Oct. 25, 1862; mustered out Jan. 4, 1866.

1,093. Joseph W. Revere, of New Jersey, Colonel 7th New Jersey Volunteers, from Oct. 25, 1862; resigned Aug. 10, 1863.

1,094. Lieut.-Colonel Alfred W. Ellett, Additional Aide-de-Camp, from Nov. 1, 1862; resigned Dec. 21, 1864.

1,095. Edwin H. Stoughton, of Vermont, Colonel 4th Vermont Volunteers, from Nov. 5, 1862; commission expired March 4, 1863.

1,096. George L. Andrews, of Massachusetts, Colonel 2d Massachusetts Volunteers, from Nov. 10, 1862; mustered out Aug. 24, 1865.

1,097. Clinton B. Fisk, of Missouri, Colonel 33d Missouri Volunteers, from Nov. 24, 1862; mustered out Sept. 1, 1866.

1,098. Colonel Henry B. Carrington, 18th U. S. Infantry, from Nov. 29, 1862; mustered out Aug. 24, 1865.

1,099. Lieut.-Colonel Robert C. Buchanan, 4th U. S. Infantry, from Nov. 29, 1862; commission expired March 4, 1863.

1,100. Captain James A. Hardie, 5th U. S. Artillery, Lieut. Colonel and Additional Aide-de-Camp, from Nov. 29, 1862; commission expired Jan. 22, 1863.

1,101. Captain William Hays, 2d U. S. Artillery, Lieut.-Colonel and Additional Aid-de-Camp, from Nov. 29, 1862; mustered out Jan. 15, 1866

1,102. Major John H. King, 15th U. S. Infantry, from Nov. 29, 1862; mustered out Jan. 15, 1866.

1,103. Major Israel Vogdes, 1st U. S. Artillery, from Nov. 29, 1862.

1,104. Major Adam J. Slemmer, 16th U. S. Infantry, from Nov. 29, 1862; mustered out Aug. 24, 1865.

1,105. Major David A. Russell, 8th U. S. Infantry and Colonel 4th Massachusetts Volunteers, from Nov. 29, 1862; killed Sept. 19, 1864.

1,106. Captain Lewis C. Hunt, 4th U. S. Infantry and Colonel 92d New York Volunteers, from Nov. 29, 1862; mustered out January 15, 1866.

1,107. Captain Thomas H. Neill. 5th U. S. Infantry and Colonel 23d Pennsylvania Volunteers, from Nov. 29, 1862; mustered out Aug. 24, 1865.

1,108. Captain Thomas G. Pitcher, 8th U. S. Infantry, from Nov. 29, 1862; mustered out April 30, 1866.

1,109. Captain Thomas W. Sweeny, 2d U. S. Infantry and Colonel 52d Illinois Volunteers, from Nov. 29, 1862; mustered out Aug. 24, 1865.

1,110. Captain Frank Wheaton, 4th U. S. Cavalry and Colonel 2d Rhode Island Volunteers, from Nov. 29, 1862; mustered out April 30, 1866.

1,111. Captain Wm. P. Carlin, 6th U. S. Infantry and Colonel 38th Illinois Volunteers, from Nov. 29, 1862; mustered out Aug. 24, 1865.

1,112. Captain John S. Mason, 11th U. S. Infantry and Colonel 4th Ohio Volunteers, from Nov. 29, 1862; mustered out April 30, 1866.

1,113. Captain Romeyn B. Ayres, 5th U. S. Artillery, from Nov. 29, 1862; mustered out April 30, 1866.

1,114. Captain Richard Arnold, 5th U. S. Artillery, from Nov. 29, 1862; mustered out Aug. 24, 1865.

1,115. Captain David McM. Gregg, 6th U. S. Cavalry and Colonel 8th Pennsylvania Cavalry, from Nov. 29, 1862; resigned Feb. 3, 1865.

1,116. Captain Wm. B. Hazen, 8th U. S. Infantry and Colonel 41st Ohio Volunteers, from Nov. 29, 1862; promoted Major-General Jan. 15, 1865.

1,117. Captain Robert O. Tyler, Asst. Quartermaster U. S. A. and Colonel 1st Connecti..ut Heavy Artillery, from Nov. 29, 1862; mustered out Jan. 15, 1866.

1,118. Captain James St. Clair Morton, Corps of Engineers, from Nov. 29, 1862; mustered out Nov. 7, 1863.

1,119. Captain Joseph A. Mower, 1st U. S. Infantry and Colonel 11th Missouri Volunteers, from Nov. 29, 1862; promoted Major-General Aug. 12, 1864.

1,120. Captain Alfred T. A. Torbert, 5th U. S. Infantry and Colonel 1st New Jersey Volunteers, from Nov. 29, 1862; mustered out Jan. 15, 1866.

1,121. First Lieut. Orlan.lo M. Poe, Topographical Engineers, U. S. A., and Colonel 2d Michigan Volunteers, from Nov. 29, 1862; commission expired March 4, 1863.

1,122. First Lieut. Geo. C. Strong, Ordnance Department, Major and Asst. Adjutant-General, U. S. Volunteers, from Nov. 29, 1862; promoted Major-General July 18, 1863.

1,123. Isham N. Haynie, of Illinois, Colonel 48th Illinois Volunteers, from Nov. 29, 1862; commission expired March 4, 1863.

1,124. D. Stuart, of Illinois, Colonel 55th Illinois Volunteers, from Nov. 29, 1862; commission expired March 11, 1863.

1,125. John F. Farnsworth, of Illinois, Colonel 8th Illinois Volunteers, from Nov. 29, 1862; resigned March 4, 1863.

1,126. F. S. Stumbaugh, of Pennsylvania, Colonel 77th Pennsylvania Volunteers, from Nov. 29, 1862; commission expired, Jan. 23, 1863.

1,127. Charles T. Campbell, of Pennsylvania, Colonel 57th Pennsylvania Volunteers, from Nov. 29, 1862; commission expired, March 4, 1863; reappointed from March 13, 1863; mustered out Aug. 24, 1865.

1,128. William H. Lytle, of Ohio, Colonel 10th Ohio Volunteers, from Nov. 29, 1862; died of wounds Sept. 20, 1863.

1,129. Gilman Marston, of New Hampshire, Colonel 2d New Hampshire Volunteers, from Nov. 29, 1862; resigned April 20, 1865.

1,130. Michael K. Lawler, of Illinois, Colonel 18th Illinois Volunteers, from Nov. 29, 1862; mustered out Jan. 15, 1866.

1,131. George D. Wagner, of Indiana, Colonel 15th Indiana Volunteers, from Nov. 29, 1862; mustered out Aug. 24, 1865.

1,132. William Dwight, of New York, Colonel 70th New York Volunteers, from Nov. 29, 1862; mustered out Jan. 15, 1866.

1,133. Lysander Cutler, of Wisconsin, Colonel 6th Wisconsin Volunteers, from Nov. 29, 1862; resigned June 30, 1865.

1,134. James W. McMillen, of Indiana, Colonel 21st Indiana Volunteers, from Nov. 29, 1862; resigned May 15, 1865.

1,135. Sullivan A. Meredith, of Pennsylvania, Colonel 56th Pennsylvania Volunteers, from Nov. 29, 1862; mustered out Aug. 24, 1865.

1,136. Joseph F. Knipe, of Pennsylvania, Colonel 46th Pennsylvania Volunteers, from Nov. 29, 1862; mustered out Aug. 24, 1865.

1,137. E. W. Hinks, of Massachusetts, Colonel 19th Massachusetts Volunteers, from Nov. 29, 1862; resigned June 30, 1865.

1,138. Joshua T. Owens, of Pennsylvania, Colonel 69th Pennsylvania Volunteers, from Nov. 29, 1862; commision expired March 4, 1863; reappointed from March 30, 1863; mustered out July 18, 1864.

1,139. John D. Stevenson, of Missouri, Colonel 7th Missouri Volunteers, from Nov. 29, 1862; commission expired March 4, 1863; reappointed from Nov. 29, 1862; resigned April 22, 1864; reappointed to rank as before, mustered out Jan. 15, 1866.

1,140. James Barnes, of Massachusetts, Colonel 18th Massachusetts Volunteers, from Nov. 29, 1862; mustered out Jan. 15, 1866.

1,141. E. N. Kirk, of Illinois, Colonel 34th Illinois Volunteers, from Nov. 29, 1862; died July 29, 1863.

1,142. N. C. McLean, of Ohio, Colonel 75th Ohio Volunteers, from Nov. 29, 1862; resigned April 20, 1865.

1,143. Theophilus T. Garrard, of Kentucky, Colonel 3d Kentucky Volunteers, from Nov. 29, 1862; mustered out April 4, 1864.

1,144. William Vandever, of Iowa, Colonel 9th Iowa Volunteers, from Nov. 29, 1862; mustered out Aug. 24, 1865.

1,145. Alexander Schemmelfinnig, of Pennsylaania, Colonel 74th Pennsylvania Volunteers, from Nov. 29, 1862; died Sept. 7, 1865.

1,146. Edward Harland, of Connecticut, Colonel 8th Connecticut Volunteers, from Nov. 29, 1862; resigned June 22, 1865.

1,147. Charles K. Graham, of New York, Colonel 74th New York Volunteers, from Nov. 29, 1862; mustered out Aug. 24, 1865.

1,148. S. K. Zook, of New York, Colonel 57th New York Volunteers, from Nov. 29, 1862; killed July 2, 1863.

1,149. Samuel Beatty, of Ohio, Colonel 19th Ohio Volunteers, from Nov. 29, 1862; mustered out Jan. 15, 1866.

1,150. Isaac Wistar, of Pennsylvania, Colonel 71st Pennsylvania Volunteers, from Nov. 29, 1862; resigned Sept. 15, 1864.

1,151. John E. Smith, of Illinois, Colonel 45th Illinois Volunteers, from Nov. 29, 1862; mustered out April 30, 1866.

1,152. Frank S. Nickerson, of Maine, Colonel 14th Maine Volunteers, from Nov. 29, 1862; resigned May 13, 1865.

1,153. Edward H. Hobson, of Kentucky, Colonel 13th Kentucky Volunteers, from Nov. 29, 1862; mustered out Aug. 24, 1865.

1,154. R. B. Buckland, of Ohio, Colonel 72d Ohio Volunteers, from Nov. 29, 1862; resigned Jan. 6, 1865.

1,155. Joseph D. Webster, of Illinois, Colonel 1st Illinois Artillery, from Nov. 29, 1862; resigned Nov. 5, 1865.

1,156. William W. Orme, of Illinois, Colonel 94th Illinois Volunteers, from Nov. 29, 1862; resigned April 26, 1864.

1,157. William Harrowe, of Indiana, Colonel 14th Indiana Volunteers, from Nov. 29, 1862 ; resigned April 20, 1865.

1,158. Joseph T. Copeland, of Michigan, Colonel 5th Michigan Cavalry, from Nov. 29, 1862 ; resigned Nov. 8, 1865.

1,159. William H. Morris, of New York, Colonel 6th New York Volunteer Artillery, from Nov. 29, 1862 ; mustered out Aug. 24, 1865.

1,160. John Beatty, of Ohio, Colonel 3d Ohio Volunteers, from Nov. 29, 1862 ; resigned Jan. 28, 1864.

1,161. Thomas H. Ruger, of Wisconsin, Colonel 3d Wisconsin Volunteers, from Nov. 29, 1862 ; mustered out Sept. 1, 1866.

1,162. T. E. G. Ransom, of Illinois, Colonel 11th Illinois Volunteers, from Nov. 29, 1862 ; died Oct. 29, 1864.

1,163. Elias S. Dennis, of Illinois, Lieut.-Colonel 30th Illinois Volunteers, from Nov. 29, 1862 ; mustered out Aug. 24, 1865.

1,164. Thomas C. H. Smith, of Ohio, Lieut.-Colonel 1st Ohio Cavalry, from Nov. 29, 1862 ; mustered out Jan. 15, 1866.

1,165. Charles A. Heckman, of New Jersey, Lieut.-Colonel 9th New Jersey Volunteers, from Nov. 29, 1862 ; resigned May 25, 1865.

1,166. Mortimer D. Leggett, of Ohio, Lieut.-Colonel 78th Ohio Volunteers, from Nov. 29, 1862 ; promoted Major-General Aug. 21, 1865.

1,167. David Tillson, of Maine, Lieut.-Colonel 1st Maine Light Artillery, from Nov. 29, 1862 ; mustered out Jan. 17, 1867.

1,168. Stephen G. Champlin, of Michigan, Major 3d Michigan Volunteers, from Nov. 29, 1862 ; died Jan. 26, 1864.

1,169. Hector Tyndale, of Pennsylvania, Major 28th Pennsylvania Volunteers, from Nov. 29, 1862 ; resigned Aug. 26, 1864.

1,170. Charles C. Dodge, of New York, Colonel 1st New York Mounted Rifles, from Nov. 29, 1862 ; resigned June 12, 1863.

1,171. Edward E. Potter, of New York, from Nov. 29, 1862 ; resigned July 24, 1865.

1,172. Thomas A. Rowley, of Pennsylvania, Colonel 102d Pennsylvania Volunteers, from Nov. 29, 1862 ; resigned Dec. 29, 1864.

1,173. Albert L. Lee, of Pennsylvania, from Nov. 29, 1862 ; resigned May 4, 1865.

1,174. Charles L. Matthies, of Iowa, Colonel 5th Iowa Volunteers, from Nov. 29, 1862 ; resigned May 16, 1864.

1,175. Marcellus M. Crocker, of Iowa, Colonel 13th Iowa Volunteers, from Nov. 29, 1862 ; died Aug. 26, 1865.

1,176. Egbert B. Brown, of Missouri, late Lieut.-Colonel 7th Missouri Volunteers, from Nov. 29, 1862 ; resigned Nov. 10, 1865.

1,177. John McNeil, of Missouri, Colonel 2d Missouri State Militia Cavalry, from Nov. 29, 1862 ; resigned April 12. 1865,

1,178. George P. McGinnis, of Indiana, Colonel 11th Indiana Volunteers, from Nov. 29, 1862 ; mustered out Aug. 24, 1865.

1,179. George W. Deitzler, of Kansas, Colonel 1st Kansas Volunteers, from Nov. 29, 1862 ; resigned Aug. 27, 1863.

1,180. Hugh Ewing, of Ohio, Colonel 13th Ohio Volunteers, from Nov. 29, 1862 ; mustered out Jan. 15, 1866.

1,181. James H. Ledlie, of New York, Colonel 3d New York Volunteer Artillery, from Dec. 24, 1862 ; commission expired March 4, 1863 ; reappointed from Oct. 27, 1863 ; resigned Jan. 23, 1865.

1,182. James M. Shackelford, of Kentucky, Colonel 8th Kentucky Cavalry, from Jan. 2, 1863; resigned Jan. 18, 1864.

1,183. Daniel Ullman, of New York, Colonel 78th New York Volunteers, from Jan. 13, 1863; mustered out Aug. 24, 1865.

1,184. John S. Phelps, of Missouri, from July 19, 1862; commission expired March 4, 1863.

1,185. Waldemir Kryzanowski, of New York, Colonel 58th New York Volunteers, from Nov. 29, 1862; commission expired March 4, 1863.

1,186. D. H. Williams, of Pennsylvania, from Nov. 29, 1862; commission expired March 4, 1863.

1,187. George J. Stannard, of Vermont, Colonel 9th Vermont Volunteers, from March 11, 1863; mustered out Aug. 24, 1865.

1,188. Henry Baxter, of Michigan, Lieut.-Colonel 2d Michigan Volunteers, from March 12, 1863; mustered out Aug. 24, 1865.

1,189. John M. Thayer, of Nebraska, Colonel 1st Nebraska Volunteers, from March 13, 1863; resigned July 19, 1865.

1,190. Halbert E. Paine, of Wisconsin, Colonel 4th Wisconsin Volunteers, from March 13, 1863; resigned May 15, 1865.

1,191. Thomas Welsh, of Pennsylvania, Colonel 45th Pennsylvania Volunteers, from March 13, 1863; died Aug. 14. 1863.

1,192. Hugh T. Reid, of Iowa, Colonel 15th Iowa Volunteers, from March 13, 1863; resigned April 4, 1864.

1,193. Abner C. Harding, of Illinois, Colonel 83d Illinois Volunteers, from March 13, 1863; resigned June 3, 1863.

1,194. Robert B. Potter, of New York, Colonel 51st New York Volunteers, from March 13, 1863; promoted Major-General Sept. 29, 1865.

1,195. Thomas Ewing, Jr., of Kansas, Colonel 11th Kansas Cavalry, from March 13, 1863; resigned Feb. 23, 1865.

1,196. J. A. J. Lightburn, of Virginia, Colonel 4th Virginia Volunteers, from March 14, 1863; resigned June 22, 1865.

1,197. Thomas G. Stevenson, of Massachusetts, Colonel 24th Massachusetts Volunteers, from March 14, 1863; killed May 10, 1864.

1,198. Patrick E. Connor, of Colorado, Colonel 3d Colorado Volunteers, from March 30, 1863; mustered out April 30, 1866.

1,199. Captain John P. Hawkins, Commissary of Subsistence and Lieut.-Colonel of Commissary Subsistence Department, from April 13, 1863; mustered out Feb. 1, 1866.

1,200. Edward A. Wild, of Massachusetts, Colonel 35th Massachusetts Volunteers from April 24, 1863; mustered out Jan. 15, 1866.

1,201. Thomas E. Bramlette, of Kentucky, late Colonel 3d Kentucky Volunteers, from April 24, 1863; declined.

1,202. First Lieut. Adalbert Ames, 5th U. S. Artillery, and Colonel 20th Maine Volunteers, from May 20, 1863; mustered out April 30, 1866.

1,203. William Birney, of New Jersey, Colonel 2d U. S. Colored Troops, from May 22, 1863; mustered out Aug. 24, 1865.

1,204. Major Daniel H. Rucker, Quartermaster, Colonel and Additional Aide-de-Camp, from May 23, 1863; mustered out Sept. 1, 1866.

1,205. Major Robert Allen, Quartermaster, Colonel and Additional Aide-de-Camp from May 23, 1863; mustered out Sept. 1, 1866.

1,206. Major Rufus Ingalls, Quartermaster, Lieut.-Colonel and Additional Aide-de-Camp, from May 23, 1863; mustered out Sept. 1, 1866.

1,207. Captain Gustavus A. De Russey, 4th U. S. Artillery and Colonel 4th New York Volunteer Artillery, from May 23, 1863; commission expired July 4, 1864; reappointed from May 23, 1863; mustered out Jan. 15, 1866.

1,208. Alexander Shaler, of New York, Colonel 65th New York Volunteers, from May 26, 1863; mustered out Aug. 24, 1865.

1,209. First Lieut. Edmund Kirby, 1st U. S. Artillery and Colonel 43d Ohio Volunteers, from May 23, 1863; died of wounds May 28, 1863.

1,210. Benjamin H. Grierson, of Illinois, Colonel 6th Illinois Cavalry, from June 3, 1863; promoted Major-General May 27, 1865.

1,211. Captain Stephen H. Weed, 5th U. S. Artillery, from June 6, 1863; killed July 2, 1863.

1,212. Robert S. Foster, of Indiana, Colonel 13th Indiana Volunteers, from June 12, 1863; resigned Sept. 25, 1865.

1,213. First Lieut. Judson Kilpatrick, 1st U. S. Artillery and Colonel 2d New York Volunteer Cavalry, from June 13, 1863; promoted Majo.-General June 18, 1865.

1,214. Captain Alexander S. Webb, 11th U. S. Infantry, Lieut.-Colonel and Asst. Inspector-General U. S. Volunteers, from June 23, 1863; mustered out Jan. 15, 1866.

1,215. Alfred N. Duffie, of Rhode Island, Colonel 1st Rhode Island Cavalry, from June 23, 1863; mustered out Aug. 24, 1865.

1,216. Walter C. Whittaker, of Kentucky, Colonel 6th Kentucky Volunteers, from June 25, 1863; must. red out Aug. 24, 1865.

1,217. Captain Wesley Merrit, 2d U. S. Cavalry, from June 29, 1863; promoted Major-General April 1, 1865.

1,218. First Lieut. George A. Custer, 5th U. S. Cavalry, Captain and Additional Aide-de-Camp, from June 29, 1863; promoted Major-General April 15, 1865.

1,219. E. J. Farnsworth, of Illinois, Captain 8th Illinois Cavalry, from June 29, 1863; killed July 3, 1863.

1,220. Edward P. Chapin, of New York, Colonel 116th New York Volunteers, from June 27, 1863; killed June 27, 1863.

1,221. Strong Vincent, of Pennsylvania, Colonel 83d Pennsylvania Volunteers, from July 3, 1863; died of wounds July 7, 1863.

1,222. Major Wm. D. Whipple, Asst. Adjutant-General, Lieut.-Colonel and Additional Aide-de-Camp, from July 17, 1863; commission expired July 4, 1864; reappointed from same date; mustered out Jan. 15, 1866.

1,223. John C. Starkweather, of Wisconsin, Colonel 1st Wisconsin Volunteers, from July 17, 1863; resigned May 11, 1865.

1,224. Captain Kenner Garrard, 5th U. S. Cavalry and Colonel 146th New York Volunteers, from July 23, 1863; mustered out Aug. 24, 1865.

1,225. James L. Kiernan, of New York, Colonel U. S. Colored Troops, from Aug. 1, 1863; resigned Feb. 3, 1864.

1,226. Captain Charles R. Woods, 9th U. S. Infantry and Colonel 76th Ohio Volunteers, from Aug. 4, 1863; mustered out Sept. 1, 1866.

1,227. John B. Sanborn, of Minnesota, Colonel 4th Minnesota Volunteers, from Aug. 4, 1863; mustered out April 30, 1866.

1,228. Giles A. Smith, of Minnesota, Colonel 8th Missouri Volunteers, from Aug. 4, 1863; promoted Major-General Nov. 24, 1865.

1,229. Samuel A. Rice, of Iowa, Colonel 33d Iowa Volunteers, from Aug. 4, 1863; died of wounds July 6, 1864.

1,230. Jasper A. Maltby, of Illinois, Colonel 55th Illinois Volunteers, from Aug. 4, 1863; mustered out Jan. 15, 1866.

1,231. Captain Frederick E. Prime, Corps of Engineers, from Aug. 4, 1863; declined.

1,232. Captain Alexander Chambers, 18th U. S. Infantry and Colonel 16th Iowa Volunteers, from Aug. 11, 1863; commission expired April 6, 1864.

1,233. Thomas K. Smith, of Ohio, Colonel 54th Ohio Volunteers, from Aug. 11, 1863; mustered out Jan. 15, 1866.

1,234. Walter Q. Gresham, of Indiana, Colonel 53d Indiana Volunteers, from Aug. 11, 1863; mustered out April 30, 1866.

1,235. Manning F. Force, of Ohio, Colonel 20th Ohio Volunteers, from Aug. 11, 1863; mustered out Jan. 15, 1866.

1,236. Robert A. Cameron, of Indiana, Colonel 34th Indiana Volunteers, from Aug. 11, 1863; resigned June 22, 1865.

1,237. John M. Corse, of Iowa, Colonel 6th Ohio Volunteers, from Aug. 11, 1863; mustered out April 30, 1866.

1,238. John A. Rawlins, of Illinois, Major and Asst. Adjutant-General of Volunteers, from Aug. 11, 1863; promoted Brig.-General U. S. A. March 31, 1865.

1,239. Captain Alvan C. Gillem, Asst. Quartermaster and Colonel 10th Tennessee Volunteers, from Aug. 17, 1863; commission expired July 4, 1864; reappointed from Aug. 17, 1863; promoted Major-General Nov. 3, 1865.

1,240. James C. Rice, of New York, Colonel 44th New York Volunteers, from Aug. 17, 1863; killed May 10, 1864.

1,241. Captain John W. Turner, Commissary of Subsistence, Colonel and Additional Aide-de-Camp, from Sept. 7, 1863; mustered out Sept. 1, 1866.

1,242. Henry L. Eustis, of Massachusetts, Colonel 10th Massachusetts Volunteers, from Sept. 12, 1863; resigned June 27, 1864.

1,243. Henry E. Davies, of New York, Colonel 2d New York Volunteer Cavalry, from Sept 16, 1863; promoted Major-General May 4, 1865.

1,244. Andrew J. Hamilton, of Texas, from Nov. 14, 1862; commission expired March 4, 1863; reappointed Sept. 18, 1863; resigned June 19, 1865.

1,245. Henry W. Birge of Connecticut, Colonel 13th Connecticut Volunteers, from Sept. 19. 1863; resigned Oct. 18, 1865.

1,246. Captain Charles G. Harker, 15th U. S. Infantry, and Colonel 65th Ohio Volunteers, from Sept. 20, 1863; died of wounds June 27, 1864.

1,247. Captain Wm. B. Sanders, 6th U. S. Cavalry, and Colonel 5th Kentucky Cavalry, from Oct. 18, 1863; died of wounds Nov. 19, 1863.

1,248. Captain Lucius Fairchild, 16th U. S. Infantry, and Colonel 2d Wisconsin Volunteers, from Oct. 19, 1863; resigned Nov. 2, 1863.

1,249. Stephen Miller, of Minnesota, Colonel 7th Minnesota Volunteers, from Oct. 26, 1863; resigned Jan. 18, 1864.

1,250. Isaac F. Shephard, of Missouri, Colonel 3d Missouri Volunteers, from Oct. 27, 1863; commission expired July 4, 1864.

1,251. Captain James H. Wilson, Corps of Engineers, Lieut.-Colonel and Asst. Inspector-General U. S. Volunteers, from Oct. 30, 1863; commission expired July 4, 1864; reappointed from Oct. 30, 1863; promoted Major General May 6, 1865.

1,252. Adin B. Underwood, of Massachusetts, Colonel 33d Massachusetts Volunteers, from Nov. 6, 1863; mustered out Sept. 1, 1865.

1,253. Augustus L. Cheslain, of Illinois, Colonel 12th Illinois Volunteers, from Dec. 18, 1863; mustered out Jan. 15, 1866.

1,254. William A. Pile, of Missouri, Colonel 33d Missouri Volunteers, from Dec. 26, 1863; mustered out Aug. 24, 1865.

1,255. Guitar Kaemerling, of Ohio, from Jan. 5, 1864; declined.

1,256. John W. Fuller, of Ohio, Colonel 27th Ohio Volunteers, from Jan. 5, 1864; resigned Aug. 15, 1865.

1,257. John F. Miller, of Indiana, Colonel 29th Indiana Volunteers, from Jan. 5, 1864; resigned Sept. 25, 1865.

1,258. Philip Regis De Trobriand, of New York, Colonel 55th New York Volunteers, from Jan. 5, 1864; mustered out Jan. 15, 1866.

1,259. Cyrus Bussey, of Iowa, Colonel 3d Iowa Cavalry, from Jan. 5, 1864; mustered out Aug. 24, 1865.

1,260. Christopher C. Andrews, of Minnesota, Colonel 3d Minnesota Volunteers, from Jan. 5, 1864; mustered out Jan. 15, 1866.

1,261. Hiram Burnham, of Maine, Colonel 6th Maine Volunteers, from April 27, 1864; killed Sept. 30, 1864.

1,262. Edward M. McCook, First Lieut. 4th U. S. Cavalry and Colonel 2d Indiana Cavalry, from April 27, 1864; mustered out Jan. 15, 1866.

1,263. Lewis A. Grant, of Vermont, Colonel 5th Vermont Volunteers, from April 27, 1864; mustered out Aug. 24, 1865.

1,264. Edward Hatch, of Iowa, Colonel 2d Iowa Cavalry, from April 27, 1864; mustered out Jan. 15, 1866.

1,265. Captain August V. Kautz, 6th U. S. Cavalry and Colonel 2d Ohio Cavalry, from May 7, 1864; mustered out Jan. 15, 1866.

1,266. Captain Francis Fessenden, 19th U. S. Infantry and Colonel 25th Maine Volunteers, from May 10, 1864; promoted Major-General Nov. 9, 1865.

1,267. John R. Brooke, of Pennsylvania, Colonel 53d Pennsylvania Volunteers, from May 12, 1864; resigned Feb. 1, 1866.

1,268. John F. Hartranft, of Pennsylvania, Colonel 51st Pennsylvania Volunteers, from May 12, 1864; mustered out Jan. 15, 1866.

1,269. Captain Samuel S. Carroll, 10th U. S. Infantry and Colonel 18th Ohio Volunteers, from May 12, 1864; mustered out Jan. 15, 1866.

1,270. Simon G. Griffin, of New Hampshire, Colonel 6th New Hampshire Volunteers, from May 12, 1864; mustered out Aug. 24, 1865.

1,271. First Lieut. Emory Upton, 5th U. S. Artillery and Colonel 121st New York Volunteers, from May 12, 1864; mustered out April 30, 1866.

1,272. Nelson A. Miles, of New York, Colonel 61st New York Volunteers, from May 12, 1864; promoted Major-General Oct. 21, 1865.

1,273. Joseph Hayes, of Massachusetts, Colonel 18th Massachusetts Volunteers, from May 12, 1864; mustered out Aug. 24, 1865.

1,274. Byron R. Pierce, of Michigan, Colonel 3d Michigan Volunteers, from June 7, 1864; mustered out Aug. 24, 1865.

1,275. Seldon Conner, of Maine, Colonel 19th Maine Volunteers, from June 11, 1864; mustered out April 7, 1866.

1,276. Joshua L. Chamberlain, of Maine, Colonel 20th Maine Volunteers, from June 18, 1864 ; mustered out Aug. 24, 1865.

1,277. Elliott W. Rice, of Iowa, Colonel 7th Iowa Volunteers, from June 20, 1864 ; mustered out Aug. 24, 1865.

1,278. William F. Bartlett, of Massachusetts, Colonel 57th Massachusetts Volunteers, from June 20, 1864 ; mustered out July 18, 1866.

1,279. Edward S. Bragg, of Wisconsin, Colonel 6th Wisconsin Volunteers, from June 25, 1864 ; mustered out Oct. 9, 1865.

1,280. Friend S. Rutherford, of Illinois, Colonel 97th Illinois Volunteers, from June 27, 1864 ; died June 20, 1864.

1,281. First Lieut. Martin D. Hardin, 3d U. S. Artillery and Colonel 12th Pennsylvania Reserve, from July 2, 1864 ; mustered out Jan. 15, 1866.

1,282. Charles J. Paine, of Massachusetts, Colonel 2d Louisiana Volunteers, from July 4, 1864 : mustered out Jan. 15, 1866.

1,283. Daniel McCook, of Ohio, Colonel 52d Ohio Volunteers, from July 16, 1864 ; died of wounds July 17, 1864.

1,284. John B. McIntosh, of Pennsylvania, Colonel 3d Pennsylvania Cavalry and Captain 5th U. S. Cavalry, from July 21, 1864 ; mustered out April 30, 1866.

1,285. Wm. McCandless, of Pennsylvania, Colonel 2d Pennsylvania Reserves, from July 21, 1864 ; declined.

1,286. George H. Chapman, of Indiana, Colonel 3d Indiana Cavalry, from July 21, 1864 ; mustered out Jan. 7, 1866.

1,287. William Grose, of Indiana, Colonel 36th Indiana Volunteers, from July 21, 1864 ; resigned Dec. 31, 1865.

1,288. Joseph A. Cooper, of Tennessee, Colonel 6th Tennessee Volunteers, from July 21, 1864 ; mustered out Jan. 15, 1866.

1,289. John T. Croxton, of Kentucky, Colonel 4th Kentucky Volunteers, from July 21. 1864 ; resigned Dec. 26, 1865.

1,290. John W. Sprague, of Ohio, Colonel of 63d Ohio Volunteers, from July 21, 1864 ; mustered out Aug. 24, 1865.

1,291. James W. Reilly, of Ohio, Colonel 104th Ohio Volunteers, from July 30, 1864 ; resigned April 20, 1865.

1,292. Luther P. Bradley, of Illinois, Colonel 51st Illinois Volunteers, from July 30, 1864 ; resigned June 30, 1865.

1,293. Charles C. Walcutt, of Ohio, Colonel 46th Ohio Volunteers, from July 30, 1864 ; mustered out Jan. 15, 1866.

1,294. William W. Belknap, of Iowa, Colonel 15th Iowa Volunteers, from July 30, 1864 ; mustered out Aug. 24, 1865.

1,295. Powell Clayton, of Kansas, Colonel 4th Kansas Volunteers, from Aug. 1, 1864 ; mustered out Aug. 24, 1865.

1,296. Major Joseph A. Haskin, 3d U. S. Artillery, Lieut.-Colonel and Additional Aide-de Camp, from Aug. 5, 1864 ; mustered out April 30, 1866.

1,297. James D. Fessenden, of Maine, Colonel and Additional Aide-de-Camp, from Aug. 8, 1864 ; mustered out Jan. 15, 1866.

1,298. Daniel D. Bidwell, of New York, Colonel 49th New York Volunteers, from Aug. 11, 1864 ; killed Oct. 19, 1864.

1,299. Captain Ely Long, 4th U. S. Cavalry and Colonel 4th Ohio Cavalry, from Aug. 18, 1864 ; mustered out Jan. 15, 1866.

1,300. Thomas W. Egan, of New York, Colonel 40th New York Volunteers, from Sept. 3, 1864 ; mustered out July 15, 1866.

1,301. Joshua B. Howell, of Pennsylvania, Colonel 85th Pennsylvania Volunteers, from Sept. 12, 1864; died Sept. 14, 1865.

1,302. Joseph R. Hawley, of Connecticut, Colonel 7th Connecticut Volunteers, from Sept. 13, 1864; mustered out Aug. 24, 1865.

1,303. William H. Seward, Jr., of New York, Colonel 9th New York Volunteer Artillery, from Sept. 13, 1864; resigned June 1, 1865.

1,304. Isaac H. Duval, of West Virginia, Colonel 9th West Virginia Volunteers, from Sept. 24, 1864; mustered out Jan. 15, 1866.

1,305. John Edwards, of Iowa, Colonel 18th Iowa Volunteers, from Sept. 26, 1864; mustered out Jan. 15, 1866.

1,306. Thomas A. Smyth, of Delaware, Colonel 1st Delaware Volunteers, from Oct. 1, 1864; died of wounds April 9, 1865.

1,307. Ferdinand Van Derveer, of Ohio, Colonel 35th Ohio Volunteers, from Oct. 4, 1864; resigned June 15, 1865.

1,308. Captain Charles R. Lowell, 6th U. S. Cavalry and Colonel 2d Massachusetts Cavalry, from Oct. 19, 1864; died of wounds Oct. 20, 1864.

1,309. William H. Powell, of Ohio, Colonel 2d Virginia Cavalry, from Oct. 19, 1864; resigned Jan. 5, 1865.

1,310. Thomas C. Devin, of New York, Colonel 6th New York Volunteer Cavalry, from Oct. 19, 1864; mustered out Jan. 15, 1866.

1,311. Captain Alfred Gibbs, 3d U. S. Cavalry, and Colonel 1st New York Dragoons, from Oct. 19. 1864; mustered out Feb. 1, 1866.

1,312. Captain Ranald S. Mackenzie, Corps of Engineers and Colonel 2d Connecticut Heavy Artillery, from Oct. 19, 1864; mustered out Jan. 15, 1866.

1,313. Rutherford B. Hays, of Ohio, Colonel 23d Ohio Volunteers, from Oct. 19, 1864; resigned June 8, 1863.

1,314. James R. Slack, of Indiana, Colonel 47th Indiana Volunteers, from Nov. 10, 1864; mustered out Jan. 15, 1866.

1,315. Thomas J. Lucas, of Indiana, Colonel 16th Indiana Mounted Infantry, from Nov. 10, 1864; mustered out Jan. 15, 1866.

1,316. E. J. Davis, of Texas, Colonel 1st Texas Cavalry, from Nov. 10, 1864; mustered out Aug. 24, 1865.

1,317. Joseph Bailey, of Wisconsin, Colonel 4th Wisconsin Cavalry, from Nov. 10, 1864; commission expired March 4, 1865; reappointed from Nov. 10, 1864; resigned July 7, 1865.

1,318. George L. Beal, of Maine, Colonel 29th Maine Volunteers, from Nov. 30, 1864; mustered out Jan. 15, 1866.

1,319. Captain Henry G. Thomas, 11th U. S. Infantry and Colonel 19th U. S. Colored Troops, from Nov. 30, 1864; mustered out Jan. 15, 1866.

1,320. Cyrus Hamlin, of Maine, Colonel 80th U. S. Colored Troops and Additional Aide-de-Camp, from Dec. 3, 1864; mustered out Jan. 15, 1866.

1,321. Patrick H. Jones, of New York, Colonel 154th New York Volunteers, from Dec. 6, 1864; resigned June 17, 1865.

1,322. John M. Oliver, of Michigan, Colonel 15th Michigan Volunteers, from Jan. 12, 1865; mustered out Aug. 24, 1865.

1,323. R. K. Scott, of Ohio, Colonel 68th Ohio Volunteers, from Jan. 12, 1865; resigned July 6, 1868.

1,324. James S. Robinson, of Ohio, Colonel 82d Ohio Volunteers, from Jan. 12, 1865; mustered out Aug. 31, 1865.

1,325. B. F. Potts, of Ohio, Colonel 32d Ohio Volunteers, from Jan. 12, 1865; mustered out Jan. 15, 1866.

1,326. John G. Mitchell, of Ohio, Colonel 113th Ohio Volunteers, from Jan. 12, 1865; resigned July 3, 1865.

1,327. James A. Williamson, of Iowa, Colonel 4th Iowa Volunteers, from Jan. 13, 1865; mustered out Aug. 24, 1865.

1,328. N. Martin Curtis, of New York, Colonel 142d New York Volunteers, from Jan. 15, 1865; mustered out Jan. 15, 1866.

1,329. Charles C. Doolittle, of Michigan, Colonel 18th Michigan Volunteers, from Jan. 27, 1865; mustered out Nov. 30, 1865.

1,330. Stephen Thomas, of Vermont, Colonel 8th Vermont Volunteers, from Feb. 1, 1865; mustered out Aug. 24, 1865.

1,331. Jar es J. Gilbert, of Iowa, Colonel 27th Iowa Volunteers, from Feb. 9, 1865; mustered out Aug. 3, 1865.

1,332. Green B. Raum, of Illinois, Colonel 56th Illinois Volunteers, from Feb. 15, 1865; resigned May 6, 1865.

1,333. Galusha Pennypacker, of Pennsylvania, Colonel 97th Pennsylvania Volunteers, from Feb. 18, 1865; resigned April 30, 1866.

1,334. Carlos J. Stolbrand, of Illinois, Major 2d Illinois Artillery, from Feb. 18, 1865; mustered out Jan. 15, 1866.

1,335. Wager Swayne, of Ohio, Colonel 43d Ohio Volunteers, from March 8, 1865; promoted Major-General June 20, 1865.

1,336. Captain Charles Ewing, 13th U. S. Infantry, Lieut.-Colonel and Asst. Inspector Volunteers, from March 8, 1865; mustered out Dec. 1, 1865.

1,337. Thomas M. Harris, from West Virginia, Colonel 10th West Virginia Volunteers, from March 29, 1865; mustered out April 30, 1866.

1,338. John H. Ketcham, of New York, Colonel 150th New York Volunteers, from April 1, 1865; resigned Dec. 2, 1865.

1,339. Major Frederick T. Dent, 4th U. S. Infantry, Lieut.-Colonel and Aide de-Camp, from April 5, 1865; mustered out April 30, 1866.

1,340. Lafayette C. Baker, of District Columbia, Colonel 1st Cavalry District Columbia, from April 26, 1865; mustered out Jan. 15, 1866.

1,341. Captain James S. Brisbin, 6th U. S. Cavalry, and Colonel 5th U. S. Colored Cavalry, from May 1, 1865; mustered out Jan. 15, 1866.

1,342. Thomas O. Osborn, of Illinois, Colonel 39th Illinois Volunteers, from May 1, 1865; resigned Sept. 28, 1865.

1,343. J. H. Potter, Major 19th U. S. Infantry and Colonel 12th New Hampshire Volunteers, from May 1, 1865; mustered out Jan. 15, 1866.

1,344. Captain James M. Warner, 8th U. S. Infantry, and Colonel 1st Vermont Artillery, from May 8, 1865; mustered out Jan. 15, 1866.

1,345. Lewis B. Parsons, of Missouri, Colonel and Additional Aide-de-Camp, from May 11, 1865; mustered out April 30, 1866.

1,346. Oliver Edwards, of Massachusetts, Colonel 37th Massachusetts Volunteers, from May 19, 1865; mustered out, Jan. 15, 1866.

1,347. Joseph E. Hamblin, of New York, Colonel 65th New York Volunteers, from May 19, 1865; mustered out Jan. 15, 1866.

1,348. Captain James W. Forsyth, 18th U. S. Infantry, Colonel and Asst. Inspector-General Volunteers, from May 19, 1865; mustered out Jan. 15, 1866.

1,349. Captain Richard H. Jackson, 1st U. S. Artillery, Colonel and Asst. Inspector-General Volunteers, from May 19, 1865; mustered out Feb. 1, 1866.

1,350. William Wells, of Vermont, Colonel 1st Vermont Cavalry, from May 19, 1865; mustered out Jan. 15, 1866.

1,351. Captain Charles H. Morgan, 4th U. S. Artillery, Colonel and Asst. Inspector-General Volunteers, from May 19, 1865; mustered out Jan. 15, 1766.

1,352. William T. Clark, of Iowa, Colonel and Asst. Adjutant-General U. S. Volunteers, from May 31, 1865; mustered out Feb. 1, 1866.

1,353. Henry A. Barnum, of New York, Colonel 149th New York Volunteers, from May 31, 1865; resigned Jan. 9, 1866.

1,354. William B. Woods, of Ohio, Colonel 76th Ohio Volunteers, from May 31, 1865; mustered out Feb. 17, 1866.

1,355. Robert F. Catterson, of Indiana, Colonel 97th Indiana Volunteers, from May 31, 1865; mustered out Jan. 15, 1866.

1,356. Americus V. Rice, of Ohio, Colonel 57th Ohio Volunteers, from May 31, 1865; mustered out Jan. 15, 1866.

1,357. George P. Este, of Ohio, Colonel 14th Ohio Volunteers, from May 31, 1865; resigned Dec. 4, 1865.

1,358. Captain Wm. H. Penrose, 33d U. S. Infantry, and Colonel 15th New Jersey Volunteers, from May 31, 1865; mustered out Jan. 15, 1866.

1,359. James H. Stokes, of New Jersey, Captain and Asst. Adjutant-General, from July 20, 1865; mustered out Aug. 24, 1865.

1,360. Francis T. Sherman, of Illinois, Colonel 88th Illinois Volunteers, from July 21, 1865; mustered out Jan. 15, 1866.

1,361. Emerson Opdycke, of Ohio, Colonel 125th Ohio Volunteers, from July 26, 1865; mustered out Jan. 1, 1866.

1,362. Captain Louis D. Watkins, 5th U. S. Cavalry, and Colonel 6th Kentucky Cavalry, from Sept. 25, 1865; mustered out Sept. 1, 1866.

1,363. William Gamble, of Illinois, Colonel 8th Illinois Cavalry, from Sept. 25, 1865; mustered out March 1, 1866.

1,364. C. H. Van Wyck, of New York, Colonel 56th New York Volunteers, from Sept. 27, 1865; mustered out Jan. 15, 1866.

1,365. William B. Tibbitts, of New York, Colonel 21st New York Volunteer Cavalry, from Oct. 18, 1865; mustered out Jan. 15, 1866.

1,366. Morgan H. Chrysler, of New York, Colonel 2d New York Veteran Volunteer Cavalry, from Nov. 11, 1865; mustered out Jan. 15, 1866.

1,367. J. A. Dewey, Colonel 111th U. S. Colored Troops, from Nov. 20, 1865; mustered out Jan. 31, 1866.

Brevet Rank.—1,170.

1,368. Col. Amos Beckwith, Add'l Aide-de-Camp U. S. Vols., from Jan. 12, 1865.
1,369. " John J. Astor, jr., " " " " March 13, "
1,370. Colonel Norton P. Chipman, Additional Aide-de-Camp U. S. Volunteers .... " " 13, "
1,371. Colonel John S. Clark, Add'l Aide-de-Camp U. S. Vols., " " 13, "
1,372. Col. Richard D. Cutts, " " " " " 13, "
1,373. Colonel W. S. Hillyer, " " " " " 13, "
1,374. " Geo. P. Ihrie, " " " " " 13, "
1,375. Col. Clark B. Lagoon, " " " " " 13, "
1,376. Colonel Wm. Myers, " " " " " 13, "
1,377. " John Riggin, " " " " " 13, "
1,378. Col. Geo. D. Ruggles, " " " " " 13, "

1,379. Col. Edw'd S. Sanford, Add'l Aide-de-Camp U. S. Vols., from March 13, 1865.
1,380. " J. Wilson Shaffer, " " " " " 13, "
1,381. " Anson Stager, " " " " " 13, "
1,382. Colonel Daniel T. Van Buren, Additional Aide-de-Camp U. S. Volunteers........................... " " 13, "
1,383. Lieut.-Colonel and Mil. Sec. Adam Badeau, Additional Aide-de-Camp U. S. Volunteers.............. " April 9, "
1,384. Major John A. Bolles, Add'l Aide-de-Camp U. S. Vols., " July 17, "
1,385. Maj. Thos. T. Eckert, " " " " March 13, "
1,386. " Wm. P. Jones, " " " " " 13, "
1,387. " T. J. McKenney, " ' " " " 13, "
1,388. " Wm. G. Mitchell, " " " " " 13, "
1,389. " William Painter, " " " " " 13, "
1,390. " Wm. R. Rowley, " " " " " 13, "
1,391. Major Verplanck Van Antwerp, Additional Aide de-Camp U. S. Volunteers.................. .... " Feb. 13, "
1,392. Maj. J. L. Van Buren, Add'l Aide-de-Camp U. S. Vols., " April 2, "
1,393. Capt. Wilson Barstow, " " " " " 2, "
1,394. Colonel Thomas J. Cram, Aide-de-Camp U. S. Vols., " " 2, "
1,395. Major John F. Anderson, " " " " 2, "
1,396. " William Cutting, " " " " 2, "
1,397. " Wm. H. Lawrence, " " " " 2, "
1,398. " Wm. M. Wherry, " " " " 2, "
1,399. " H. E. Tremaine, " " " Nov. 30, "
1,400. Lt.-Col. Theodore Read, Asst. Adj.-Gen. U. S. Vols., " Sept. 29, 1864.
1,401. Lieut.-Colonel Andrew J. Alexander, Asst. Adjutant-General U. S. Volunteers......................... " Jan. 5, 1865.
1,402. Lt.-Col. Fred. T. Locke, Asst. Adj.-Gen. U. S. Vols., " April 1, "
1,403. Lieut.-Colonel and Mil. Sec. Ely S. Parker, Asst. Adjutant-General U. S. Volunteers.................... " " 9, "
1,404. Lt.-Col. Chas. A. Whittier, Asst. Adj.-Gen. U. S. Vols., " " 9, "
1,405. " Chas. A. Carleton, " " " " arch 13, "
1,406. Lieut.-Colonel Christian T. Christensen, Asst. Adjutant-General U. S. Volunteers.................... " " 13, "
1,407. Lt.-Col. George B. Drake, Asst. Adj.-Gen. U. S. Vols., " " 13, "
1,408. " Jos. S. Fullerton, " " " " " 13, "
1,409. " O. H. Hart, " " " " " 13, "
1,410. " John Hough, " " " " " 13, "
1,411. " Adam E. King, " " " " " 13, "
1,412. " H. W. Perkins, " " " " " 13, "
1,413. " Lewis Richmond, " " " " " 13, "
1,414. " E. W. Smith, " " " " " 13, "
1,415. " Duncan S. Walker, " " " " " 13, "
1,416. " Francis A. Walker, " " " " " 13, "
1,417. " Louis E. York, " " " " " 13, "
1,418. " Alex. C. McClurg, " " " " Sept. 18, "
1,419. Maj. John H. Hammond, " " " " Oct. 31, 1864.
1,420. " Simon F. Barstow, " " " " March 13, 1865.
1,421. " J. A. Campbell, " " " " " 13, "
1,422. " Henry M. Cist, " " " " " 13, "

1,423. Maj. Wm. Hyde Clarke, Asst. Adj.-Gen. U. S. Vols., from March 13, 1865.
1,424. "   Joseph Dickinson,   "   "   "   "   "   13, "
1,425. "   L. G. Estes,   "   "   "   "   "   13. "
1,426. "   Charles G. Halpine,   "   "   "   "   "   13, "
1,427. "   Charles Hamlin,   "   "   "   "   "   13, "
1,428. "   Hiram C. Rogers,   "   "   "   "   "   13, "
1,429. "   W. Radwood Price,   "   "   "   "   "   13, "
1,430. "   Walter B. Scates,   "   "   "   "   "   13, "
1,431. "   Alex. Von Schrader,   "   "   "   "   "   13, "
1,432. "   G. P. Thruston,   "   "   "   "   "   13, "
1,433. "   Chas. H. Whittelsey,   "   "   "   "   "   13, "
1,434. Major Maxwell V. L. Woodhull, Asst. Adjutant-General U. S. Volunteers ....   "   "   13, "
1,435. Major Charles Mundee, Asst. Adj.-Gen. U. S. Vols.,   " April   2, "
1,436. "   Hazard Stevens,   "   "   "   "   "   2, "
1,437. "   Wm. H. Morgan,   "   "   "   "   "   20, "
1,438. Capt. G. H. McKibbin,   "   "   "   " Dec.   2, 1864.
1,439. "   E. B. Harlan,   "   "   "   " March 13, 1865.
1,440. Lt.-Col. Peter S. Michie, Asst. Insp.-Gen. U. S. Vols.,   " Jan.   1, "
1,441. "   Wm. Hartsuff,   "   "   "   "   "   24, "
1,442. Lieut.-Colonel Andrew Hickenlooper, Asst. Inspector-General U. S. Volunteers ....   " March 13, "
1,443. Lt.-Col. Wm. H. Thurston, Asst. Insp. Gen. U. S. Vols.,   "   "   13, "
1,444. "   Wm. E. Strong,   "   "   "   "   "   21, "
1,445. "   H'y C. Bankhead,   "   "   "   " April 1, "
1,446. Maj. Henry L. Burnett, Judge-Advocate U. S. Vols.,   " March 13, "
1,447. "   H. H. Bingham,   "   "   " April 9, "
1,448. Col. George S. Dodge, U. S. Vol. Quartermaster Dept.,   " Jan. 15, "
1,449. "   Herman Biggs,   "   "   "   " March 8, "
1,450. "   Jas. A. Ekin,   "   "   "   "   "   8, "
1,451. Colonel Richard N. Batchelder, U. S. Volunteer Quartermaster Department ....   "   "   13, "
1,452. Colonel Marshall J. Ludington, U. S. Volunteer Quartermaster Department ....   "   "   13, "
1,453. Colonel W. L. James, U. S. Vol. Quartermaster Deptartment.....................................   "   "   1, 1866.
1,454. Colonel Roeliff Brinkerhof, U. S. Volunteer Quartermaster Department....................... ....   " Sept. 20, "
1,455. Lieut.-Colonel James T. Conklin, U. S. Volunteer Quartermaster Department.......... .. ..   " March 13, 1865.
1,456. Lieut.-Colonel Wm. G. LeDuc, U. S. Volunteer Quartermaster Department ....   "   "   13, "
1,457. Lt.-Col. Jas. Dunlap, U. S. Vol. Quartermaster Dept.,   "   "   13, "
1,458. Lieut.-Colonel Charles B. Norton, U. S. Volunteer Quartermaster Department......................   "   "   13, "
1,459. Capt. Joseph F. Boyd, U. S. Vol. Quartermaster Dept.,   "   "   13, "
1,460. Captain S. Lockwood Brown, U. S. Volunteer Quartermaster Department ....   "   "   13, "
1,461. Captain J. J. Elwell, U. S. Vol. Quartermaster Dept ,   "   "   13, "
1 562. Capt. Chas. H. Hoyt,   "   "   "   "   "   13, "

1,463. Captain Andrew J. Mackay, U. S. Volunteer Quartermaster Department........ ....from March 13, 1865.
1,464. Capt. S. H. Manning, U. S. Vol. Quartermaster Dept., " " 13, "
1,465. Captain Reese M. Newport, U. S. Volunteer Quartermaster Department......... .. .. " " 13, "
1,466. Captain Henry L. Robinson, U. S. Volunteer Quartermaster Department....... .... " " 13, "
1,467. Captain George V. Rutherford, U. S. Volunteer Quartermaster Department........... .... " " 13, "
1,468. Captain R. C. Rutherford, U. S. Volunteer Quartermaster Department.............................. " " 13, "
1,469. Captain Henry M. Whittlesey, U. S. Volunteer Quartermaster Department....................... ...... " " 13, "
1,470. Capt. George D. Wise, U. S. Vol. Quartermaster Dept , " " 13, "
1,471. " Jas. F. Rusling, " " " " Feb. 16, 1866.
1,472. Lieut.-Colonel John C. Cox, Volunteer Commissary Subsistence Department. .... " July 4, 1863.
1,473. Lieut.-Colonel G. W. Balloch, Volunteer Commissary Subsistence Department...................... ..... " March 13, 1865.
1,474. Lieut.-Colonel D. Remick, Volunteer Commissary Subsistence Department................ .... " " 13, "
1,475. Lieut.-Colonel Daniel D. Wiley, Volunteer Commissary Subsistence Department....... .... " " 13, "
1,476. Lieut.-Colonel Thomas Wilson, Volunteer Commissary Subsistence Department............. .. .. " " 13, "
1,477. Lieut.-Colonel Joseph S. Smith, Volunteer Commissary Subsistence Department .. .. " July 11, "
1,478. Capt. Francis Darr, Vol. Commissary Subsistence Dep., " March 13, "
1,479. Maj. B. Rush Cowen, Add'l Paymaster U. S. Vols..... " " 13, "
1,480. " John B. Dennis, " " " .... " " 13, "
1,481. " Matthew McEwen, Surgeon U. S Volunteers... " " 13, "
1,482. Col. Benj. F. Fisher, Chief Signal Officer U. S. Vols.. " " 13, "
1,483. Lt.-Col. Jonathan P. Cilley, 1st Regt. Maine Vol. Cav., " June 2, "
1,484. " Andrew B. Spaulding, 2d Regt. Me. " " March 26, "
1,485. Colonel Russell B. Shepherd, 1st Regiment Maine Volunteer Heavy Artillery............................ " " 13, "
1,486. Lieut.-Colonel Thomas H. Talbot, 1st Regiment Maine Volunteer Heavy Artillery......................... " " 13, "
1,487. Lt.-Col. Jas. A. Hall, 1st Bat'n Maine Vol. Light Art., " " 7, "
1,488. Colonel Thomas W. Hyde, 1st Regt. Maine Vol. Inf., " April 2, "
1,489. " George Varney, 2d " " " March 13, "
1,490. " Charles W. Roberts, 2d " " " " 13, "
1,491. " Clark S. Edwards, 5th " " " " 13, "
1,492. " John D. Rust, 8th " " " " 13, "
1,493. " Henry Boynton, 8th " " " " 13, "
1,494. " Wm. M. McArthur, 8th " " " " 13, "
1,495. " Geo. Fred. Granger, 9th " " " June 12, "
1,496. " Jonathan A. Hill, 11th " " " April 9, "
1,497. Lt.-Col. Chas. P. Baldwin. 11th " " " " 1, "
1,498. Colonel William R. Kimball, 12th " " " March 13, "

1,499. Colonel Henry Rust, Jr., 13th Regt. Maine Vol. Inf., from March 13, 1865.
1,500.   "   Isaac Dyer,   15th   "   "   "   "   13,   "
1,501. Lt.-Col. Benj. B. Murray, 15th   "   "   "   "   13,   "
1,502. Colonel Charles W. Tilden, 16th   "   "   "   "   13,   "
1,503.   "   George W. West,   17th   "   "   " Dec.   2, 1864.
1,504.   "   Chas. P. Mattocks, 17th   "   "   " March 13, 1865.
1,505. Lt-Col. William Hobson,   17th   "   "   " April   6,   "
1,506. Colonel Francis Heath,   19th   "   "   " March 13,   "
1,507.   "   Isaac W. Starbird, 19th   "   "   "   "   13,   "
1,508.   "   Elias Spear,   20th   "   "   "   "   13,   "
1,509.   "   Thos. H. Hubbard, 30th   "   "   " June 30,   "
1,510. Lt.-Col. Geo. W. Randall, 30th   "   "   " March 13,   "
1,511. Colonel Daniel White,   31st   "   "   "   "   13,   "
1,512.   "   Mark F. Wentworth, 32d   "   "   "   "   13,   "
1,513. Lieut.-Colonel John Marshall Brown, 32d Regiment
        Maine Volunteer Infantry.........................   "   "   13,   "
1,514. Colonel John L. Thompson, 1st Regt. N. H. Vol. Cav.,   "   "   13,   "
1,515.   "   Joab N. Patterson, 2d Regt. N. H. Vol. Inf.,   "   "   13,   "
1,516. Lt.-Col. Frank S. Fiske,   2d   "   "   "   "   13,   "
1,517. Colonel John Bedel,   3d   "   "   "   "   13,   "
1,518.   "   Joseph C. Abbott, 7th   "   "   " Jan.   5,   "
1,519.   "   Herbert B. Titus, 9th   "   "   " March 13,   "
1,520. Col. Michael T. Donohoe,   10th   "   "   "   "   13,   "
1,521. Lieut.-Col. John Coughlin, 10th   "   "   " April   9,   "
1,522. Colonel Walter Harriman,   11th   "   "   " March 13,   "
1,523.   "   Aaron F. Stevens, 13th   "   "   " Dec.   8, 1864.
1,524.   "   Alex. Gardiner,   14th   "   "   " Sept. 19,   "
1,525. Capt. Theodore A. Ripley, 14th   "   "   " March 13, 1865
1,526. Colonel J. M. Clough,   18th   "   "   "   "   3,   "
1,527.   "   Chas. P. Stoughton, 4th Regt. Vt. Inf. Vols., "   "   13,   "
1,528.   "   George P. Foster, 4th   "   "   " Aug.   1, 1864.
1,529.   "   John R. Lewis,   5th   "   "   " March 13, 1865.
1,530. Lieut.-Col. Asa P. Blunt, 6th   "   "   "   "   13,   "
1,531. Colonel Edward H. Ripley, 9th   "   "   " Aug.   1, 1864.
1,532.   "   William W. Henry, 10th   "   "   " March 7, 1865.
1,533.   "   Horace B. Sargent, 1st Regt. Mass. Vol. Cav., "   " 21, 1864.
1,534. Lieut.-Colonel Samuel E. Chamberlain, 1st Regiment
        Massachusetts Volunteer Cavalry.................   " Feb. 24, 1865.
1,535. Lieut.-Col. Greely S. Curtis, 1st Regt. Mass. Vol. Cav., " March 13,   "
1,536. Col. Casper Crowninshield, 2d   "   "   "   "   13,   "
1,537.   "   Thomas E. Chickering, 3d   "   "   "   "   13,   "
1,538. Major S. Tyler Reed,   3d   "   "   "   "   13,   "
1,539. Colonel Francis Washburn, 4th   "   "   " April   6,   "
1,540. Col. Horatio Jenkins, Jr., 4th   "   "   " March 13,   "
1,541. Col. H'y S. Russel, 5th Colored Regt. Mass. Vol Cav., "   "   13,   "
1,542. Colonel Chas. F. Adams, Jr., 5th Colored Regiment
        Massachusetts Volunteer Cavalry.................   "   "   13,   "
1,543. Col. Jones Frankle, 2d Regt. Mass. Vol. Heavy Art.,   " Sept.   3,   "
1,544.   " Wm. S. Abert, 3d   "   "   "   " March 13,   "
1,545.   " Wm. S. King,   4th "   "   "   "   "   13,   "

1,546.	Colonel Wm. Coggswell,	2d	Regt. Mass. Vol. Inf.,	from Dec.	15, 1864.
1,547.	" Thomas D. Johns,	7th	" "	" March	13, 1865.
1,548.	Col. Patrick Robert Guiney,	9th	" "	" "	13, "
1,549.	Colonel William Blaisdell,	11th	" "	" June	23, 1864.
1,550.	" Thos. H. Dunham,	11th	" "	" March	13, 1865.
1,551.	" George H. Ward,	15th	" "	" July	2, 1863.
1,552.	" Thos. J. C. Amory,	17th	" "	" Oct.	7, 1864.
1,553.	" Arthur F. Devereux,	19th	" "	" March	13, 1865.
1,554.	Col. Wm. Raymond Lee,	20th	" "	" "	13, "
1,555.	Colonel Francis W. Palfrey,	20th	" "	" "	13, "
1,556.	" Paul Joseph Revere,	20th	" "	" July	2, "
1,557.	Lt.-Col. Arthur R. Curtis,	20th	" "	" March	13, "
1,558.	Maj. Henry Lyman Patten,	20th	" "	" Sept.	10, 1864.
1,559.	Colonel George P. Hawkes,	21st	" "	" March	13, 1865.
1,560.	" William S. Tilton,	22d	" "	" Sept.	9, 1864.
1,561.	Lt.-Col. Thos. Sherwin, Jr.,	22d	" "	" March	13, 1865.
1,562.	Colonel Francis A. Osborn,	24th	" "	" "	13, "
1,563.	Lt.-Col. Albert Ordway,	24th	" "	" "	13, "
1,564.	" Rob't H. Stevenson,	24th	" "	" "	13, "
1,565.	Colonel Josiah Pickett,	25th	" "	" "	13, "
1,566.	" Edward F. Jones,	26th	" "	" "	13, "
1,567.	" Horace C. Lee,	27th	" "	" "	13, "
1,568.	Lt.-Col. Luke Lyman,	27th	" "	" "	13, "
1,569.	Col. Nathan A. M. Dudley,	30th	" "	" Jan.	19, 1865.
1,570.	Lt.-Col. Francis H. Whittier,	30th	" "	" March	13, "
1,571.	Col. J. Cushing Edmonds,	32d	" "	" "	13, "
1,572.	" George L. Prescott,	32d	" "	" June	18, 1864.
1,573.	Lieut.-Colonel Luther Stephenson, Jr., 32d Regiment Massachusetts Volunteer Infantry.................			" March	13, 1865.
1,574.	Lieut.-Colonel James A. Cunningham, 32d Regiment Massachusetts Volunteer Infantry............			" April	1, "
1,575.	Colonel George D. Wells,	34th Regt. Mass. Vol. Inf.,		" Oct. 12,	1864.
1,576.	" William S. Lincoln,	34th	" "	" June	23, 1865.
1,577.	" Sumner Carruth,	35th	" "	" April	2, "
1,578.	Lt.-Col. Wm. F. Draper,	36th	" "	" March	13, "
1,579.	Lt.-Col. Arthur A. Goodell,	36th	" "	" "	13, "
1,580.	Colonel Timothy Ingraham,	38th	" "	" Oct.	2, "
1,581.	" Charles L. Pierson,	39th	" "	" March	13, "
1,582.	" Guy V. Henry,	40th	" "	" Oct.	28, 1864.
1,583.	Colonel Augustus B. R. Sprague, 51st Regiment Massachusetts Volunteer Infantry......................			" March	13, 1865.
1,584.	Colonel John W. Kimball, 53d Regt. Mass. Vol. Inf.,			" "	13, "
1,585.	Colonel Edward N. Hallowell, 54th Regiment Massachusetts Colored Volunteer Infantry...............			" June	27, "
1,586.	Colonel Alfred S. Hartwell, 55th Regiment Massachusetts Colored Volunteer Infantry.............. ..			" Dec.	30, 1864.
1,587.	Col. Stephen M. Weld, Jr., 56th Regt. Mass. Vol. Inf.,			" March	13, 1865.
1,588.	Colonel Napoleon B. McLaughlin, 57th Regiment Massachusetts Volunteer Infantry.....................			" Sept.	30, 1864.
1,589.	Colonel Ansell D. Wass, 60th Regt. Mass. Vol. Inf.,			" March	13, 1865.

1,590. Colonel Charles F. Walcott, 61st Regt. Mass. Vol. Inf., from April   9, 1865.
1,591. Colonel Charles H. Tompkins, 1st Regiment Rhode
   Island Volunteer Light Artillery.................. " Aug.   1, 1864.
1,592. Major John G. Hazard, 1st Regiment Rhode Island
   Volunteer Light Artillery......................... " March 13, 1865.
1,593. Colonel Charles R. Brayton, 3d Regiment Rhode Island
   Volunteer Heavy Artillery........................ "   "   13, "
1,594. Colonel William Ames, 3d Regiment Rhode Island
   Volunteer Heavy Artillery.... .... "   "   13, "
1,595. Lieut.-Colonel Geo. W. Tew, 5th Regiment Rhode Island Volunteer Heavy Artillery....... .... "   "   13, "
1,596. Major Joseph P. Balch,   1st Regt. R. I. Vol. Inf.,   "   "   13, "
1,597.   "   William Goddard,   1st   "   "   "   "   13, "
1,598. Colonel Horatio Rodgers, Jr., 2d   "   "   "   "   13, "
1,599.   "   Wm. H. P. Steers,   4th   "   "   "   "   13, "
1,600.   "   Erastus Blakeslee, 1st Regt. Conn. Vol. Cav.,   "   "   13, "
1,601.   "   Brayton Ives,   1st   "   "   "   "   13, "
1,602.   "   Edw'd W. Whitaker, 1st   "   "   "   "   13, "
1,603. Colonel James Hubbard, 2d Regiment Connecticut
   Volunteer Heavy Artillery.................... .... " April   6, "
1,604. Colonel Alfred P. Rockwell, 6th Regt. Conn. Vol. Inf., " March 13, "
1,605.   "   John L. Otis,   10th   "   "   "   "   13, "
1,606.   "   Edwin S. Greeley,   10th   "   "   "   "   13, "
1,607. Lieut.-Colonel Ellsworth D. S. Goodyear, 10th Regiment Connecticut Volunteer Infantry.............. " April   2, "
1,608. Colonel Griffin A. Steadman, Jr., 11th Regiment Connecticut Volunteer Infantry....................... " Aug.   5, 1864.
1,609. Lieut.-Col. Frank H. Peck, 12th Regt. Conn. Vol. Inf., " Sept. 19, "
1,610. Colonel Theodore G. Ellis, 14th   "   "   "   " March 13, 1865.
1,611. Major James B. Coit,   14th   "   "   "   "   "   13, "
1,612. Colonel Wm. H. Noble,   17th   "   "   "   "   "   13, "
1,613.   "   William C. Ely,   18th   "   "   "   "   "   13, "
1,614.   "   Samuel Ross,   20th   "   "   "   " April 13, "
1,615.   "   Arthur H. Dutton,   21st   "   "   "   " May   16, 1864.
1,616. Col. Alonzo W. Adams,   1st Reg't N. Y. Vol. Cav.,   " March 13, 1865.
1,617.   "   Alanson M. Randol,   2d   "   "   "   " June 24,   "
1,618. Major Edwin F. Cook,   2d   "   "   "   " March 13,   "
1,619. Col. John Hammond,   5th   "   "   "   "   "   13,   "
1,620.   "   Charles L. Fitzhugh, 6th   "   "   "   "   "   13,   "
1,621.   "   Edmond M. Pope,   8th   "   "   "   "   "   13,   "
1,622. Lt.-Col.Wm. H. Benjamin,   8th   "   "   "   "   "   13,   "
1,623. Col. Wm. H. Sackett,   9th   "   "   "   " June 10, 1864.
1,624.   "   George S. Nichols,   9th   "   "   "   " March 13, 1865.
1,625.   "   Matthew H. Avery,   10th   "   "   "   "   "   13,   "
1,626. Lt.-Colonel Wm. Irvine,   10th   "   "   "   "   "   13,   "
1,627. Col. Henry S. Gansevoort, 13th   "   "   "   " June 24, 1864.
1,628.   "   Nelson B. Sweitzer, 16th   "   "   "   " March 13, 1865.
1,629. Lt.-Col. Chas. Fitzsimmons, 21st   "   "   "   "   "   13,   "
1,630. Col. Walter C. Newberry,   24th   "   "   "   "   "   31,   "
1,631. Lt.-Col. Ferris Jacobs, Jr., 26th   "   "   "   "   "   13,   "

1,632. Colonel Thos. J. Thorp, 1st Regiment New York Volunteer Dragoons.............................. ....from March 13, 1865.

1,633. Lieut.-Colonel Rufus Scott, 1st Regiment New York Volunteer Dragoons............................ " " 13, "

1,634. Colonel Edwin V. Sumner, 1st Regiment New York Volunteer Mounted Rifles............. .... " " 28, "

1,635. Colonel John S. Platner, 1st Regiment New York Volunteer Veteran Cavalry .... " " 13, "

1,636. Colonel Charles S. Wainwright, 1st Regiment New York Volunteer Light Artillery .... " Aug. 1, 1864.

1,637. Lieut.-Colonel Edward R. Warner, 1st Regiment New York Volunteer Light Artillery .... " April 9, 1865.

1,638. Colonel Joseph N. G. Whistler, 2d Regiment New York Volunteer Heavy Artillery .... " March 13, "

1,639. Lieut.-Colonel Thomas R. Allcock, 4th Regiment New York Volunteer Heavy Artillery.................... " " 13, "

1,640. Colonel Samuel Graham, 5th Regiment New York Volunteer Heavy Artillery......................... " " 13, "

1,641. Lieut.-Colonel Edward Murray, 5th Regiment New York Volunteer Heavy Artillery .... " " 13, "

1,642. Colonel J. Howard Kitching, 6th Regiment New York Volunteer Heavy Artillery...................... " Aug. 1, 1864.

1,643. Colonel Joseph J. Morrison, 16th Regiment New York Volunteer Heavy Artillery............. .... " March 13, 1865.

1,644. Lieut.-Colonel Thomas J. Strong, 16th Regiment New York Volunteer Heavy Artillery .... " " 13, "

1,645. Colonel Edward W. Serrell, 1st Regiment New York Volunteer Engineers...................... . ... " " 13, "

1,646. Colonel James F. Hall, 1st Regiment New York Volunteer Engineers .... " Feb. 24, "

1,647. Lieut.-Colonel Ira Spaulding, 50th Regiment New York Volunteer Engineers.......... .... " April 9, "

1,648. Colonel J. Fred. Pièrson,   1st Regt. N. Y. Vol. Inf.,   " March 13, "
1,649.   "   Sidney W. Park,   2d   "   "   " " 13, "
1,650.   "   John E. Mulford,   3d   "   "   " July 4, 1864.
1,651. Major T. Ellery Lord,   3d   "   "   " March 13, 1865.
1,652. Colonel John D. McGregor, 4th   "   "   " " 13, "
1,653.   "   Hiram Duryea,   5th   "   "   " " 13, "

1,654. Captain Paul A. Oliver, 5th Regiment New York Veteran Volunteer Infantry....... .... " " 8, "

1,655. Colonel William Wilson, 6th Regt. N. Y. Vol. Infantry,   " " 13, "
1,656.   "   George W. Von Schaak, 7th Regiment New York Veteran Volunteers......................... " " 13, "

1,657. Colonel Rush C. Hawkins, 9th Regt. N. Y. Vol. Inf.,   " " 13, "
1,658.   "   John E. Bendix,   10th   "   "   " " 13, "
1,659.   "   Joseph Howland,   16th   "   "   " " 13, "
1,660.   "   Joel J. Seaver,   16th   "   "   " " 13, "
1,661.   "   Henry S. Lansing, 17th   "   "   " " 13, "

1,662. Lieut.-Colonel Edward Jardine, 17th Regiment New York Veteran Volunteer Infantry.................. " Nov. 2, "

13*

1,663. Colonel George R. Myers, 18th Regt. N. Y. Vol. Inf.. from March 13, 1865.
1,664.   "   Baron Ernest Von Vegesack, 20th Regiment
  New York Volunteer Infantry......................   "   "   13,   "
1,665. Colonel William F. Rogers, 21st Regt. N. Y. Vol. Inf.,   "   "   13,   "
1,666.   "   Walter Phelps, Jr., 22d   "   "   "   "   13,   "
1,667.   "   Henry C. Hoffman, 23d   "   "   "   "   13,   "
1,668. Col. Charles A. Johnson, 25th   "   "   "   "   13,   "
1,669. "   William H. Christian, 26th   "   "   "   "   13,   "
1,670. "   Francis E. Pinto, 32d   "   "   "   "   13,   "
1,671. "   Byron Lafflin, 34th   "   "   "   "   13,   "
1,672. "   S. B. Hayman, 37th   "   "   "   "   13,   "
1,673. "   Joseph Gerhardt, 46th   "   "   "   "   13,   "
1,674. "   William B. Barton, 48th   "   "   "   "   13,   "
1,675. "   Charles W. Le Gendre, 51st   "   "   "   "   13,   "
1,676. "   John G. Wright, 51st   "   "   "   "   13,   "
1,677. "   Paul Frank, 52d   "   "   "   "   13,   "
1,678. "   Eugene A. Kozlay, 54th   "   "   "   "   13,   "
1,679. "   Waldimir Kryzanowski, 58th   "   "   "   "   2,   "
1,680. "   William A. Olmsted, 59th   "   "   "   April   9,   "
1,681. Lt.-Col. Lester S. Wilson, 60th   "   "   "   March 13.   "
1,682. Colonel George W. Scott, 61st   "   "   "   "   13,   "
1,683. Lt.-Col. R. C. Bentley, 63d   "   "   "   "   13,   "
1,684.   "   William Glenny, 64th   "   "   "   "   13,   "
1,685. Col. Henry C. Fisk, 65th   "   "   "   April   6,   "
1,686. "   Joseph C. Pinckney, 66th   "   "   "   March 13,   "
1,687. Lt.-Col. John S. Hammell, 66th   "   "   "   "   13,   "
1,688. Colonel Felix Prince Salm Salm, 68th Regiment New
  York Volunteer Infantry ....   "   April   13, 1865.
1,689. Colonel Robert Nugent, 69th Regt. N. Y. Vol. Inf.,   "   March 13,   "
1,690. Lieut.-Col. Thomas Holt, 70th   "   "   "   "   13,   "
1,691. Colonel Wm. R. Brewster, 73d   "   "   "   Dec.   2, 1864.
1,692. Lieut.-Colonel Willoughby Babcock, 75th Regiment
  New York Volunteer Infantry ....   "   Sept.   19,   "
1,693. Col. Wm. P. Wainwright, 76th Regt. N. Y. Vol. Inf.,   "   March 13, 1865.
1,694. Lt.-Col. Winser B. French, 77th   "   "   "   "   13,   "
1,695. Col. Addison Farnsworth, 79th   "   "   "   Sept.   27,   "
1,696. "   David Morrison, 79th   "   "   "   March 13,   "
1,697. Lt.-Col. Samuel M. Elliott, 79th   "   "   "   "   13,   "
1,698. Col. Theodore B. Gates, 80th   "   "   "   "   13,   "
1,699. "   Jacob B. Hardenbergh, 80th   "   "   "   "   13,   "
1,700. Lt.-Col. David B. White, 81st   "   "   "   "   13,   "
1,701. Major Allen Rutherford, 83d   "   "   "   "   13,   "
1,702. Col. Edward B. Fowler, 84th   "   "   "   "   13,   "
1,703. "   Enrico Fardella, 85th   "   "   "   "   13,   "
1,704. "   Harrison S. Fairchild, 89th   "   "   "   "   13,   "
1,705. Lt.-Col. Nelson Schaurman, 90th   "   "   "   "   13,   "
1,706. Col. Jonathan Tarbell, 91st   '   "   "   "   13,   "
1,707. "   John S. Crocker, 93d   "   "   "   "   13,   "
1,708. Major Ambrose L. Cassidy, 93d   "   "   "   "   13,   "
1,709.   "   Samuel McConihe, 93d   "   "   "   "   13,   "

1,710. Major Stephen Moffitt, 96th Regt. N. Y. Vol. Inf., from March 13, 1865.
1,711.   "   Charles Wheelock, 97th "   "   " Aug. 9, 1864.
1,712.   "   John P. Spofford, 97th "   "   " March 13, 1865.
1,713.   "   George B. Dandy, 100th "   "   "   " 13, "
1,714. Lt.-Col. Calvin N. Otis, 100th "   "   "   " 13, "
1,715. Col. Thos. B. Van Buren, 102d "   "   "   " 13, "
1,716.   "   William Heine, 103d "   "   "   " 13, "
1,717. Colonel Baron F. W. Von Egloffstein, 103d Regiment
    New York Volunteer Infantry...................... "   " 13, "
1,718. Col. Alexander S. Diven, 107th Regt. N. Y. Vol. Inf., " Aug. 30, 1862.
1,719.   "   Miron M. Crane, 107th "   "   " March 13, 1865.
1,720.   "   Oliver H. Palmer, 108th "   "   "   " 13, "
1,721.   "   Benjamin F. Tracy, 109th "   "   "   " 13, "
1,722.   "   De Witt C. Littlejohn, 110th "   "   "   " 13, "
1,723. Col. Clinton D.McDougall, 111th "   "   " Feb. 25, "
1,724. Col. Samuel R. Per Lee, 114th "   "   " March 13, "
1,725. Lt.-Col. Henry B. Morse, 114th "   "   "   " 13, "
1,726. Col. George M. Love, 116th "   "   "   " 7, "
1,727.   "   William R. Pease, 117th "   "   "   " 13, "
1,728.   "   Rufus Daggett, 117th "   "   " Jan. 15, "
1,729.   "   George F. Nichols, 118th "   "   " March 13. "
1,730.   "   John T. Lockman, 119th "   "   "   " 13, "
1,731.   "   Richard Franchot, 121st "   "   "   " 13, "
1,732.   "   James C. Rogers, 123d "   "   "   " 13, "
1,733.   "   A. Van Horn Ellis, 124th "   "   " July 2, 1863.
1,734.   "   William Gurney, 127th "   "   " May 19, 1865.
1,735.   "   James Smith, 128th "   "   " March 13, "
1,736.   "   Nicholas W. Day, 131st "   "   "   " 13, "
1,737. Lt.-Col. Geo. H. Hitchcock, 132d "   "   " June 28, "
1,738.   "   Anthony J. Allaire, 133d "   "   " March 18, "
1,739. Col. Samuel H. Roberts, 139th "   "   " Oct. 28, 1864.
1,740. Lt.-Col. Thomas Mulcahy, 139th "   "   " March 13, 1865.
1,741.   "   Elwell S. Otis, 140th "   "   "   " 13, "
1,742.   "   And'w J. McNett, 141st "   "   " July 28, 1866.
1,743. Col. Roscius W. Judson, 142d "   "   " March 13, 1865.
1,744.   "   Albert M. Barney, 142d "   "   "   " 11, "
1,745.   "   Horace Boughton, 143d "   "   "   " 13, "
1,746.   "   James Grindlay, 146th "   "   "   " 13, "
1,747.   "   John B. Murray, 148th "   "   "   " 13, "
1,748.   "   Alfred B. Smith, 150th "   "   "   " 13, "
1,749. Lt.-Col. James E. Curtis, 152d "   "   "   " 13, "
1,750. Col. Edwin P. Davis, 153d "   "   " Oct. 19, 1864.
1,751.   "   Jacob Sharpe, 156th "   "   " March 13, 1865.
1,752. Lt.-Col. Alfred Neafie, 156th "   "   "   " 13, "
1,753. Col. Wm. H. McNary, 158th "   "   "   " 13, "
1,754. Lt.-Col. Wm. B. Kinsey, 161st "   "   "   " 13, "
1,755. Col. Lewis Benedict, 162d "   "   " April 9, 1864.
1,756.   "   Justus W. Blanchard, 162d "   "   " March 13, 1865.
1,757. Lt.-Col. Wm. De Lacey, 164th "   "   "   " 13, "
1,758. Major Felix Agnus, 165th "   "   "   " 13, "

1,759. Col. Alonzo Alden, 169th Regt. N. Y. Vol. Inf., from Jan. 15, 1865.
1,760. " John McConihe, 169th " " " June 1. 1864.
1,761. Lt.-Col. Wm. M. Green, 173d " " " May 14, "
1,762. Lieut.-Colonel Mellen T. Holbrook, 173d Regiment New
      York Volunteer Infantry................ .... " March 13, 1865.
1,763. Lt.-Col. John A. Foster, 175th Regt. N. Y. Vol. Inf., " Sept. 28, "
1,764. Col. William M. Gregg, 179th " " " April 2, "
1,765. " Gustavus Sniper, 185th " " " March 13, "
1,766. " Bradley Winslow, 186th " " " April 2, "
1,767. " John McMahon, 188th " " " June 30, "
1,768. " John V. Van Petten, 193d " " " March 13, "
1,769. " Charles Roome, 37th Regiment N. Y. S. M...... " " 13, "
1,770. Lt.-Col. Walter R. Robbins. 1st Regt. N. J. Vol. Cav., " " 13, "
1,771. Col. Jonah Karge, 2d " " " " 13, "
1,772. " Alex. C. M. Pennington, 3d " " " July 15, "
1,773. Lt.-Col. Wm. P. Robeson, Jr., 3d Regiment New Jer-
      sey Volunteer Cavalry... .... " April 1, "
1,774. Col. Edward L. Campbell, 4th Regt. N. J. Vol. Inf., " June 2, "
1,775. Major David Vickers, 4th " " " March 13, "
1,776. Col. George C. Burling, 6th " " " " 13, "
1,777. " Louis R. Francine, 7th " " " July 2, 1863.
1,778. " Francis Price, 7th " " " March 13, 1865.
1,779. " James Stewart, Jr., 9th " " " " 13, "
1,780. " John William, 12th " " " April 9, "
1,781. " Ezra A. Carman, 13th " " " March 13, "
1,782. " William S. Truex, 14th " " " April 2, "
1,783. Lt.-Col. Caldwell K. Hall, 14th " " " March 13, "
1,784. " Jos. C. Jackson, 26th " " " " 13, "
1,785. " Edward W. West, 33d " " " " 13, "
1,786. Colonel William Hudson Laurence, 34th Regiment
      New Jersey Volunteer Infantry............... " " 13, "
1,787. Lt.-Col. Timothy C. Moore, 34th Regiment New Jersey
      Volunteer Infantry-......................... " " 13. "
1,788. Col. E. Burd Grubb, 23d and 37th Regt. N. J. Vol. Inf., " " 13, "
1,789. " Abram C. Wildrick, 39th " " " April 2, "
1,790. " John P. Taylor, 1st Regt. Penn. Vol. Cav., " Aug. 4, "
1,791. " Richard B. Price 2d " " " March 13, "
1,792. " S. B. M. Young, 4th " " " April 9, "
1,793. Lt.-Col. William E. Doster, 4th " " " March 13, "
1,794. Col. Robert M. West, 5th " " " April 1, "
1,795. " Charles L. Leiper, 6th " " " March 13, "
1,796. " Chas. C. McCormick, 7th " " " " 13, "
1,797. " Pennock Huey, 8th " " " " 13, "
1,798. " Thomas J. Jordon, 9th " " " Feb. 25, "
1,799. " Samuel P. Spear, 11th " " " March 13, "¶
1,800. " Franklin A. Stratton, 11th " " " " 13, "
1,801. " Marcus A. Reno, 12th " " " " 13, "
1,802. Lt.-Col. Jas. A. Congdon, 12th " " " " 13, "
1,803. Col. William J. Palmer, 15th " " " Nov. 6, 1864.
1,804. Lt.-Col. John R. Robison, 16th " " " March 13, 1865.

1,805. Colonel Theophilus F. Rodenbough, 18th Regiment
Pennsylvania Volunteer Cavalry ....from April 13, 1865.
1,806. Col. Alexander Cummings, 19th Regt. Penn. Vol. Cav., "   " 19, "
1,807. " Oliver B. Knowles, 21st "   " " March 13, "
1,808. Lieut.-Colonel Benjamin Griffin Barney, 2d Prov. Regiment Pennsylvania Volunteer Heavy Artillery.... "   " 13, "
1,809. Colonel Joseph Roberts, 3d Regiment Pennsylvania
Volunteer Heavy Artillery........................ " April 9, "
1,810. Colonel Charles Barnes, 6th Regiment Pennsylvania
Volunteer Heavy Artillery........................ " Sept. 28, "
1,811. Colonel William C. Tulley, 1st Regiment Reserves
Pennsylvania Volunteer Infantry .. .. " March 13, "
1,812. Lieut.-Colonel William W. Stewart, 1st Regiment Reserves Pennsylvania Volunteer Infantry .... "   " 13, "
1,813. Colonel Wellington H. Ent, 6th Regiment Reserves
Pennsylvania Volunteer Infantry.................. "   " 13, "
1,814. Lieut.-Colonel William D. Dixon, 6th Regiment Reserves Pennsylvania Volunteer Infantry .... "   " 13, "
1,815. Colonel H. C. Bolinger, 7th Regiment Reserves Pennsylvania Volunteer Infantry .... "   " 13, "
1,816. Lieut.-Colonel Robert M. Henderson, 7th Regiment
Reserves Pennsylvania Volunteer Infantry......... "   " 13, "
1,817. Colonel Silas M. Bailey, 8th Regiment Reserves Pennsylvania Volunteer Infantry....................... "   " 13, "
1,818. Colonel Samuel M. Jackson, 11th Regiment Reserves
Pennsylvania Volunteer Infantry.................. "   " 13, "
1,819. Colonel Thomas F. Gallagher, 11th Regiment Reserves
Pennsylvania Volunteer Infantry.................. "   " 13, "
1,820. Lieut.-Colonel Robert A. McCoy, 11th Regiment Re- "   " 13, "
serves Pennsylvania Volunteer Infantry........... "   " 13, "
1,821. Lt.-Col. Robert L. Bodine, 26th Regt. Penn. Vol. Inf., "   " 13, "
1,822. Col. John Flynn, 28th "   " "   " 13, "
1,823. " Samuel M. Zulick, 29th "   " "   " 13, "
1,824. " John K. Murphy, 29th "   " "   " 13, "
1,825. " John J. Curtin, 45th "   " " Oct. 12, 1864.
1,826. " James L. Selfridge, 46th "   " " March 16, 1865.
1,827. " J. P. Shindel Gobin, 47th "   " "   " 13, "
1,828. " Joshua K. Sigfried, 48th "   " " Aug. 1, 1864.
1,829. " George W. Gowan, 48th "   " " April 2, 1865.
1,830. Lt.-Col. Henry Pleasants, 48th "   " " March 13, "
1,831. Col. William H. Irvin, 49th "   " "   " 13, "
1,832. " B. C. Christ, 50th "   " " Aug. 1, 1864.
1,833. Lt.-Col. Sam'l K. Schwenk, 50th "   " " July 24, 1865.
1,834. Col. William J. Bolton, 51st "   " " March 13, "
1,835. " Henry M. Hoyt, 52d "   " "   " 13, "
1,836. Lt.-Col. Jno. A. Hennessy, 52d "   " "   " 13, "
1,837. Col. Wm. M. Mintzer, 53d "   " "   " 13, "
1,838. " Jacob M. Campbell, 54th "   " "   " 13, "
1,839. " Wm. J. Hoffman, 56th "   " " Aug. 1, 1864.
1,840. " George Zinn, 57th "   " " April 6, 1865.

1,841. Lt.-Col. Cecil Clay, 58th Regt. Penn. Vol. Inf........from March 13, 1865.
1,842. Col. Jacob Bowman Sweitzer, 62d Regiment Pennsyl-
　　　　vania Volunteer Infantry.......................... " 　 " 　 13, "
1,843. Major Harry White, 67th Regt. Penn. Vol. Inf., " 　 " 　 2, "
1,844. Lt.-Col. Robt. E. Winslow, 68th " 　 " 　 " 　 " 　 13, "
1,845. 　 " 　 John Markoe, 71st " 　 " 　 " 　 " 　 13, "
1,846. Col. D. W. C. Baxter, 72d " 　 " 　 " 　 " 　 13, "
1,847. " 　 John S. Littell, 76th " 　 " 　 " Jan. 15, "
1,848. " 　 Thomas E. Rose, 77th " 　 " 　 " July 22, "
1,849. Lt.-Col. Wm. A. Robinson, 77th " 　 " 　 " March 13, "
1,850. Col. Henry A. Hambright, 79th " 　 " 　 " June 7, "
1,851. " 　 Isaac C. Bassett, 82d " 　 " 　 " Dec. 12, 1864.
1,852. " 　 Orpheus S. Woodward, 83d " 　 " 　 " March 13, 1865.
1,853. " 　 Samuel M. Bowman, 84th " 　 " 　 " 　 " 　 13, "
1,854. " 　 Louis Wagner, 88th " 　 " 　 " 　 " 　 13, "
1,855. " 　 Peter Lyle, 90th " 　 " 　 " 　 " 　 13, "
1,856. Lt.-Col. Wm. A. Leech, 90th " 　 " 　 " 　 " 　 13, "
1,857. Col. John F. Ballier, 98th " 　 " 　 " July 13, 1864.
1,858. " 　 Edwin R. Biles, 99th " 　 " 　 " March 13, 1865.
1,859. Lt.-Col. Peter Fritz, Jr., 99th " 　 " 　 " March 13, "
1,860. Col. Norman J. Maxwell, 100th " 　 " 　 " April 18, "
1,861. " 　 Wm. W. H. Davis, 104th " 　 " 　 " March 13, "
1,862. " 　 Turner G. Morehead, 106th " 　 " 　 " 　 " 　 13, "
1,863. " 　 Thomas F. McCoy, 107th " 　 " 　 " April 1, "
1,864. Lt.-Col. Jas. M. Thompson, 107th " 　 " 　 " March 13, "
1,865. Col. Wm. D. Lewis, Jr., 110th " 　 " 　 " 　 " 　 13, "
1,866. " 　 Geo. A. Cobham, Jr., 111th " 　 " 　 " July 19, 1864.
1,867. " 　 Thomas M. Walker, 111th " 　 " 　 " 　 " 　 5, 1865.
1,868. " 　 Robert E. Patterson, 115th " 　 " 　 " March 13, "
1,869. Lt.-Col. Robt. Thompson, 115th " 　 " 　 " 　 " 　 13, "
1,870. 　 " 　 Chas. P. Herring, 118th " 　 " 　 " 　 " 　 13, "
1,871. 　 " 　 Gideon Clark, 119th " 　 " 　 " 　 " 　 13, "
1,872. Col. Mat. R. McClennan, 138th " 　 " 　 " April 2, "
1,873. " 　 Frederick H. Collier, 139th " 　 " 　 " March 13, "
1,874. " 　 John Frazer, 140th " 　 " 　 " 　 " 　 13, "
1,875. " 　 Edmund L. Dana, 143d " 　 " 　 " July 26, "
1,876. " 　 Hiram L. Brown, 145th " 　 " 　 " Sept. 3, 1864.
1,877. Lieut.-Colonel David B. McCreary, 145th Regiment
　　　　Pennsylvania Volunteer Infantry .... " March 13, 1865.
1,878. Colonel Ario Pardee, Jr., 147th Regt. Penn. Vol. Inf., " Jan. 12, 1865.
1,879. 　 " 　 James A. Beaver, 148th " 　 " 　 " Aug. 1, 1864.
1,880. 　 " 　 Roy Stone, 149th " 　 " 　 " Sept. 7, "
1,881. 　 " 　 Langhorne Wister, 150th " 　 " 　 " March 13, 1865.
1,882. 　 " 　 Harrison Allen, 151st " 　 " 　 " 　 " 　 13, "
1,883. 　 " 　 William H. Blair, 179th " 　 " 　 " 　 " 　 13, "
1,884. 　 " 　 James C. Lynch, 183d " 　 " 　 " 　 " 　 13, "
1,885. 　 " 　 Henry A. Frink, 186th " 　 " 　 " Oct. 4, "
1,886. Col. Wm. R. Hartshorne, 190th " 　 " 　 " March 13, "
1,887. Lt.-Col. Joseph B. Pattee, 190th " 　 " 　 " April 9, "
1,888. Colonel James Carle, 191st " 　 " 　 " March 13, "

1,889.	Colonel Joseph W. Fisher,	195th Regt. Penn.Vol. Inf., from Nov.				4, 1865.
1,890.	Col. Jas. C. Briscoe,188th & 199th	"	"	"	March 13,	"
1,891.	" C. W. Diven,	200th	"	"	"	"	25,	"
1,892.	Lt.-Col. Wm. H. H. McCall,	200th	"	"	"	April	2,	"
1,893.	Colonel Charles Albright,	202d	"	"	"	March	7,	"
1,894.	Col. Joseph A. Mathews,	205th	"	"	"	April	2,	"
1,895.	" Robert C. Cox,	207th	"	"	"	"	2,	"
1,896.	" Alfred B. McCalmont,	208th	"	"	"	March 13,	"
1,897.	" Levi A. Dodd,	211th	"	"	"	April	2,	"
1,898.	" David B. McKibbin,	214th	"	"	"	March 13,	"
1,899.	" Daniel Woodall,	1st Regt Del.	"	"	June 15,	"
1,900.	Lt.-Col. James M. Deems,	1st Regt. Md.	Vol. Cav.,	"	March 13,	"
1,901.	Col. C. Carroll Tevis,	3d	"	"	"	"	13,	"
1,902.	Lt.-Col. Byron Kirby,	3d	"	"	"	Sept.	6,	"
1,903.	Col. David L. Stanton,	1st	"	Vol. Inf.,	"	April	1,	"
1,904.	Lt.-Col. J. Eugene Duryee,	2d	"	"	"	March 13,	"
1,905.	Col. Rich'd N. Bowerman,	4th	"	"	"	April	1,	"
1,906.	Col. John W. Horn,	6th	"	"	"	Oct.	19, 1864.
1,907.	" Charles E. Phelps,	7th	"	"	"	March 13, 1865.
1,908.	Lt.-Col. John A. Steiner,	13th	"	"	"	"	13,	"
1,909.	Col. David H. Strother,	3d Regt. W.Va.Vol. Cav.,	"	Aug.	23,	"
1,910.	Lt.-Col. John S. Witcher,	3d	"	"	"	March 13,	"
1,911.	Col. George R. Latham,	6th	"	"	"	"	13,	"
1,912.	Lt.-Col. Rufus E. Fleming,	6th	"	"	"	"	13,	"
1,913.	Col. John H. Oley,	7th	"	"	"	"	13,	"
1,914.	Col. Wm. H. Enochs,	1st Vet. "	"	"	"	13,	"
1,915.	Col. Van H. Bukey,	11th Regt. W.Va.Vol. Inf.,	"	"	13,	"
1,916.	" William B. Curtis,	12th	"	"	"	"	13,	"
1,917.	Lieut.-Colonel Robert S. Northcott, 12th Regiment West Virginia Volunteer Infantry	"	"	13,	"
1,918.	Col. Wm. R. Brown,	13th Regt. W.Va.Vol. Inf.,	"	"	13,	"
1,919.	" Milton Wells,	15th	"	"	"	"	13,	"
1,920.	Colonel William C. Bartlett, 2d Mounted Regiment North Carolina Volunteer Infantry........	"	"	13,	"
1,921.	Col. George E. Spencer,	1st Regt. Ala. Vol. Cav.,	"	"	13,	"
1,922.	Major Francis L. Cramer,	1st	"	"	"	"	13,	"
1,923.	Col. D. J. Keily,	2d Regt. La.	"	"	"	13,	"
1,924.	" William O. Fiske,	1st	"	Vol. Inf.,	"	"	13,	"
1,925.	" Charles Everett,	2d	"	"	"	"	13,	"
1,926.	" M. La Rue Harrison,	1st Regt. Ark. Vol. Cav.,	"	"	13,	"
1,927.	" John E. Phelps.	2d	"	"	"	"	13,	"
1,928	Lt.-Col. Hugh Cameron,	2d	"	"	"	"	13,	"
1,929.	Col. J. M. Johnson,	1st	"	Vol. Inf.,	"	"	13,	"
1,930.	" Robert Johnson,	1st Regt. Tenn. Vol. Cav.,	"	"	13,	"
1,931.	" James P. Brownlow,	1st	"	"	"	"	13,	"
1,932.	" Wm. B. Stokes,	5th	"	"	"	"	13,	"
1,933.	" William J. Smith,	6th	"	"	"	July	16,	"
1,934.	Lt.-Col. Isaac R. Hawkins,	7th	"	"	"	March 13,	"
1,935.	Col. George Spalding,	12th	"	"	"	"	21,	"
1,936.	" Ely H. Murray,	3d Regt. Ky.	"	"	"	25,	"

1,937.	Col. David A. Enyart,	1st Regt. Ky. Vol. Inf., from March 13, 1862.
1,938.	" Henry C. Dunlap,	3d	"	"	"	"	13, "
1,939.	" George W. Monroe,	7th	"	"	"	"	13, "
1,940.	" George H. Cram,	9th	"	"	"	"	13, "
1,941.	" George W. Gallop,	14th	"	"	"	"	13, "
1,942.	" Alexander M. Stout,	17th	"	"	"	"	13, "
1,943.	" William J. Landran,	19th	"	"	"	"	13, "
1,944.	" S. W. Price,	21st	"	"	"	"	13, "
1,945.	Lt.-Col. Thos. J. Williams,	55th	"	"	"	Sept.	22, "
1,946.	Col. Beroth B. Eggleston,	1st Regt. Ohio Vol. Cav.,	"	March 13,	"
1,947.	" A. Bayard Nettleton,	2d	"	"	"	"	13, "
1,948.	" Louis Zahn,	3d	"	"	"	"	13, "
1,949.	" Horace N. Howland,	3d	"	"	"	"	13, "
1,950.	" Thomas T. Heath,	5th	"	"	"	Dec.	15, 1864.
1,951.	" William Stedman,	6th	"	"	"	March 13, 1865.
1,952.	" Israel Garrard,	7th	"	"	"	June	20, "
1,953.	" Samuel A. Gilbert,	8th	"	"	"	March 13, "
1,954.	" William D. Hamilton,	9th	"	"	"	April	9, "
1,955.	Lt.-Col. William Stough,	9th	"	"	"	March 13, "
1,956.	Col. Thos. W. Sanderson,	10th	"	"	"	"	13, "
1,957.	" Robert W. Ratliff,	12th	"	"	"	"	13, "
1,958.	Lt.-Col. Robert H. Bentley,	12th	"	"	"	"	13, "
1,959.	Colonel Horatio G. Gibson, 2d Regiment Ohio Volunteer Heavy Artillery	"	"	13, "
1,960.	Colonel James Barnett, 1st Regiment Ohio Volunteer Light Artillery................................	"	"	13, "
1,961.	Col. E. Bassett Langdon,	1st Regt. Ohio Vol. Inf.,	"	"	13, "
1,962.	James H. Godman,	4th	"	"	"	"	13, "
1,963.	Lt.-Col. Franklin Sawyer,	8th	"	"	"	"	13, "
1,964.	Col. Joseph W. Burke,	10th	"	"	"	"	13, "
1,965.	" Carr B. White,	12th	"	"	"	"	13, "
1,966.	" Dwight Jarvis, Jr.,	13th	"	"	"	"	13, "
1,967.	" Franklin Askew,	15th	"	"	"	July	14, "
1,968.	" Durbin Ward,	17th	"	"	"	Oct.	18, "
1,969.	" Timothy R. Stanley,	18th	"	"	"	March 13, "
1,970.	Colonel Charles H. Grosvenor, 18th Veteran Regiment Ohio Volunteer Infantry.....................	"	"	13, "
1,971.	Col. C. F. Manderson,	19th Regt. Ohio Vol. Inf.,	"	"	13, "
1,972.	" James M. Comly,	23d	"	"	"	"	13, "
1,973.	Lt.-Col. Russell Hastings,	23d	"	"	"	"	13, "
1,974.	Col. Wm. P. Richardson,	25th	"	"	"	Dec.	7, 1864.
1,975.	Lt.-Col. Nath'l Haughton,	25th	"	"	"	March 13, 1865.
1,976.	Lt.-Col. Mendal Churchill,	27th Regt. Ohio Vol. Inf.,	"	"	13, "
1,977.	Col. Augustus Moor,	28th	"	"	"	"	13, "
1,978.	" Theodore Jones,	30th	"	"	"	"	13, "
1,979.	" Moses B. Walker,	31st	"	"	"	"	27, "
1,980.	Lt.-Col. H'y V. N. Boynton,	35th	"	"	"	"	13, "
1,981.	Col. Hiram F. Duval,	36th	"	"	"	"	13, "
1,982.	Lieut.-Colonel Louis Von Blessingh, 37th Regiment Ohio Volunteer Infantry	"	"	13, "

1,983.	Col. Edward F. Noyes,	39th Regt. Ohio Vol. Inf., from March 13, 1865.
1,984.	" Jonathan Cranor,	40th	"	"	"	"	3,	"
1,985.	Colonel Aquila Wiley,	41st	"	"	"	"	13,	"
1,986.	Lieut.-Colonel Ephraim S. Holloway, 41st Regiment
	Ohio Volunteer Infantry......................	"	"	13,	"
1,987.	Captain James McCleery,	41st Regt. Ohio Vol. Inf.,	"	"	13,	"
1,988.	Colonel Lionel A. Sheldon,	42d	"	"	"	"	13,	"
1,989.	Lt.-Col. Dow A. Pardee,	42d	"	"	"	"	13,	"
1,990.	" Walter F. Herrick,	43d	"	"	"	"	13,	"
1,991.	Major Henry H. Giesy,	46th	"	"	"	May	28, 1864.
1,992.	Colonel Augustus C. Parry,	47th	"	"	"	March 13, 1865.
1,993.	Lieut.-Col. Thos. T. Taylor,	47th	"	"	"	"	13,	"
1,994.	Colonel Peter J. Sullivan,	48th	"	"	"	"	13,	"
1,995.	" William H. Gibson,	49th	"	"	"	"	13,	"
1,996.	" Silas A. Strickland,	50th	"	"	"	May	27,	"
1,997.	Lt.-Col. George R. Elstner,	50th	"	"	"	Aug.	8, 1864.
1,998.	Colonel Wells S. Jones,	53d	"	"	"	March 13, 1865.
1,999.	" John C. Lee,	55th	"	"	"	"	13,	"
2,000.	" Wm. H. Raynor,	56th	"	"	"	"	13,	"
2,001.	Lt.-Col. Samuel R. Mott,	57th	"	"	"	"	13,	"
2,002.	Col. Stephen J. McGroarty,	61st	"	"	"	May	1,	"
2,003.	Lt.-Col. Henry R. West,	62d	"	"	"	July	13,	"
2,004.	" Charles E. Brown,	63d	"	"	"	March 13,	"
2,005.	" Horatio N. Whitbeck, 65th Regiment Ohio
	Volunteer Infantry	"	"	13,	"
2,006.	Lt.-Col. Orlow Smith,	65th Regt. Ohio Vol. Inf.,	"	"	13,	"
2,007.	Colonel Charles Candy,	66th	"	"	"	"	13,	"
2,008.	Lt.-Col. Lewis C. Hunt,	67th	"	"	"	"	13,	"
2,009.	" George E. Welles,	68th	"	"	"	"	13,	"
2,010.	Col. Joseph R. Cockerill,	70th	"	"	"	"	13,	"
2,011.	" Henry K. McConnell,	71st	"	"	"	"	13,	"
2,012.	Lt.-Col. Jame H. Hart,	71st	"	"	"	"	13,	"
2,013.	" Charles G. Eaton,	72d	"	"	"	"	13,	"
2,014.	Colonel Orlando Smith,	73d	"	"	"	"	13,	"
2,015.	Lt.-Col. Samuel H. Hurst,	73d	"	"	"	"	13,	"
2,016.	Colonel Granville Moody,	74th	"	"	"	Jan.	12,	"
2,017.	" Josiah Given,	74th	"	"	"	March 13,	"
2,018.	" Andrew L. Harris,	75th	"	"	"	"	13,	"
2,019.	" Greenbury F. Wiles,	78th	"	"	"	"	13,	"
2,020.	" Henry G. Kennett,	79th	"	"	"	"	13,	"
2,021.	Lt.-Col. Azariah W. Doan,	79th	"	"	"	"	13,	"
2,022.	Colonel Robert N. Adams,	81st	"	"	"	"	13.	"
2,023.	Lt.-Col. David Thompson,	82d	"	"	"	"	13,	"
2,024.	Col. Frederick W. Moore,	83d	"	"	"	"	26,	"
2,025.	Lt.-Col. Wm. H. Baldwin,	83d	"	"	"	Aug.	22,	"
2,026.	Colonel George W. Neff,	88th	"	"	"	March 13,	"
2,027.	" John A. Turley,	91st	"	"	"	"	13,	"
2,028.	Col. Benjamin F. Coates,	91st	"	"	"	"	13,	"
2,029.	" Benjamin D. Fearing,	92d	"	"	"	Dec.	2, 1864.
2,030.	Lt.-Col. Wm. H. Martin,	93d	"	"	"	June	8, 1865.

2,031. Col. Joseph W. Frizell, 94th Regt. Ohio Vol. Inf., from March 13, 1865.
2,032. Lt.-Col. Rue P. Hutchins, 94th " " " " 13, "
2,033. " Jefferson Brumback, 95th Regiment Ohio Volunteer Infantry.................................. " " 13, "
2,034. Colonel John Q. Lane, 97th Regt. Ohio Vol. Inf., " " 13, "
2,035. Lt.-Col. John S. Pearce, 98th " " " " 13, "
2,036. Colonel Patrick S. Sleven, 100th " " " " 13, "
2,037. Lt.-Col. Edwin L. Hayes, 100th " " " Jan. 12, "
2,038. Colonel Isaac M. Kirby, 101st " " " " 12, "
2,039. Lt.-Col. John Messer, 101st " " " March 13, "
2,040. Colonel William Given, 102d " " " " 13, "
2,041. " John S. Casement, 103d " " " Jan. 25, "
2,042. Lt.-Col. Philip C. Hayes, 103d " " " March 13, "
2,043. Colonel John R. Bond, 111th " " " " 13, "
2,044. Lt.-Col. Moses R. Brailey, 111th " " " " 13, "
2,045. " Isaac R. Sherwood,111th " " " Feb. 27, "
2,046. Colonel James A. Wilcox, 113th " " " " 13, "
2,047. Lt.-Col. Darius B. Warner, 113th " " " " 13, "
2,048. Colonel John H. Kelly, 114th " " " " 13, "
2,049. " Thomas L. Young, 118th " " " " 13, "
2,050. Lt.-Col. Edgar Sowers, 118th " " " " 13, "
2,051. " William Slocum, 120th " " " " 13, "
2,052. Colonel Wm. H. Ball, 122d " " " Oct. 19, 1864.
2,053. " Wm. T. Wilson, 123d " " " March 13, 1865.
2,054. " Oliver H. Payne, 124th " " " " 13, "
4,055. " Benj. F. Smith, 126th " " " " 26, "
2,056. Lt.-Col. Wm. S. Pierson, 128th " " " " 13, "
2,057. Colonel John R. Hurd, 173d " " " " 13, "
2,058. " John S. Jones, 174th " " " " 13, "
2,059. Lt.-Col. Daniel McCoy, 175th " " " " 13, "
2,060. Colonel Edwin C. Mason, 176th " " " June 3, "
2,061. " Joab A. Stafford, 178th " " " March 13, "
2,062. " John O'Dowd, 181st " " " " 13, "
2,063. " George W. Hoge, 183d " " " " 13, "
2,064. " H'y S. Commager, 184th " " " " 13, "
2,065. " John E. Cummins, 185th " " " " 13, "
2,066. " Thos. F. Wildes, 186th " " " " 11, "
2,067. Col. Andrew R. Z. Dawson, 187th " " " Nov. 21, "
2,068. " Jacob E. Taylor, 188th " " " March 13, "
2,069. " Henry D. Kingsbury, 189th " " " " 10, "
2,070. " Robert L. Kimberly, 191st " " " " 13, "
2,071. " Eugene Powell, 193d " " " " 13, "
2,072. " Anson G. McCook, 194th " " " " 13, "
2,073. Lt.-Col. O. C. Maxwell, 194th " " " " 13, "
2,074. " Marcellus J. W. Holter, 195th Regiment Ohio
Volunteer Infantry .... " " 13, "
2,075. Colonel Robert P. Kennedy, 196th Regiment Ohio
Volunteer Infantry .... " " 13, "
2,076. Lt.-Colonel Gersham M. Barber, 197th Regiment Ohio
Volunteer Infantry .... " " 13, "

2,077. Colonel Giles W. Shurtleff, 5th U. S. Colored, or 127th
    Regiment Ohio Volunteer Infantry ....from March 13, 1865.
2,078. Colonel Thornton F. Broadhead, 1st Regiment Michi-
    gan Volunteer Cavalry........................... " Aug. 30, 1862.
2,079. Colonel Peter Stagg,   1st Regt. Mich. Vol. Cav.,   " March 13, 1865.
2,080.   "   John K. Mizner,   3d   "   "   "   "   13,   "
2,081. Lt.-Col. Benj. D. Pritchard, 4th   "   "   "   May   10,   "
2,082. Lt.-Col. Edward M. Lee,   5th   "   "   "   March 13,   "
2,083. Colonel James H. Kidd,   6th   "   "   "   "   13,   "
2,084. Lt.-Col. H'y E. Thompson, 6th   "   "   "   "   13,   "
2,085.   "   A. C. Litchfield,   7th   "   "   "   "   13,   "
2,086. Colonel Elisha Mix,   8th   "   "   "   "   13,   "
2,087.   "   George S. Acker,   9th   "   "   "   "   13,   "
2,088.   "   Israel C. Smith,   10th   "   "   "   "   13,   "
2,089.   "   Sam'l B. Brown,   11th   "   "   "   Jan.   31,   "
2,090. Lt.-Col. Chas. E. Smith, 11th   "   "   "   March 13,   "
2,091. Colonel Cyrus O. Loomis, 1st Regiment Michigan Vol-
    unteer Light Artillery............................ " June 20,   "
2,092. Colonel Wm. P. Innes, 1st Regiment Michigan Volun-
    teer Engineers...................... .... " March 13,   "
2,093. Colonel Charles V. De Land, 1st Regiment Michigan
    Volunteer Sharpshooters................ .... "   "   13,   "
2,094. Colonel Ira C. Abbott,   1st Regt. Mich. Vol. Inf.,   "   "   13.   "
2,095. Lt.-Col. Wm. A. Throop,   1st   "   "   "   "   13.   "
2,096. Colonel Wm. Humphrey,   2d   "   "   "   Aug.   1, 1861.
2,097. Lt.-Col. Moses B. Houghton, 3d   "   "   "   March 13, 1865.
2,098. Colonel Jairus W. Hall,   4th   "   "   "   "   13,   "
2,099. Lt.-Col Mich'l J. Vreeland, 4th   "   "   "   "   13,   "
2,100. Colonel John Pulford,   5th   "   "   "   "   13,   "
2,101. Lieut.-Colonel Solomon S. Matthews, 5th Regiment
    Michigan Volunteer Infantry .... "   "   13,   "
2,102. Colonel Ralph Ely,   8th Regt. Mich. Vol. Inf.,   "   April   2,   "
2,103.   "   John G. Parkhurst, 9th   "   "   "   May   22,   "
2,104. Lieut.-Colonel Christopher J. Dickerson, 10th Regi-
    ment Michigan Volunteer Infantry................. " March 13,   "
2,105. Colonel Dwight May,   12th Regt. Mich. Vol. Inf.,   "   "   13,   "
2,106.   "   Henry R. Mizner, 14th   "   "   "   "   13,   "
2,107. Col. Fred. S. Hutchinson, 15th   "   "   "   May   24,   "
2,108.   "   Benj. F. Partridge,   16th   "   "   "   March 31,   "
2,109.   "   Wm. H. Withington, 17th   "   "   "   "   13,   "
2,110. Lt.-Col. Fred. W. Swift,   17th   "   "   "   "   13,   "
2,111. Colonel Adolphus W. Williams, 20th Regiment Michi-
    gan Volunteer Infantry .... "   "   13,   "
2,112. Colonel Heber Le Favour, 22d Regt. Mich. Vol. Inf.,   "   "   13,   "
2,113. Lt.-Col. Wm. Sanborn,   22d   "   "   "   "   13,   "
2,114. Col. Oliver L. Spaulding,   23d   "   "   "   June   25,   "
2,115. Lt.-Col. Mark Flanigan,   24th   "   "   "   March 13,   "
2,116. Col. Henry H. Wells,   26th   "   "   "   June   3,   "
2,117.   "   Charles Waite,   27th   "   "   "   April   2,   "
2,118.   "   Byron M. Cutcheon, 27th   "   "   "   March 13,   "

2,119.	Lt.-Col. Geo. T. Shaffer,	28th Regt. Mich. Vol. Inf., from March 13, 1865.					
2,120.	Colonel Grover S. Wormer (late Lt.-Col. 8th Michigan Cavalry),	30th Regt. Michigan Volunteer Infantry..	"	"	13,	"	
2,121.	Colonel Thomas H. Butler.	5th Regt. Ind. Vol. Cav.,	"	"	13,	"	
2,122.	Lt.-Col. John Woolley,	5th	"	"	"	"	13, "
2,123.	Colonel James Biddle,	6th	"	"	"	"	13, "
2,124.	"　　Thomas M. Browne,	7th	"	"	"	"	13, "
2,125.	"　　Thos. J. Harrison,	8th	"	"	"	Jan.	31, "
2,126.	"　　Fielder A. Jones,	8th	"	"	"	March 13, "	
2,127.	Col. Gilbert M. L. Johnson,	13th	"	"	"	"	13, "
2,128.	"　Ira G. Grover,	7th	"	Vol. Inf.,	"	"	13, "
2,129.	"　David Shurk.	8th	"	"	"	Feb.	9, "
2,130.	Lt.-Col. Wm. P. Laselle,	9th	"	"	"	March 13, "	
2,131.	Colonel Daniel Macauley,	11th	"	"	"	"	13, "
2,132.	"　　Reuben Williams,	12th	"	"	"	"	13, "
2,133.	"　　John T. Wilder,	17th	"	"	"	Aug.	7. 1864.
2,134.	Lt.-Col. Frank White,	17th	"	"	"	March 13, 1865.	
2,135.	Colonel Jacob G. Vail,	17th	"	"	"	"	13, "
2,136.	Lt.-Col. Wm. W. Dudley,	19th	"	"	"	"	13, "
2,137.	"　　John M. Lindley,	19th	"	"	"	"	13, "
2,138.	Colonel Wm. T. Spicely,	24th	"	"	"	"	26, "
2,139.	"　　Silas Colgrove,	27th	"	"	"	Aug.	4, 1864.
2,140.	"　　John Coburn,	33d	"	"	"	March 13, 1865.	
2,141.	"　　Benj. F. Scribner,	38th	"	"	"	Aug.	8, 1864.
2,142.	Lt.-Col. Dan'l F. Griffin,	38th	"	"	"	March 13, 1865.	
2,143.	Colonel Abel D. Streight,	51st	"	"	"	"	13, "
2,144.	"　　Edward H. Wolfe,	52d	"	"	"	"	13, "
2,145.	"　　George P. Buell,	58th	"	"	"	Jan.	12, "
2,146.	"　　Thos. A. McNaught,	59th	"	"	"	Aug.	4, "
2,147.	"　　Israel N. Stiles,	63d	"	"	"	Jan.	31, "
2,148.	"　　DeWitt C. Anthony,	66th	"	"	"	March 13, "	
2,149.	"　　Thos. W. Bennett,	69th	"	"	"	"	5, "
2,150.	"　　Benj. Harrison,	70th	"	"	"	Jan.	23, "
2,151.	"　　Abram O. Miller,	72d	"	"	"	March 13, "	
2,152.	"　　Milton S. Robinson,	75th	"	"	"	"	13, "
2,153.	"　　Frederick Knefler,	79th	"	"	"	"	13, "
2,154.	"　　Morton C. Hunter,	82d	"	"	"	"	13, "
2,155.	Lt.-Col. Andrew J. Neff,	84th	"	"	"	"	13, "
2,156.	Colonel George F. Dick,	86th	"	"	"	"	13, "
2,157.	"　　Newell Gleason,	87th	"	"	"	"	13, "
2,158.	"　　Louis J. Blair,	88th	"	"	"	"	13, "
2,159.	"　　John Mehringer,	91st	"	"	"	"	13, "
2,160.	"　　DeWitt C. Thomas,	93d	"	"	"	"	13, "
2,161.	"　　Thomas J. Brady,	117th	"	"	"	"	13, "
2,162.	"　　Reuben C. Kise,	120th	"	"	"	"	13, ..
2,163.	Col. John C. McQuiston,	123d	"	"	"	"	13, "
2,164.	"　Richard P. De Hart,	128th	"	"	"	"	13, "
2,165.	"　Jasper Packard,	128th	"	"	"	"	13, "
2,166.	"　Charles S. Parish,	130th	"	"	"	"	13, "
2,167.	"　Will A. Adams,	145th	"	"	"	"	13, "

2,168. Col. Lafayette McCrillis, 3d Regt. Ill. Vol. Cav., from Sept. 4, 1864.
2,169. " Robert K. Carnahan, 3d " " " Oct. 28, 1865.
2,170. Lt.-Col. James M. Ruggles, 3d " " " March 13, "
2,171. Col. Martin R. M. Wallace, 4th " " " " 13, "
2.172. " John McConnell, 5th " " " " 13, "
2,173. Lt.-Col. David R. Clendenin, 8th " " " Feb. 20, "
2,174. Major George A. Forsyth, 8th " " " " 13, "
2,175. " John M. Waite, 8th " " " " 13, "
2,176. Colonel Otto Funke, 11th " " " " 13, "
2,177. " Hasbrook Davis, 12th " " " " 13, "
2,178. Lieut.-Colonel Thomas W. Grosvenor, 12th Regiment
Illinois Volunteer Cavalry .... " " 13, "
2,179. Lt.-Col. Hamilton B. Dox, 12th Regt. Ill. Vol. Cav., " " 13, "
2,180. Col. Joseph Warren Bell, 13th " " " " 13, "
2,181. " Albert Erskine, 13th " " " " 13, "
2,182. " Horace Capron, 14th " " " " 13, "
2,183. Lt.-Col. Robert W. Smith, 16th " " " " 13, "
2,184. Col. John L. Beveridge, 17th " " " " 7, "
2,185. Colonel Ezra Taylor, 1st Regiment Illinois Volunteer
Light Artillery..................................... " " 13, "
2,186. Major Charles Houghtaling, 1st Regiment Illinois Volunteer Light Artillery............... .... " " 13, "
2,187. Colonel Thomas S. Mather, 2d Regiment Illinois Volunteer Light Artillery............................ " Sept. 28, "
2,188. Lieut.-Colonel William L. Duff, 2d Regiment Illinois
Volunteer Light Artillery .... " March 13, "
2,189. Col. Richard Rowett, 7th Regt. Ill. Vol. Inf., " " 13, "
2,190. " Josiah A. Sheets, 8th " " " " 13, "
2,191. " August Mersy, 9th " " " " 13, "
2,192. Lt.-Col. Jesse L. Phillips, 9th " " " " 13, "
2,193. Col. John Tillson, 10th " " " " 10, "
2,194. " James H. Coates, 11th " " " " 13, "
2,195. Lt.-Col. Arthur C. Ducat, 12th " " " " 13, "
2,196. Major James R. Hugunin, 12th " " " " 13, "
2,197. Lt.-Col. Fred.W. Partridge, 13th " " " " 13, "
2,198. Col. Cyrus Hall, 14th " " " " 13, "
2,199. " George C. Rodgers, 15th " " " " 13, "
2,200. Major Adam Nase, 15th " " " " 13, "
2,201. Col. Robert F. Smith, 16th " " " " 13, "
2,202. " Daniel H. Brush, 18th " " " " 13, "
2,203. Lt.-Col. Jules C. Webber, 18th " " " " 13, "
2,204. Col. James A. Mulligan, 23d " " " July 23, "
2,205. Lt.-Col. Ira J. Bloomfield, 26th " " " March 13, "
2,206. " Wm. A. Schmitt, 27th " " " " 13, "
2,207. Col. Loren Kent, 29th " " " " 22, "
2,208. " Warren Shedd, 30th " " " " 13, "
2.209. " Lyndorf Ozburn, 31st " " " " 13, "
2,210. Lt.-Col. Robert N. Pearson, 31st " " " " 13, "
2,211. Col. Charles E. Lippincott, 33d " " " Feb. 17, "
2,212. " Isaac H. Elliott, 33d " " " March 13, "

2,213.	Col. John Charles Black,	37th Regt. Ill. Vol. Inf., from March 13, 1865.							
2,214.	Lt.-Col. Eugene B. Payne,	37th	"	"	"	"	13,	"
2,215.	" Orrin L. Mann,	39th	"	"	"	"	13,	"
2,216.	Col. Isaac C. Pugh,	41st	"	"	"	"	10,	"
2,217.	" Adolph Engelman,	43d	"	"	"	"	13,	"
2,218.	" Wallace W. Barrett,	44th	"	"	"	"	13,	"
2,219.	Lt.-Col. John O. Duer,	45th	"	"	"	July	12,	"
2,220.	Col. David W. Magee,	47th	"	"	"	March 13,	"
2,221.	Lt.-Col. Edward Bonham,	47th	"	"	"	"	13,	"
2,222.	Col. Phineas Pease,	49th	"	"	"	"	13,	"
2,223.	Lt.-Col. William Hanna,	50th	"	"	"	"	13,	"
2,224.	Col. Gilbert W. Cumming,	51st	"	"	"	"	13,	"
2,225.	Capt. Theodore F. Brown,	51st	"	"	"	"	13,	"
2,226.	Col. John S. Wilcox,	52d	"	"	"	"	13,	"
2,227.	" Grenville M. Mitchell,	54th	"	"	"	Aug.	22,	"
2,228.	" William F. Lynch,	58th	"	"	"	Jan.	31,	"
2,229.	" Robert W. Healy,	58th	"	"	"	March 13,	"
2,230.	" P. Sidney Post,	59th	"	"	"	Dec.	16, 1864.
2,231.	" Wm. B. Anderson,	60th	"	"	"	March 13, 1865.
2,232.	" James M. True,	62d	"	"	"	"	6,	"
2,233.	" John Morrill,	64th	"	"	"	"	13,	"
2,234.	Lt.-Col. Jos. S. Reynolds,	64th	"	"	"	July	11,	"
2,235.	Col. Daniel Cameron,	65th	"	"	"	March 13,	"
2,236.	" W. Scott Stewart,	65th	"	"	"	"	13,	"
2,237.	" Frederick A. Starring,	72d	"	"	"	"	13,	"
2,238.	Lt.-Col. Joseph Stockton,	72d	"	"	"	"	13,	"
2,239.	Col. John E. Bennett,	75th	"	"	"	April	6,	"
2,240.	Lt.-Col. Wm. M. Kilgour,	75th	"	"	"	June	20,	"
2,241.	Col. Samuel T. Busey,	76th	"	"	"	April	9,	"
2,242.	" David P. Grier,	77th	"	"	"	March 26,	"
2,243.	Lt.-Col. Erastus N. Bates,	80th	"	"	"	"	13,	"
2,244.	" Edward S. Salomon,	82d	"	"	"	"	13,	"
2,245.	Col. Arthur A. Smith	83d	"	"	"	"	13,	"
2,246.	" Louis H. Waters,	84th	"	"	"	June	18,	"
2,247.	" Caleb J. Dilworth,	85th	"	"	"	March 13,	"
2,248.	Lt.-Col. George W. Smith,	88th	"	"	"	"	13,	"
2,249.	Col. Charles T. Hotchkiss,	89th	"	"	"	"	13,	"
2,250.	" Henry M. Day,	90th	"	"	"	"	26,	"
2,251.	Lt.-Col. Benjamin F. Sheets,	93d	"	"	"	"	13,	"
2,252.	Col. John McNulta,	94th	"	"	"	"	13,	"
2,253.	Lieut.-Colonel Rankin G. Laughlin, 94th Regiment Illinois Volunteer Infantry					"	"	13,	"
2,254.	Col. Leander Blanden,	95th Regt. Ill. Vol. Inf.,	"	"	26,	"
2,255.	" Thos. W. Humphrey,	95th	"	"	"	June	10, 1864.
2,256.	" Thomas E. Champion,	96th	"	"	"	Feb.	20, 1865.
2,257.	Lt.-Col. John C. Smith,	96th	"	"	"	June	20,	"
2,258.	" Victor Vifquain,	97th	"	"	"	March 13,	"
2,259.	" Edward Kitchell,	98th	"	"	"	"	13,	"
2,260.	Col. Franklin C. Smith,	102d	"	"	"	"	13,	"
2,261.	" Daniel Dustin,	105th	"	"	"	"	16,	"

2,262.	Lt.-Col. Everell F. Dutton,	105th Regt. Ill. Vol. Inf., from March 16, 1865.					
2,263.	" Henry Yates,	106th	"	"	"	"	13, "
2,264.	Col. Charles Turner,	108th	"	"	"	"	26, "
2,265.	" James S. Martin,	111th	"	"	"	Feb.	28, "
2,266.	" Thos. J. Henderson,	112th	"	"	"	Nov.	30, 1864.
2,267.	" George B. Hoge,	113th	"	"	"	March 13, 1865.	
2,268.	Lt.-Col. John F. King,	114th	"	"	"	"	13, "
2,269.	" Samuel Shoup,	114th	"	"	"	"	13, "
2,270.	Col. Jesse H. Moore,	115th	"	"	"	May	15. "
2,271.	" John G. Fonda,	118th	"	"	"	June	28, "
2,272.	" Thomas J. Kinney,	119th	"	"	"	March 26, "	
2,273.	" John I. Rinaker,	122d	"	"	"	"	13, "
2,274.	Lt.-Col. Jonathan Biggs,	123d	"	"	"	"	13, "
2,275.	" John H. Howe,	124th	"	"	"	"	13, "
2,276.	Col. Hamilton N. Eldridge,	127th	"	"	"	"	13, "
2,277.	" Henry Case,	129th	"	"	"	"	16, "
2,278.	" Nathaniel Niles,	130th	"	"	"	"	13, "
2,279.	" Rollin V. Aukeny,	142d	"	"	"	"	13, "
2,280.	" Hiram F. Sickles,	147th	"	"	"	"	13, "
2,281.	" Wm. C. Kneffner,	149th	"	"	"	"	13, "
2,282.	" Stephen Bronson,	153d	"	"	"	Sept.	28, "
2,283.	" Gustavus A. Smith,	155th	"	"	"	March 13, "	
2,284.	" Lewis Merrill,	2d Regt. Mo. Vol. Cav.,	"	"	13, "		
2,285.	Lt.-Col. Theo. A. Switzler,	6th	"	"	"	"	13, "
2,286.	Col. William D. Wood,	11th	"	"	"	"	13, "
2,287.	Lieut.-Colonel George W. Schofield, 2d Regiment Missouri Volunteer Light Artillery........				"	Jan.	26, "
2,288.	Col. Eli Bowyer,	11th Regt. Mo. Vol. Inf.,	"	March 13, "			
2,289.	" Hugo Wangelin,	12th	"	"	"	"	13, "
2,290.	" Joseph Conrad,	15th	"	"	"	"	13, "
2,291.	" Charles S. Sheldon,	18th	"	"	"	"	13, "
2,292.	" Madison Miller,	18th	"	"	"	"	13. "
2,293.	" David Moore,	21st	"	"	"	Feb.	21, "
2,294.	" James K. Mills,	24th	"	"	"	March 13, "	
2,295.	" Chester Harding, Jr.,	25th	"	"	"	May	27, "
2,296.	" Thomas Curly,	27th	"	"	"	March 13, "	
2,297.	Lt.-Col. Dennis T. Kirby,	27th	"	"	"	"	13, "
2,298.	Col. John S. Cavender,	29th	"	"	"	"	13, "
2,299.	Lt. Col. Joseph S. Gage,	29th	"	"	"	June	15, "
2,300.	" Samuel P. Simpson,	31st	"	"	"	March 13, "	
2,301.	" Gustav Heinrichs,	41st	"	"	"	"	13, "
2,302.	Col. Robert C. Bradshaw,	44th	"	"	"	"	13, "
2,303.	" Thomas C. Fletcher, 31st and 47th Regiment Missouri Volunteer Infantry.........................				"	"	13, "
2,304.	Col. Oscar H. La Grange,	1st Regt. Wis. Vol. Cav.,	"	"	13, "		
2,305.	Lt.-Col. Henry Harnden,	1st	"	"	"	"	13. "
2,306.	Col. William Hawley,	3d	"	Vol. Inf.,	"	"	16, "
2,307.	" Amasa Cobb,	5th	"	"	"	"	13, "
2,308.	" Thomas S. Allen,	5th	"	"	"	"	13, "
2,309.	" John A. Kellogg,	6th	"	"	"	April	9, "

2,310. Lt.-Col. Rufus R. Dawes, 6th Regt. Wis. Vol. Inf., from March 18, 1865.
2,311.   "   Hollon Richardson, 7th   "   "   "   " 13, "
2,312. Col. Charles E. Salomon, 9th   "   "   "   " 13, "
2,313. " Charles L. Harris, 11th   "   "   "   " 13, "
2,314. " James K. Proudfit, 12th   "   "   "   " 13, "
2,315. " William P. Lyon, 13th   "   "   " Oct. 26, "
2,316. " Lyman M. Ward, 14th   "   "   " March 13, "
2,317. " Cassius Fairchild, 16th   "   "   "   " 13, "
2,318. " Adam G. Malloy, 17th   "   "   "   " 13, "
2,319. " Horace T. Sanders, 19th   "   "   " April 19, "
2,320. Lt.-Col. Sam'l K. Vaughan, 19th   "   "   " Aug. 9, "
2,321. Col. Henry Bertram, 20th   "   "   " March 13, "
2,322. " Harrison C. Hobart, 21st   "   "   " Jan. 12, "
2,323. " Joshua J. Guppy, 23d   "   "   " March 13, "
2,324. " Milton Montgomery, 25th   "   "   "   " 13, "
2,325. Lt.-Col. Jeremiah M. Rusk, 25th   "   "   "   " 13, "
2,326.   "   Fred. C. Winkler, 26th   "   "   " June 15, "
2,327. Col. Conrad Krez, 27th   "   "   " March 26, "
2,328. " Francis H. West, 31st   "   "   "   " 13, "
2,329. " Charles H. De Groat, 32d   "   "   "   " 13, "
2,330. " Jonathan B. Moore, 33d   "   "   "   " 26, "
2,331. " Samuel Harriman, 37th   "   "   " April 2, "
2,332. " James Bintliff, 38th   "   "   "   " 2, "
2,333. " Ezra T. Sprague, 42d   "   "   " June 20, "
2,334. " Frederick S. Lovell, 46th   "   "   " Oct. 11, "
2,335. " George C. Ginty, 47th   "   "   " Sept. 28, "
2,336. " Uri B. Pearsall, 48th   "   "   " March 18, "
2,337. " Samuel Fallows, 49th   "   "   " Oct. 24, "
2,338. " William Thompson, 1st Regt. Iowa Vol. Cav., " March 13, "
2,339. Lt.-Col. Alex. G. McQueen, 1st   "   "   "   " 13, "
2,340. Col. Datus E. Coon, 2d   "   "   "   " 8, "
2,341. " John W. Noble, 3d   "   "   "   " 13, "
2,342. " Edward F. Winslow, 4th   "   "   " Dec. 12, 1864.
2,343. " William W. Lowe, 5th   "   "   " March 13, 1865.
2,344. " Samuel M. Pollock, 6th   "   "   "   " 13, "
2,345. Lt.-Col. John Pattee, 7th   "   "   "   " 13, "
2,346. Major Geo. M. O'Brien, 7th   "   "   "   " 13, "
2,347. Col. Matthew M. Trumbull, 9th   "   "   "   " 13, "
2,348. " James B. Weaver, 2d   " Vol. Inf., "   " 1C, "
2,349. Major John Williams, 6th   "   "   "   " 13, "
2,350. Lt.-Col. James C. Parrott, 7th   "   "   "   " 13, "
2,351. Col. James L. Geddes, 8th   "   "   " June 5, "
2,352. " John H. Stibbs, 12th   "   "   " March 13, "
2,353. " James Wilson, 13th   "   "   "   " 13, "
2,354. " John M. Hedrick, 15th·   "   "   "   " 13, "
2,355. Lt.-Col. George Pomutz, 15th   "   "   "   " 13, "
2,356. Col. Alex. Chambers, 16th   "   "   "   " 13, "
2,357. Lieut.-Colonel Addison H. Saunders, 16th Regiment
    Iowa Volunteer Infantry... .... "   " 13, "
2,358. Col. David B. Hillis, 17th Regt. Iowa Vol. Inf., "   " 13, "

2,359. Col. Clark R. Wever,   17th Regt. Iowa Vol. Inf., from Feb.   9, 1865.
2,360. Lt.-Col. John Bruce,   19th   "   "   " March 13,   "
2,361. Col. Wm. McE. Dye,   20th   "   "   "   " 13,   "
2,362. Lt.-Col. Joseph B. Leake, 20th   "   "   "   " 13,   "
2,363. Col. Wm. M. Stone,   22d   "   "   "   " 13,   "
2,364. "   Harvey Graham,   22d   "   "   " July 25,   "
2,365. "   Samuel L. Glasgow,   23d   "   "   " Dec. 19, 1864.
2,366. "   Ed. Wright,   24th   "   "   " March 13, 1865.
2,367. "   Geo. A. Stone,   25th   "   "   "   " 13,   "
2,368. "   Thos. H. Benton, Jr., 29th   "   "   " Dec. 15, 1864.
2,369. Lieut.-Colonel Robert F. Patterson, 29th Regiment
         Iowa Volunteer Infanty........................   " March 13, 1865.
2,370. Col. Geo. W. Clark,   34th Regt. Iowa Vol. Inf., "   " 13,   "
2,371. "   Sylvester G. Hill,   35th   "   "   " Dec. 15, 1864.
2,372. Lt.-Col. Francis M. Drake, 36th   "   "   " Feb. 22, 1865.
2,373. "   Jos. O. Hudnutt,   38th   "   "   " March 13,   "
2,374. Col. Robt. N. McLaren,   2d Regt. Minn. Vol. Cav.,   " Dec. 14,   "
2,375. "   William Colville, Jr., 1st   "   Vol. Inf.,   " March 13,   "
2,376. Lt.-Col. Charles P. Adams, 1st   "   "   "   " 13,   "
2,377. Col. Judson W. Bishop,   2d   "   "   " June   7,   "
2,378. "   John E. Tourtelotte, 4th   "   "   " March 13,   "
2,379. "   Lucius F. Hubbard,   5th   "   "   " Dec. 16, 1864.
2,380. "   John T. Averill,   6th   "   "   " Oct. 18, 1865.
2,381. "   Wm. R. Marshall,   7th   "   "   " March 13,   "
2,382. "   Minor T. Thomas,   8th   "   "   " Feb. 10,   "
2,383. "   James H. Baker,   10th   "   "   " March 13,   "
2,384. Lt.-Col. Sam'l P. Jennison, 10th   "   "   "   " 13,   "
2,385. Col. George. S. Evans,   2d Regt. Cal. Vol. Cav.,   "   " 13,   "
2,386. "   Edward McGarry,   2d   "   "   "   " 13,   "
2,387. Lt.-Col. Ambrose E. Hooker, 2d   "   "   "   " 13,   "
2,388. "   Francis J. Lippitt, 2d   "   Vol. Inf.,   "   " 13,   "
2,389. "   Thomas F. Wright,   2d   "   "   "   " 13,   "
2,390. "   James F. Curtis,   4th   "   "   "   " 13,   "
2,391. "   Geo. W. Bowie,   5th   "   "   "   " 13,   "
2,392. "   Chas. W. Lewis,   7th   "   "   "   " 13,   "
2,393. "   Allen L. Anderson, 8th   "   "   "   " 13,   "
2,394. Col. Wm. R. Judson,   6th Regt. Kan. Vol. Cav.,   "   " 13,   "
2,395. "   Thomas Moonlight,   11th   "   "   " Feb. 13,   "
2,396. "   Charles W. Blair,   14th   "   "   "   " 13,   "
2,397. Lt.-Col. Geo. H. Hoyt,   15th   "   "   " March 13,   "
2,398. "   Samuel Walker,   16th   "   "   "   " 13,   "
2,399. Major James Ketner,   16th   "   "   "   " 13,   "
2,400. Colonel John Ritchie, 2d Regiment Kansas Indian
         Home Guard...................................   " Feb. 21,   "
2,401. Col. John A. Martin,   8th Regt. Kan. Vol. Inf.,   " March 13,   "
2,402. Lt.-Col. Edw'd F. Schneider, 8th   "   "   "   " 13,   "
2,403. Col. Chas. W. Adams,   12th   "   "   " Feb. 13,   "
2,404. "   Thomas M. Bowen,   13th   "   "   "   " 13,   "
2,405. Colonel Christopher Carson, 1st Regiment New Mexico
         Volunteer Cavalry ....   " March 13,   "

XIII.—14

2,406. Colonel Robert R. Livingston, 1st Regiment Nebraska
 Volunteer Cavalry.......... ....from June 21, 1865.
2,407. Colonel James H. Ford, 2d Regiment Colorado Volunteer Cavalry................ .... " Dec. 10, "
2,408. Lt.-Col. Fred. E. Trotter, 1st Regt. Vet. Res. Corps, " March 13, 1865.
2,409. Col. George A. Morgan,   2d   "   " " " 13, "
2,410. " Frederick D. Sewall, 3d   "   " " July 21, "
2,411. Major Wm. H. H. Beadle, 3d   "   " " March 16, 1866.
2,412. " Benj. F. Harris,   4th   "   " " " 13, 1865.
2,413. Col. Ambrose A. Stevens 5th   "   " " " 7, "
2,414. Lieut.-Colonel Calvin H. Frederick, 5th Regiment
 Veteran Reserve Corps......................... " " 13, "
2,415. Col. Moses N. Wisewell,   6th Regt. Vet. Res. Corps, " " 13, "
2,416. " Edward P. Fyffe,   7th   "   " " " 13, "
2,417. Lt.-Col. John B. Callis,   7th   "   " " " 13, "
2,418. Col. Benjamin J. Sweet,   8th   "   " " Dec. 20, 1864.
2,419. " George W. Gile,   9th   "   " " May 6, 1865.
2,420. " D. P. De Witt,   10th   "   " " March 13, "
2,421. Lt.-Col. Benezst F. Foust, 10th   "   " " " 13, "
2,422. Col. J. Egbert Farnum,   11th   "   " " Jan. 3, 1866.
2,423. " John Mansfield,   12th   "   " " March 13, 1865.
2,424. Lt.-Col. John H. Bell,   12th   "   " " Nov. 30, "
2,425. Col. John Hendrickson,   13th   "   " " March 13, "
2,426. Lt.-Col. Horace Neide,   13th   "   " " " 13, "
2,427. Col. Sam'l D. Oliphant,   14th   "   " " June 27, "
2,428. " James C. Strong   15th   "   " " March 13, "
2,429. Lt.-Col. Martin Flood,   15th   "   " " " 13, "
2,430. Colonel Charles M. Prevost, late 118th Pennsylvania
 Volunteers, 16th Regiment Veteran Reserve Corps, " " 13, "
2,431. Col. A. J. Warner,   17th Regt. Vet. Res. Corps, " " 13, "
2,432. " Oscar V. Dayton,   19th   "   " " " 13, "
2,433. " Noah L. Jeffries,   20th   "   " " " 30, "
2,434. Lieut.-Colonel George A. Washburn, 20th Regiment
 Veteran Reserve Corps......................... " " 13, "
2,435. Maj. Jas. R. O. Beirne,   22d Regt. Vet. Res. Corps, " Sept. 26, "
2,436. Col. Wm. H. Browne,   24th   "   " " March 13, "
2,436b. " William H. Morgan,   3d U. S. Vet. Vol. Inf., " " 13, "
2,437. " Oliver Wood,   4th   "   " " " 13, "
2,438. Lt.-Col. Aaron S. Daggett, 5th   "   " " " 13, "
2,439. Major Edward S. Meyer,   5th   "   " " " 13, "
2,440. Col. C. E. La Motte,   6th   "   " " " 13, "
2,441. " P. P. Browne, Jr.,   7th   "   " " " 13, "
2,442. " Francis E. Pierce,   8th   "   " " " 13, "
2,443. Lt.-Col. William G. Mauk 8th   "   " " " 13, "
2,444. Colonel Hiram Berdan, 1st Regiment U. S. Sharpshooters...... .... " " 13, "
2,445. Col. C. A. R. Dimon,   1st Regt. U. S. Vol. Inf., " " 13, "
2,446. " Carroll H. Potter,   6th   "   " " " 13, "
2,447. " Jephtha Garrard,   1st Regt. U. S. Col. Cav., " " 13, "
2,448. Lt.-Col. Frank J. White,   2d   "   " " " 13, "

2,449. Capt. Albert G. Lawrence, 2d Regt. U. S. Col. Cav., from March 25, 1865.
2,450. Col. Embury D. Osband, 3d " " " Oct. 5, 1864.
2,451. " Jas. Grant Wilson, 4th " " " March 13, 1865.
2,452. " James F. Wade, 6th " " " Feb. 13, "
2,453. " John E. McGowan, 1st " " Art., " March 13, "
2,454. " Herman Leib, 5th " " " " 13, "
2,455. " Bernard G. Farrar, 6th " " " " 9, "
2,456. Lt.-Col. Jas. D. McBride, 8th " " " " 13, "
2,457. Col. Charles A. Hartwell, 10th " " " Dec. 2d, "
2,458. " J. Hale Sypher, 11th " " " March 13, "
2,459. " John H. Holman, 1st " " Inf., " " 13, "
2,460. " Benj. C. Tilghman, 3d " " " April 13, "
2,461. Lt.-Col. George Rogers, 4th " " " March 13, "
2,462. Col. John W. Ames, 6th " " " Jan. 15, "
2,463. " Jas. Shaw, Jr., 7th " " " March 13, "
2,464. " Sam'l C. Armstrong, 8th " " " " 13, "
2,465. " Elias Wright, 10th " " " Jan. 15, "
2,466. " Chas. R. Thompson, 12th " " " April 13, "
2,467. Lieut.-Colonel Theodore Trauernicht, 13th Regiment
    U. S. Colored Infantry.................... .... " March 13, "
2,468. Col. Henry C. Corbin, 14th Regt. U. S. Col. Inf., " " 13, "
2,469. " Thos. J. Morgan, 14th " " " " 13, "
2,470. Lt.-Col. Nicholas J. Vail, 14th " " " " 13, "
2,471. Colonel Wm. R. Shafter, 17th " " " " 13, "
2,472. Lt.-Col. William Welsh, 19th " " " " 13, "
2,473. Col. Milton S. Littlefield, 21st " " " Nov. 26, "
2,474. " Cleveland J. Campbell, 23d " " " March 13, "
2,475. " Orlando Brown, 24th " " " Jan. 6, 1866.
2,476. " Albert M. Blackman, 27th " " " Oct. 27, 1864.
2,477. " Chas. S. Russell, 28th " " " July 30, 1864.
2,478. " Delavan Bates, 30th " " " " 30, "
2,479. " Henry O. Ward, 31st " " " Nov. 29, 1865.
2,480. Lt.-Col. W. E. W. Ross, 31st " " " March 11, "
2,481. Col. Wm. T. Bennett, 33d " " " May 25, "
2,482. " Wm. W. Marple, 34th " " " March 13, "
2,483. " James C. Beecher, 35th " " " " 13, "
2,484. " Alonzo G. Draper, 36th " " " Oct. 28, 1864.
2,485. Lt.-Col. Benj. F. Pratt, 36th " " " March 13, 1865.
2,486. Col. Nathan Goff, Jr., 37th " " " " 13, "
2,487. " Robert M. Hall, 38th " " " " 13, "
2,488. Lt.-Col. Dexter E. Clapp, 38th " " " " 13, "
2,489. " Lucius H. Warren, 38th " " " " 13, "
2,490. Col. Fred. W. Lister, 40th " " " " 13, "
2,491. " Llewellyn F. Haskall, 41st " " " " 13, "
2,492. " Stephen B. Yeoman, 43d " " " " 13, "
2,493. Lt.-Col. H. Seymour Hall, 43d " " " " 13, "
2,494. Col. Lewis Johnson, 44th " " " " 13, "
2,495. " Ulysses Doubleday, 45th " " " " 11, "
2,496. " Eliphalet Whittlesey, 46th " " " " 13, "
2,497. " Hiram Schofield, 47th " " " " 13, "

2,498.	Col. Fred. M. Crandal,	48th Regt. U. S. Col. Inf., from				Oct. 24, 1865.		
2,499.	" Chas. A. Gilchrist,	50th	"	"	"	March 26,	"
2,500.	" A. Watson Webber,	51st	"	"	"	" 26,	"
2,501.	" George M. Ziegler,	52d	"	"	"	" 13,	"
2,502.	" Orlando C. Risdon,	53d	"	"	"	" 13,	"
2,503.	" Thomas D. Seawell,	57th	"	"	"	" 13,	"
2,504.	" Simon M. Preston,	58th	"	"	"	Dec. 30,	"
2,505.	" Edward Bouton,	59th	"	"	"	Feb. 28,	"
2,506.	" John G. Hudson,	60th	"	"	"	March 13,	"
2,507.	" Theodore H. Barrett,	62d	"	"	"	" 13,	"
2,508.	" John Eaton, Jr.,	63d	"	"	"	" 13,	"
2,509.	" Samuel Thomas,	64th	"	"	"	" 13,	"
2,510.	" Alonzo J. Edgerton,	65th	"	"	"	" 13,	"
2,511.	Lt.-Col. George Baldey,	65th	"	"	"	" 13,	"
2,512.	Col. Wm. T. Frohock,	66th	"	"	"	" 13,	"
2,513.	" J. Blackburn Jones,	68th	"	"	"	" 13,	"
2,514.	" Henry W. Fuller,	75th	"	"	"	" 13,	"
2,515.	" Chas. W. Drew,	76th	"	"	"	" 13,	"
2,516.	" Samuel B. Jones,	78th	"	"	"	" 31,	"
2,517.	" James M. Williams,	79th	"	"	"	July 13,	"
2,518.	" William S. Mudgett,	80th	"	"	"	March 13,	"
2,519.	" John F. Appleton,	81st	"	"	"	" 13,	"
2,520.	Lt.-Col. Isaac S. Bangs,	81st	"	"	"	" 13,	"
2,521.	Col. Samuel J. Crawford,	83d	"	"	"	" 13,	"
2,522.	" William H. Dickey,	84th	"	"	"	" 13,	"
2,523.	" Henry N. Frisbie,	92d	"	"	"	" 13,	"
2,524.	" Samuel M. Quincy,	96th	"	"	"	" 13,	"
2,525.	" George D. Robinson,	97th	"	"	"	" 13,	"
2,526.	" Reuben D. Mussey,	100th	"	"	"	" 13,	"
2,526b.	Lt.-Col. Henry G. Davis,	101st	"	"	"	" 13,	"
2,527.	Col. Henry L. Chipman,	102d	"	"	"	" 13,	"
2,528.	" Stewart L. Woodford,	103d	"	"	"	May 12,	"
2,529.	" Douglas Frazer,	104th	"	"	"	March 13,	"
2,530.	" Wm. R. Revere, Jr.,	107th	"	"	"	" 13,	"
2,531.	" Orion A. Bartholomew, 109th Regiment of U. S. Colored Infantry...................................					" 13,	"
2,532.	Col. Lewis G. Brown,	117th Regt. U. S. Col. Inf.				" 13,	"
2,533.	" John C. Moon,	118th	"	"	"	Nov. 21,	"
2,534.	" Chas. G. Bartlett,	119th	"	"	"	March 13,	"
2,535.	" Samuel A. Porter,	123d	"	"	"	" 13,	"
2,536.	" Chas. H. Howard,	128th	"	"	"	Aug. 15,	"
2,537.	" Benj. C. Ludlow, U. S. Colored Troops,					Oct. 28, 1864.	

GENERAL OFFICERS OF STATES

WHO ENTERED THE SERVICE WITH THE QUOTAS OF THEIR RESPECTIVE STATES IN APRIL, 1861, FOR THREE MONTHS.—(12.)

New York.

2,538. Major-General Charles W. Sandford, mustered out August 15, 1861.

New Jersey.

2,539. Brig.-General Theodore Runyon, mustered out July 30, 1861.

Pennsylvania.

2,540. Major-General Robert Patterson, mustered out July 27, 1861.

2,541. Brevet Major-General George C. Cadwallader, mustered out July 19, 1861.

Ohio.

2,542. Major-General George B. McClellan, appointed Major-General U. S. Army.

2,543. Brig.-General J. D. Cox, appointed Brig.-General U. S. Volunteers

2,544. Brig.-General N. Schleich, mustered out July 30, 1861.

2,545. Brig.-General J. H. Bates, mustered out August 27, 1861.

Indiana.

2,546. Brig.-General T. A. Morris, mustered out July 27, 1861.

Wisconsin.

2,547. Brig.-General Rufus King, appointed Brig.-General U. S Volunteers.

Massachusetts.

2,548. Brig.-General Benjamin F. Butler, appointed Major-General U. S. Volunteers.

Connecticut.

2,549. Brig.-General Daniel Tyler, mustered out August 8, 1861.

GENERAL OFFICERS DECEASED WHILE IN THE SERVICE.—(102.)

2,550. Brig.-General Thomas Williams, killed Aug. 5, 1862, at Battle of Baton Rouge, La.

2,551. Brig -General Robert L. McCook, killed Aug. 6, 1862, near Dechard, Tenn., by guerillas.

2,552. Brig.-General Henry Bohlen, killed Aug. 22, 1862, at Freeman's Ford, Rappahannock River, Va.

2,553. Major-General Philip Kearney, killed Sept. 1, 1862, at Chantilly, Va.

2,554. Major-General Isaac I. Stevens, killed Sept. 1, 1862, at Chantilly, Va.

2,555. Brig. General Pleasant A. Hackelman, killed Oct. 3, 1862, at Corinth, Miss.

2,556. Brig.-General James S. Jackson, killed Oct. 8, 1862, at Perryville, Ky.

2,557. Brig.-General Wm. R. Terrill, killed Oct. 8, 1862, at Perryville, Ky.

2,558. Brig.-General Conrad Feger Jackson, killed Dec. 13, 1862, at Fredericksburg, Va.

2,559. Brig.-General Joshua W. Sill, killed Dec. 31, 1862, at Stone River, Tenn.

2,560. Major-General Hiram G. Berry, killed May 2, 1863, at Chancellorsville, Va.

2,561. Major-General John F. Reynolds, killed July 1, 1863, at Gettysburg, Pa.

2,562. Brig.-General Stephen W. Weed, killed July 2, 1863, at Gettysburg, Pa.

2,563. Brevet Major-General S. K. Zook, killed July 2, 1863, at Gettysburg, Pa.

2,564. Brevet Brig.-General A. Van Horn Ellis, Colonel 124th N. Y. Volunteers, killed July 2, 1863, at Gettysburg, Pa.

2,565. Brevet Brig.-General Lewis Benedict, Colonel 162d N. Y. Volunteers, killed April 9, 1864, at Port Hudson, La.

2,566. Brevet Major-General Alex. Hays, U. S. Volunteers, killed May 5, 1864, at the Wilderness, Va.

2,567. Brevet Major-General James S. Wadsworth, U. S. Volunteers, killed May 6, 1864, at the Wilderness, Va.

2,568. Major-General John Sedgwick, U. S. Volunteers, killed May 9, 1864, at Spottsylvania Court-house, Va.

2,569. Brig.-General Thomas G. Stevenson, U. S. Volunteers, killed May 10, 1864, at Spottsylvania Court-house, Va.

2,570. Brig.-General James C. Rice, U. S. Volunteers, killed May 10, 1864, at Laurel Hill, Va.

2,571. Brevet Brig.-General Henry H. Giesy, Major 46th Ohio Volunteers, killed May 28, 1864, at Dallas, Ga.

2,572. Brevet Brig.-General John McConihe, Colonel 169th N. Y. Volunteers, killed June 1, 1864, at Cold Harbor, Va.

2,573. Brevet Brig.-General Thomas W. Humphrey, Colonel 95th Illinois Volunteers, killed June 10, 1864, at Grentown, Mo.

2,574. Brevet Brig.-General Wm. Blaisdell, Colonel 11th Massachusetts Volunteers, killed June 23, 1864, before Petersburg, Va.

2,575. Brevet Brig.-General George A. Cobham, Jr., Colonel 111th Pennsylvania Volunteers, killed July 20, 1864, at Peach-tree Creek, Ga.

2,576. Major-General James B. McPherson, U. S. Volunteers, killed July 22, 1864, before Atlanta, Ga.

2,577. Brevet Brig.-General Griffin A. Stedman, Colonel 11th Connecticut Volunteers, killed Aug. 6, 1864.

2,578. Brevet Brig.-General George E. Elstner, Lt.-Colonel 50th Ohio Volunteers, killed Aug. 8, 1864, before Atlanta, Ga.

2,579. Brevet Major-General David A. Russell, U. S. Volunteers, killed Sept. 19, 1864, at Winchester. Va.

2,580. Brevet Brig.-General Frank H. Peck, Lt.-Colonel 12th Connecticut Volunteers, killed Sept. 19, 1864, at Winchester, Va.

2,581. Brig.-General Hiram Burnham, U. S. Volunteers, killed Sept. 30, 1864, at Chapin's Farm, Va.

2,582. Brevet Brig.-General George D. Wells, Colonel 34th Massachusetts Volunteers, killed Oct. 13, 1864, at Cedar Creek, Va.

2,583. Brig.-General Daniel D. Bidwell, U. S. Volunteers, killed Oct. 19, 1864, at Cedar Creek, Va.

2,584. Brevet Brig.-General Sylvester G. Hill, Colonel 35th Iowa Volunteers, killed Dec. 15, 1864, at Nashville, Tenn.

2,585. Brevet Major-General Frederick Winthrop, Colonel 5th New York Veteran Volunteers, killed April 1, 1865, at Five Forks, Va.

2,586. Brevet Brig.-General George W. Gowan, Colonel 48th Pennsylvania Volunteers, killed April 2, 1865, near Petersburg, Va.

2,587. Brevet Brig.-General Theodore Read, Major and Asst. Adjutant-General Volunteers, killed April 6, 1865, at High Bridge, Va.

Died of Wounds Received in Action—(29).

2,588. Brig.-General Wm. H. L. Wallace, U. S. Volunteers, died April 10, 1862, at Savannah, Tenn.. of wounds received at Shiloh, Tenn.

2,589. Brig.-General George W. Taylor, U. S. Volunteers, died Aug. 31, 1862, at Alexandria, Va., of wounds received near Cub Run, Va.

2,590. Brevet Brig.-General Thornton F. Broadhead, Colonel 1st Michigan Cavalry, died Sept. 2, 1862, of wounds received at Bull Run, Va.

2,591. Major-General Jesse L. Reno, U. S. Volunteers, died Sept. 14, 1862, of wounds received in battle of South Mountain, Md.

2,592. Major-General Joseph K. F. Mansfield, U. S. Volunteers, died Sept. 18, 1862, of wounds received in battle of Antietam, Md.

2,593. Brig.-General Isaac P. Rodman, U. S. Volunteers, died Sept. 30, 1862, of wounds received in battle of Antietam, Md.

2,594. Major-General Israel B. Richardson, U. S. Volunteers, died Nov. 3, 1862, at Sharpsburg, Md., of wounds received in battle of Antietam, Md.

2,595. Brig.-General George D. Bayard, U. S. Volunteers, died Dec. 14, 1862, of wounds received at the battle of Fredericksburg, Va.

2,596. Major-General Amiel W. Whipple, U. S. Volunteers, died May 7, 1863, at Washington, D.C., of wounds received at Chancellorsville, Md.

2,597. Brig.-General Edmund Kirby, U. S. Volunteers, died May 28, 1863, at Washington, D. C., of wounds received at Chancellorsville, Md.

2,598. Brevet Brig.-General George H. Ward, Colonel 15th Massachusetts Volunteers, died July 2, 1863, of wounds received at Gettysburg, Pa.

2,599. Brevet Brig.-General Paul Joseph Revere, Colonel 20th Massachusetts Volunteers, died July 5, 1863, of wounds received at Gettysburg, Pa.

2,600. Brevet Brig.-General Louis R. Francine, Colonel 7th New Jersey Volunteers, died July 16, 1863, of wounds received at Gettysburg, Pa.

2,601. Major-General George C. Strong, U. S. Volunteers, died July 30, 1863, of wounds received in the assault on Fort Wagner, S. C.

2,602. Brig.-General Wm. H. Lytle, U. S. Volunteers, died Sept. 20, 1863, of wounds received at Chickamauga, Ga.

2,603. Brig.-General William P. Sanders, U. S. Volunteers, died Nov. 19, 1863, of wounds received before Knoxville, Tenn.

2,604. Brevet Brig.-General Wm. N. Green, Lt.-Colonel 173d New York Volunteers, died May 14, 1864, of wounds received in action.

2,605. Brevet Brig.-General Arthur H. Dutton, Colonel 21st Connecticut Volunteers, died June 4, 1864, of wounds received in action.

2,606. Brevet Brig.-General Wm. H. Sackett, Colonel 9th New York Cavalry Volunteers, died June 10, 1864, of wounds received in action.

2,607. Brevet Brig.-General George L. Presscott, Colonel 32d Massachusetts Volunteers, died June 19, 1864, of wounds received in action.

2,608. Brig.-General Charles G. Harker, U. S. Volunteers, died June 27, 1864, of wounds received before Marietta, Ga.

2,609. Brig.-General Samuel A. Rice, U. S. Volunteers, died July 6, 1864, of wounds received at Jenkins' Ferry, Ark.

2,610. Brevet Brig.-General James A. Mulligan, Colonel 23d Illinois Volunteers, died July 26, 1864, of wounds received at Winchester, Va.

2,611. Brevet Brig.-General Henry Lyman Patten, Major 20th Massachusetts Volunteers, died September 10, 1864, of wounds received in action.

2,612. Brevet Brig.-General Willoughby Babcock, Lieut.-Colonel 75th New York Volunteers, died October 6, 1864, of wounds received in action.

2,613. Brevet Brig.-General Alexander Gardiner, Colonel 14th New Hampshire Volunteers, died October 7, 1864, of wounds received at Opequan, Va.

2,614. Brevet Brig.-General J. Howard Kitching, Colonel 6th New York Volunteer Artillery, died Jan 10, 1865, of wounds received in action.

2,615. Brevet Major-General Thomas A. Smyth, U. S. Volunteers, died April 9, 1865, of wounds received near Farmville, Va.

2,616. Brevet Brig.-General Francis Washburn, Colonel 4th Massachusetts Cavalry, died April 22, 1865, of wounds received in action.

Died of Disease and Other Causes—(35).

2,617. Brevet Brig.-General John Garland, Colonel 8th U. S. Infantry, at New York City, June 5, 1861.

2,618. Brevet Major-General George Gibson, U. S. Army, at Washington, D. C., Sept. 29, 1861.

2,619. Brig.-General Frederick W. Lander, U. S. Volunteers, at Camp Chase, on the Upper Potomac, Va., March 2, 1862.

2,620. Major-General Charles F. Smith, U. S. Volunteers, at Savannah, Tenn., April 25, 1862.

2,621. Brig.-General Wm. H. Keim, U. S. Volunteers, at Harrisburg, Pa., May 18, 1862.

2,622. Brig.-General Joseph B. Plummer, U. S. Volunteers, at Corinth, Miss., August 9, 1862.

2,623. Major-General Wm. Nelson, U. S. Volunteers, at Louisville, Ky., Sept. 29, 1862.

2,624. Major-General Ormsby M. Mitchell, U. S. Volunteers, at Beaufort, S. C., Oct. 30, 1862.

2,625. Brig.-General Charles D. Jamison, U. S. Volunteers, at Old Town, Me., Nov. 6, 1862.

2,626. Brig.-General Francis E. Patterson, U. S. Volunteers, Nov. 6, 1862.

2,627. Brevet Brig.-General Sylvester Churchill, Colonel U. S. A., at Washington, D. C., Dec. 7, 1862.

2,628. Major-General Edwin V. Sumner, U. S. Volunteers, at Syracuse, N. Y., March 21, 1863.

2,629. Brig.-General James Cooper, U. S. Volunteers, at Columbus, Ohio, March 28, 1863.

2,630. Brig.-General E. N. Kirk, U. S. Volunteers, at Chicago, Ill., July 29, 1863.

2,631. Brig.-General Thomas Welsh, U. S. Volunteers, at Cincinnati, Ohio, Aug. 14, 1863.

2,632. Major-General John Buford, U. S. Volunteers, at Washington, D. C., Dec. 16, 1863.

2,633. Brig.-General Michael Corcoran, U. S. Volunteers, at Fairfax Court House, Va., Dec. 22, 1863.

2,634. Brig.-General Stephen G. Champlin, U. S. Volunteers, at Grand Rapids, Mich., Jan. 26, 1864.

2,635. Brevet Major-General Joseph G. Totten, Chief Engineer U. S. A., at Washington, D. C., April 22, 1864.

2,636. Brig.-General Joseph P. Taylor, U. S. A., at Washington, D. C., June 29, 1864.

2,637. Brig.-General Daniel P. Woodbury, U. S. Volunteers, at Key West, Fla., Aug. 15, 1864.

2,638. Brig.-General Joshua B. Howell, U. S. Volunteers, near Petersburg, Va., Sept. 14, 1864.

2,639. Brevet Brig.-General Thomas J. C. Amory, Colonel 17th Massachusetts Volunteers, at Beaufort, N. C., Oct. 7, 1864.

2,640. Major-General David B. Birney, U. S. Volunteers, at Philadelphia, Pa., Oct. 18, 1864.

14*

2,641. Brevet 'Major-General T. E. G. Ransom, U. S. Volunteers, at Rome, Ga., Oct. 29, 1864.

2,642. Brevet Brig.-General Chas. Wheelock, Colonel 97th New York Volunteers, Jan. 21, 1865.

2,643. Brevet Brig.-General David P. Shunk, Colonel 8th Indiana Volunteers, Feb. 21, 1865.

2,644. Brevet Brig.-General Cleaveland J. Campbell, Colonel 23d U. S. Colored Troops, at Charlestown, N. Y., June 13, 1865.

2,645. Brig.-General George Wright, U. S. Volunteers, lost at sea by wreck of steamer Jonathan, en route from San Francisco to Columbia River, July 30, 1865.

2,646. Brig.-General M. M. Crocker, U. S. Volunteers, at Washington, D. C., Aug. 26, 1865.

2,647. Brevet Brig.-General Alonzo G. Draper, 36th U. S. Colored Troops, by accidental gunshot wound, Sept. 3, 1865.

2,648. Brig.-General Alexander Schimmelfennig, U. S. Volunteers, at Wernersville, Pa., Sept. 7, 1865.

2,649. Brevet Brig.-General Wm. R. Revere, Jr., Colonel 107th U. S. Colored Troops, at Morehead City, N. C., Sept. 20, 1865.

2,650. Brevet Brig.-General René E. DeRussy, Colonel Corps of Engineers, U. S. A.. at San Francisco, Cal., Nov. 23, 1865.

2,651. Brevet Major-General Wm. W. Morris, Colonel 2d U. S. Artillery, at Baltimore, Md., Dec. 15, 1861.

INDEX TO NAMES.

Ball, William H., 2,052
Ballier, John F., 1,857
Balloch, G. W., 1,473
Bangs, Isaac S., 2,520
Bankhead, Henry C., 1,445
Banks, Nathaniel P., 169
Banning, Henry B., 564
Barber, Gersham M., 2,076
Barlow, Francis C., 284, 1,073
Barnard, John G., 70, 893
Barnes, Charles, 1,810
    James, 390, 1,140
    Joseph K., 65, 610
Barnett, James, 1,960
Barney, Albert M., 1,744
    Benjamin Griffin, 1,808
    Lewis T., 532
Barnum, Henry A., 392, 1,353
Barrett, Theodore H., 2,507
    Wallace W., 2,218
Barriger, John W., 660
Barry, H. W., 581
    William F., 119, 313, 865
Barstow, Simon F., 1,420
    Wilson, 1,393
Bartholomew, Orion A., 2,531
Bartlett, Charles G., 2,534
    Joseph J., 302, 1,086
    William C., 1,920
    William F., 391, 1,278
Barton, William B., 1,674
Bassett, Isaac C., 1,851
Batchelder, Richard N., 1,451
Bates, Delavan, 2,478
    Erastus N., 2,243
    J. H., 2,545
Baxter, DeWitt C., 1,846
    Henry, 467, 1,188
Bayard, George D., 998, 2,595
Beadle, William H. H., 2,411
Beal, George L., 393, 1,318
Beatty, John, 1,160
    Samuel, 366, 1,149
Beaver, James A., 1,879
Beckwith, Amos, 62, 1,368
    Edward G., 737
Bedel, John, 1,517
Beecher, James C , 2,483
Belknap, William W., 383, 1,294
Bell, John H., 2,424

Bell, Joseph Warren, 2,180
    George, 658
Bendix, John E., 1,658
Benedict, Lewis, 1,755, 2
Benham, Henry W., 73, 394, 858
Benjamin, William H., 1,622
Bennett, John E., 2,239
    Thomas W., 2,149
    William T., 2,481
Bentley, Richard C., 1,683
    Robert H., 1,958
Benton, Thomas H., Jr , 2,368
    William P., 460, 1,007
Berdan, Hiram, 2,444
Berry, Hiram G., 242, 953, 2,560
Bertram, Henry, 2,321
Beveridge, John L., 2,184
Biddle, Charles J., 872
    James, 2,123
Bidwell, Daniel D., 1,298, 2,583
Biggs, Herman, 1,449
    Jonathan, 2,274
Biles, Edwin R., 1,858
Bingham, Henry H., 1,447
    Judson D., 644
Bintliff, James, 2,332
Birge, Henry W., 345, 1,245
Birney, David B., 259, 941, 2,640
    William, 395, 1,203
Bishop, Judson W., 2,377
Black, John Charles, 2,213
Blackman, Albert M., 2,476
Blair, Charles W., 2,396
    Frank P., 249, 1,052
    Lewis J., 2,158
    William H., 1,883
Blaisdell, William, 1,549, 2,574
Blake, George A. H., 710
Blakeslee. Erastus, 1,600
Blanchard, Justus W., 1,756
Blandon, Leander, 2,254
Blenker, Louis, 849
Bloomfield, Ira J., 2.205
Blunt, Asa P., 1,530
    James G., 245, 973
Bodine, Robert L., 1,821
Bohlen, Henry, 1,008, 2,552
Bolinger, H. C., 1,815
Bolles John A., 1,384
Bolton, William J., 1,834

Graham, Harvey, 2,364
    Lawrence P., 721, 870
    Samuel, 1,640
    William M., 733
Granger, George Frederick, 1,495
    Gordon, 97. 219, 969
    Robert S., 151, 363, 1,091
Grant, Lewis A., 321, 1,263
    Ulysses S., 1. 2, 10, 174, 825
Greeley, Edwin S., 1,606
Green, William N., 1,761, 2,604
Greene, George S., 359, 1,012
    James D., 764
    Oliver D., 627
Gregg, David McM., 308, 1,115
    John Irvin, 545, 728
    William M., 1,764
Gregory, Edgar M., 547
Gresham, Walter Q.. 410, 1,234
Grier, David P., 2,242
    William N., 711
Grierson, Benjamin H., 113, 286, 1,210
Griffin, Charles, 128, 280, 1,018
    Daniel F., 2,142
    Simon G., 468, 1,270
Grindlay, James, 1,746
Grose, William, 495, 1,287
Grosvenor, Charles H., 1,970
    Thomas W., 2,178
Grover, Cuvier, 139, 319, 976
    Ira G., 2,128
Grubb, E. Burd, 1,788
Guiney, Patrick Robert, 1,548
Guppy, Joshua J., 2,323
Gurney, William, 1,734
Guss, Henry R., 548
Gwyn James, 551

Hackleman, Pleasant A., 1,003, 2,555
Hagner, Peter V., 704
Haines, Thomas J., 656
Hall, Caldwell K., 1,783
    Cyrus, 2,198
    H. Seymour, 2,493
    Jairus W., 2,098
    James A., 1,487
    James F., 1,646
    Robert M., 2,487
Halleck, Henry W., 8
Hallowell, Edward N., 1,585

Halpine, Charles G., 1,426
Hamblin, Joseph E., 473, 1,347
Hambright, Henry A., 1,850
Hamilton, Andrew J., 1,244
    Charles S., 220. 828
    Schuyler, 218, 924
    William D., 1,954
Hamlin, Charles, 1,427
    Cyrus, 411, 1,320
Hammill, John S., 1,687
Hammond, John, 1,619
    John H., 1,419
    William A., 595
Hancock, Winfield S., 15, 233, 609, 898
Hanna, William, 2,223
Hardenburgh, Jacob B., 1,699
Hardie, James A., 40, 1,100
Hardin, Martin D., 743, 1,281
Harding, Abner C., 1,193
    Chester, Jr., 2,295
Harker, Charles G., 1,246, 2,608
Harlan, Emory B., 1.439
Harland, Edward, 1,146
Harnden, Henry, 2,305
Harney, W. S., 27, 585
Harriman, Samuel, 2,331
    Walter, 1,522
Harris, Andrew L., 2,018
    Benjamin F., 2,412
    Charles L., 2,313
    Thomas M., 470, 1,337
Harrison, Benjamin, 2,150
    M. La Rue, 1,926
    Thomas J., 2,125
Harrow, William, 1,157
Hart, James H., 2,012
    Orson H., 1,409
Hartranft, John F., 458, 1,263
Hartshorne, William R., 1,886
Hartsuff, George L., 35, 246, 977
    William, 1,441
Hartwell, Alfred S., 1,586
    Charles A., 2,457
Hascall, Milo S., 988
Haskell, Llewellyn F., 2,491
Haskin, Joseph A., 732, 1,296
Hastings, Russell, 1,973
Hatch, Edward, 112, 331, 1,264
    John P., 355, 722, 907
Haughton, Nathaniel, 1,975